BUCKNELL REVIEW

Mappings of the Biblical Terrain:
The Bible as Text

STATEMENT OF POLICY

BUCKNELL REVIEW is a scholarly interdisciplinary journal. Each issue is devoted to a major theme or movement in the humanities or sciences, or to two or three closely related topics. The editors invite heterodox, orthodox, and speculative ideas and welcome manuscripts from any enterprising scholar in the humanities and sciences.

This journal is a member of the Conference of Editors of Learned Journals

Contributors should send manuscripts with a self-addressed stamped envelope to the Editors, Bucknell University, Lewisburg, Pennsylvania, 17837.

BUCKNELL REVIEW

Mappings of the Biblical Terrain: The Bible as Text

Edited by
VINCENT L. TOLLERS
and
JOHN MAIER

LEWISBURG
BUCKNELL UNIVERSITY PRESS
LONDON AND TORONTO: ASSOCIATED UNIVERSITY PRESSES

Associated University Presses
440 Forsgate Drive
Cranbury, NJ 08512

Associated University Presses
25 Sicilian Avenue
London WC1A 2QH, England

Associated University Presses
P.O. Box 488, Port Credit
Mississauga, Ontario
Canada L5G 4M2

The paper used in this publication meets the requirements
of the American National Standard for Permanence of Paper
for Printed Library Materials Z39.48-1984.

Library of Congress Cataloging-in-Publication Data

Mappings of the biblical terrain : the Bible as text / edited by
Vincent L. Tollers and John Maier.
    p.   cm.—(Bucknell review; v. 33, no. 2)
    Includes bibliographical references.
    ISBN 0-8387-5172-5 (alk. paper)
    1. Bible—Criticism, interpretation, etc.   2. Bible as literature.
I. Tollers, Vincent L.   II. Maier, John R.   III. Series.
BS511.2.M33   1990
220.6'6—dc20   89-42567
                                                                    CIP

(Volume XXXIII, Number 2)

PRINTED IN THE UNITED STATES OF AMERICA

Contents

Charts of Biblical Texts

Recent Issues of BUCKNELL REVIEW

Notes on Contributors

JOHN I. ADES teaches English and biblical literature at Southern Illinois University at Edwardsville. His recent publications include "Lamb's Correspondence with Thomas Manning: Reflections on Epistolary Friendship," in *The Wordsworth Circle*, and "Fit Letters though Few: Dryden's Correspondence," in *Papers on Language and Literature*.

JOHN BLIGH has recently retired from the Department of English of the University of Guelph. He has published on Saint Paul, Shakespeare, and various novelists in British, American, and Canadian journals.

DANIEL BOYARIN is an associate professor of Talmud and Midrash at Bar Ilan University in Israel. He has published papers on Midrash and literary theory in *Poetics Today* and *Representations*. His article in this volume of *Bucknell Review* is a version of a chapter from a book in progress on this subject.

DIANE T. EDWARDS is an associate professor of English at the University of Victoria, where she teaches biblical literature and modern literature. She has published articles in *Seven, Studies in Short Fiction, Renascence*, and *Recent Research on Anglo-Irish Writers*.

ANN W. ENGAR teaches in the Honors and Liberal Education Programs at the University of Utah. She has published a number of articles on women, eighteenth-century, and popular fiction writers.

LYLE ESLINGER teaches Hebrew Bible in the Department of Religious Studies at the University of Calgary. His special interest is biblical narrative, and he is currently working on a hypertext catalogue of literary allusion in the Bible.

KEN FRIEDEN is an assistant professor of Near Eastern and Judaic Languages and Literatures at Emory University. His books include *Genius and Monologue* (1985) and *Freud's Dream of Interpretation* (1990).

RAYMOND-JEAN FRONTAIN is an instructor of English at the University of Tennessee. Coeditor of *The David Myth in Western Literature* (1980)

9

and *Poetic Prophecy in Western Literature* (1984), several of his articles on English Renaissance literature treat the literary uses made of the David story.

ESTHER FUCHS is an associate professor of Hebrew literature at the University of Arizona. She is the author of *Israeli Mythogynies: Women in Contemporary Hebrew Fiction* (1987) and of *Sexual Politics in the Biblical Narrative*. She is also a specialist in the fiction of S. Y. Agnon.

ALEXANDER GLOBE, professor of English at the University of British Columbia, has published several articles on the Bible and a book on *Peter Stent: London Printseller circa 1642–1665*.

NORMAN K. GOTTWALD is W. W. White professor of biblical studies at the New York Theological Seminary. He is the author of *The Tribes of Yahweh: A Sociology of the Religion of Liberated Israel, 1250–1050 B.C.E.* and *The Hebrew Bible: A Socio-Literary Introduction*. He is also a frequent contributor to periodicals, anthologies, and dictionaries in the field of biblical studies.

DAVID LYLE JEFFREY is professor of English language and literature at the University of Ottawa. General editor for *The Dictionary of Biblical Tradition in English Literature*, he is also the author of books and monographs on medieval and modern English literature and a translator of texts of medieval spirituality.

HERBERT J. LEVINE, associate professor of English at Franklin and Marshall College, teaches courses on the Psalms at the National Havurah Summer Institutes. In addition to biblical scholarship in *Prooftexts*, he has published a book on Yeats and articles on George Eliot and Whitman in *Journal of English Literary History* and *American Literature*.

AARON LICHTENSTEIN teaches at The City University of New York in the fields of language and literature at the Baruch College and English at the Borough of Manhattan Community College. He is the author of *The Seven Laws of Noah* (1986), a study combining ancient history, law, and religion.

JOHN MAIER is professor of English at the State University of New York College at Brockport and the coauthor of *The Bible in Its Literary Milieu* (with Vincent L. Tollers), *Gilgamesh* (with John Gardner and

Richard A. Henshaw), and *Myths of Enki: The Crafty God* (with Samuel Noah Kramer).

MICHAEL PAYNE is John P. Crozer professor of English at Bucknell University. His recent publications include studies of The Song of Songs and of Ecclesiastes and a review of recent scholarship on biblical literature for *Papers on Language and Literature*. He is editing a volume on Frank Kermode for the Andrew W. Mellon Series on Literary Theory for the Bucknell University Press.

GILA RAMRAS-RAUCH is professor of Hebrew literature at Hebrew College, Boston, and at Brandeis University. Her most recent book is *The Arab in Israeli Literature*.

GARY A. RENDSBURG is an assistant professor of Near Eastern Studies at Cornell University, where he teaches courses in Hebrew Bible and Semitic languages. He is the author of *The Redaction of Genesis* (1986) and has published many articles in leading journals in Europe and the United States.

S. N. ROSENBAUM is an associate professor of Classics and Religion at Dickinson College, where he coordinates the Judaic Studies Program. His work includes a monograph on Amos and essays in *The Christian Century, Hebrew Union College Annual, Encounter, Journal of Ecumenical Studies, Midstream*, and many other journals.

JOSEPH C. SITTERSON, JR. is an associate professor of English at Georgetown University. He has published articles on critical theory and on Romantic poetry in *University of Toronto Quarterly, Studies in Philology, Journal of English and Germanic Philology, PMLA*, and elsewhere.

THEODORE L. STEINBERG is a professor of English at the State University of New York at Fredonia, where he teaches courses in biblical, medieval, and Renaissance literature. He is currently working on a study of the prophetic tradition and *Piers Plowman*.

LEONARD L. THOMPSON is professor of Religious Studies and Dean of the Faculty at Lawrence University. He is the author of *Introducing Biblical Literature* and *The Book of Revelation: Apocalypse and Empire*. He has also published in journals in the biblical and classical fields.

VINCENT L. TOLLERS is professor of English at the State University of New York College at Brockport. He has published *A Bibliography of Matthew Arnold* (1974), is coauthor (with John Maier) of *The Bible in Its Literary Milieu* (1979), and edited *Literary Research* (1976–1986).

DEEANNE WESTBROOK is an associate professor of English at Portland State University. She has published articles on metaphor and mythology, and writes and publishes fiction and poetry. She is at work on a book on the North in myth, folklore, and literature.

Introduction:
"With Wand'ring Steps and Slow"

They looking back, all th' Eastern side beheld
Of Paradise, so late thir happy seat,
Wav'd over by that flaming Brand, the Gate
With dreadful Faces throng'd and fiery Arms:
Some natural tears they dropp'd, but wiping them soon;
The World was all before them, where to choose
Thir place of rest, and Providence thir guide:
They hand in hand with wand'ring steps and slow,
Through *Eden* took thir solitary way.
—*Paradise Lost* 12. 641–49

THAT intrepid rereader and rewriter of biblical narratives, John Milton, in these often-repeated lines brought *Paradise Lost* to an optimistic, if appropriately sober, close. For Milton the World that was "all before" Adam and Eve was not a world merely of empirical facts but a world that was always and already a text in need of interpretation. The World was also, as the hermeneutical tradition can appreciate, "all before them," ambiguously close by or infinitely removed from their vision. *Paradise Lost* was a pivotal interpretation of the Hebrew Bible in the turn of Western thought. Milton was fighting a rearguard battle against the forces that were coming to define "modernity," scientific skepticism, and even for the first time since antiquity, atheism. Milton had to know that he stood across a divide not all that different from the gap between Paradise and Eden. He could no longer live merely in the innocence of an unmediated hearing/reading of the divine Word.

It is not surprising, then, that the last quarter of the twentieth century, increasingly dominated by "interpretive strategies" and sophisticated theories of reading the arts, literature, and anthropology, should witness intense concern for approaches to the Bible, "as literature"—so the popular college courses proclaim—but even more basically as *text*. When we set out some ten years ago to map the territory increasingly being claimed by literary critics and biblical scholars (in *The Bible in Its Literary Milieu: Contemporary Essays*), it was still necessary to point out that "literary criticism" meant one thing to the critics and another to the scholar. The explosion of mainly Continental literary theory in the American academy has made that attempted mapping curiously naive. What this new collection of

essays shows is that the dividing line between literary criticism and
biblical scholarship has all but disappeared as each group draws from
the methods of the other.

   Like those first moments of human existence, as Milton imagined
them, the attempts to see into this new world are "wandr'ing steps
and slow." The paths turn off in a number of directions, and it is not
clear from our vantage point if they are headed toward anything like a
common end. Most obvious is the "solitary way" the writers in this
collection seem to take.
   Some trends are, however, observable. One trend seems to be
emerging. Jewish tradition, long separated from the interpretive traditions of Western Christianity even when the object of attention was
the Hebrew Bible, is now making an important claim for recognition.
Rabbinical interpretation, according to Susan A. Handelman in her
1982 *The Slayers of Moses*, constitutes a very different *type* of interpretive
strategy than the Hellenic mode of abstract thinking that came to
dominate early Christian readings of Scripture. She claims that the
rabbinical tradition of interpretation, forced underground through
most of the Common Era, has reemerged in some of the most powerful
thinkers in the modern world, including Freud, Jacques Lacan, Jacques Derrida, and Harold Bloom. If this analysis is correct, the often
antagonistic relationship between Judaism and Christianity may be
taking a more positive direction. As a number of these essays in this
special issue of the *Bucknell Review* attempt to show, the Hebrew Bible
must be reconsidered in its own right and in association with the
Christian appropriation of it as the Old Testament. In that vein a
detailed study of one type of rabbinical interpretation, the study of the
exegetic *mashal* offered by Daniel Boyarin, for example, takes on much
greater significance than it might have in earlier days. (On the other
hand, the exegetic *mashal* is not really the free play of interpretation
Susan Handelman thinks characterizes the rabbinical tradition.)
   One area to which the study of the Bible has made a major contribution is gender studies. Literary-critical studies of biblical texts by
women and from feminist perspectives are far more common now
than they were only ten years ago. Milton would doubltess have been
shocked by that development. Indeed, citing Milton here might
almost be considered an affront to feminist scholarship on the Bible,
for he certainly thought women were not as capable as men in the
noble work he was about. Milton's division of mental faculties and
powers into masculine and feminine, a veritable paradigm of androcentric, patriarchal, and hierarchical thinking, is too well-known and

painful to rehearse here. But even Milton imagined Adam and Eve "hand in hand," taking their (solitary) way into Eden without the bickering that had marred their lives immediately after the Fall. In a way the poet anticipated a development that was to take place hundreds of years after he had written.

As Elisabeth Schüssler Fiorenza, in her 1987 presidential address to the Society of Biblical Literature (*Journal of Biblical Literature* [March 1988]), pointed out, women have had little voice in the biblical scholarship of the last one-hundred years. That, however, is changing rapidly. Several essays in this collection bear that out. One aspect of the change can be glimpsed in the renewed interest in the figure of the trickster. The experimental journal for biblical criticism, *Semeia*, devoted an issue to the trickster. In 1988, J. Cheryl Exum and Johanna W. H. Bos edited a special issue of *Semeia* (No. 42), which they named *Reasoning with the Foxes: Female Wit in a World of Male Power*. The *Semeia* came out too late to be useful to the contributors to this collection of essays. But, as the essays by Esther Fuchs, Ann W. Engar, Gila Ramras-Rauch, Raymond-Jean Frontain, and Ken Frieden demonstrate in very different ways, the trickster is of major interest to scholars, and it is by no means exclusively an interest of women scholars. But it is a topic driven these days by a double interest in women's studies and in literary hermeneutics.

As might be expected, the contemporary authors most often cited by the essayists in our collection are Robert Alter, Meir Sternberg, and Frank Kermode, whose works are at the meeting place of literary theory and critical applications of biblical texts, especially narratives. Kermode's 1979 *The Genesis of Secrecy*, Alter's 1981 *The Art of Biblical Narrative*, Sternberg's 1985 *Poetics of Biblical Narrative*, and Alter's and Kermode's 1987 *The Literary Guide to the Bible* are by far the works most often mentioned in the essays. Nearly all the well-known literary theorists are here, though they are not necessarily treated uncritically: Harold Bloom, Geoffrey Hartman, J. Hillis Miller, Stanley Fish, Norman Holland, and a host of others. However, Northrop Frye is more conspicuous than any of the poststructuralists. (More surprisingly, perhaps, Jacques Derrida is almost entirely absent from the discussions—surprising, but maybe fitting for one who is bent on overcoming a metaphysics of presence.) A very wide range of scholarly and critical opinion is represented in this work—from Terry Eagleton and Fredric Jameson to Susan Wittig and Elisabeth Schüssler Fiorenza. Freud, Nietzsche, Kierkegaard, Bakhtin, Propp, Greimas, Buber, and Auerbach turn up, but the overall impression confirms the extraordinary plurality of new voices engaged in discourse on the literary dimensions of the Bible.

This collection was gathered in the main from three sources: contributors to a volume in the Modern Language Association of America's series on Teaching World Masterpieces, *Teaching the Hebrew Bible*, edited by Barry N. Olshen and Yoel Feldman; sections on the Bible as Literature at the 1986 Modern Language Association annual meeting; and sections on the Bible as Literature at the 1985–88 annual meetings of the College English Association. We wish to extend our thanks, in particular, to Jason Rosenblatt and to Michael Payne for their assistance in making this special issue a reality.

All of the contributors take their solitary ways through the biblical terrain. The aim of the collection is to present something of the range of scholarly interests by students of literature and by biblical scholars at a certain moment in history. As mentioned earlier, several broad divisions can be detected in the essays that were finally accepted for the volume. Some essays are mainly theoretical, some apply a new social or literary-critical theory to a specific text, and others consider specific biblical texts in some detail. Our notes on the essays place the individual pieces within the larger divisions we saw emerge while the volume was taking shape.

CONTOURS OF INTERPRETATION

In the most comprehensive of the essays in the collection, NORMAN GOTTWALD surveys three areas of scholarly concern, in the past separate domains, which he thinks are converging "toward a hermeneutical horizon where all are complementary and mutually enriching aspects of a single biblical landscape." The three are literary-critical practice, social criticism, and theology. Gottwald is most interested in the places where the three lines intersect. While he considers only the Hebrew Bible in his survey, Gottwald's "mappings of the biblical terrain" might productively be extended to include New Testament studies as well. While narrative theory developed in an examination of secular literature has yielded impressive results, the critics like Harold Bloom have not been as successful in dealing with the text and its readers when it sees *only* a will to power exercised in interpretation. In an examination of the New Testament parable, JOSEPH SITTERSON sees the parable as part of a complex speech act that does not evade the tension between interpretation and experiential story, between narrative and creed, as secular hermeneutics evades the tension. DANIEL BOYARIN focuses on one type of Midrashic *mashal*, or "likeness," favored in the rabbinical tradition: the exegetic *mashal*, in which a verse of the Bible is interpreted by means of a parable. The exegetic *mashal* takes an unusual interpretive step, one that might look to us like the most extreme form of unconstrained play. Boyarin points out that, to the contrary, the exegetic *mashal* is not at all indeterminate (unlike the views of New Testament parables popular today). There is hardly room for interpretation once the *mashal* provides a "handle" to the Torah. Unquestioned in the making of such *meshalim* is the ground upon which the "likeness" is raised to fill in gaps: the history of God's tender treatment of the people.

LYLE ESLINGER argues that historical criticism of the Hebrew Bible, the critical method developed to organize knowledge about the Bible, "unhindered by the trammels of faith," is limited in a way that contemporary "narratology" is not. Narratology, as a description of narratives in the Western literary tradition, is useful to an under-standing of the narrative voices and "narratorial situations"—"the variety of narrative ontologies and epistemologies from which an author may choose to frame his story," a concept taken from Franz Stanzel—found in biblical texts like Genesis, Nehemiah, 1 Samuel, and Job. In particular, the "external unconditioned narrator" relates the biblical story and its teller in a way that remained undetected by historical criticism. Where most of the essays draw on contemporary literary theories to provide readings of biblical texts, S. N. ROSEN-BAUM's essay argues that a close attention to the word is likely to "inhibit, if it does not positively preclude," the appreciation of the Bible "as literature." Rosenbaum follows Edward Sapir in insisting on a careful knowledge of the original language of the text, a Semitic language that cannot adequately be translated into Indo-European languages. The triliteral root system of Hebrew, word play, and number symbolism require a knowledge of the language that is often ignored by literary critics of biblical texts. The contexts in which the under-standing of the ancient Hebrew word can be understood are outlined by Rosenbaum, who advocates a "semantic field theory" approach to such terms as "wisdom," the "regulation" of women by men, and the notorious controversy over "virgin" in Isaiah 7:14. In sharp contrast to Rosenbaum, who deals with the smallest elements of the biblical text and those elements most difficult to extend to other contexts with-in the Bible, DIANE EDWARDS applies concepts of literary unity, espe-cially the sense of closure, to the largest organizational patterns of the Bible. Edwards points out the important differences in the way the Hebrew Bible, the Septuagint, and the Christian Bible close the col-lection of Hebrew Scriptures. Complete closure is resisted or deferred in Genesis, Exodus, Deuteronomy, while the New Testament Book of Revelation was positioned for its strong closure. Edwards traces the concern for a "garden" to which we can no longer return and for the great symbol of "the city" to which we are led forward.

VOICEPRINTS, MALE AND FEMALE

DEEANNE WESTBROOK begins with Harold Bloom's comments on the Yahwist as the "author of authors," and she sets about exploring the "unresolved antitheses" in the Yahwist narrative of creation and fall. The two trees in the Yahwist garden are polar opposites. The play of truth and falsehood involved in Eve's ethical decision to eat of the fruit fills the story with enigmatic irony. The pair of antitheses, life and death, is embodied in the figures of God and the woman (reduced from her ancient status of mother goddess). In contrast to the cycles of existence that dominate the religion of the mother goddess, Yahwist culture sees existence as linear. The woman, the serpent, the tree of the knowledge of good and evil, exist in agonistic relationship with God and life. Ironically, the polarities reverse as the creator becomes associated with dust, and death, while the "mother of all living" comes to dominate the human world of sexuality, generation, and consciousness. Where Westbrook's is a subtle rereading of a key biblical story from a feminist perspective, ESTHER FUCHS directly challenges what she calls the "poeticism now in vogue" in the literary study of the Bible. She claims that the supposed objectivity of biblical criticism has in fact obscured the more important point: the patriarchal ideology informing not only the biblical text but the modern critics' work as well.

While the heroes of the Bible are mainly men of faith and obedience rather than intelligence, ANN ENGAR discusses the women in the biblical stories that are marked by a certain kind of intelligence much valued in the ancient world: Rebekah, Leah, Tamar, Ruth, and Esther are prominent among many examples from the Hebrew Bible. The trickster stories involve women ensuring their own security as mothers, saving their people from war and subjugation, and helping men to recognize the will of the Lord. Later stories emphasize the temptress who uses her beauty along with her intelligence to overcome her enemies. GILA RAMRAS-RAUCH asks, Can a female protagonist be regarded as a biblical protagonist in the fullest sense? From an analysis of the four aspects typifying the biblical protagonist—promise, trial, dialogue, and exile—Ramras-Rauch argues that the woman is "part of the divine scheme" and parallels the major male protagonists. Two narratives are reexamined—the story of Dinah and the story of Jephthah and his daughter—to show that, almost unique in the ancient world, woman has a definite legal status, and that both women and men in the biblical narratives are moored in their humanity, including vulnerability and mortality. RAYMOND-JEAN FRONTAIN examines deception in the David narrative. Early in his career, David plays the trickster in order to survive and preserve the life of his people; he is, as Frontain notes, an "irrepressible life force." Once sure of his position, though, David's use of deception changes, leading him close to the ruthlessness Yahweh had warned of in the king the people demanded. As if to check David's trickery, others arise to trick the trickster, especially Nathan and Joab. The cycle of deception ends with the trickster, apparently, "justly tricked." A puzzling dream text in Freud's *The Interpretation of Dreams*, considered one way by Freud and another way by KEN FRIEDEN, links Sigmund (Solomon) to a major theme in the Hebrew Bible, the theme of exile. Like Joseph and Daniel, Freud experienced the powerlessness of exile and found power through the interpretation of dreams. Frieden finds in Freud's unconscious wish to alleviate the modern Jewish exile a connection with a long tradition of interest in dreams and language as the means of Jewish self-assertion.

Charts of Biblical Texts

The result of interpretation is not only scholarly discussion. Interpretation can take the form, as it does in Michelangelo's Sistine Chapel ceiling, of a visual rereading. The unity of scenes has been open to question, and chronology seems to be violated in the arrangement. AARON LICHTENSTEIN argues that the arrangement is unified. Michelangelo's use of other biblical works (e.g., Jeremiah) and commentaries for the artist's understanding of Genesis explain the apparent distortions of the biblical stories. GARY RENDSBURG shows that the tendency today to see unity in the shape of biblical narratives often conflicts with earlier redaction criticism and source criticism of the Bible. The Documentary Hypothesis in particular is called in question when what appear to be "secondary" and unrelated additions to a story turn out to be part of a larger narrative structure. Rendsburg joins the Joseph story to the Primeval History, the Abraham cycle, and the Jacob cycle as a fourth unified whole in Genesis. The structure is chiastic, evident in the intricacy of balanced "theme-words," with the pivot point the episode in which Joseph reveals himself to his brothers. ALEXANDER GLOBE argues that the apparent disunity in Judges is the result, not of late additions to an early text, but of a "writerly" style that exploits nonsequential rhetorical, thematic, and symbolic patterns in what might appear a haphazard mix of stories. A close analysis of the work shows an ideal of the judge that, in the author's evaluation of this age, gives way to depravity. Order gives way to chaos when strict monotheism is contaminated by foreign influences. Even the ring composition of the work, a device to give a narrative unity, shows the theme of disintegration as the age of judges slips into depravity.

While the Book of Ruth initially appears to be about Ruth's faithfulness, the careful reader discovers that, like Caesar's Brutus, its meaning is found through another, Naomi. VINCENT TOLLERS argues that by using Naomi to advance the plot and by seeing much of the story through her eyes, the author subtly shows the biblical theme of self-help: God's plan is unconsciously carried out by the Naomis of this world who think they are only working out their own destiny. JOHN ADES finds complexities in the Hebrew concepts of an afterlife in an analysis of 1 Samuel 28. The episode of Saul at En-dor brings together several beliefs about the afterlife (which is not the same as "immortality," although the concepts anticipate in some ways ideas about immortality that are found in the New Testament). Ades finds six features of the afterlife in that episode and notes the skillful literary art that is evident especially at the end of the episode. Mikhail Bakhtin's concept of a dialogic discourse is discovered in prose narratives, but HERBERT LEVINE argues that it is involved in a complex way in the poetry of Psalms as well. Quoting another's words permits the interplay of many voices and allows the voices to retain their linguistic diversity. A dimension that has been ignored in the literary study of the Bible, dialogic discourse is a rhetorical use of double-voicedness: the psalmists quarrel with the authoritative God-voice, with the words of the wicked, and even with the words of an earlier self, turning their quarrels into speaking voices.

Writers of the biblical genre that is typically called "prophecy" were determined in the manner of their address to the reader by the special imposition of their vocation. Unlike most writers, they often represent themselves as writing (or speaking) against their will. They would prefer to eschew the task. According to DAVID JEFFREY, rhetoric, rather than narrative, pervades the basic structure of their work. Grammatical juxtaposition and stylistic alterations reenforce the rhetorical strategies of the prophets. Although much is made of the poetry in the Bible, recent scholarship often fails to distinguish "poetry" from "verse." THEODORE STEINBERG treats Isaiah as a unified whole and examines the imaginativeness, the development, and the logic of images employed by the poet. Images, sometimes disparate and yoked together, disclose an elaborate wordplay that takes the work beyond verse to the "intricately rich communication" of poetry. JOHN BLIGH's study of The Wisdom of Solomon is prompted by a pedagogical aim. The apocryphal Wisdom of Solomon deserves a place in courses on "The Bible as Literature" because of the links it offers between the Hebrew Bible and the New Testament. Bligh considers the structure and purpose of the work in its historical situation. At the center of the Wisdom is a concept of kingship that owes as much to the Greeks as to biblical history. Beyond the study of a work in its historical situation, Bligh's essay is a defense of the very notion of "The Bible as Literature" as a valid study in the modern, secular university.

Theologian Joseph S. O'Leary in *Questioning Back* (1985) uses Jacques Derrida's method of deconstruction in a project toward the "overcoming of metaphysics" in the Christian tradition. One of the texts he deconstructs is the Gospel of John, which he rereads in light of a "new trinity" of emptiness, phenomenality, and immediacy. O'Leary suggests that contact between early Christianity and an earlier Semitic tradition would allow a countermetaphysical reading of the Bible that would "free faith from the morose, introspective provincialism characteristic of metaphysical theology." He leaves that contact mainly unexplored. JOHN MAIER, however, contends that the contact can be documented not only by the Hebrew Bible but by earlier ancient Near Eastern works as well. LEONARD THOMPSON is concerned with demonstrating the unity of "horizontal" (narrative) and "vertical" (metaphor) structures in the last New Testament work in the traditional canon. The essay catalogues in great detail three types of unity Thompson finds in the biblical text: narrative unity, metaphoric unity, and mythic unity. One feature of Revelation Thompson notices, ring composition, or what he calls its "circularity," is receiving a great deal of attention from students of ancient literature and also from scholars working on the differences between oral tradition and literacy. MICHAEL PAYNE notes the early Christian unconcern with visual images and a corresponding emphasis on the voice. Related to that emphasis is the tendency to incorporate symbolic and abstract metaphors in Revelation. The work moreover discloses a highly self-conscious author who has found a narrative design—the *menorah*, a kind of ring composition—to unify voice, metaphor, and narrative in a work that stubbornly resists the attempt of framing devices to contain the vision of the end. Like Thompson, Payne is interested in the archetectonics of an ancient work that is very close to an oral tradition, but one that carries the mark of the literate author.

VINCENT L. TOLLERS
JOHN MAIER

BUCKNELL REVIEW

Mappings of the Biblical Terrain:
The Bible as Text

Contours of Interpretation

Literary Criticism of the Hebrew Bible: Retrospect and Prospect

Norman K. Gottwald

New York Theological Seminary

AS an informed and sympathetic outsider to the biblical literary critical guild, I have been invited to assess the achievements of literary criticism of the Hebrew Bible, particularly in terms of its bearing on biblical studies as a whole. At the same time I shall be noting feedback from other forms of biblical criticism which may prove instructive for the literary critical task. This is a daunting undertaking which requires me both to choose a large enough frame for the presentation to set forth a point of view and to select and focus my "case studies" concretely enough to be pertinent to the actual work we do as biblical interpreters.

My basic argument is that there exist a number of coordinate dimensions to biblical texts which carry equal weight for interpretation and imply their own methods of disclosure. While these coordinates securely possess their own integrity, they nonetheless imply and require one another to interpret the fullness of the texts. I shall divide my discussion into three parts:

1) I shall specify three coordinates under the rubrics of "literary," "social," and "theological," and underscore how the history of the development of the different types of criticism has emphasized the autonomy of each coordinate while paying little corresponding attention to the ways they imply and require one another.

2) Taking the literary coordinate as the principal interest, I shall indicate some of the points in current research where the literary coordinate and its appropriate methods encounter the other coordinates and their methods, with the result that new opportunities arise to sharpen the work of each critical practice and to invite collaboration in forwarding the complex task of biblical interpretation. These "points of meeting" will be set forth as a series of "examples" or "case studies" in the interreading of the coordinates.

27

3) Finally, I shall raise the issue of a satisfactory literary theory which will be able to frame and give intellectual warrant to the interreading of the literary, social, and theological practices. The work of the literary theorists Terry Eagleton and Fredric Jameson will be proposed as one way of plotting and interconnecting the coordinates.

Literary, Social, and Theological Critical Practices

In recent decades, literary and social critical practices have arisen alongside—and at times in opposition to—the older historical critical practice, while the much older theological approach has undergone revision in step with the new complexity of biblical inquiry. These critical practices have been pursued with unrelenting vigor and with enough payoffs to have attracted enthusiastic practitioners and to have shaken up the way the field is construed and divided up for working purposes.

In the main these critical practices have proceeded along highly independent lines, appropriate to their corresponding coordinates and often with the overt or tacit assumption that they are not only different but incompatible mappings of the biblical terrain, so radically dissimilar in starting points that their findings cannot be expected to meet other than disjunctively. After a brief look at the circumstances and grounds of this presumed incompatibility of critical practices, I will contend that amid and beyond all the pronounced disjunctions that separate the literary, social, and theological worlds of the Bible, they do in fact converge toward a hermeneutical horizon where all are complementary and mutually enriching aspects of a single biblical landscape. Moreover, I shall urge that the convergence of these perspectives and practices does not come simply at the end of study, as a final moment of integration, but informs the entire process of study, since each of the criticisms uses data and raises questions that call the other forms of criticism into play.[1]

Literary Critical Practice

It is virtually impossible to overstate the scope and impact of the explosion of literary studies of the Bible. Biblical scholars have at long last come to employ the full arsenal of literary criticism and not merely its genetic aspects related to source criticism, form criticism, tradition criticism, and redaction criticism. As Leonard Thompson puts it, drawing on a phrase of Robert Penn Warren, there opens before us "a more fantastic country," the realm of structured and structuring speech which need not serve immediate historical and social reconstruction or distill theological truths to be a plausible and compelling world.[2] This fictive world can be explored, as Edgar McKnight notes, according to any or all of four literary elements: the work itself, the author of the work, the universe imitated in the work, or the audience receiving the work.[3]

Now in order to bring this literary world fully into the consciousness of biblical scholarship as a legitimate object of study, it has been methodologically and psychically necessary to open wide the gulf between the literary coordinate and the history and society associated with it and the theological constructs expressed in it. This emphatic declaration of independence by biblical literary critics has been productive in authorizing their undertakings and carving out a recognizable space for their work. Once the sphere of literary critical practice is securely established, however, the question of the long-range status of literary criticism vis-à-vis the other types of criticism emerges with growing insistence. How are the literary findings to be communicated to other kinds of critics and how are literary critics to receive feedback from specialists in the other critical practices? Unless this problem of communication and collaboration is faced, literary criticism may settle into balkanized dogma, isolated from the larger body of biblical scholarship.

Social Critical Practice

Studies of the social coordinate in biblical interpretation have followed a course very much like that of literary studies. Social inquiry into biblical traditions has been able to uncover the contours of social organization and social change which underlie and pervade the checkered political and religious history of ancient Israel. The dike restraining social scientific criticism from a full engagement with the Bible has been breached at so many points that we have passed irreversibly beyond compiling social data as random realia to a deepening clarification of how biblical people lived as social beings and how their social struggles, self-interests, and utopian aspirations are expressed directly and indirectly in the texts. Here too, alongside the literary world, unfolds "a more fantastic country," the social world of a people who were not simply speakers or writers on religious subjects but also producers and reproducers of a determinate social existence which encompassed all aspects of life. Just as literary critical practice has removed forever the uncritically read text, so social critical practice has taken away for all time the uncritically assumed society, whether of wandering nomads or of religiously preoccupied students of sacred texts.

In order to validate the systemic examination of the Bible's social fabric, it has been necessary to sharpen the gulf between social structure and process and what is written both in its literary form and in its theological content. The favorite label for this maneuver by those who don't like it is "reductionism," generally not noticing the "reduction" practiced by their own methods. This assertive declaration of independence, analogous to the situation in literary criticism, has laid new foundations and fashioned new tools for recovering the conflictual social world previously dissipated into history and culture narrowly or fuzzily conceived. But exactly as in the literary fold, so too within social critical practice there looms the threat of stagnating dogma unless the social critical results can find their way into the give-and-take of commonly addressed hermeneutical and exegetical tasks.

Theological Critical Practice

The study of the theological coordinate has developed differently than studies of the literary and social coordinates. After all, theological methods of inquiry into the Bible have been at work far longer than the full-bodied literary and social practices. By instinct, theological critics want to be the integrating and synthesizing interpreters of the Bible. That task was difficult enough when theology had to wrestle with the results of historical criticism. With the eruption of new critical practices onto the biblical scene, theology faces a disorienting array of choices. On which of the critical practices should it draw and in what depth and over what range? Should it try to stand back from the thick of the fray in the other critical practices, wary of being trapped in fads? But if it does "stand back," on what material content will its theological reflection stand? The main historic roots of theological criticism of the Bible are in the classical theological and philosophical traditions which do not offer ready means to appropriate the literary and social understandings deeply and substantively. Thus, theological criticism must run "to keep up" with its own object of study.

Where recent theological criticism of the Hebrew Bible has been strongest is in laying hold of the expanded literary dimensions of historical critical practice by turning form criticism, tradition criticism, and redaction criticism to its purposes. Yet it cannot be said that "stream-of-tradition"/trajectory theological constructs or canon critical schemes are closely in touch either with literary or social critical practices as they are now carried on with rigor and sophistication. While theological criticism hopes to take advantage of the new openings, it has great difficulty with the elusive imagination of the literary coordinate and with the cold secularity of the social coordinate. Unless new theological discourse can bridge the chasms between it and the other critical practices, theological study of the Hebrew Bible may more and more resemble notions from past ages of biblical scholarship uninformed by a vital enagement with the full range of our current ways of recovering the richness of the Bible in its several facets.

The Ground of All Critical Practices

But what if the literary, social, and theological coordinates are so autonomous that there is no way to overcome their differentia as separate subject matters? Why, we necessarily ask, is there reason to believe that these types of criticism can cooperate and cohere in a larger project of biblical interpretation? The "reason" I advance may seem deceptively commonsensical and possibly so truistic that it amounts to little. I believe, however, that it is the bedrock from which we start any form of critical practice.

At bottom the three critical worlds we have surveyed do share a common ground and currency, even though that ground is not directly accessible to us. In the critical practices associated with the three coordinates are disclosed the simultaneous expressions of human beings who lived in communities of a certain social character and who wrote their thoughts and feelings in texts of certain types and who found meaning in their life together through religious categories of a specific sort. These literary, social, and theological "worlds" which we split for analysis were inhabited by real people for whom those worlds were dimensions of their lived experience and shared meanings. The three coordinates which we are trying to bring together coexisted in their collective lives and interpreting minds, filtered through linguistic and cultural socialization processes.

To be sure these worlds are separable and distinctive with respect to their particularities as speech, as social patterning, and as religious symbol and practice, and they require separable treatments according to varying methods. Always, however, the analysis begins from and returns to the unifying ground of a people speaking, associating, and generating religious meaning. What we are challenged to attempt is a way of seeing the literary, social, and theological artifacts in their specificity and in their ensemble, synchronically as function and diachronically as process. So the "trick" in critical practice is to keep the *distinctions* that matter while seeing the *assemblage* of dimensions and elements at work in the whole social formation. The test of whether this holistic approach is more than a slogan and self-deception is to be able to negotiate the interconnections among the coordinates as they appear in texts, without lapsing into detached piecework or vaulting into uncontrolled abstractions. This means to pay attention to the kind of information that can be productively passed from coordinate to coordinate at the "synapses" between them.

WHERE THE CRITICAL PRACTICES MEET

It seems to me that the way to work toward better covering theory, able to overarch and intercommunicate among the different critical practices, is to attend to the "joins" or "synapses" at the points where the practices do or may touch one another. As it stands, the varying critical "answers" are usually presented as incommensurates, or, if in some way on the same plane, regarded as rivals in an uneasy truce or stalemate. Instead, we need to inquire as to exactly what these literary, historical, social, and theological "answers" consist of, the "questions" they do and do not address, and whether the interfacing and interreading of these various "answers" teaches us anything that can sharpen the practice of each and that can lead on to collaboration because we come to see exactly why and how the subject of study in all its complexity truly requires more than the one critical practice we are best at.

Since our orientation for this discussion is the literary coordinate, I shall note some of the ways in which the results of literary criticism present themselves at the boundary points, the "joins" or "synapses" between the coordinates, interfacing and prompting dialogue with historical, social, and theological criticisms and new kinds of inquiry internal to literary criticism which this encounter provokes. In choosing my examples or case studies, I have drawn freely from different types of literary criticism, such as the study of biblical rhetoric or poetics, structuralism, and deconstruction, without any attempt to adjudicate among them on literary critical grounds.

The Meeting of Literary and Historical Practices

First, I call attention to the meeting points between literary critical practice and recognizably older forms of historical critical practice. With respect to the endeavor to write a history of ancient Israel, one devastating effect of literary criticism has been to undermine the positivist tendencies of the historical critical approach, and perhaps even to throw into doubt the possibility of writing more than a sketch of most periods of biblical history insofar as the Bible constitutes the primary or sole source of information. For example, recent literary analysis of the two accounts of the war of Deborah and Barak against the Canaanites in Judges 4–5[4] and of the Succession Narrative of David in 2 Samuel 9–20 and 1 Kings 1–2[5] caution severely against reading these texts as eyewitness accounts, since literary compression, expansion, and transposition of events are underscored in all the texts and since the aims of the texts were far afield from what we take as documented historiography. I have no doubt about the wisdom of this caution.

On the other hand, this literary "de-composition" of presumed historical sources may give us useful units of historical reflection. If the literary materials yield certain themes or programs, such as "Yahweh's use of weak women to confound strong men" in Judges 4–5 or of "David's giving and grasping" in family and political affairs in the Succession Narrative, we may ask if these construals of the original events accord with other information about them, and also what connection obtains between the events of the times of the judges and David and the situations in which the literary profiles were created. This may seem a very "weak" form of historical reconstruction, but, provided we acknowledge its indirection and imaginative ingredient, this too is an aspect of history as "the past remembered in a certain way."

In my judgment there is also an overlooked direct contribution of the newer literary criticism to source criticism proper, even though this may come as a surprise to literary critics who have generally distanced themselves from source critical questions for understandable reasons. We now have a substantial body of work, notably by Robert Alter and Meir Sternberg, which sets forth nuanced descriptions of literary techniques in biblical narrative, for example forms of characterization and types of repetition.[6] Much of this work has been done precisely in the pentateuchal narratives regarded as constituent of the J, E, and P sources. Would it not make sense to apply these newly refined literary criteria to the designated pentateuchal sources in order to determine if differentia in characterization, repetition, and other literary devices do or do not support the classical divisions of the text into sources? As far as I know, no one has taken up this task.

The Meeting of Literary and Social Practices

The location of the "synapses" between literary critical practice and social critical practice may be more tenuous and problematic, since these two practices are relative newcomers to the field in their present developed forms. By the nature of the case there are a good many "blanks" or "gaps" about social history and social change that we are trying to fill in because they are not directly addressed in the texts. At the same time, literary criticism is far from having adequately treated all sections of the Hebrew Bible.

Let me first speak of the possibilities in comparative literary studies, which may turn out to be a heuristic aid that will increase precision in both the literary and the social critical practices. I will illustrate with the historylike saga genre, whose sociohistorical context we find hard to pin down to the particularities of any one period, either with respect to the oldest horizons the stories contain or in respect to the times of their final composition. These double horizons of *oldest reference* and *time of composition* are presently distributed by various scholars over a span of 1500 years from the Early Bronze Age to the exile. It seems to me that to make progress on this issue we need to look to places outside Israel where we have a body of sagas that is more closely controlled by attendant historical and social data than is the case in ancient Israel. I believe that a likely place to begin the search is with the Icelandic sagas and their parallel chronicles within the setting of the history of Iceland's settlement by Norwegian peoples who were fleeing the introduction of kingship in their homeland and who retained a loose tribal structure for many centuries.[7] Once we have determined, if possible, what sorts of historical and social conditions are coordinate with the literary features of the Icelandic sagas, we may have some controlled grids for reexamining the pentateuchal sagas in Israelite history and society. It may also be worth looking at recent advances in the historical and social clarification of the circumstances surrounding the King Arthur legends for similar comparative literary and social controls possibly applicable to the sagas in ancient Israel.

Another promising boundary-confronting aspect of literary practice is the manner in which structuralist or formalist analysis of narrative programs in the Israelite sagas yield semantic themes that are fraught with connotations alluding to or issuing from the social formation. In Joshua, for instance, Robert Polzin claims that the "first" Deuteronomistic voice of authoritarian dogmatism shows us a unified people of one origin and status, while the "second" voice that speaks for critical traditionalism attests to a miscellaneous assortment of peoples, the majority of whom are in one way or another "outsiders" to the male assembly of "true" Israelites: Rahab and her family, Gibeonites and their allies, women, children, resident aliens, Levites, etc. Polzin sums up: "As the narrative describes Israel-the-community settling within Israel-the-land, it never ceases to emphasize how much of the 'outside,' both communally and territorially is 'inside' Israel."[8]

Rather similar issues about who is "in" and who is "out," as well as who is "in control," are suggested in David Jobling's analyses of the narrative programs of Numbers 11–12 concerning murmuring and rebellion in the wilderness and in Numbers 32 and Joshua 22 concerning the disposition of tribes on either side of the Jordan.[9] In the former case, the program has to do with getting through the wilderness safely to Canaan. A leading semantic theme is the people of Israel arranged in a hierarchy which, from top down, runs like this: Moses, Aaron, people, Miriam, rabble. The corresponding semantic theme concerns provision of true knowledge of how to get through the wilderness, which is guaranteed by obedience to the instructions of Moses and Aaron at the top of the hierarchy. In the latter case, the program has to do with getting the tribes properly arranged on either side of the Jordan without splitting apart in distrust and alienation. The semantic themes are the unity of Israel, the proper scope of Israel's land, and the place of women and children and the coming generations in securing the unity of the people in the land. There is a great deal of "touchiness" about the full Israelite status of the Transjordanian tribes.

As an aspect of the structuralist analysis of the texts in Numbers 32 and Joshua 22, Jobling attempts to test the appropriateness of the immigration and revolt models of the settlement of Palestine as clarifiers of the structuralist literary data. He does not succeed in coming to a firm conclusion. Instead, the patterning of the dealings among the tribes is analyzed with the aid of conflict resolution theory from social psychology so that various scenarios of avoidance and of procedural resolution of conflict are seen at play within the accounts. Little is made of the wider import of such an analysis, but it might be promising to undertake a conflict resolution analysis of groups of stories in the Hebrew Bible in order to see if preferences for particular strategies typify particular literary traditions, historical periods, or levels of social and political organization. Somewhat along these lines, William Herbrechtsmeier attempts to correlate the original stratum of Deuteronomic legislation with types of third-party adjudication construed according to a theory of evolution of law correlated to levels of political organization.[10]

In short, I am arguing that the social structural and conflictual implicates of these narrative programs bear careful examination, not in a narrow historicist sense but in terms of broad patterns which can be cautiously assessed in terms of approximate historical periodization. For instance, does the "touchiness" about Israel's composite and compromised origins stem solely from collective insecurity in a late monarchic/exilic Deuteronomistic horizon, or does it reach back to memories of the premonarchic formation of intertribal Israel out of diverse groups of previously unrelated peoples?

My boundary-breaching examples between the literary and social coordinates have so far been taken from narrative genres. I wish now to mention the covenant or treaty genre as a stellar instance of the same phenomenon. The notion that Israel's covenant form is an adaptation of the suzerainty treaty from imperial politics is widely championed among biblical scholars, although many see this model as primarily Deuteronomic and not at all characteristic of earlier Israel. It so happens that the literary evidence for the suzerainty model is so fractured and scattered in the Bible—probably because of the reshaping of liturgical texts and literary redaction—that the decision of the comparativist to collect it all into a typical or modular form of suzerainty treaty is highly arbitrary.

It is possible, however, that this "literary" question may also be approached by another route, namely, through comparative sociology and politics. If we compare the sociopolitical organization underlying the suzerainty treaty in the ancient Near East with the sociopolitical organization of premonarchic Israel, the likelihood is strengthened that the suzerainty treaty was *not* the model of the premonarchic Israelite covenant except insofar as it may be an "antimodel" by which Israel cancels out imperial politics as a realm without any claim on its thinking and on its manner of life. I mean by this that the suzerainty treaty presupposes autonomous long-existing states that enter relations at narrowly specified points, leaving the rest of their existence untouched, and who do so as a normal part of international politics concerning which there is no cause for exceptional comment. By contrast, Israel has only recently been constituted a people, and its "treaty" between God and people, and among the peoples themselves, is in fact a "constituting instrumentality" which creates its own sovereignty de novo, in a manner that breaks sharply with the way "covenants" are conceived among the nations and thus we may conclude that there was some justification for Israel to think of itself as unique on specifically sociopolitical and religious organizational grounds (a point treated theologically by the doctrine of the chosen people).

The Meeting of Literary and Theological Practices

Lastly, I will mention some meeting points of literary critical practice and theological critical practice which appear to be instructive in generating research possibilities that will refine the literary conclusions and the theological conclusions. I want first to comment on the tendency of some literary critics, beginning at least with Erich Auerbach,[11] to round out their detailed literary analyses with attempts to explain the literary features of the Bible as a product of the religion or theology of Israel. Robert Alter, for instance, attributes the literary power of the Bible to the monotheistic belief of Israel, and Meir Sternberg sees the biblical literature as shot through with and shaped by an ideologizing of history. At times, perhaps because the theological treatment is far briefer than the literary, these explanations read almost like "spontaneous generation" theories, the faith, as it were, directly producing the literature so that the literary and the theological cease to be coordinates and the former is subsumed under the latter.

Alter at least has been quick to admit the impressionistic character of his suggestion so that it more nearly amounts, I think, to a question to pursue than it constitutes a satisfying answer. Others have noted that it is odd, if Alter and Sternberg are right, that it was just when the monotheistic and ideologizing forces grew strongest in Israel, namely in the exile and restoration, that the literary power of the narratives waned. It seems that some other mediating terms are needed between the high levels of theology or ideology and the literary expressions. I suggest that we look at sociopolitical forms, especially the conflictual wrenching from Egyptian-Canaanite servitude to tribal freedom to independent monarchy and return to servitude under Assyria and Babylon, as the likely matrix and resource for developing crisp and laconic stories that are highly contentious and materially bound to issues of immediate communal crisis. In this connection, it is relevant, I think, to attend to the suggestion of one scholar in regarding the short story as a virtual creation of the Yahwistic revolution at the beginning of Israel's intertribal social and religious formation, "designed to portray the radical effect of a new and great commitment upon the part of a new people who were once not a people. . . . The literary form was new, the people were new, the purpose was new."[12] In a broad sense this construal of the Israelite short story fits with Alter's attribution of the narrative skill to a religious source, but it does so not by the invocation of something so general as "monotheism" but by a correlation of the social features of the early Israelite movement and the earthy themes of the stories coincident with Yahwism of a certain type specific to the premonarchic period, which we probably do well not to call monotheism.

I mention here only one other mediation candidate in accounting for the lapidary narrative art in early Israel. I refer to the notion that early Israel, like early Greece, stood in a creative tension on the boundary between an oral culture and a rapidly developing literary culture, a tension which is aesthetically very creative.[13] Of course this oral-written passageway needs to be looked at in terms of its sociopolitical and religious correlates.

A tentative summary of the interaction of the coordinates in producing superb narrative might be as follows: when Yahwism was spawned in conjunction with intertribal sovereignty and prevailing oral genres and then extended under monarchic sovereignty nurturing writing, the narrative power was generated and sustained, but as sociopolitical sovereignty and religion were disjoined from the exile on, the narrative power to synthesize the social-theological combination lost much of its earlier force and edge.

To illustrate, let me cite an instance of a literary-theological "synapse" where the structurally analyzed narrative contradictions parallel theological contradictions. A vivid case in point is an actantial analysis of Genesis 2–3 according to which Yahweh is the initial sender/giver of the human cultivator Adam as object to the whole created earth as receiver, in order to till its waiting soil.[14] The program is compromised, however, and nearly destroyed, with Yahweh "coming off" as a deceptive giver, a folkloristic villain, since he in fact withholds the human cultivator from the whole earth by keeping him in the garden as a personal attendant. The original program can only be carried out by Yahweh appearing in a second role as helper when he creates the serpent and the man-woman pair out of the undifferentiated human. The serpent by tempting and the human pair by succumbing to temptation together become the subjects/protagonists who facilitate the blocked transfer of the human being as cultivator of the soil to the outside world. In the process, however, Yahweh must take on a third role as opponent who punishes the man in such a way that he enters the outside world as a greatly impaired cultivator since the soil will now produce poor yields.

This fascinating structural reading gives what amounts to a narratized transformation of the theological enigmas that have plagued interpreters of the story over the centuries and constituted major debating points within Christian theology. Yahweh's conflicted roles of sender, helper, and opponent are ways of alluding to the unresolved problems about divine justice, goodness, and power and about human freedom, guilt, and responsibility which are posed by the prohibition and the punishment for its violation. It can be said that we have a theological puzzle because we have a narrative program in which Yahweh appears to have put himself and the human pair in a "no win" situation hedged by a "double bind." Message one reads: "Don't eat the fruit! Stay here in the garden. But of course then you will not 'know' and human life in the real world will never begin!" Message two reads: "Eat the fruit! Gain knowledge and start living in the historical world. But of course you will live a frustrated and limited life lacking the social harmony and physical abundance of the garden!"

In short, if this account is looked at as an actual transcript of the first human events and of the mind and behavior of God assumed to possess the attributes assigned him in many later theologies, the story is out of joint. If, however, it reflects some of the major contradictions of human experience and does not hesitate to involve God (not necessarily here congruent with later notions of deity), the literary, social, and theological "faces" of the story will be less a puzzle to us and more a revelation of how certain contradictions of corporate human life were imagined in certain contexts in ancient Israel.

What form should theology take if it is to attend to literary critical practice? It seems to me that a proper beginning point for a theology of the Hebrew Bible is to take account of everything that the Bible says about God, everything that God says, and everything that people say to God. This would be to follow radically and faithfully the course of the text. It would be an enormous task of registering and grouping the data. Unless and until this is done, however, theological criticism will continue to build very selectively on narrow bases of God-talk and perhaps often with assumptions about how that language functions which a fresh look might alter. Of course a mere adding up of all the theological formulations according to some classification system will not produce theology, but interpretation would I think be better founded and more consistently answerable to a wider range of data than is now the case.

A LITERARY THEORY TO ENCOMPASS THE CRITICAL PRACTICES

How shall we conceive and give theoretical formulation to the interplay of the coordinate critical practices? It will have to be theory that does justice to all the practices as truthful ways of uncovering aspects of textual meaning. When I say that the literary, the social, and the theological are coordinate dimensions and coordinate critical practices, I mean that they are of equal rank and importance as specifiic "moments" or "instances" within an interpretive process that links or coordinates them as indispensable aspects of recovering meaning.

I would, however, like to stress that coordinate in rank and significance does not mean coordinate in the sense that any and every possible way of proceeding to interrelate the coordinates is advisable or productive. I take it, for instance, that literary criticism has effectively established that we begin with the text and we begin with it as a whole, from which point the literary genetics can be traced and the social and theological coordinates can be brought into play at every stage in the synchronic and diachronic literary treatments. This assumes that we are practicing literary, social, and theological criticism of a text called *Bible*. It is appropriate, and sometimes necessary, to supplement critical practices on the text with study of the social history or of the history of theological thought, etc., and then a first step would not necessarily be to consider the texts as wholes.

If, however, we attempt to convert the strategic first place of the literary coordinate in textual study into an assumption about its priority in rank and significance, we overstep the coordinating frame and truly "reduce" everything to the closed world of the text. We must have a theory that explains how the widest realities of life generate meanings in the text—how the text is open in certain ways to penetration and formation by the limits and conditions of history, society, and theology/ideology.

Simultaneously, we must recognize that the social and theological worlds enter the text through mediations of a complex sort. As we cannot let all the meaning of the text collapse into a self-constituting structure impervious to the rest of life, so we cannot rupture the aesthetic integrity of the text by making it a mere veiled set of signs about external conditions and happenings. No projection or mirror theory claiming that history, society, or ideology simply "toss off" or "exude" textual meanings will possibly do. The sui generis character of linguistic activity within the whole of human action must be respected and specified as a special way of rendering meaning that is in itself inseparable from the human life activities it refers to. So, an adequate theory of the coordinate critical practices must leave space to specify this oblique relation of literature to life, while also eschewing the impression that literature is free-floating from life and unqualified by it.

Among contemporary literary critics known to me, Terry Eagleton and Fredric Jameson come closest in my judgment to meeting the above desiderata. I comment only on some of their signal emphases. Eagleton locates a text within wider and narrower frames of constraint. The wider frame is the predominant mode of production interacting with the prevailing ideology. The narrower frame is the literary mode of production and ideology associated with a particular aesthetic ideology which is given a twist by the specific authorial ideology of the writer. The result of writing within these frames is a text with its own ideology. This text is not a mere passive product of the mentioned constraints but a particular formation in the force field which works so as "to actively determine its own determination," thereby presenting an ideology unique to the text. The ideology of the text does not preexist the text but is coexistent with the text, as it constitutes a peculiar expression of the general ideology or of some oppositional ideology locked in contest with the prevailing ideology.

When we take our stance within a work of fiction—and I would say also within a biblical historylike genre as well—whose relation to the historical is not straightforward, we discover that part of the text's very ideology as text is to present itself, as it were, outside of history or, at best, to be a reference to a general human condition uncluttered by historical specificity. This feature, which Eagleton calls "the pseudo-real" of the text, is an aspect of its guise as literature and in this act of self-hiding we see the text's ultimate residual connection to history.

> The text, we may say, gives us certain socially determined representations of the real cut loose from any particular real conditions to which those representations refer. It is in this sense that we are tempted to feel that it is self-referential, or conversely (the twin idealist error) refers to "life" or the "human condition," since if it denotes no concrete state of affairs it must denote either itself, or states of affairs in general. But it is precisely in this absence of the particular real that the text most significantly refers—refers not to concrete situations, but to an ideological formation (and hence, obliquely, to history) which "concrete situations" have actually produced. The text gives us such ideology without its real history alongside it, as though it were autonomous. . . . If it seems true that at the level of the text's "pseudo-real"—its imaginary figures and events—"anything can happen," this is by no means true of its ideological organization; and it is precisely because *that* is not true that the free-wheeling contingency of its pseudo-real is equally illusory. . . . The truth of the text is not an essence but a practice—the practice of its relation to ideology, and in terms of that to history. . . . Like private property, the literary text thus appears as a "natural" object, typically denying the determinants of its productive process. The function of criticism is to refuse the spontaneous presence of the work—to deny that "naturalness" in order to make its real determinants appear.[15]

Jameson, following Althusser's notion of "history as absence" and reworking Greimas's binary oppositions as a way of mapping the "ideological closures" that texts effect, has developed sophisticated analyses of how the limits of the social and ideological worlds of the author are mediated or refracted into limit situations in the fictional works. Much of his attention is given to what the text excludes in its way of seeing the problematic of the story or in its way of recognizing live options for the characters. His tracings of these "ideological closures" in Balzac and Conrad are elaborately done and succeed in bringing out the historical and social ground while also accenting the distinctive shape of the plot and characterization, unique in the very moment that they manifest the history which is strictly absent from them. Jameson thus tries to show how the conflicts of the text, especially what it excludes or omits as possibility, have a significant correlation to what is experienced and deemed as centrally disputed, actual, possible, or impossible in the lived fabric of the society experienced by the writer:

> History is *not* a text, not a narrative, master or otherwise, but, as an absent cause, it is inaccessible to us except in textual form, and our approach to it and to the Real itself necessarily passes through its prior textualization, its narrativization in the political unconscious. . . . Ideology is not something which informs or invests symbolic production: rather the aesthetic act is itself ideological, and the production of aesthetic or narrative form is to be seen as an ideological act in its own right, with the function of inventing imaginary or formal "solutions" to unresolvable social contradictions. . . . History is therefore the experience of Necessity, and it is this alone which can forestall its thematization or reification as a mere object of representation or as one master code among many others. Necessity is not in that sense a type of content, but rather the inexorable *form* of events; it is therefore a narrative category in the enlarged sense of some properly narrative political unconscious which has been argued here, a retextualization of History which does not propose the latter as some new representation or "vision," some new content, but as the formal effects of what Althusser, following Spinoza, calls an "absent cause." Conceived in this sense, History is what hurts, it is what refuses desire and sets inexorable limits to individual as well as collective praxis, which its "ruses" turn into grisly and ironic reversals of their overt intention. But this History can be apprehended only through its effects, and never directly as some reified force. This is indeed the ultimate sense in which History as ground and untranscendable horizon needs no particular theoretical justification: we may be sure that its alienating necessities will not forget us, however much we might prefer to ignore them.[16]

To date, the explicit use of literary theoretical mappings of this sort in biblical studies has been minimal. In conceptualizing Deutero-Isaiah and Lamentations for teaching and writing purposes, I have employed Eagleton's categories and am impressed by their "utility" in forcing clarity of questions and in compelling careful and frequent interreadings among the coordinates. Only more recently have I become aware of Jameson and have yet to fully "cash in" on the points where he seems to advance beyond Eagleton. A recent "Jamesonian reading" of Psalm 72 by David Jobling does a skillful job of opening up the "differences" in a royal psalm so as to show how the operation of political centralization and the tributary mode of production in Israel effect the very structuration of the psalm as literary work.[17]

Finally, let me add that nothing I have said is intended to lay out flatly this sort of boundary crossing as a project for every literary critic, or for every biblical critic of whatever stripe. What I am contending is that the community of literary critics—and all the other critical communities—must include these boundary-searching projects with agendas that challenge and stretch the rest of us. We must encourage and support colleagues who venture on this course by offering them our constructive criticism. And of course in so complex and heady a work nothing can prevent results that are slipshod or nonsensical, some proportion of which must be tolerated for the sake of the health and productivity of all the critical practices which depend upon the lively interchange among them.

Notes

1. For fuller discussion, see Norman K. Gottwald, *The Hebrew Bible—A Socio-Literary Introduction* (Philadelphia: Fortress Press, 1985), pp. 6–34, 596–609.

2. Leonard L. Thompson, *Introducing Biblical Literature: A More Fantastic Country* (Englewood Cliffs, N.J.: Prentice-Hall, 1978).

3. Edgar V. McKnight, *The Bible and the Reader: An Introduction to Literary Criticism* (Philadelphia: Fortress Press, 1985).

4. D. F. Murray, "Narrative Structure and Technique in the Deborah and Barak Story," Supplements to *Vetus Testamentum* 30 (1979): 155–89; Alan J. Hauser, "Judges 5: Parataxsis in Hebrew Poetry," *Journal of Biblical Literature* 99 (1980): 23–41.

5. R. N. Whybray, *The Succession Narrative* (London: Student Christian Movement Press, 1968); David M. Gunn, *The Story of King David: Genre and Interpretation* (Sheffield: Journal for the Study of the Old Testament Press, 1978).

6. Robert Alter, *The Art of Biblical Narrative* (New York: Basic Books, 1981) and *The Art of Biblical Poetry* (New York: Basic Books, 1985); Meir Sternberg, *The Poetics of Biblical Narrative: Ideological Literature and the Drama of Reading* (Bloomington: Indiana University Press, 1985).

7. Njördur P. Njardvik, *Birth of a Nation: The Story of the Iceland Commonwealth* (Reykjavik: Iceland Review, 1978); Jona Kristjánsson, *Icelandic Sagas and Manuscripts* (Reykjavik: Iceland Review, 1980).

8. Robert Polzin, *Moses and the Deuteronomist: A Literary Study of the Deuteronomic History* (New York: Seabury Press, 1980), p. 145.

9. David Jobling, *The Sense of Narrative: Three Structural Analyses in the Old Testament—1 Samuel 13–31, Numbers 11–12. 1 Kings 17–18* (Sheffield: Journal for the Study of the Old Testament Press, 1978), pp. 26–52; Jobling, "'The Jordan a Boundary': A Reading of Numbers 32 and Joshua 22," *Society of Biblical Literature Seminar Papers* 19 (1980): 183–207.

10. William Herbrechtsmeier, "False Prophecy and Canonical Thinking" (Ph.D. diss., Columbia University, 1987), drawing on Katherine S. Newman, *Law and Economic Organization: A Comparative Study of Preindustrial Societies* (New York: Cambridge University Press, 1983).

11. Erich Auerbach, *Mimesis: The Representation of Reality in Western Literature* (Garden City, N.Y.: Doubleday, 1957).

12. Edward E. Campbell, Jr., *Ruth*, The Anchor Bible (Garden City, N.Y.: Doubleday, 1975), pp. 8–9.

13. H. A. Innis, *The Bias of Communication* (Toronto: University of Toronto Press, 1951).

14. David Jobling, "The Myth Semantics of Genesis 2:4b–3:24," *Semeia* 18 (1980): 41–49.

15. Terry Eagleton, *Criticism and Ideology: A Study of Marxist Literary Theory* (New York: Schocken Books, 1976), pp. 73–74, 101.

16. Fredric Jameson, *The Political Unconscious: Narrative as a Socially Symbolic Act* (Ithaca: Cornell University Press, 1981), pp. 35, 79, 102.

17. David Jobling, "Deconstruction and the Political Analysis of Biblical Texts: A Jamesonian Reading of Psalm 72" (unpublished paper for Society of Biblical Literature annual meeting, 1986).

Will to Power in Biblical
Interpretation

Joseph C. Sitterson, Jr.
Georgetown University

PARTLY by having reached limits to its own form and historical criticism, biblical study recently has shifted its focus: the biblical text formerly seen as transparent or culturally translucent to the Word of God is now, in the words of James M. Robinson, "not a secondary, distorting objectification of meaning that must be removed to free the meaning behind the language," but instead "an interpretative proclamation of that meaning."[1] Critics on both sides consequently have suggested that biblical hermeneutics can learn something from secular hermeneutics. About narrative theory, these critics are right; about relations between readers and texts, however, biblical hermeneutics should be skeptical of what much recent secular theory has to offer it. I believe that an influence should flow in the other direction, that biblical hermeneutics offers us a chastening perspective on our role in the creation of textual meaning, secular and sacred. The allusion in my title, then, is by way of Nietzsche to Harold Bloom, who writes that "No critic . . . can evade a Nietzschean will to power over a text, because interpretation at last is nothing else."[2] I shall argue this to be at best only a partial understanding of interpretation.

Let us look first at parable, on which a number of contemporary secular critics call to illuminate Bloom's scenario for the relation of textual meaning to interpretive subjects. It is perhaps telling that the parable cited in this context is not from the Bible but from Kafka: "Leopards break into the temple and drink to the dregs what is in the sacrificial pitchers; this is repeated over and over again; finally it can be calculated in advance, and it becomes a part of the ceremony."[3] This parable is quoted by Geoffrey Hartman, Susan Handelman, and Frank Kermode, and all interpret it allegorically.[4] I shall present a synthesis of Hartman and Handelman, who use it to explicate Bloom. (Kermode differs significantly in ways I shall not discuss here.)

The temple is culture; the sacred pitchers are its canonical texts. The leopards are the subsequent interpreters of the texts; their actions, breaking into the temple and emptying the pitchers, are their interpretations of the texts. The parable then supposedly illustrates the following claims about both interpretation and canon formation. First, acts of interpretation are instinct-derived—the leopards are thirsty, humans need meaning. Second, such acts become recorded and remembered in a culture's self-definition only if they are somehow strong interpretive acts—if leopards could not break into the temple, they could not become part of the ceremony, never having gotten there in the first place. Third, such acts are otherwise undifferentiated from one another—all leopards are the same; in Hartman's words, "there can be no progress, only repetition and elaboration—more ceremonies, sacrifices, lies, defenses. That we esteem these is the woe and wonder Bloom constantly commemorates."[5] Fourth, the cultural canon continues to be formed by the accumulation of such acts, such subsequent interpretive texts, added to earlier texts because the culture needs to master by incorporation what appears to it violent, barbarous, or incomprehensible behavior.

Here modern biblical parable study has learned from secular narrative theory to distrust simple allegory and to look more closely at the parable itself. Such study, as part of biblical hermeneutics' larger focal shift that I mentioned at the outset, has gone well beyond the uncritical belief that parables are always, in John Drury's critical words, allegorical "windows upon the world behind them," with "Interpreters [their] window-cleaners."[6] When we study this particular window-glass, we find enigmatic depths invisible to its secular allegorizers, who seem to see so clearly through it. Supposing it a parable about interpretation, is it about all interpretation? Are all interpreters—including the allegorizers—like leopards, animals acting solely out of some kind of thirst? Who is calculating in advance their appearance? Who is responding to the ceremony, and how? Are canonical texts containers, like sacred pitchers, of some liquid meaning that can be drunk up? I suggest, in keeping with the emphasis we have just noted on parabolic enigma, that Kafka's parable raises such issues without allegorizing their final interpretation. This suggestion interestingly brings Kafka's parable into the genre of biblical parable as characterized by recent interpreters like John Dominic Crossan: "story grown self-conscious and self-critical,"[7] a characterization I want to pursue later.

But let us look now at a second, biblical parable, this one also generally interpreted to be about interpretation: the synoptic Gospels' parable of the sower, whose seed we recall falls respectively to birds, rocks, thorns, and good soil. It is a "parable about parable," says J. Hillis Miller, who details its paradoxes, its self-conscious enigmas, which define the genre. First, "if you can understand the parables, you do not need them. If you need them, you cannot hope to understand them"—a paradox whose strong Markan version is explored further by Kermode. Second, the disciples, who, Jesus says, can understand the parables, don't; so he explains it to them. Third, Christ "The Word cannot speak the Word" directly, but only in "the limitations of [fallen] human language." This final paradox, "the parables of the Gospels as at once Word of God and at the same time humanly comprehensible words," Miller finds analogous to "the mystery of the Incarnation [itself], in which God and humanity become one across the barrier of the impossibility of their union."[8]

All three synoptic writers narratively situate us as readers with Jesus and the disciples, since we overhear their dialogue as well as his parables. We therefore might suppose ourselves superior to the people, the outsiders who hear only the parables.[9] Except that the disciples demonstrate repeatedly failures to understand, and except that we are not overhearing a dialogue but reading a text, outside it and outside the events it recounts. So that we are left in our attempts to interpret the Word with words, not the Word itself; just as, most strikingly, Mark originally left off his story with words about the tomb emptied of Jesus, explicitly identified in John with the Word, and with words about the fearful human silence that followed that emptiness. And even the resurrection appearances in Matthew and Luke insistently, if less strikingly, show the disciples' failures to believe and, as Robinson observes, do not show a resurrected Jesus "liberated from the shackles of the flesh"—and of human words—"in the glory of a luminous heavenly body or bodilessness, teaching esoteric Gnostic truth."[10]

At this point the customary postmodern move is obvious: absence, presence deconstructed, meaning endlessly deferred—these would be the allegorical interpretations of the sower parable and Mark's empty tomb alike. And presumably it would follow that subsequent Gospel assertions of meaning and presence derive not from original meaning and presence, but from human needs and drives, what Bloom and others see as a defensive will to power.

But let us reencounter the text. Unlike Kafka's, the biblical parable is not disembodied, standing alone.[11] It is instead presented within the narrative as part of a complex speech act. Within that narrative people, including Jesus, act. The disciples are not, as the very existence of the Gospels evidences, finally paralyzed into contemplative inactivity by their uncomfortably paradoxical role in the narrative containing the sower parable. So if we situate ourselves as outsiders, like others within the narrative, then we must also see that not all outsiders react the same way to enigmatic meaning.

The sower parable has other specifically biblical contexts. Let me

mention two of them and what I shall argue to be their similar interpretive consequences. First, although I have been discussing it as a
synoptic parable, it of course has three different forms, each in the
service of a different narrative. The biggest difference is between two
small Greek words, *hina* and *hoti*. Just before giving the sower parable,
in Mark Jesus explains to the disciples that "for those outside everything is in parables; so that [*hina*] they may indeed see but not perceive, and may indeed hear but not understand; lest they should turn
again, and be forgiven"; in Matthew, he says that "I speak to them in
parables, because [*hoti*] seeing they do not see, and hearing they do
not hear, nor do they understand." This difference to Kermode and
others makes all the difference: "One says the stories are obscure on
purpose to damn the outsiders; the other . . . says that they are not
necessarily impenetrable, but that the outsiders, being what they are,
will misunderstand them anyway." "The desire to change *hina* to *hoti*,"
Kermode continues, "is a measure of the dismay we feel at our arbitrary and total exclusion from the kingdom, or from the secret sense of
the story," and "Matthew took the first step toward reducing th[is]
bleak mystery." Kermode's point is well argued, but we should notice
that Matthew's first step is actually an enigmatic one: as Kermode
himself admits, "it is Matthew who remarks, at the moment when he
is explaining the difference between insiders and outsiders . . . that 'to
him who has will more be given . . . but from him who has not, even
what he has will be taken away.'"[12] And we should notice also that
Luke, while he omits Mark's emphatic "lest they should turn again,
and be forgiven," retains *hina*: "for others they ["the secrets of the
kingdom of God"] are in parables, so that [*hina*] seeing they may not
see, and hearing they may not understand." There is then, I am
arguing, a parabolic continuity here as significant as its intertextual
difference. I suggest further that the difference, between Mark's sense
that parable is uninterpretable and a later sense that it is interpret-
able, is itself parabolic: Drury observes that "the parable [is] a riddle
for which an interpretation and an interpreter are not optional but
necessary"[13]—but, he implies, the interpretation is not necessarily a
sufficient one.

When we look at a second, larger context I believe we can extend
this principle of continuity and difference to become a hermeneutic
principle. For example, in relation to the synoptics the Gospel of John
marks the end, as Drury puts it, "of Christianity as popular narrative. . . . A great age of Christian doctrine begins. Stories will yield to
creeds." And yet he also rightly says that "for all John's perception of
the eternal, his long speeches floating over the historical narrative, his
grounding beyond history of the one who utters them—it still tells a

story," like the synoptics.[14] Similarly, the Bible as a whole embodies such a tension between interpretation and experiential story. To Joseph Blenkinsopp, the "creative tension" in the Hebrew Bible is Law, or "normative order," versus Prophecy, which attacks "misplaced confidence arising out of possession of a law written down, edited, and authoritatively interpreted." This tension is not an accident of the canon; "those responsible for the editing of the biblical material did not on the whole expunge views in conflict with their own," he argues, "but rather allowed them to exist side by side in a state of unresolved tension or unstable equilibrium."[15] This argument, he suggests, extends to the Christian Bible,[16] where Crossan finds a similar tension between what he calls "the binary and polar opposites" of biblical story: myth, "that gives one the final word," versus parable, "that subverts final words"; and while Crossan believes that the primitive church sought to allegorize Jesus' parables into myth, the Gospels still present not one but both.[17]

The reader's relation, to the single parable and its differing versions, to its Gospel context(s), to the Bible, must then also be tension-filled if he or she is not to assume either a godlike transcendence of the text or a complete submission to the text and its meaning taken as dominating, clear, and absolute.

Secular hermeneutics too often evades this tension. On one side, the "every man his own interpreter" position, as exemplified by Norman Holland, simply ignores it by ignoring the cultural constraints operating on any single interpreter.[18] On the same side Stanley Fish transfers interpretive authority from the individual to his or her "interpretive community" and thereby frees individuals of both their individual authority and any possible resulting tension with their community.[19] For both Holland and Fish the reader, whether purely individual for Holland, or culturally determined for Fish, dominates and eventually replaces with his or her own the text's cultural context (to the extent that context has not become somehow "part of" the reader or the reader's interpretive community). On the other side, for T. S. Eliot the text's cultural context (including all of its history as part of "the" collection of great works of art) dominates, even subsumes, the individual subject into its "tradition," to the point of what Eliot calls "a continual self-sacrifice, a continual extinction of personality," "depersonalization."[20] Bloom, though his preference is clear, at least writes about both possibilities—that the reader either replaces the text's cultural context with his or her own or is subsumed into the text's cultural context.

But the two are finally for Bloom the only, and mutually exclusive, alternatives. I suggest that all these theories of textual meaning, au-

thority, and power—Bloom's in particular—fundamentally mislocate
that meaning because they suppose it to be a positivist entity, locatable "in" the reader or "in" the text. In Bloom's oedipal model for the
will to power, there can be only two ultimate centers or locations of
meaning, authority, and power—father (text) and son (reader), and
these two inevitably contest for primacy. And for all Bloom's emphasis on reading as an agonistic process,[21] it always comes to an end in
that only one of the two can survive—father (Bloom's "strong precursor" writer who subsumes the weak interpreter son) or son (Bloom's
"strong misreader" who replaces—in his own mind anyway—the
father-text with his own reading or version of it). But these alternatives, father or son, winning or losing, are based on a misunderstanding of the Oedipus complex. Bloom writes: "The poetic ego is a
kind of paranoid construct founded upon the ambivalency of opposition [complete independence] and identity [complete dependence]
between the ephebe [later poet or reader] and the precursor."[22] His
misunderstanding supposes that one subject's identity either is
achieved through complete independence from its "father" or cultural
context or is lost through complete dependence on that context.

These are indeed the two extremes of oedipal "resolution." But why
do we suppose that the complex is "resolved" in some final sense in
every or even in most cases? Sons, children, subjects, and later texts
do not usually achieve some final resolution of their tension-filled relations with their fathers, parents, cultures, and earlier texts, and those
who believe that they do so I suspect believe it out of their own desire
for permanence, not because it is in fact true. Even if we suppose such
resolution, it is not necessarily the "winner take all" ending which
Bloom envisions. Paul Ricoeur hypothesizes "fatherhood as a process
rather than a structure," enabling us to see how arrested is Bloom's
oedipal literary structure, frozen in an "infantile omnipotence" from
which "proceeds the phantasm of a father who would retain the
privileges which the son must seize if he is to be himself." The alternative, Ricoeur suggests, is "the degree [to which] our desire, by
renouncing omnipotence, assents to the representation of a mortal
father whom it is no longer necessary to kill but who can be
recognized."[23] I would add here only that such recognition is not
always free from tension.

One final example, again from the Gospels. Robinson argues for a
tension, of the same sort I and others have suggested is essential to the
Hebrew and the Christian Bibles, between the narrative of Mark and
the sayings of Q—along with Mark an hypothesized common source of
Matthew and Luke. The canonizing process, he continues, sought to
correct Q's neglect of narrative by omitting it, and to correct Mark's

neglect of sayings "by sandwiching it in between Matthew and Luke and hence ultimately degrading it into what was taken to be an abridgement of Matthew, to play a negligible role in the history of Christianity."[24] So Robinson reminds us that such tension can be threatening and consequently canonically minimized. I am not then claiming a consistently deliberate and self-conscious human preservation of this tension in the various biblical canons. But I am suggesting that defensive will to power is not adequate to explain the pervasiveness there of parabolic tension, whether intratextual or intertextual, and that consequently will to power is not adequate to explain canonizing in particular or interpreting in general. Mark is still there, after all. The continuing existence of this tension—intertextually between Old Testament and New, between Law and Prophecy, between one Gospel and another, between one version of a parable and another, even between one word and another, and intratextually between parable and its narrative, even within the parable itself—suggests that power and meaning are not easily locatable and do not simply stay with or pass from one text, interpretation, or subject to another. It suggests also that the human subjects who grow up, create, and interpret in tension sometimes recognize that tension not as barbarous or incomprehensible, to be overcome, but as partly constituting their subjectivity.[25]

Notes

All biblical quotations are from the Revised Standard Version of the Bible.

1. James M. Robinson, "Hermeneutic since Barth," *The New Hermeneutic*, ed. Robinson and John B. Cobb, Jr. (New York: Harper & Row, 1964), pp. 6–7.

2. Harold Bloom, "From J to K, or The Uncanniness of the Yahwist," in *The Bible and the Narrative Tradition*, ed. Frank McConnell (New York: Oxford University Press, 1986), p. 21.

3. Franz Kafka, *Parables and Paradoxes*, 2d. rev. ed. (New York: Schocken Books, 1961), p. 93.

4. Geoffrey H. Hartman, *Criticism in the Wilderness: The Study of Literature Today* (New Haven: Yale University Press, 1980), p. 55; Susan A. Handelman, *The Slayers of Moses: The Emergence of Rabbinic Interpretation in Modern Literary Theory* (Albany: State University of New York Press, 1982), pp. 222–23; Frank Kermode, *The Genesis of Secrecy: On the Interpretation of Narrative* (Cambridge: Harvard University Press, 1979), pp. 26–27.

5. Hartman, *Criticism in the Wilderness*, p. 55.

6. John Drury, *The Parables in the Gospels: History and Allegory* (New York: Crossroad, 1985), p. 2.

7. John Dominic Crossan, *The Dark Interval: Towards a Theology of Story* (Niles, Ill.: Argus, 1975), p. 57.

8. J. Hillis Miller, "Parable and Performative in the Gospels and in Modern Literature," in *Humanizing America's Iconic Book*, ed. Gene M. Tucker and Douglas A. Knight (Chico, Calif.: Scholars Press, 1982), pp. 62, 63, 70.

9. See Luke T. Johnson, *The Writings of the New Testament: An Interpretation* (Philadelphia: Fortress Press, 1986), p. 158.

10. James M. Robinson, "The Gospels as Narrative," in McConnell, ed., *Bible and Narrative*, p. 103.

11. In one sense Kafka's parables are not alone, but parts of larger works. This parable is not, however, given an explicit narrative context by its contemporary interpreters.

12. Kermode, *Genesis of Secrecy*, pp. 32, 33, 31.

13. Drury, *Parables in the Gospels*, p. 13.

14. Ibid., pp. 164, 158–59.

15. Joseph Blenkinsopp, *Prophecy and Canon: A Contribution to the Study of Jewish Origins* (Notre Dame: University of Notre Dame Press, 1977), pp. 2, 38, 94. See also Robert Alter, *The Art of Biblical Narrative* (New York: Basic Books, 1981), pp. 34–35.

16. Blenkinsopp, *Prophecy and Canon*, p. 140.

17. Crossan, *The Dark Interval*, pp. 57, 128, 123–27.

18. See Norman Holland, *5 Readers Reading* (New Haven: Yale University Press, 1975). This may seem unfair to Holland, since one of his chapters is titled "From Subjectivity to Collectivity" (pp. 232–49). But he moves untroubled from one to the other using the same model of an "identity theme," a particular "constancy that informs everything a human being says or does" (p. 56), and that determines how each person interprets a text: "The individual (considered as the continuing creator of variations on an identity theme [stemming from "a pleasure principle of change"]) relates to the world as he does to a poem or a story: he uses its physical reality as grist with which to re-create himself, that is, to make yet another variation in his single, enduring identity" (pp. 128–29). "One can then understand the group as a macroperson, having an identity theme. . . . In this sense, one grasps the whole style of the group outright, as one would abstract the personality of one of these five readers" (p. 245). Tension in this model, we should notice, exists only to be overcome or avoided. Holland does not change his model substantially in his most recent book *The I* (New Haven: Yale University Press, 1985).

19. Stanley Fish, *Is There a Text in This Class? The Authority of Interpretive Communities* (Cambridge: Harvard University Press, 1980).

20. T.S. Eliot, "Tradition and the Individual Talent" (1919), *Selected Essays* (New York: Harcourt, Brace & World, 1950), p. 7. Eliot says that the tradition, the "ideal order" of artworks, "is modified by the introduction of the new (the really new) work of art among them," and thus "the past [is] altered by the present as much as the present is directed by the past" (p. 5). Given his insistence on the artist's (and interpreter's) "extinction of personality," his explanation for such change seems either magical or absent.

21. For example, Harold Bloom, "The Breaking of Form," in *Deconstruction and Criticism* (New York: Seabury Press, 1979), pp. 5–6, and Bloom, *The Breaking of the Vessels* (Chicago: University of Chicago Press, 1982), p. 104.

22. Harold Bloom, *Poetry and Repression: Revisionism from Blake to Stevens* (New Haven: Yale University Press, 1976), p. 145.

23. Paul Ricoeur, "Fatherhood: From Phantasm to Symbol," *The Conflict of Interpretations*, ed. Don Ihde (Evanston, Ill.: Northwestern University Press, 1974), pp. 469, 470, 473. Elsewhere Ricoeur's analysis can be taken as an even more precise critique of Bloom. Bloom's dominant figure, among many, for poetic influence is "apophrades," the return of the dead: "A poet [is] a man rebelling against being spoken to by a dead man (the precursor) outrageously more alive than himself." In *A Map of Misreading* (New York: Oxford University Press, 1975), p. 19. Ricoeur writes: "on the level of phantasm, there is a death of the father, but it is a murder; this murder is the work of omnipotent desire, which dreams of itself as immortal; it gives birth, by the interiorization of the paternal image, to a complementary phantasm, that of the father immortalized beyond the murder" (p. 491). I would go so far as to say that Bloom's reading of the

entire Romantic tradition fundamentally mistakes the imagination for this phantasy of omnipotent desire.

24. Robinson, "Gospels," in McConnell, ed., *Bible and Narrative*, p. 103.

25. I thank my former colleague Jouette Bassler, now at the Perkins School of Theology, Southern Methodist University, and my colleagues Eric Cheyfitz, Elizabeth McKeown, and Jason Rosenblatt for their thoughtful readings of an earlier version of this essay, which I read at "The Bible and Literary Theory" program of the Religious Approaches to Literature division of MLA, 29 December 1986.

History Becomes Parable:
A Reading of the Midrashic *Mashal*

Daniel Boyarin

Bar Ilan University

THE meaning and typology of figurative narrative is a subject that has held the interest of literary critics at least since Aristotle. In the last century, a whole small library has been written about the parables of the Gospels attempting to arrive at generic definitions and classifications.[1] The study of the midrashic *mashal* (pl. *meshalim*) has played an increasingly important role in this research, but it, itself, has rarely been studied on its own terms.[2] The house of *mashal* has in fact several rooms, and in this essay I would like to enter one of these, the exegetic *mashal* as it is found in tannaitic Midrash.[3] The term *exegetic mashal* intends that in these texts a verse of the Bible is being interpreted by means of a parable. The relation of the verse to the parable (and indeed, the very nature of these parables) will be the subject of my text.

Susan Wittig's very clear analysis of the semiosis of the gospel parable and its congeners in later Western literature will make an effective backdrop for my study.[4] Her argument is that in normal denotation a sign vehicle refers to a *denotatum*, "which has or could have physical existence in the extra-linguistic world (e.g. 'The householder went out early in the morning to hire workers for his vineyard.')."[5] In the parabolic system, however, the denotatum, in turn, becomes a sign in itself, "designating an *unstated designatum*, a conceptual referent which exists only in a work of moral and physiological abstraction, which cannot be perceived in the extra-linguistic world, and which must be supplied by the perceiver of the sign (e.g. 'The spirit of God at the beginning of time began to seek out righteous men.')."[6]

The structure of this duplex semiotic gains its energy and effectiveness from the nature of the semantic relationships which link its components. The first order linguistic sign vehicle is linked *conventionally* and *arbitrarily* to its denotatum, as are nearly all linguistic signs; the second order material sign vehicle, however, is linked *iconically* to its object in the same way that the structure of a diagram formally exemplifies and exhibits the structure of its object.[7]

54

However, Wittig goes much further than this in her discussion. She argues that the parable is an indeterminate text in Wolfgang Iser's sense of text marked by "*hiatus*—the lack of syntactic or semantic connections—and *indeterminacy*—the omission of detail—and which invite the reader to establish his own connections between the lines of the text, so to speak, and to create his own significant detail, when the text does not offer it."[8] The parables of the Gospels are in Wittig's view just such texts. The "indeterminacy" of meaning is suggested by the fact that the "second order denotatum" is not stated in the text (a definition governed, incidentally, by the assumption—common but nevertheless an assumption—that the applications of the parables in the Gospels are not an original part of the text).[9] The reader, by being forced to interpret such texts, comes up against his/her own "expectations and preconceptions—his own meaning-system."[10] Then:

> In semiotic terms, such texts are self-reflexive in a metacommunicative dimension, calling to our attention not their syntactic or semantic structures, but the variety of ways in which those structures are actualized in our minds, are made to yield their potential meanings. When we read a text characterized by the quality of indeterminacy, as the parables are, we are reading ourselves as well as the text, and are being forced to an awareness of the creation of meaning in our own minds, as well as to an awareness of the meaning itself.[11]

Now, whether or not Wittig's characterization of the Gospel parables as "indeterminate" texts is successful,[12] it can be used as an effective backdrop for the midrashic *mashal*, precisely because the latter manifests a quite different structure. Let us see an example of the midrashic *mashal* and see the differences which this text shows from Wittig's description (and indeed from the Gospel parables, if she is correct):[13]

> And the angel of God, going before the Camp of Israel, moved and went behind them. And the Pillar of Cloud moved from before them and went behind them [Exod. 14:19]. R. Yehuda said: "This is a Scripture enriched from many places. He made of it a mashal; to what is the matter similar? To a king who was going on the way, and his son went before him. Brigands came to kidnap him from in front. He took him from in front and placed him behind him. A wolf came behind him. He took him from behind and placed him in front. Brigands in front and the wolf in back; he (He) took him and placed him in his (His) arms, for it says, "I taught Ephraim to walk, taking them on My arms [Hos. 11:3]." . . . The son began to suffer; he (He) took him on his shoulders, for it is said, "in the desert which you saw, where the Lord, Your God carried you [Deut. 1:31]." The son began to suffer from the sun; he (He) spread on him His

cloak, for it is said, "He has spread a cloud as a curtain [Ps. 105:39]." He became hungry; he (He) fed him, for it is said, "Behold I send bread, like rain, from the sky [Exod. 16:4]." He became thirsty; he (He) gave him drink, for it is said, "He brought streams out of the rock [Ps. 78:16]."[14]

A semiotic analysis of this text will reveal how far it is from the description of the Gospel parables we have been summarizing. Let us begin by questioning the term *mashal* itself. It translates as "likeness" in English, a translation expanded as well by the phrase, "to what is the matter similar?" in the introduction formula to the midrashic *mashal*. The very semantics of the *mashalic* terminology seem therefore to support at this level Wittig's analysis of the parable as an iconic sign. However, this support is only apparent, because the *mashal* is not iconic of an abstraction, of a *designatum*, which is not present in the text itself as in Wittig's account, but precisely of other signs which are present and even primary. Moreover, that of which the *mashal* is an iconic sign is itself a narrative, and indeed a narrative which is more concrete in reference than the narrative in the *mashal*, namely, in this case, the story of God's tender treatment of the Jews in the wilderness. There seems to be some kind of a reversal of structure here. While in the parables of the gospel a story is told, which, in Wittig's words, does or could have real reference in the world and designates another meaning which is not referential, in the midrashic text it is the biblical narrative which is being interpreted by the *mashal*. Now the biblical narrative certainly makes referential claims—much more strongly than that of the denotatum of a parable. It not only claims that it could possibly be something that happened out there in the world, but that it certainly *did* happen. Moreover, the *mashal* makes no claim in its discourse that it did or even really could have happened. It usually, in fact, is either quite schematic in its characterizations and plot or even quite unrealistic. Finally, the *mashal* as an interpretive structure is anything but indeterminate. There is indeed hardly any room for interpretation at all of the *mashal*. Its meaning is rigidly controlled by its textual form. Hardly any gaps are found—neither hiatus nor indeterminacy—in the *mashalic* narrative. The *mashal* is a closed text —not an open one—at least insofar as any text can be closed.

Let us see then what this text does do. The narrative in the verse upon which R. Yehuda is commenting is gapped. The motivation for the movement of the angel of God that was accustomed to go before the people is not made clear. Moreover, there is a doubling in the verse. "The angel of God who was accustomed to go in front of the Israelite army, moved and went behind them. And the pillar of cloud shifted from in front of them and took its place behind them." The higher critics place a join between J and E in the middle of this verse.[15] R. Yehuda puts in his story. This paradoxical moving around of first angel then pillar is explained as part of a pattern of God's protective behavior toward the Jews in the wilderness,[16] as a father would protect his infant son. The story which R. Yehuda puts in and which answers to the gapping in the verse is built up entirely out of materials drawn from other parts of the biblical canon itself, as he himself avers by his statement, "This is a Scripture enriched from many places." What then is the function of the *mashal?* I suggest that it is a structure (genre/code) which enables and constrains at the same time the possibility of new narrative to fill in the gap. As such, it can hardly in itself be indeterminate and enigmatic.

The Midrash has described the function of *mashal* as interpreting the hermetic Torah, not by any means of being hermetic itself. The Torah is encoded; the *mashal* is the code book by which it was encoded and through which it may therefore be decoded. In the introduction to the Midrash on Song of Songs, which the rabbis read as a *mashal* itself,[17] we read:

> Another interpretation: "Song of Songs," This is what Scripture has said: "And not only that Kohellet was wise." (*Ecclesiastes* 12:9) Had another man said them, you would have had to bend your ears and hear these words; "and not only that"—it was Solomon who said them. Had he said them on his own authority, you would have had to bend your ear and hear them; "and not only that"—he said them by the Holy Spirit. "And not only that Kohellet was wise, he moreover taught knowledge to the people, and proved and researched, and formulated many *meshalim:"*—"and proved" words of Torah; "and researched" words of Torah; he made handles[18] for the Torah. You will find that until Solomon existed, there was no *dugma*).[19]

Kohellet is, of course, Solomon. According to biblical tradition, that wise king wrote three books—Song of Songs, Proverbs, and Ecclesiastes (Kohellet).[20] Therefore, the verse of Ecclesiastes which tells us of his intellectual activity in general is appropriately referred to all three of his works. Now this activity is characterized as "teaching knowledge to the people," which for the rabbis means ineluctably teaching Torah. It follows that he "proved and researched" the words of Torah. And this interpretive activity is designated by the verse itself as "making of many *meshalim,*" this last glossed by the Midrash as *dugma*, that is, figure, simile, or paradigm.[21] The interpretive activity that Solomon engaged in was the making of figurative stories which are "handles to the Torah," that is, as I shall argue, which render the axiological meaning of the narratives of the Torah accessible.[22]

We see, therefore, that on the rabbis' own account, the *mashal* is anything but an enigmatic narrative. Its whole function is to teach knowledge to the people, to make handles for the Torah, so that the people (not an elect) can understand. Now the filling in of gaps as a major force in midrashic reading certainly has been seen before me.[23] What I wish to question here is the origin and authority of the narrative which fills in the gaps. The material for the filling in of the gaps in Midrash is generated by the intertext in two ways. First of all, as we have seen, the narrative material is created often (if not always) out of other scriptural materials having a more or less explicit reference to the narrative at hand. Second, the plot—the narrative action—and the characters of the narrative gap-filling are also given in the intertext. They are the *mashal*. That is to say, on my reading, the *mashal* is a culturally determined narrative schema which creates and constrains the possibilities for filling in the hiatus and resolving the indeterminacy of the biblical narrative text. The *mashal*, on my view, corresponds then to what Wittig has called "the 'meaning system,' the organized stable gestalt of beliefs and values held by the perceiver,"[24] except that I would locate this system not in the perceiver but in the cultural code. This is what the Midrash above means when it characterizes the *mashal* as *dugma*, paradigm.

In order to understand better the function that I am claiming for the *mashal* I will discuss it in the light of Frank Kermode's *The Genesis of Secrecy*, although not in regard to his chapter on parable but rather to the one in which he discusses the generation of the gospel narrative. In an extraordinarily elegant and lucid discussion which I can hardly hope to reproduce in shortened form, Kermode presents there something like the following model by which the gospel story has been generated. There was/is[25] a primitive fable underlying the text as we have it today. Kermode discusses the Passion narrative as having been generated from such a primitive fable. His theory is that originally (diachronically or synchronically understood) the fable existed. The fable is a series of actions—a plot:

> The primitive "ado"[26] must, insofar as it is a series of actions, have agents, and these agents, insofar as ado or fable acquires extension, must transcend their original type and function, must cease to be merely Hero, Opponent, and so on, and acquire idiosyncracies, have proper names. The more elaborate the story grows—the more remote from its schematic base—the more these agents will deviate from type and come to look like "characters."[27]

The fabula underlying the gospel has according to Kermode an appearance quite similar to the deep structure of the folk tale as hypothesized by Propp or Greimas.[28] "Let us then presuppose a *fabula*, progressively interpreted: first by Mark, then by Matthew and Luke using Mark, and by John, who perhaps used a not dissimilar but not identical original."[29] Kermode calls this process of narrative elaboration interpretation because "the redaction of an existing narrative was, in these circumstances, a pre-exegetical interpretative act; instead of interpreting by commentary, one does so by a process of augmenting the narrative."[30] This primitive gospel fable had the following narrative acts: Leavetaking, Arrest, Trial, Execution, and Reunion. Now, this narrative sequence requires that there be a betrayer. In Kermode's words:

> The necessity, in a circumstantial and history-like story, of having a character to perform the Betrayal is obvious enough. Depending how one looks at it, he plays the role of Helper or Opponent; by opposing the Hero he serves the logic of the narrative, as Satan did in Job. Satan's name means "adversary" or "Opponent"; so here, when, as Luke and John report, he entered into Judas, we have a case of a character being possessed by his narrative role. Of course by opposing he helps; his evil act, like Satan's, is permissive, ultimately a means to good.
>
> So Betrayal becomes Judas. . . . And for Mark, that is the end of Judas. He has done his narrative part. So in this gospel there is not a great deal to distinguish Judas from a more abstract agency—he might be called simply "the Betrayer," or "Betrayal," as in some morality play.[31]

Now what I would like to propose is that in the Midrash text which includes the written Torah story, the *mashal*, and the narrative filling which the Midrash provides, the *mashal* is the (necessarily synchronic) fabula underlying the narrative elaboration of the biblical text together with its midrashic expansion. That is, in effect the *mashal* accomplishes its work by assigning a structural description to the elliptic narrative of the Torah, which enables the completion of its syntactic structure. Moreover, since, as we know, structural description on the syntactic level is also semantic description, this assigning of an underlying structural description to the narrative declares a meaning as well.

We find a very elegant example of this hermeneutic technique in the *Mekilta* in the following passage:

> And Moses stretched out his hand over the sea (*Exod.* 14:21). The Sea began to stand against him. Moses said, "in the Name of the Holiness," but it did not yield. The Holiness Blessed be He, revealed Himself; the Sea began to flee, as it says, "The Sea saw and fled (*Ps.* 114:3)." Its *mashal*; to

what is the matter similar? To a king of flesh and blood, who had two gardens, one inside the other. He sold the inner one, and the purchaser came to enter, but the guard did not allow him. He said to him, "in the name of the king," but he did not yield. He showed him the signet, but he did not yield until the king came. Once the king came, the guard began to flee. He said, "all day long I have been speaking to you in the name of the king and you did not yield. Now, why are you fleeing?" He said, "not from you am I fleeing, but from the king am I fleeing." . . . Similarly, Moses came and stood at the sea. He said to him, "in the name of the Holiness," and it did not yield, until the Holiness, Blessed be He, revealed Himself in His glory. The sea began to flee, as it is said, "The Sea saw and fled (Ps. 114:3)." Moses said to him, "all day long I have been speaking to you in the name of the Holiness, Blessed be He, and you did not submit. Now, what ails you, O Sea that you flee? (Ps. 114:5)" He answered him, "Not from before you do I flee, son of Amram, but, from before the Lord, tremble Earth, from before the God of Jacob (Ps. 114:7–8)."[32]

This text is a commentary on the verse, "And *Moses* stretched out his hand over the Sea, and the *Lord* moved the Sea with a strong wind. (*Exod.* 14:21)." The question that the interpreter is tacitly asking is what is the meaning of this sequence of events? Why did Moses stretch out his hand over the sea if it is God who is doing the moving? Or alternatively, if it is Moses who is performing the miracle, why does it say that the Lord moved the Sea? Magical staff or divine aid? Surely one does not need both. It is fascinating to note that modern Bible critics place precisely here a join between two sources for the Pentateuch, revealing their perception of a hiatus here in the story.[33] The solution of the Midrash is implicitly created by reading the text of Psalm 114 as a commentary on this passage. The dialogue of the psalm is inserted right into the middle of the verse between "And Moses stretched out his arm," and "And God moved the Sea." It is important that we have a look at the whole text of this small poem to appreciate the moves of the Midrash.

When Israel went out from Egypt; the House of Jacob from a foreign nation. Judah became His holy one; Israel His dominion. The Sea saw and fled; the Jordan turned back. The mountains danced like rams; the hills like lambs. What has happened to you, O Sea, that you flee; O Jordan that you turn back? O mountains that you dance like rams; O hills like lambs? From before the Master, tremble Earth, from before the God of Jacob.

The rhetorical question of the psalm is turned in the midrashic text into an actual colloquy between Moses and the Sea. That is to say, the figurative usage of the poem, the personification of the Sea, is contextualized historically and dramatized. This minidrama is then correlated with the verse in Exodus which is the subject of the Midrash, and that verse is situated dramatically as well. Out of the two texts is created a third, a new text, which has qualities, both semantic and aesthetic, which neither had alone. The verse in Exodus is now motivated. The answer has been given to the question why Moses stretched out his hand, but then God was the motivating force behind the movement of the sea. The text of the psalm has been sharpened. We now understand what the Sea saw. Instead of a vague "When Israel went out from Egypt," we have a specific moment. Instead of the somewhat enigmatic "What has happened to you O Sea?" we have a specific, why did you not flee till now, or rather why now and not before?

The function of the *mashal* here is to provide a narrative structure or pattern, within which the text from Exodus and the text from Psalms can be read together and provide mutual interillumination.[34] The hiatus in the narrative has been resolved through a double intertextual reading—double because both the text of the psalm and the *mashal*—the paradigm—are involved in the creation of the narrative material which fills the hiatus. The Midrash is therefore performing an operation of reading which is almost identical to that which is theorized by Iser for all readers of narrative. However, more than that is happening here, because by establishing the characters of the biblical narrative, that is, the Sea, Moses, and God as owner, guardian and purchaser, a system of values is also being invoked, which has power over the *indeterminacy* of the story. We are being told via this *mashal* that the Sea was not an independent power, but only a servant of God in this matter; his opposition to Moses was not against God's will but in (perhaps mistaken) obedience to God's will in making him guardian of these borders. The fact that it is only the inner garden which is sold is a figure of the contingency of the right that Moses (Israel) had to disturb the fundamental rules of nature, and that only God, the Creator, can change the rules at all.[35] We have here historical interpretation at its very intersection with fiction. In the words of Hayden White:

A historical interpretation, like a poetic fiction, can be said to appeal to its readers as a plausible representation of the world by virtue of its implicit appeal to those "pre-generic plot-structures" or archetypal story forms that define the modalities of a given culture's literary endowment. Historians, no less than poets, can be said to gain an "explanatory effect"—over and above whatever formal explanations they may offer of specific historical events—by building into their narratives patterns of meaning similar to those more explicitly provided by the literary art of the cultures to which they belong.[36]

What is the *mashal* if not such a narrative pattern of meaning?

We see this semiotic structure in another text from the *Mekilta*, where the authoritative and axiological power of the *mashal* is explicit:

> And Amaleq attacked [Exod. 17:8]. R. Yehoshua and R. El'azar Hasama say, this scripture is unclear[37] and it is interpreted by Job, where it says, "Can the rush grow without a swamp; can reeds wax large without water? [Job 8:11]" Is it possible for the rush to grow without a swamp; or is it possible for the reed to grow without water? So it is impossible for Israel to exist unless they busy themselves with the words of the Torah. And because they separated themselves from the Torah the enemy came upon them, because the enemy only comes because of sin and transgression.[38]

The text of Exodus is declared unclear, because the connection between this passage and the immediately preceding one is not explicit in the biblical text. The immediately preceding verses tell a story of the arrival of the Israelites in a place called Refidim, where they have no water to drink. The people become quite rebellious, and even threaten violence against Moses until God intervenes and sends water miraculously. The narrative finishes with the statement "He called the name of the place Trial and Strife, because of the strife of the Israelites and their trying of God, saying, 'Is God among us, or is He not?' (v. 7)." And then immediately, "And Amaleq attacked." What is the connection between the two events, or rather, what is the meaning of the second following hard on the first? This is the gap that the Midrash wishes to fill here. The text of Job is invoked as a solution to this hiatus or indeterminacy. In my reading of this text, the actual words cited from Job are only part of the text mobilized here in the interpretation. In order to understand how the text works, we ought to have a look at the quoted verse of Job in its context:

> Can the rush grow without a swamp; can reeds wax large without water? While it is still in its youth, will it not be cut down, and be dry before any grass? *So* are the ways of those who forget God, and the hope of the scornful will be lost.

Now it can be seen that the text from Job is itself a simple parable, so by utilizing this parable to solve the indeterminacy of the Exodus text the rabbis are performing precisely the same sort of hermeneutic operation we have been considering until now. The explicit meaning of the Job text is that sinners will be punished, and the implication is that those who do not sin will not be, as is, indeed, the message of the whole speech from which this is a quotation. This message is placed into the gap of the Torah text which is now no longer unclear. The attack of Amaleq is a direct result of the previous events. Since they were forgetters of God ("Is God among us or is He not?"), therefore they were doomed to early death, and the connection is explained. However, we can go even further than this. In the story of the Torah, the problem has to do with water. The people have arrived at a desert place and there is no water for them to drink; they complain and ask for water. Their request is heavily condemned as rebellion. Now this narrative presents problems of its own, for if they are indeed in the depths of the desert, and there is no water for them to drink, their desperation and crying out for water is quite understandable. This problem exercises interpreters of Exodus until the present day. Our Midrash, by using the *mashal* of Job, solves this problem as well. The lack of water which is spoken of is itself to be understood figuratively as lack of Torah, just as in the Job text those who forget God are compared to a stand of reeds whose water has dried up. Accordingly, we see that it is the neglect of Torah which leads to the forgetting of God and then to sin and the punishment for sin is that "the hope of the scornful will be lost."

We see here once more precisely the semiotic structure that we have seen in the previous texts. A gapped narrative in the Torah is disambiguated by the application to it of a *mashal*, which is composed of verses from another part of the canon. The narrative gap-filling is structured both in plot and ideology by the *mnashal* structure. "What the historian must bring to his consideration of the record are general notions of the *kinds of stories that might be found there*."[39] The *mashal* structure therefore has the function of intertext—it controls the possible messages which can be sent and received in the midrashic culture; it is an explicit representation of the "meaning system," making reading possible. The *mashal* itself has either the authority of Scripture or that of being anonymous code, the intertext. Another text about the *mashal* in the introduction to the Midrash on Song of Songs makes this idea clearer:

The rabbis say: Do not let this *mashal* be light in your eyes, for by means of this *mashal* one comes to comprehend the words of Torah. A *mashal* to a king who has lost a golden coin from his house or a precious pearl[40]—does he not find it by means of a wick worth a penny? Similarly, let not this *mashal* be light in your eyes, for by means of this *mashal* one comes to comprehend the words of Torah. Know that this is so, for Solomon, by means of this *mashal*[41] understood the exact meaning of the Torah. Rabbi Judah says: it is to teach you that everyone who teaches words of Torah to the many is privileged to have the Holy Spirit descend upon him.[42] From

whom do we learn this? From Solomon, who because he taught words of
Torah to the many was privileged to have the Holy Spirit descend upon
him and uttered three books, *Proverbs*, *Ecclesiastes*, and *Song of Songs*.[43]

This passage gives us some very important insight into the nature of
the *mashal*. It is figured here as something which does not cost much,
but nevertheless has great value. What is the meaning of this figure?
I suggest that it refers to the fact that the *meshalim* are themselves
a closed corpus of well-known narrative themes, characters, and
actions. This point about the *meshalim* themselves has been made
before,[44] but it has not been shown that this is *essential* to the signifying
structure of the *mashal* form of interpretation. Our text does make this
clear. The *mashal* is "common coin" and this is precisely its value.
Since it comes from the common stock of possible characters and
possible actions and motivations, it provides the possible ways to fill
in and understand the hidden biblical narrative. This wick which is so
common that it is worth only a penny is an excellent figure, it seems,
for the intertext in the sense of the cultural code, the anonymous
cultural code whose origins have been forgotten.

Our analysis up until now suggests that the *mashal* is not truly a
narrative at all, but a narrative structure or scheme. It is a code which
allows for the creation of narrative within the culture (if anything,
paradoxically, it seems analogous to the functions of the Proppian
system). The *mashal* does not stand beside the concrete situation but
creates it, or allows it to be created. The very story did not exist before
the *mashal*; it is enfolded within it. The *mashal* is the matrix or code out
of which the narrative of the Torah has been generated—both syntactic and semantic structural description, necessarily then as conventional and schematic, as fixed, as the morphology of the folk tale described by Propp. It answers then to Kermode's fabula.

Kermode finally sums up his theory in the following way:

The matter of this chapter is really quite simple. Of an agent there is
nothing to be said except that he performs a function: Betrayal, Judgement.
. . . The key to all this development—from fable to written story, from
story to character, from character to more story—is interpretation. At
some point a narrative achieves a more or less fixed form; in the case of
the gospels this was the formation of a more or less fixed canon. There
were many other gospels, but their failure to achieve canonicity cost them
their lives; four remain, and each illustrates in its own way the manner
in which pre-canonical interpretation works. Some of the differences
between them are no doubt due to the varying needs and interests of the
communities for whom the evangelists originally wrote, and to their own
diverse theological predispositions; but many are induced by the pressure

of narrative interpretation, not independent of these other pressures, *but quite different from the kinds of institutional commentary and exegesis that typically constitute post-canonical interpretation.* For these early interpretations take the form of new narrative whether by a reorganization of existing material or by the inclusion of new material. In the first stage this new material characteristically derives from texts—Old Testament texts tacitly regarded as somehow part of the same story.[45]

Now in some ways Kermode's description seems to me to be a perfect description of Midrash. Here also, as we have amply seen, we have narrative expansion derived from other texts tacitly—or not so tacitly—regarded as part of the same story. As such, however, it presents several paradoxes. The most obvious is that Kermode claims this type of interpretation to be characteristic only of the precanonical situation, whereas Midrash is obviously postcanonical. Moreover, Kermode's description wavers on the very crucial point of the status of the "primitive fable." Although Kermode himself presents them as if they were equal alternatives,[46] it is in fact one thing to state that there was an early account which was elaborated by midrashic techniques or other sorts of narrative expansions and quite another to claim this fabula as the underlying synchronic structure of the gospel stories without positing its or their historical reality. Just how fraught this issue is will become clear when we pursue our application of Kermode to the *mashal* a little further. It is clear that the *mashal* can only fit the synchronic version of the primitive fable theory; there is no possible claim that there was a historical story about such agents as a king, his son, and robbers which was somehow elaborated into the Torah's account. But the whole genre of the Torah requires that its narrative be taken seriously as a "true" story. As Sternberg has cogently remarked, "By incorporating the definition and command and observance, the narrative . . . illegitimates all thought of fictionality on pain of excommunication."[47] If the midrashic reading is a claim that the *mashal* represents the ideological/narrative matrix from which the Bible text is derived, how can that text claim—in the view of the Midrash—to be true? Stated baldly, how can a true story have a primitive fabula underlying it?

What we need here is a model that accounts for two structures, in a sense one that answers to both of the alternatives which Kermode has raised. The issue is not whether we consider the biblical narrative as fiction with its synchronically underlying fabula or as historiography with the fabula as diachronic "kernel of truth," or ancient eyewitness account, but something much more complex and sophisticated. The Bible must be read as historiography; that much has been made clear

by Sternberg, but it is ideologized historiography, as also shown by
him. Indeed, according to White all historiographical narrative is
structured by plots and genres in ways that are controlled by the personal and social ideology of the writer of the history. Historical narratives are for White "metaphorical statements which suggest a relation
of similitude between such events and processes and the story types
that we conventionally use to endow the events of our lives with culturally sanctioned meanings."[48] Writing history is the articulation "of
a complex of symbols which gives us directions for finding an icon of
the structure of those events in our literary tradition,"[49] in a word, a
mashal. I claim, therefore, that if the Bible is historiography, then
Midrash is precisely metahistoriography. The biblical narrative, at
least as much as any historiography, is structured by metaphor at its
very heart; it is not, or could it be, a mere transparent chronicle of
events. The midrashic *mashal* is to be understood as a raising to consciousness of the unstated tropics of the biblical history. It is the
schematic statement of the icons of the structures of events in the
literary tradition, the Prophets and Writings, as the Midrash says, "of
them it is *interpreted* in the tradition."

Louis Marin in an article on a parable of Pascal's has brilliantly
addressed precisely this use of the parable form. In Pascal's text, the
speaker is addressing a young nobleman and in trying to teach him
some truth about his place in the world tells him a classic sort of
parabolic tale about a man who is stranded on an isolated island,
where he discovers the people have lost their king. Since he has the
appearance of the king, he is taken as such by the people, and after a
period of some hesitation accepts the role, remembering however that
it is only a role. Now on one mode of reading we could take this as a
moral parable of a fairly simple semiotic structure. You are the cast-
away, young friend. Know that you have no more right by nature to
be a nobleman than did that man, but accept your role and perform it
with self-knowledge. Indeed, on one level, Pascal's text authorizes
such a straight reading of it. Marin does much more. He shows how
the parable is not merely analogously related to an application
thereof—to an interpretation of its meaning—but that it is the underlying structure of the biography of his interlocutor. Thus:

> One perceives how narrative and code function in relation to each other in
> the construction of Pascalian discourse: the first narrative is (in its textual
> manifestation) the figural development of the notion of chance occurrence
> contained in the second code. This notion appears in the narrative only in
> the form of an "image," without being expressly manifested: the tempest,
> the disappearance of the island's king, the shipwreck, and finally the cast-

away's corporal and facial resemblance to the lost king, are all so many figures of contingency, the notion of which permits the deciphering of the parabolic narrative by another narrative which is unveiled in its turn, as it comes into contact with the "parable," at a point of articulation marked by the term "chance occurrence." *This other narrative is the biographical "structure" of the interlocutor: his birth as son of a duke, his finding himself "in" the world, the marriage of his parents and all those of his ancestors, a thousand unforeseen events which left their mark on his family and whose narration would constitute the family tradition.*[50]

The analogy to our midrashic *meshalim* is exact. In these as well it is a "family tradition" and a "biographic structure" which are being interpreted. These traditions and biographies are real stories, just as they are in the case of Pascal's young duke. However, by themselves they have no meaning. They are merely data. *They must be made into fictions before they can signify.* The function of the *mashal* is to reveal the fictionality of the true story of the Torah, that is to take its recital of events—gapped as it is, and by assigning it a place in the cultural codes articulated by simple narrative functions and structures to allow it to signify. That is why until Solomon created the *mashal* the Torah was like a basket of fruit which no one could carry. Again in Marin's words:

The function of the parabolic narrative therefore appears through an ambiguity which gives it great practical efficacy: the parable designates in its fiction a real narrative (situation, position) that it assimilates to itself in the process of showing that this narrative is the revealing figure of one term of the code by which the parable was encoded into a fictive narrative.[51]

The parable in Marin's analysis has as its designatum not an abstraction but the "true story" itself. This is precisely what I have claimed for the midrashic *mashal* as well. Its designatum is the very biblical narrative. This narrative is assimilated to the *mashal*—the history itself is shown to be a figure of the code which the *mashal* represents. The *mashal* then stands in an ambiguous position similar to the one that Marin discusses. Is there a story or is there not? Is it history or is it fiction? This ambiguity is greatly heightened in our texts, for in both the two narratives are physically assimilated to each other. Ostensibly R. Yehuda begins by telling a fictive narrative of a king and a king's son, which we would expect to be placed beside a real narrative of God and the people, but as soon as he begins it becomes clear that only one story is being told at all, for God is the king and Israel is the son. This ambiguity is embodied in such sentences as: "He [the son] became hungry, He [who, the king or God?] fed him, as it says, 'Behold I [God] will rain bread down!' "[52] A similar kind of ambiguity is present in the story of Moses and the Sea, where the real story is begun by saying "The Sea began to stand against him," before the introduction of the *mashal* pattern, and then it is continued after that.[53] The very structure of these texts reveals therefore that the *mashal* is the code which generates the midrashic reading—indeed the code which generates the Torah text in the sense of text as interaction between writing and reader—Written and Oral Torah.

The function of the *mashal* in the *Mekilta* can be described in terms very similar to those by which theorists such as Iser describe the activity of reading of narrative. The biblical text as written is characterized by hiatus and indeterminacy in many points.[54] Into these fissures in the text the rabbis introduce other biblical texts, founded again on their insight that the Bible is a single semiotic system—in hermeneutic terms, a self-glossing work.[55] The rabbis however were conscious of the fact that their reading must be ideologically constrained—as indeed is all reading but usually unconsciously so. They have often then represented on the surface of their hermeneutic texts precisely the ideological codes which allow and constrain their interpretation. The *mashal* is the most clearly defined of those codes which generate interpretation by narrative expansion. The *mashal* is a basic narrative structure whose characters and actions belong to the common coin of the intertext. These basic narrative structures are thus the carriers of values and ideology in the culture. The biblical story, referential and historical in its generic claims, is made to signify by being read with its rabbinic intertext. By this practice, history becomes parable.

Notes

A much earlier version of this analysis can be found in *Prooftexts* 5 (1985): 269–76, along with disagreement of David Stern, there, pp. 276–80. The reader of those texts will be able to see how I have tried here to answer Stern's arguments against my original somewhat primitive formulation. The scope of the present paper does not allow for a full discussion of Stern's position versus mine, and I reserve that, therefore, for my book-length essay on the Midrash currently in progress. All translations from Hebrew (including the Bible) are mine.

1. For an excellent survey of the *status quaestionis* and the literature, see Robert Johnston, "Parabolic Interpretations Attributed to Tannaim" (Ph.D. diss., Hartford Seminary Foundation, 1977), pp. 1–118.

2. The most important exception that I know of is David Stern's dissertation and his article cited below, n. 22.

3. That is, the earlier period of Midrash, roughly up to and including the second Christian century. I will henceforth use the term midrashic *mashal*, although I am speaking only of the exegetic *meshalim* of this period.

4. Susan Wittig, "Meaning and Modes of Signification: Toward a Semiotic of the Parable," in *Semiology and Parables*, ed. Daniel Patte (Pittsburgh: Pickwick, 1976), pp. 319–47.

5. Ibid., p. 323.

6. Ibid.

7. Ibid., p. 324.

8. Ibid., p. 334.

9. See Stern's paper cited below, n. 22, for discussion of this point and Johnston, "Parabolic Interpretations," for the literature on this issue.

10. Wittig, "Meaning and Modes," p. 335.

11. Ibid., p. 336.

12. See the discussion of her paper in Patte, ed., *Semiology and Parables*, on pp. 348–84.

13. Whatever the results of this type of semiotic structural comparison, they do not prejudice the question of possible genetic dependence or influence between the two literatures, on which question, see most recently, David Flusser, "The Parables of Jesus and the Parables in Rabbinic Literature," in his *Jewish Sources in Early Christianity* (Tel Aviv: Sifriat Hapoalim, 1979), pp. 150–209. Even if we allow common origin for *meshalim* and parables, it is still eminently possible that they perform quite different functions in the literary system.

14. *Mekilta De-rabbi Ishmael*, ed. J. Z. Lauterbach, 3 vols. (Philadelphia: Jewish Publication Society of America, 1933), 1:224–25. The text given here has been drawn from my new edition of the *Mekilta*. This text has been completely corrupted in current editions, both vulgate and critical, and may only be restored by recourse to the oldest manuscripts. All the texts discussed in this paper are taken from this, one of the oldest, midrash. Midrash is produced for nearly a thousand years and is very heterogeneous, so the claims being made here should be understood as being of tentative validity for the whole body of midrash.

15. Brevard S. Childs, *The Book of Exodus* (Philadelphia: Westminster Press, 1974), p. 220. See also below, n. 33, another example of this phenomenon.

16. See Johnston, "Parabolic Interpretations," pp. 227–28.

17. See below and my forthcoming "Song of Songs—Lock or Key?," to appear in *The Book and the Text*, ed. Regina Schwartz (Oxford: Blackwell).

18. The word for "handles" and the word "proved" come from the same root in Hebrew. "Handles" is being used in a sense very similar to that of the modern English colloquial phrase, "I can't get a handle on that idea," i.e., a place of access. See Bruns's work cited n. 55 below.

19. *Song of Songs Rabbah*, ed. Shimshon Dunasky (Jerusalem: Dvir, 1980), p. 5.

20. That is to say, the Bible explicitly or implicitly ascribes these three works to Solomon; it was the rabbis who explained that the first was written in his youth, the second in his maturity, and the third in his old age, thus providing a sort of typology of the three ages of man.

21. Compare the following use of this term from the same midrash, "Your eyes are doves,"— like doves, your figure (*dugma*) is similar to a dove (*Song of Songs Rabbah*, p. 100). *Dugma* is accordingly practically an etymological equivalent of *figura*.

22. See David Stern, "Rhetoric and Midrash: The Case of the Mashal," *Prooftexts* 1 (1981):261–91.

23. Notably in the classic work of Isaac Heinmann, *The Ways of the Agada* (Jerusalem: Magnes Press, 1954), pp. 56–70.

24. Wittig, "Meaning and Modes," p. 339.

25. See below n. 46 on this ambiguity.

26. "Ado" is cited by Kermode from James.

27. Frank Kermode, *The Genesis of Secrecy: On the Interpretation of Narrative* (Cambridge: Harvard University Press, 1979), p. 77.

28. Ibid., p. 80.

29. Ibid., p. 81.

30. Ibid. Kermode even calls this process *midrash*, mistakenly in my view. He is closer to midrash when he speaks on p. 82 of collections of "Old Testament" testimonia about the messiah underlying the Gospel stories.

31. Ibid., p. 85.

32. Lauterbach, ed., *Mekilta*, 1:227–29.

33. See Childs, *Book of Exodus*, pp. 221 and 227. See also above, n. 15. This is an elegant demonstration of another point made by Wittig, namely that, meaning "is a product as well of the analytical system by which the perceiver has decided to interpret" ("Meaning and Modes," p. 339). The gap is there; the question is what do we do with it.

34. I shall be dealing at much greater length with the interpretation of this fascinating text in another essay entitled, "Reification and Resistance: The Personal Landscape in Midrash", *Poetics Today* 10, no. 4 (forthcoming).

35. Defense of this reading is beyond the scope of the present essay. For the moment, suffice it to say that it is grounded at least partly in parallel texts which raise it to the surface. Nevertheless, I will not claim that it is the only possible interpretation of the *mashal*.

36. Hayden White, *Tropics of Discourse* (Baltimore: Johns Hopkins University Press, 1978), p. 58.

37. The Hebrew term here is *rashum*, which has been itself interpreted to mean *mashal*, a meaning which would not be altogether unwelcome here. However, I have shown in a Hebrew article in the *Moshe Held Memorial Volume* (Jerusalem: Magnes Press, 1988), pp. 23–35, that this word is a synonym of *hatum* and *satum*, both of which mean "sealed," also with reference to texts, and which are moreover used as antonyms of *meforash*, which as here means "interpreted," "explicit," "clear."

38. Lauterbach, ed., *Mekilta*, 2:135.

39. White, *Tropics of Discourse*, p. 59.

40. Yet another image for the hermetic Torah, now that which was possessed but is lost.

41. I.e., the Song of Songs, as I demonstrate in the paper cited above, n. 17.

42. Hence, the analogy between Solomon and the rabbis. Solomon is a sort of proto-rabbi for the Midrash.

43. *Song of Songs Rabbah*, p. 6. This is the sequel to the above-quoted passage. The order of Solomon's works deviates from both the chronological and canonical ones because this passage is an introduction to the Midrash on Song of Songs, and its author wishes therefore to end his discourse mentioning that book.

44. Stern, "Rhetoric."

45. Kermode, *Genesis of Secrecy*, pp. 98–99 (emphasis added).

46. "It is at least convenient to think of the methodologically describable *fabula* as having historical existence." Kermode, ibid., p. 79.

47. Meir Sternberg, *The Poetics of Biblical Narrative: Ideological Literature and the Drama of Reading* (Bloomington: Indiana University Press, 1985), p. 31. For Kermode on this question see there, pp. 101–25.

48. White, *Tropics of Discourse*, pp. 69–70.

49. Ibid., p. 88.

50. Louis Marin, "On the Interpretation of Ordinary Language: A Parable of Pascal," *Textual Strategies*, ed. Josue Harari (Ithaca: Cornell University Press, 1979), p. 245 (emphasis added).

51. Ibid., p. 246.

52. The printed texts of the *mashal* of R. Yehuda have partially occulted this ambiguity by separating out the parable from its "application," telling us first the metaphorical narrative of a man and his son, and then, "So did the Holy One etc." and retelling the whole story once again and then quoting the verses. However, this text is not supported by *any* manuscript. Moreover, even in the printed version the ambiguity remains, as pointed out by Johnston: "Another not-

able aspect of this item is the blurred distinction between *Bild* and *Sache* as worked out in the application. Sun, hunger, and thirst are repeated as sun, hunger, and thirst. More strikingly, the son is still 'the son,' and not Israel, as one might expect" ("Parabolic Interpretations," p. 229). We see now that this blurring is an uneradicated relic of the original ambiguity of reference at the very heart of the *marshal*, which on my reading is present in fact in every *mashal*. This reading renders impossible any question of the originality of the connection between the *Bildwort* and the *Sachwort* in this type of text (Johnston, pp. 229 and 243).

53. There is even a manuscript—a very venerable one at that—in which the quotation of the text from Psalms is begun before the *mashal* is told. The parallels to this text also leave the *mashal* unexpressed on the surface.

54. The classic statement on this issue is now Meir Sternberg's chapter entitled "Gaps, Ambiguities, and the Reading Process," *Poetics of Biblical Narrative*, pp. 186–229.

55. See Gerald Bruns, "Midrash and Allegory," *The Literary Guide to the Bible*, ed. Robert Alter and Frank Kermode (Cambridge: Harvard University Press, 1987), pp. 626–27. I wish to thank Professor Bruns for letting me have a prepublication copy of this very important text.

Narratorial Situations in the Bible

Lyle Eslinger
The University of Calgary

HISTORICAL CRITICISM AND LITERARY CRITICISM

BETWEEN modern and traditional biblical interpretation there is one primary difference: the critical stance of the former. The critical method was developed to organize knowledge about the Bible, unhindered by the trammels of faith. As we all know, the movement that resulted was historical criticism. It has taken hold of academic biblical study and established a monopoly that, for a time, successfully rebuffed all competition.

As its name suggests, the organizing principle of historical criticism —a name that has become synonymous with biblical criticism—is history. By reorganizing the data of biblical literature within a historical framework, the historical critic creates a logical, noncontradictory representation of the events described in biblical narrative. Through this process the critic also generates another narrative about the literary history of the biblical narratives. That is, the historical critic creates two historical frameworks to explain biblical narrative because the critic perceives two different kinds of data requiring organization. The primary concern, at least in the beginning, is with the participants, actions, and events described in the narrative; historical organization of this plane of the Bible's narrative literature culminates in a history of Israel. But to write accurate histories of Israel, the historical critic must also take into account another level in biblical narrative, the compositional plane of the author. This plane intervenes between the critic and the events described in the narrative; historical organization of it results in histories of Israelite literature.[1]

The binocular analytical framework of historical criticism is the product of two factors, one methodological, the other a generic feature of narrative writing. It is a fundamental rule of history writing that one must be circumspect about one's sources. One must always be aware, when using documents as sources, of the influence of the author's own historically conditioned situation on his composition. This awareness is encouraged by the appearance of narrative itself, which is typically a story related by someone, a narrator. As the narrator tells his story he leaves traces of his attitudes and opinions about the

72

subject matter of his story in his narrative account. These traces
reflect the author's[2] own existential and historical situations and it is
these traces that allow the circumspect critic to take his literary
source's biases into account.

Such traces vary in the degree of information that they reveal about
the teller. The scale extends from the simple phenomenon of tagged
speech, "he said"—which only allows us to know that there is a
teller—to seemingly forthright, evaluative comments about the story
(e.g., "Notwithstanding they would not hear, but hardened their
necks, like to the neck of their fathers, that did not believe in the Lord
their God," 2 Kings 17:14). Here a vivid reflection of the teller's
values seems to appear, though ironic assertions are common enough
that one must be careful. But for historical critics such traces of supposed authorial bias are consistently treated as reliable revelations
of the compositional circumstance in which the work was written.
The note of disapproval in Genesis 25:34, for example, seems to betray the narrator's allegiance to Jacob, prompting a historical critical
reader such as H. Gunkel to comment: "Die Sage lacht den dummen
Esau aus, der seine ganz Zukunft um ein Linsengericht verkauft hat;
and jubelt über den klugen Jacob in dem die Erzähler ihr eigenes Bild
wiederkennen." [The legend derides the silly Esau who sold his entire
future for a bowl of lentils and exults over the crafty Jacob in whom
the narrator recognizes his own image.][3]

Whichever of the two levels the historical critic addresses, the ultimate goal of historical reconstruction absolutely depends on literary
analysis.[4] To get at the actual history (the history of Israel) lying
behind the events recorded in the biblical stories, the historical critic
must get past any authorial/narratorial bias. To neutralize the influence of authorial distortion on our perception of the events described, the critic must place the author and his story in the relativiz-
ing framework of literary history. To write literary history the critic
must isolate and consolidate all traces of authorial self-revelation in
the narrative. And to decide which of the multitudinous evaluations
and statements in a narrative are to be attributed to the author, the
critic must engage in literary analysis and, more particularly, in analysis of the question of point of view. Therein lies the problem that
plagues all historical criticism and, from the perspective of the new
biblical narratology, vitiates most existing historical-critical readings
of biblical narrative.

In its hasty, but enlightened, pursuit of the historical truth about
the events described in Bible stories, historical criticism paused only
briefly—did it pause at all?—to develop crude, makeshift tools for
literary analysis of the variety of phenonema bearing on the category

of narrative features known as "point of view." Unfortunately, the literary theory that supported these rudimentary tools was frequently a product of critics' casual acquaintance with the literary works of their contemporaries or with literary theories developed to explain modern European literature. Certainly there are many parallels between ancient and modern literature—we "moderns" are not that distant from the literate cultures that have preceded us in human history—but the theories derived from the study of contemporary European literature require, as we know now, adaptation to the peculiarities of ancient Hebrew narrative style. Some features of narrative literature, such as manipulation of narrative ontology and "point of view" are common; others, such as Hebrew narrative's manipulation of redundancy and repetition are less so. Without a constant view to adaptation and an inductive approach to the study of biblical literary technique, anachronistic analysis was inevitable and many of the conclusions drawn were hampered by it.

Narrative Ontology

The attempt to relativize authorial distortion in description of events is a good example of what I am talking about. Every narrative is a combination of a story that is told and a teller that relates it. Franz Stanzel identifies this literary trait—"mediacy of presentation"—as the distinguishing generic characteristic of all narrative literature.[5] The author of a narrative creates both a story and a narrating voice or view that mediates the story. Depending on the manner in which an author chooses to frame this relationship between narrator and story world, there is frequently (almost always in biblical narrative) a hierarchy of authority within the fictive literary cosmos. Only the reader who understands the nature of this hierarchy will be able to draw valid conclusions about the author's views.

The implications for historical criticism's unremitting focus on the biblical author's sociohistorically bound discourse are tremendous. If one is concerned to understand the view of the author of the Deuteronomistic narrative (Joshua–2 Kings) so as to reach a correct assessment of the document's date and the sociohistorical context within which it came to expression, it is obvious that one must first be certain that one is reading the author's views and not the pilloried quotation of a view in fact opposed by the author and his narrative.[6]

Most biblical narrative is rendered using one common "narrative situation,"[7] which can be sketched as follows:

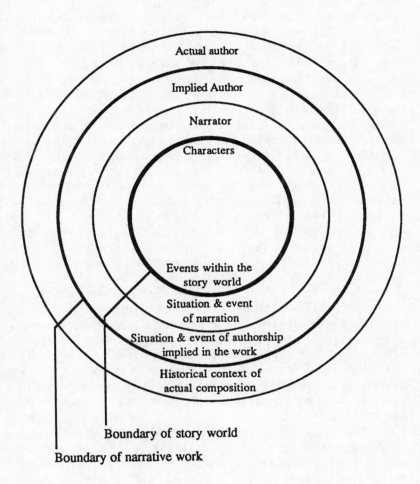

Actual author

Implied Author

Narrator

Characters

Events within the
story world

Situation & event
of narration

Situation & event of authorship
implied in the work

Historical context of
actual composition

Boundary of story world

Boundary of narrative work

Concerned to know the historical truth about the events described in the story, historical critics must relativize at least three levels of literarily (characters, narrator) or historically (actual author) conditioned perception before they can even begin to evaluate the historical value of the story.[8] If they do not relativize either the literary or historical tiers that bar them from the history for which they search, their reconstructions are predestined to certain delusion.

In fact, however, historical-critical analyses have run roughshod over the hierarchical narrative ontology. The complex narrative layering of varying views of characters, the comments of narrators, and the overarching structural and thematic implications of the implied author have all been lumped together in a literary-historical hypothesis that sees the narrative literature as a flat, two-dimensional mass of opinions from the long line of actual authors who have contributed to these stories. The third dimension, that of the hierarchical narrative ontology, is entirely overlooked in conventional historical-critical treatments. And aspects of the narrative that are, without presupposing anything beyond the generic conventions of narrative literature, part of the third dimension—the narrative's vertical ontology—have been mistaken for the products of compositional production through time.

A prime example of the danger of the two-dimensional historical interpretation of biblical narrative is the treatment of 1 Samuel 8–12, in which historical critics have seen the hands of numerous authors and redactors of varying opinions about the value of a monarchy. No matter whether it is Samuel, God, or the people speaking in the narrative, all statements are directly ascribed to a real author[9] who stands immediately behind the voice in the narrative and voices his own disagreeing views over against the other authors of this text, whose contrary voices are heard directly through the other characters or the narrator's own voice. When one pays some attention to the hierarchy of perspectival levels within the narrative, it is not difficult to see correlations between particular views expressed in the narrative and particular characters or perspectival levels.[10] The dissonant voices can be heard and understood within the framework of the story world and the ontology of that particular narrative. Samuel, for example, criticizes the proposed monarchy because he stands to lose his preeminent position of authority.[11]

If historical critics had seen the existential matrix that conditioned Samuel's view, which is relative to his personal situation in the story world, I doubt that they would have posited the existence of a dissenting author behind this character. That hypothesis was, after all, supposed to resolve a literary conflict in the narrative that could not be resolved except by resort to literary history. The hypothetical explanation of historical criticism, in which contrary perspectives are explained by recourse to the inference of varying authorial opinions that now find expression in one conglomerate narrative, is a second-order interpretation whose complexity and conjectural foundation makes it easy prey for a literary explanation in terms of narrative ontology.[12] The elegance of the narratological explanation is best appreciated after hearing the multitude of hypothetical literary histories promoted as explanations of the perspectival layers in 1 Samuel 8–12. Like phlogiston, the pro- and antimonarchic sources (or traditions, or redactions) are a plausible, if unverifiable, explanation of a phenomenon. Now that a first-order alternative presents itself such conjectures should, if one subscribes to Occam's dictates, be put aside.

BIBLICAL NARRATOLOGY

To improve the state of literary affairs in the study of biblical narrative biblical scholars are beginning to devise a literary theory and method that accounts for the multileveled mediation of events. To the good fortune of biblical studies a rich source of theory about narrative is already available in the separate field of literary criticism now known as narratology.[13] Just as the founding fathers of historical criticism frequented the domains of folklorists and historians, contemporary biblical scholars are beginning to explore the methods of narratology to gain new insights into biblical narrative.

Narratology is the organized study and description of the characteristic features of the narrative genre in the Western literary tradition. Based on the distinguishing generic characteristic "mediacy of presentation"[14] that distinguishes narrative from other kinds of literature, narratology focuses on the mechanics of narrative composition. Narrative has two primary components, a tale and a teller; narratology analyzes the two parts as *story*, the events, actions, and characters that are described, and *discourse*, the means of communicating the content to the reader.[15] An important aim of narratology is to describe how authors can manipulate discourse as a tool to affect the meaning of story. Narratology devotes greater attention to the discourse that relates story because it is the only medium in narrative literature that is directly aimed at the reader.[16] No voice within the story world of the narrative can address the reader directly without breaking the conventions that govern this literary form.

In developing a biblical narratology, then, one takes the theoretical developments of narratology and combines them with an ongoing inductive study of Hebrew narrative, its idiomatic style and devices. Because narratology has been developed within a cross-cultural, generically defined field, its theories and analyses are well-suited to an interdisciplinary study of biblical literature. In addition to the inherent adaptability of the discipline of narratology, which tends on the whole toward the study of narrative as a genre rather than specific instances of narrative technique, the consciousness of all would-be biblical narratologists that they are primarily students of Hebrew narratology and that their best teacher is Hebrew narrative should protect this promising new approach to biblical narrative against the imperialistic tendencies that have sometimes accompanied method-ological developments in biblical studies.

Just how suitable is narratology as a tool for biblical study? Approx-imately sixty-four percent of biblical literature is prose. Of that per-centage only the pentateuchal legal texts appear to stand outside the narrative genre, but even the laws are enclosed within a narrative context. And even those seemingly antiliterary texts have narrative qualities and can be interpreted as literature when the conventions within which they were written are understood.[17]

All biblical narrative is mediated by a narrator. The narrator is the reader's guide, a medium for the duration of the story. The reader is closer to the narrator than to any of the characters in the story. The narrator intervenes between the reader and the world of the story just as our own senses and conceptual faculties intervene between us and our own world.[18] As readers, all that we can know about the fictional story world is already filtered and interpreted for us by our ears, eyes, and nose—the biblical narrator.

There are many different types of narrator, each having his own degree of prominence and influence on the reader's perception of the story. In the Bible the scale of narratorial prominence is unevenly balanced. Narrators such as those of Ezekiel of the revelations, prom-inent in self-references using the first person pronoun "I," are in the minority; the majority are impersonal observers who report only what they see and rarely draw attention away from the story onto them-selves or the existential situation from which they tell their story. The consequent appearance of unconditioned objectivity is a literary con-vention of great utility to the biblical authors. Given the extreme prej-udice with which their readers were (are) accustomed to viewing the subject matter of biblical narrative, it was expedient for the authors to endow their narrators with every available bit of credibility; if their renditions of the age-old stories were to be heard at all, appearances of partisan bias had to be carefully concealed behind a veil of impar-tiality.

   The qualities of narrator visibility and personalization, or depersonalization as is the case in the Bible, are produced by more fundamental choices that each author makes about the type of narrator
that he employs. There are two primary variables to manipulate in the
narratorial situation.[19] They are the ontological and temporal vantage
from which the descriptions of the story world and its characters are
described.[20] A narrator can be situated in being and/or time either
within the world of the story, or outside it. The narrator's existential/
temporal stance is visible in his pronominal usages—"I" tending to
include the narrator in, or relate him to, the story world; "he" tending
to exclude or separate him from it—and in the tenses of his verbal
descriptions—the present associating the narrator with the story
world and the preterite separating him from it. The combination of
first person pronominal self-references and the present tense usually
defines a narrator standing squarely in the story world, while the preterite and third person references to characters in the story are indications of a narrator speaking from outside the spatio-temporal bounds
of the story world.[21] These pronominal and verbal manifestations of
the narrator's spatio-temporal stance are supported by his usage of
demonstratives and temporal adverbs. The internal narrator's here
and now is the external narrator's then and there.
   The single most important difference between these two narratorial
situations is their variable perceptual and epistemological potentiali-
ties. The narrator who shares or has shared space and time with his
characters is subject (or was when he experienced the events he describes) to the same environmental constraints and existential limitations as they. Everything he says is relative to his ontological ties to
the story world and his motivation to narrate is also conditioned by
the bond.[22] His perceptions are conditioned and relative to the story
world.
   In contast the external narrator is untouched by the limitations that
the story world imposes on all its inhabitants. His existential im-
munity makes for more potential reliability in objective perception
and description of events and characters within the story.[23] Of course
this seemingly superhuman ability to know the truth of things, unhindered by the common misperceptions and ignorance attendant on
mankind, is only a literary convention. Like all artistic conventions we
tend to forget the fictionality that inheres, however, allowing ourselves
the aesthetic luxury of accepting conventional fictions as actual, if
fleeting, facts. The doctrine of scriptural inspiration may be seen, in
part, as an attempt to dogmatize and prolong the experience of
accepting the convention. The "truths" revealed by means of the literary convention of an external narrator who has unconditioned access

to the truth are enshrined as real, enduring, and guaranteed by God himself.

A good illustration of the privilege that the external narrator owes to his narratorial position is his exemption from the physical limitations that attend life within the story. The external, unconditioned narrator can hop about in space and time as it suits his narratorial purpose, the sole determinant of his represented momentary perceptions. The narrator of Job demonstrates this unlimited mobility. In 1:1–5 he describes the land of Uz from an unnamed position with an unrestricted view. In verses 4–5, which take a maximum of twenty seconds of narrating time, he covers the entire yearly cycle of Job's family activity. Suddenly in verse 6, without apology or explanation, he shifts his focus to heaven to look in on the heavenly council. By way of contrast the first person narrator who lives in the story world in the Book of Nehemiah takes four verses (2:12–15) just to describe his nocturnal tour of the walls of Jerusalem.[24]

Related to the perceptual characteristics of the two major narratorial situations are their epistemological properties. A narrator's access to informtion is a matter of degree. The possibilities extend from the conditioned, limited knowledge of an ordinary human witness who can tell his reader only as much as any other attendant person could,[25] to the unconditioned knowledge of the narrator who seems to know about all times and places (e.g., Genesis 1:1–26, prior to the creation of the first human being) and can even tell us what God himself thinks and feels (e.g., Genesis 6:6, "And the Lord repented that he had made man"). As a rule external narrators sit on the unconditioned end of the scale and internal narrators are epistemologically limited in keeping with their station in human life.[26]

Aside from the two narratorial situations of external and internal narrators there is a third possibility in which the prominence of the narratorial situation all but disappears and the events of the story are told as reflected in the mind and senses of one or several of the characters.[27] Such a narrative situation is by definition limited and incomplete, the logical extension of the direction taken with a first person internal narrator. The decision to use such a narrative mode constitutes a statement about access to meaning and order in human existence; it stands in opposition to that made by the author who chooses an external narrator who can know anything and tells a tale similarly complete and meaningful.

BIBLICAL NARRATIVE SITUATIONS

What, then, are the narratorial situations in the Bible? A survey

reveals a preference for external, unconditioned narrators. Such a
narratorial situation extends through the Pentateuch, the Deuteronomistic narrative (Joshua–2 Kings), and the books Jonah, Haggai,
Ruth, Esther, Daniel, Ezra, and Chronicles. It also appears briefly in
the poetic collection in Jeremiah 32–45 and in the narrative brackets
in the Book of Job. Remaining is approximately eleven percent of biblical narrative, all mediated by a "first person" internal narrator
(Nehemiah, retrospective; Ezekiel, prophetic). The Bible does not
contain any lengthy continuous narrative representation of events
seen solely through the eyes of a character in the story.[28]

Genesis 1

As a rule the opening sentence or paragraph of a narrative reveals the
type of narratorial situation used throughout, though, as Bal points
out, there is sometimes a switch in situations midway through.[29] The
introduction also provides some indications as to why this type of
narration was chosen to mediate the story.[30] The introduction to biblical narrative is no exception. Genesis 1:1 begins "In the beginning."
This is an ultimate beginning at the dawn of creation, before any
human observer was created. Yet here is our narrator telling us what
happened then. Obviously he is not limited to any position in space
and time, especially not to the singularity of place and time that gov-
erns all normal human existence. The fact that he can tell us something that no human character within the story could (humans are not
created for another twenty-six verses) shows that he is existentially
immune to conditions that will govern characters within the story
world and readers in the real. But it is not only what the narrator tells
that separates him from the story, it is also how he tells it. The Genesis narrator reveals his temporal separation from the event by describing God's action with a preterite verb—"In the beginning God created": he stands subsequent to the event of creation, as do all other
human beings both inside and outside the story, yet he is able to see
back to that primeval event. What an extraordinarily perceptive
fellow!

The narrator's distinctive vision is made more so by his failure to
identify the source of his knowledge. He does not say, "In the beginning I saw," or "I dreamt that in the beginning," or even "God told
me that in the beginning"; he simply says "In the beginning." His
superhuman ability is unapologetically unconditioned. He simply
knows. The content of this first disclosure suggests that there is little if
anything to do with the cosmos that this narrator could not know.

The narrator continues to display his unconditioned knowledge in
verse 2 by describing physical conditions prior to God's imposition of

law and order on the cosmos. The human characters within the story all depend on this very created order for all facets of their existence. But the narrator is free of such dependence and knows about things outside that order and prior to it; his unconditioned knowledge puts a wide existential and epistemological gap between him and his characters. As his readers we are temporarily privileged to rise above our limitations to share his unobstructed perspective and insight. While reading, the reader gains an Olympian overview of the story world. This perspective is unavailable to any of the human characters in the story and normally unavailable to the reader who seeks to understand his own world, which is at least analogous to the story world. The overview is freed from the human limitations of viewing the world from within. With this narrator we stand outside looking in.

In verses 3–4 the narrator's dispassionate neutrality toward the world of the story contrasts with God's affection. When God calls light into existence the narrator reports objectively, "There was light." God, on the other hand, "saw that the light was good," an evaluation that implicates him in the story world. And, at the very moment when the narrator is revealing God's involvement in the story world he is also demonstrating his own separation from it by displaying his ability to know the minds of the characters who inhabit that world, including even the mind of God. Moreover, while God sees that the light is good the narrator's knowing of God's mind is not even represented by a cognitive verb let alone a perceptual one. God, however supreme and omnipotent compared to the human denizens of the story world, is definitely implicated and subordinated by his involvement to the all-seeing wisdom and insight of the external, unconditioned narrator.[31] The contrast illumines the extreme ontological separation between this narratorial situation and the story world; it also reveals the insufficiency of the conventional description of this narrator as "omniscient." The epistemological adjective is an inaccurate exaggeration. The narrator never claims he knows all, nor does his creator, the author, make that claim for him. At the same time the adjective falls short of complete description. For the sorts of observations the Genesis narrator makes, his detachment from the story world is as important as his wide-ranging cognitive powers. A more accurate description of this narrator is that he is external and his ability to know about events or characters is unconditioned, not subject to the constraints attendant on normal human observers or even on the involved divine participant in his story.

Nehemiah 1

Genesis 1 introduces the biblical story and the dominant narrative situation in the Bible. The fact that the majority of biblical authors chose this mode of narrative mediation suggests that they found it most advantageous as a vehicle for their kind of stories. The availability of other narrative modes is shown by the existence of books such as Nehemiah and Ezekiel, which are narrated from an entirely different narratorial situation. A brief glance at the introduction of Nehemiah illustrates the difference.[32]

In Nehemiah 1:1 the narrator also employs preterite description of events within the story. There is an indeterminate temporal gap between the events in the story and the event of narration. But the suggestion of any existential separation between the narrator and the world of the story is canceled by his inclusion in that world by means of the emphatic self-reference, "and *I* was in Shushan." The narrator's ties to the story world are made even more concrete when he gives the exact date and location of his past involvement in it. Here preterite narration provides only temporal separation between events in the story and the event of narration. Both the actions of the character referred to as "I" and the narrator's act of narrating take place on the same existential plane; both are subject to the same limitations and conditions. Only temporally external to the story world, this narrator presents an ontologically internal view of it. He remains in and of the world he describes.

The former existence of the narrator in the story world is the single most important difference between the discourse of Nehemiah and that of Genesis, with its absolute separation of story world and narratorial situation. The two different situations create radically different epistemological possibilities, which in turn result in distinct portraits of human existence. Especially important are the differences in the presentation of man's interaction with God, the dominant biblical theme. The internal narrator can only give the reader a common, limited view of the interaction. His narratorial view is superior to the characters' views only by advantage of hindsight. The external narrator obviously has a much better opportunity of presenting a new perspective on the ways of God with man.

In verses 2–3 the narrator of Nehemiah reveals just how conditioned his narration by means of his own past first person experiences will be. The narratorial view is limited to the "then and there" of his former spatio-temporal position. Knowledge of other times or places necessarily comes to the narrator through the communications of other characters in the story. We learn about the conditions in Jerusalem while the narrator was in Shushan only through some characters who have come from Jerusalem. They describe the situation in Jerusalem in response to a query from our narrator. By way of contrast the external, unconditioned narrator of 2 Kings 24–25 shifts his focus back and forth several times between scenes in Babylon and the plundered city of Jerusalem without once explaining how he knows about what is happening in either city.

The internal narrator's knowledge of the divine character is even more restricted, hindsight being no advantage in this respect. In verses 4–11 the narrator describes his prayer about the bad turn that Israel's state affairs have taken, but he cannot tell us what God thought or did in response to his prayer. Hindsight is no advantage this time and God's response can only be deduced later from the course that events later take (2:8, 18). Unlike the external narrator of Genesis, who discloses nothing about himself but much about God, the internal narrator/character of Nehemiah bares his soul to the reader of his prayer but can say nothing about God, who is a closed book both to the praying character, the retrospective narrator, and so also to the reader.

The internal narrator's prominent display of his past existence in the story world is the exact opposite of the ghostly presence of the nonincarnate, external narrator.[33] By confining his representations strictly to the limited viewpoint of his principal character (himself), the narrator forces his reader to view the other characters and the events in which all were caught up through his own eyes. The reader can see things only through the biased view of the narrator at that time but subject to additional self-justifying qualifications. Consequently, all of the narrator's actions are supplied with rationales or rationalizations, but other characters' acts are unjustified, inexplicable, and even reprehensible. The conditioned, internal narrator gives his side of the story and, in giving it exclusively so, tries to coerce his reader's acceptance.[34] Whether or not the reader accepts this narrator's evaluative norms or not will depend on individual readers' idiosyncrasies, but beyond them no one can go with any certainty.

The restricted view is a product of the narrator's ties to the principal character; his motivation for telling his story is existentially conditioned.[35] In fact the internal narrator of Nehemiah exposes his narratorial strategies by repeatedly asking his intended reader, God, to remember all his good deeds and reward him for them (13:14, 22, 31) and to remember the bad deeds of other characters and punish them (13:29). Obviously the first person internal narratorial situation meets this narrator's needs perfectly.

If the narratorial motivation of the internal narrator is the product of his entanglement in the conditions of his story, what motivates the external, unconditioned narrator of books like Genesis? And what affect does his external perspective have on his story? The external, unconditioned narratorial situation draws the reader away from entangling involvements on the level of the characters within the story world. The detached objectivity of this vantage is a rare perceptual mode unavailable in the reader's real world where the biblical traditions were/are charged with religious and existential significance. The reader's interest is refocused on the larger horizon rather than on localized details. Though the narrator can override the inherent neutrality of his external viewpoint with explicit commentary, he usually does not. An example from 1 Samuel will illustrate.

1 Samuel 8–12

In 1 Samuel 8 a crucial moment in Israel's covenantal relationship with Yahweh is described. The future of Israel's theocratic government is at stake. Here, if anywhere, we might expect the narrator to supply his reader with some commentary to guide the reader in the way that he ought to go.

A crisis arises when Israel requests a human to replace God as king (v. 5; cf. vv. 7–8; 10:19). The request is a radical rejection of the theocracy established at Sinai, a denial of Isra-el's identity as the "God-ruled" (שׂרר אל) people. Both God and his servant Samuel denounce the request (vv. 6–8), but the narrator remains silent. He does balance out the denunciation by describing the circumstances that provoked the request (vv. 1–3), a provocation also validated by the chain of events previously described in chapters 2–7. But just as he does not explicitly support the denunciation, he does not say, in so many words, "The request is just." Instead he maintains the neutrality afforded by his external perspective and presents characters and events from a nonpartisan viewpoint. He even promotes the objectivity of his external view by using his unlimited access to enter the minds of characters on both sides of the issue. The reader is privileged with an overview of the misunderstandings, the cross-purposes, and the genuine, laudable motivations on each side of the dispute. The narratorial perspective is a synthetic view with its center focused on the problem of divine-human relationship and interaction within a political framework, not on the pedestrian question of who is right and who is wrong. From the normal human perspective the answer to that question is all too obvious.

The example from 1 Samuel is characteristic of the external, unconditioned narrator's treatment of evaluation. Instead of directly evaluating the actions of characters he uses his privileged access to reveal the often unpublished thoughts or words of one character about another. Even in the saying repeated throughout the Deuteronomistic history that "Israel did evil," the apparent directness of the evaluation is removed by the concluding ascription to a character: "in the sight of the Lord." Obviously the neutrality of the external narratorial situation is amenable to the unconditioned narrator who uses his situation and power to achieve a single end. But why did the biblical authors want to present such a perspective on a subject—God and man, or more to the point, God and Israel—that history had made so volatile?

The answer that is suggested by my reading—I do not believe we are yet at the point, in our study of biblical narratology, where we can make anything more than working suggestions—is that this narratorial situation is aimed precisely at the emotional piety and prejudice with which these traditions were/are approached by the normal, conditioned consciousness of the reader. Whether or not the view presented by the external narrator is neutral or not, it is made to appear so and the reader is invited to explore this otherwise unavailable perspective on the old, well-worked traditions. The reader is asked to step across the usual bounds of human understanding about God's motives, to cross over the theological barrier described by God in the well-known passage from Isaiah (55:6-8). God's motives can be known and they are not always the most complimentary (e.g., Exodus 7:3-5 in the light of Exodus 5, especially vv. 22-23; 1 Samuel 2:25). For the biblical God, the end does justify the means.

Similarly the reader is asked to transcend conventional views about human suffering, in which the combination of piety and human ignorance about divine motives leads to a theodicy based on man's universal feeling of guilt. Job does not suffer because he sinned; he suffers because God made a bet with Satan that Job feared God out of pure motives (1:8-12). Job suffers for God's honor. This example may seem to reveal a narratorial bias against God because of the biblical reader's usual piety toward the biblical God, but the narrator never once criticizes God for the bet.[36] It is simply a case of the actual state of affairs being presented by the narrator to the shocked chagrin of the pious reader.

Judges 2

One final example gives a more characteristic view of the affect of this narrative mode on the meaning of the biblical traditions. Israel's repeated political disasters are piously attributed to Israel's idiotic disobedience throughout the prophetic books (e.g., Hosea 7:2, 8-16). The external, unconditioned narrator of Judges suggests a revision. The Exodus from Egypt was the divine act of benefaction upon which the call to covenantal obedience at Sinai was based. By the time Israel

entered the promised land, however, there remained only two individuals, Joshua and Caleb, who had seen that event (Numbers 14:6–
38, especially vv. 22–23). In spite of the fact that nobody but these
two men had seen the deed upon which the demand of obedience to
the law was based, Israel served God while the witnesses were alive
(Judges 1:7). It was only when Joshua died and a new generation
arose that did not know Yahweh or the works he did for Israel
(Judges 2:10) that Israel "did evil in the sight of the Lord" (v. 11).
Moreover the subsequent cycle of apostasy and punishment was not
exclusively the product of Israel's ignorance of the Exodus. God has
his own share in the ignorance and misunderstanding that fuels
Israel's history. The narrator grants the reader a privileged audition
of a divine monologue through which we learn that God is punishing
Israel not for ignorance of the Exodus event, but for disobedience to
the covenant that he imposed on the fathers (2:20–22). God does not
seem to know that Israel does not know about the Exodus without
which he has no claim to Israel's loyalty.

The narrator blames neither God nor Israel. He simply reports the
problem using the tools provided by his external, unconditioned viewpoint. And to the reader he offers a fresh insight into the problem of
God and Israel. Existing as they do on two different levels of being,
God and Israel constantly misunderstand each other. Divine omniscience may be a reality for the uninvolved God, but for the one that
has chosen to mix with man in history it seems to fade. The history of
Israel, traced in the Deuteronomistic narratives, is a history of misunderstanding and cross-purposes that ends, as it must, in failure.

It is this existential gap between God and man that is the main-
spring of much biblical narrative and it is the genius of biblical
authors to have developed a narratorial vehicle—the external, unconditioned narrator—to explore what would otherwise be a no-man's-
land of misconception and ignorance. The key to understanding biblical narrative, it seems to me, is neither history nor literary history,
but an appreciative acceptance of the revelations of these extraordinary narrators. Without them and in the measure that we cannot be
what they are, we will fail just as miserably as the human characters
in their stories to understand the way of God with man.

Notes

The translations used when quoting the Bible are my own.

1. Roman Ingarden makes similar observations about the analysis of literature in general:
"In fact, in reading a work, our attention is likewise directed primarily at represented objectivi-

ties. We are attuned to them, and our intentional gaze finds in them a certain peace and satisfaction; whereas we pass by the other strata with a certain degree of inattention, and, at any rate, we notice them incidentally, only to the extent that this is necessary for the thematic apprehension of objects. Some naïve readers are interested solely in the vicissitudes of represented objects, while everything else is nearly nonexistent for them. In works in which represented objects are engaged in the function of representation, such readers wish only to *find out* something about the *represented* world. And since the represented world, usually the real world, which then constitutes the main focus of interest, is conceived as something existing only for itself and performing no function, the world represented in a literary work of art is also conceived in the same sense. It is quite in keeping with this that works of literary history on the whole deal mainly with represented objects and, after some analysis of the properties of the "language" or of the nature of "images" used by the author, go into various problems of the work's genesis." In *The Literary Work of Art*, trans. G. G. Grabowicz (Evanston: Northwestern University Press, 1973), pp. 288–89.

2. Though it is common enough in the study of narrative literature to make a distinction between the narrator of a narrative and the author of a narrative, historical criticism has been unaware of this distinction's importance for the comprehension of meaning in narrative literature. Biblical critics have mostly assumed that all statements, especially evaluative assertions, in the narrative are the expressions of an author's own views or beliefs. No distinction is made between character voices or that of the narrator: all, democratically, are vehicles for the direct expression of the author's own views.

In the narrative study of the Bible one need observe only one distinction: between the voices of the author, the narrator, and the characters. For the moment, however, you will have to accept my alignment of narratorial and authorial points of view for purposes of argument. The alignment can and will be demonstrated later in this essay.

3. H. Gunkel, *Genesis* (Göttingen: Vandenhoeck & Ruprecht, 1902), p. 264.

4. "Historic and literary study are equal in importance: but for priority in order of time the literary treatment has the first claim. The reason of this is that the starting point of historic analysis must be that very existing text, which is the sole concern of the morphological study. The historic inquirer will no doubt add to his examination of the text light drawn from other sources; he may be led in his investigation to alter or rearrange the text; but he will admit that the most important single element on which he has to work is the text as it has come down to us. But, if the foundation principle of literary study be true, this existing text cannot be truly interpreted until it has been read in the light of its exact literary structure. In actual fact, it appears to me, Biblical criticism at the present time is, not infrequently, vitiated in its historical contentions by tacit assumptions as to the form of the text such as literary examination might have corrected." R. G. Moulton, *The Literary Study of the Bible*, rev. ed. (Boston: Heath, 1908), p. ix. Moulton and others who voiced similar warnings went unheeded in the early part of this century. Historical criticism's triumphs over traditional literalist readings of the Bible allowed it the unfortunate liberty of ignoring all opposing claims, regardless of their validity. Only more recently has the same sentiment been able to gain an audience, mainly because the passage of time has allowed the deficiencies in the historical-critical method to come to light and so to criticism more willingly heard, e.g., Robert Polzin, *Moses and the Deuteronomist: A Literary Study of the Deuteronomistic History* (New York: Seabury Press, 1980), p. 6, who voices a similar caution to Moulton's.

5. Franz Stanzel, *A Theory of Narrative*, trans. C. Goedsche (Cambridge: Cambridge University Press, 1984), p.4.

6. See Polzin's discussion of "ultimate semantic authority," *Moses and the Deuteronomist*, p. 20.

7. "Narrative situation" is a term coined by Stanzel in *Narrative Situations in the Novel*, trans, J. P. Pusack (Baltimore: Johns Hopkins University Press, 1971) to describe the variety of narrative ontologies and epistemologies with which an author may choose to frame his story. Stanzel

tries to summarize all possible narrative situations in three categories (*Theory of Narrative*, p. xvi).

8. The actual events that the story is based on are not represented in the diagram. Imagine them as lying in the paper of the page upon which the diagram is printed. You may catch a direct glimpse of them if you look at the page edgewise. The edgewise view, though slim, is about as close as we can come to a view that is not conditioned by the multiple levels of relativized perception in biblical narrative.

9. I use the noun *author* to describe all authorial roles, variously described by biblical scholars as "redactors" (editors), compilators, glossators, and sources.

10. L. Eslinger, "Viewpoints and Point of View in 1 Samuel 8–12," *Journal for the Study of the Old Testament* 23 (1983): 61–76; *Kingship of God in Crisis: A Close Reading of 1 Samuel 1–12* (Sheffield: Almond Press, 1985).

11. Eslinger, *Kingship*, pp. 260–62.

12. Moulton, *Literary Study*, p. ix, provides the following early example of an elegant obviation of a second-order explanation: "In the latter part of our Book of Micah a group of verses (vii. 7–10) must strike even a casual reader by their buoyancy of tone, so sharply contrasting with what has gone before. Accordingly Wellhausen sees in this changed tone evidence of a new composition, product of an age different in spirit from the age of the prophet: 'between v. 6 and v. 7 there yawns a century.' What really yawns between the verses is simply a change of speakers. . . . At this point the Man of Wisdom speaks, and the disputed verses change the tone to convey the happy confidence of one on whose side the divine intervention is to take place. . . . I submit that in this case a mistaken historical judgment has been formed by a distinguished historian for want of that preliminary literary analysis of the text for which I am contending."

13. Curiously, English speaking historical-critical scholars react negatively at the mention of this study, feigning innocent exasperation at another neologistic "-ology." It is difficult to understand how such academics, who also for the most part know some Greek, have any more difficulty with narrato-logy than they do with bio-logy, cosm- ology, or the-ology.

14. Stanzel, *Narrative Situations*, p. 15.

15. Seymour Chatman, *Story and Discourse: Narrative Structure in Fiction and Film* (Ithaca: Cornell University Press, 1978), p. 19.

16. According to G. Genette it is also more appropriate for narratology to study discourse, since that is the distinctive modal character of this genre alone. See the comments of Gerald Prince, "Review of G. Genette, *Nouveau discours du récit*," *Poetics Today* 5(1984):867.

17. David Damrosch, "Leviticus," *The Literary Guide to the Bible*, ed. Robert Alter and Frank Kermode (Cambridge: Harvard University Press, 1987), pp. 66–77 has offered one such reading of the Book of Leviticus. According to Damrosch: "Rather than a sterile opposition between law and narrative, the text shows a complex but harmonious interplay between two *forms* of narrative. Law and history meet on a common ground composed of ritual, symbolic, and prophetic elements."

18. K. Friedemann, *Die Rolle des Erzählers in der Epik* (Leipzig: Hässel, 1910), p. 26.

19. The "narratorial situation" is the perspectival, existential situation from which the narrator speaks.

20. See Stanzel, *Narrative Situations*, p. 23; N. W. Visser, "Temporal Vantage Point in the Novel," *Journal of Narrative Technique* 7 (1977): 81–93; G. Genette, *Narrative Discourse: An Essay in Method*, trans. J. E. Lewin (Ithaca: Cornell University Press, 1980), pp. 185–94, 215–37.

21. Both Stanzel (*Narrative Situations*, pp. 108–47) and Genette (*Narrative Discourse*, pp. 243–52) provide detailed discussion of pronominal indications of narratorial situation. Mieke Bal, *Narratology: Introduction to the Theory of Narrative*, trans. C. van Boheemen (Toronto: University of Toronto Press, 1985), pp. 120–34, offers many detailed observations about the differences that are roughly categorized here by means of pronominal indications of narratorial stance vis-à-vis the story world. W. J. M. Bronzwaer, *Tense in the Novel* (Groningen: Wolters-Noordhoff, 1970), pp. 41–80 describes the variation of verb tense to create different temporal distances between

narratorial situation and story world. (See also Stanzel, *Narrative Situations*, pp. 22–37; Chatman, *Story and Discourse*, pp. 79–84; Genette, *Narrative Discourse*, pp. 215–27. In ancient narrative one must also take prophetic and predictive temporal modulations into account (Genette, *Narrative Discourse*, p. 216). In the biblical examples, the prophetic and apocalyptic books, the verbal descriptions usually maintain the separation of narratorial situation and story world at the time of narration, but also allow for increasing contact between the two with the passage of time.

22. See Stanzel, *Theory of Narrative*, pp. 121–27; Bal, *Narratology*, p. 124.

23. See Dorrit Cohn, "The Encirclement of Narrative," *Poetics Today* 2 (1981): 164: "first person narration posits a relationship of existential contiguity between discourse and story, authorial [third person] narration posits a merely mental, cognitive relationship between these two functional spheres."

24. See Bal, *Narratology*, p. 109: "The way in which a subject is presented gives us information about that object itself and about the focalizer [viewer]." We know that the narrator in the Book of Nehemiah was bound, as he tells his story, to the physical constraints of the story world and we know that the narrator of the Book of Job is not.

25. See N. Friedman, "Point of View in Fiction: The Development of a Critical Concept," *PMLA* 70 (1955): 1174–75.

26. See Stanzel, *Theory of Narrative*, p. 90.

27. See Chatman, *Story and Discourse*, pp. 166–95; Genette, *Narrative Discourse*, pp. 185–94; Bal, *Narratology*, p. 105, "internal focalization."

28. A so-called reflector character; see Stanzel, *Theory of Narrative*, p. 59.

29. Bal, *Narratology*, pp. 105–6.

30. See Franz Stanzel, "Teller-Characters and Reflector-Characters in Narrative Theory," *Poetics Today* 2 (1981): 5–15.

31. On this point I disagree with the position that seems to be shared by three notable commentators on biblical narrative: Robert Alter, Robert Polzin, and Meir Sternberg. All three authors seem to believe that the biblical narrator consciously subordinates his perspective and views to the deity also known as the character Yahweh or God in the narrative. Sternberg is most explicit on this point: "The very choice to devise an omniscient narrator serves the purpose of staging and glorifying an omniscient God." *The Poetics of Biblical Narrative: Ideological Literature and the Drama of Reading* (Bloomington: Indiana University Press, 1985), p. 89. God's omniscience and his power are certainly "staged" in the narratives of the Bible, but is often an exposition of which the character in the narrative would disapprove. Many times the insights that the narrator's own unlimited access to information provide expose attitudes, thoughts, or practices of the deity that he clearly hides from his human partners in the drama of human history. In the narrative God is secretive precisely because his, as anyone's, hidden motives or actions might be reprehensible from the point of view of interpersonal interactions and fidelities. God, for example, may in fact learn from his experience in interacting with his human creatures, as 1 Samuel 15 suggests. See L. Eslinger, "'A Change of Heart': 1 Samuel 16," *Ascribe to the Lord: Biblical and Other Studies in Memory of Peter C. Craigie*, ed. L. Eslinger and J. G. Taylor (Sheffield: Journal for the Study of the Old Testament Press, 1988). But God does not want his human counterpart to know that. So he chides Samuel for the reasonable assumption that because God chose a big fellow for his first king that he would be likely to do the same in the case of the second. Another important example is the uncomplimentary difference between the actual reason for the failure of total conquest (Judges 2:23, a narratorial revelation), and what God wants to believe is the reason (Judges 2:21) and what he tells Israel, in public, is the reason (Judges 2:3). Although such insights into the machinations of the divinity in the Bible are not condemnations, neither are they laudatory; they are not, in any obvious sense, "glorifying." Sternberg's view seems less a consideration of the perspective presented by the external, unconditioned narrator than an assumption about what the ancient authors of sacred writ probably wrote for. See M. Bal, "The Bible as Literature: A Critical Escape," *Diacritics* 16 (1986): 72:

"The biblical narrator duplicating God's omniscience, thanks to divine inspiration, is he [Sternberg] claims, not a religious dogma. . . . This way of putting it is, however, symptomatic of the critic's ideological commitment to the text and his use of poetics to support it, if not to impose it"; N. Segal, "Review of M. Sternberg, *The Poetics of Biblical Narrative*," *Vetus Testamentum* 38 (1988): 243–49: "How is it possible, except by complacency, to avoid reading the author/narrator as controlling his chief character, as more god than God?"

Instead of ideological commitment supporting the deity that he describes acting in his story world, the external, unconditioned narrator is neutral, his interests being to reveal the hidden workings of divine-human interaction and to understand. Understanding: that is central. The simple fact that so many of these insights expose what God would keep hidden does, however, evoke, at least initially, a certain sense of shock and repugnance from the reader.

32. The introductory superscription, "The words of Nehemiah, son of Hacaliah," are not part of the narrative. Rather, they function as a descriptive title for the subsequent narrative.

33. Stanzel, *Theory of Narrative*, p. 126, describes the internal first person narrator as "Ich mit Leib," a characterization well-suited to this conditioned and limited narratorial situation.

34. See Wayne Booth, *The Rhetoric of Fiction* (Chicago: University of Chicago Press, 1961), p. 155.

35. See Stanzel, *Theory of Narrative*, pp. 126–27.

36. Frequently readings such as I present here—e.g., the readings of D. M. Gunn, *The Fate of King Saul: An Interpretation of a Biblical Story* (Sheffield: Journal for the Study of the Old Testament Press, 1980); "The 'Hardening of Pharaoh's Heart': Plot, Character and Theology in Exodus 1–14," *Art and Meaning: Rhetoric in Biblical Literature*, ed. D. J. A. Clines, D. M. Gunn, and A. J. Hauser (Sheffield: Journal for the Study of the Old Testament Press, 1982), pp. 72–96—are mistaken for a dark, perverted misreading of biblical narrative. It is only against the ponderous sanctimony that has characterized so much of the pious apologetic that passes for exegesis that descriptions of the objective narration of the Bible seems bleak. But as Herbert Schneidau has pointed out, the Bible is a book that constantly challenges and provokes the reader; it is alienating literature that constantly exposes established dogmas to new searching and criticism: "what the Bible offers culture is neither an ecclesiastical structure nor a moral code, but an unceasing critique of itself." See *Sacred Discontent: The Bible and Western Tradition* (Berkeley: University of California Press, 1976), p. 16. I, for one, would apply this to the biblical narrator's critique of the theological dogmas contained within their very narratives.

In the Beginning Is the Word

S. N. Rosenbaum

Dickinson College

REVIEWING Alter's and Kermode's recent *The Literary Guide to the Bible*, George Steiner concludes: "the voice and that which it speaks can never be considered as separate."[1] He faults the volume for trying to enforce such a separation, and this desire is, indeed, the besetting problem of Bible-as-literature teachers. C. S. Lewis was more blunt when he wrote, "those who read the Bible as literature do not read the Bible."[2] I have to wonder, though, whether Steiner knows how serious the problem is. As for Lewis, he is part of the problem. It's not only the voice we need to hearken to, but also the tongue.

In the case of Tanach (often wrongly termed the Old Testament), that tongue is Hebrew. Not that the literary/religious fraternity is unaware of this. In 1958, in a little book about the Psalms, Lewis fatuously claims that a lack of biblical Hebrew makes him better able to explain Scripture than someone who has knowledge of the language.[3] I can just imagine the howls of English professors if some Israeli made the same claim about teaching Shakespeare in modern Hebrew. (In fact, I recall a Hebrew subtitle for a line in the movie version of Marlowe's *Dr. Faustus*: the character says, "I bid thee sweet night, fair friend"; the subtitle reads *Leilah tov, habibi*, which back-translates as something akin to "G'night, buddy.")

Twenty-five years after Lewis, Northrop Frye gives us *The Great Code*. Like his predecessor, he pays some heed to his own lack of language. This is apparent already in the subtitle, *The Bible and Literature*. To his credit, Frye acknowledges that Scripture in translation is "second best."[4] He and I differ as to how distant a second. Frye implies that the LXX (Septuagint, allegedly translated ca. 280 B.C.E. by seventy scholars who, working independently, arrived at identical translations), or Greek Bible, is a decent translation that was rejected by Jews after they saw the uses to which Christians put it (see below).

In reality, I would assert there are no decent translations and there cannot be any, regardless of one's theology, because we cannot effectively translate between a Semitic and an Indo-European language. As Edward Sapir puts it, each language has its own "cut":[5] texture, we might say. To translate in the face of this is, I submit, an act of cultural imperialism masquerading as expediency.

I have another problem with Frye, though, that is even more serious. His insistence on considering the Christian New Testament along with Hebrew Scripture is misplaced on literary grounds. As Nietzsche observed:

> to have glued this New Testament, a kind of rococo of taste in every respect, to the Old Testament to make *one* book . . . that is, perhaps, the greatest audacity and "sin against the spirit that literary Europe has on its conscience."[6]

Here and elsewhere, commenting on the content of the two Scriptures, Nietzsche expresses admiration for the three-dimensionality and profundity of the Old Testament while expressing his usual contempt for New Testament.

Nietzsche was no philologist—nor phil-anything, for that matter. But he has a point. English steals words or spawns them while Hebrew generally milks meaning from a limited number of (mostly) triliteral roots. As I've written elsewhere, English is a "horizontal" language, Hebrew a "vertical" one.[7] For example, the root *n-ḥ-š* gives us two nouns, "serpent" and "bronze," and the verb "to divine." If one knows this, the story in Numbers 21 comes alive and we see Moses being told to invent the caduceus.[8]

The very sounds of Hebrew have different associations than ours do. Thus, *Torah* (meaning "teaching" or "instruction" but erroneously rendered into English as "law") rhymes with *'orāh*, "light," giving us a wordplay possibility absent in English (though present in the Latin *lex/lux*). The "music" of language was of interest to Philo, around Jesus' time, and to Abraham Abulafia, the thirteenth-century mystic. It should be of interest to us as well. Abulafia writes:

> Know that the method of *Tzeruf* [the combination of letters] can be compared to music; for the ear hears sounds from various combinations in accordance with the melody and the instrument.[9]

I hear this echoed in the character of Leo Tzuref in Philip Roth's excellent short story "Eli, the Fanatic" (the concluding story in the collection *Good-bye, Columbus*). Tzuref is the headmaster of a yeshiva for displaced children that casts up in a suburb of New York after the war. He has *eighteen* boys in his charge, as the story is at pains to make clear. Eighteen, of course, stands for "life" in Hebrew number mysticism. The Bible is chock-a-block with numbers that must similarly be understood.

Frye is right about one thing: "too many scholarly fields are relevant."[10] Doing text criticism—what the last century contemptuously refers to as the "lower" criticism—reminds me of Tolstoy's "How Much Land Does a Man Need?" In my profession, we might ask, How many fields does a person need? The answer is, All of them, dammit! If we don't drop dead trying to encompass all the knowledge that we wish to bring to bear upon Bible studies, we eventually plow it back into our home field, the Bible.

We must do this because the Bible is our story. As Sam Gamgee, a kind of working-class Everyman in J. R. R. Tolkien's religious-fantasy epic *The Lord of the Rings* realizes, we are part of the story we tell.[11] I can understand Lewis or Frye being eager to get on with the business of telling our story. But what they tell will be richer, ultimately, if they have the patience to acquire some of the tools of a Hebrew storyteller before going too far.

We could profitably begin with an examination of the pericope, of the sentence, or of the individual lexical item—the word. Each of these approaches has something to recommend it; ultimately, all must be taken into account. But as I am here engaged in the particularities of semantics, I restrict myself to the last. In the beginning is the word. The Hebrew word.

If the reader needs additional convincing, consider the celebrated "virgin" of Isaiah 7:14. Christianity, for centuries, pilloried Judaism for failing to accept this signal prediction of Jesus' birth made some seven hundred years in advance of the event. In fact, as Hebrew readers know, Isaiah said no such thing. LXX took *'almāh* ("young woman") and read *parthenos* ("young woman or virgin") and Jerome translated *virgo*. The church anathematized anyone who used the Greek text in preference to the Latin and a crucial error was set in stone for a thousand years. (Hebrew has a separate word for "virgin"; it is *b'tûlāh*.)[12]

Assuming we can now avoid theologically dictated errors of the cruder sort, how do we go about getting at the meaning of Hebrew words? The answer, of course, is through their context. But here we must identify at least four kinds of context, all of which have some part to play. They are, in no particular order: 1) the sentence in which a word is found; 2) every sentence in which that word is found; 3) the word's semantic field (and its mirror-image or antonymic field); and 4) similar words in the cognate languages. We could, I suppose, add a fifth—the versional material—but I've already indicated my distrust of it on both linguistic and theological grounds. Besides, the first four will keep us more than well enough occupied.

James Barr is particularly keen on the sentence as the primary locus of theological meaning for items within it.[13] Certainly, one cannot take such a loaded word as *nefesh* and translate it on any sort of one-for-one basis. The *nefesh ḥayyah* is "in the blood" and that's why the Israelites could not eat meat with the blood in it. But David asks (Psalm 137:12) to be delivered from the *nefesh* of his enemies. Clearly, the word has more than one English extension. Most Hebrew words do.

A careful scholar will also consider *every* biblical occurrence of a given word. (Computers make the task easier, perhaps too much so.) We have to recall that our text is composed of pieces that span a one-thousand-year time period, from Judges 5 (Song of Deborah, ca. 1225 B.C.E.) to Daniel (ca. 165 B.C.E.). It is highly unlikely that words used in Joshua's time retained their parameters intact until the Maccabean period. Bible scholars are aware of the problem, which we call synchronic versus diachronic reading of the text. Too many of us, I think, read the text synchronically, as though it were all from the same period. Of course, the other way is almost impossible; it implies that no biblical text necessarily sheds light on another. But we should remember that there is a problem here.

For example, when King Josiah died (608 B.C.E.) the "people of the land" elected one of his sons, Jehoahaz, to succeed him—probably because this son had pro-Babylonian political views similar to his father's. These electors were the substantial citizens of the kingdom of Judah. In Jesus' time, six hundred years and a lot of history later, the same term, *'amê hā'āretz*, is used to designate "yokels," "rabble," "rubes."

It is not possible always to rely on inner biblical evidence for help. Sapir asserts:

> totally unrelated languages (may) share in one culture, closely related languages—even a single language (may) belong to distinct cultural spheres.[14]

As Lawrence Durrell said of Coventry Patmore, Sapir wrote better than he knew. The most recent complication in the field of biblical Hebrew is the investigation of dialects within the language.

Few of us have had the audacity to do much with this. James Davila is working on the thesis that Ecclesiastes is influenced by a "northern" Hebrew,[15] and my own work on Amos points in the same direction.[16] If we are at all correct, it could mean that what seems the same word in the mouths of different biblical characters is not the same at all: compare "torch" in the mouths of British and American English speakers or "soda" to a Chicagoan and to a Bostonian.

But if this is true of English dialects in the twentieth century, how much less reliable is the "evidence" from cognate languages in the biblical period? One snare the unwary literature teacher may fall afoul of is secondary Bible criticism that depends upon other Semitic languages, notably Arabic, to elucidate obscure biblical words. Cognomania seems to have been born in the nineteenth century when F. Max Muller discovered connections between Sanskrit and Greek.[17] Later, redoubtable German explorers such as Eduard Meyer and Alois Musil felt they could penetrate the recesses of Hebrew culture and thought by reference to the manners and customs of modern Bedouin.[18] If there is no other context—the biblical term is *hapax legomenon*—then cognate cultures must be pressed into service, however reluctantly. The results may be downright misleading.

For years scholars identified the prophet Amos as some sort of migrant worker because the word *bôlēs* in 7 : 14 may be cognate with an Ethiopic term meaning "pinch" or "gash." Amos, then, is a pincher (to expedite fertilization) of sycamore figs: a rather lowly occupation, it would seem. In fact, there is also an Aramaic cognate that means "inspector," and ramifications of this are far different. We have to remember that cognates are not always identical twins.

The way out of this difficulty, I think, lies through the use of semantic field theory. As defined by Ullmann, a semantic field is

> a closely knit and articulated lexical sphere where the significance of each unit is determined by its neighbors, with their semantic areas reciprocally limiting one another and dividing up and covering the whole sphere between them.[19]

A corollary to this would be Nelson Goodman's observation that in a natural language there are no synonyms.[20] One might, of course, argue with this assertion; medieval Jewish scholars in fact did just that.[21] But, certainly, there is some truth to the claim.

Consider the case of *'ôyēb* ("enemy") and *rāšā'* ("wicked person")[22] in Psalms. In Psalms alone these two words are used 83 and 74 times respectively (along with about two dozen congeners used much less frequently). The whole weight of this semantic field (which I called "antagonist" in my dissertation)[23] is such that Lewis is appalled by what he sees as a continuous pleading in Psalms to destroy Israel's "enemies."[24]

In fact, as I discovered (along with Othmar Keel),[25] the two main terms mean "foreign" and "domestic" enemies respectively. The whole field breaks down into two primary groups: foreigners—what an Israelite Kipling might call "lesser breeds without the law"—and

Israelites, whose knowledge of the covenant and *mitzvot* ("command-ments") holds them to a higher standard of behavior. Few foreigners are termed "wicked," while fewer Israelites earn the appellation "enemy."

Speaking of enemies, my coursings through the concordance in pre-computer days turned up the rare form *'êvāh* in Genesis 3:15.[26] I rec-ognized the root *'-y-b* (n. *'ôyēb*) and wondered what weight of ill-will continues to inform mankind's relationship with serpentkind. I found that the Ur-serpent and all his generations are our mortal enemies because their progenitor, in effect, "murdered" Adam and Eve by destroying their immortality.[27]

Another area in which words should be carefully differentiated is the so-called Wisdom Literature: Job, Proverbs, Ecclesiastes, and some psalms. (I say "so-called" because of my continuing uneasiness with categories we have coined for the academic dissection of religious literature. Dissected frogs don't jump.)

Job, of course, is a special case because he is so beloved of the liter-ary guild. I have taught MacLeish's *J. B.* myself, but the very suscep-tibility of the book to dramatic interpretation turns our attention away from its careful use of vocabulary. The words in the semantic field we may as well call "wisdom" that Job chooses show a philo-sophical concern which has long gone unnoticed.

Exegesis begins to get off track in New Testament times when James's Epistle (5:11f.) points out Job as a "pattern" of patience. The Jewish view of Job is quite other, namely, that he was impatient with God's justice, demanding a trial in which he was sure to be vindi-cated. But there is a third view, neither Jewish nor Greek, that Job is mainly concerned with the question of how we know what we know, that is, with epistemology.[28]

Job uses seven terms from the field "wisdom," but three of them are marked by their multiple occurrence as more importkant than the others: *ḥokmāh*, *bînāh*, and *dā'at*. Expositors have often assumed they are synonyms because they are so often used in poetic "parallelism."[29] This essay is not the place to dispute the too easy division of Hebrew texts into prose and poetry,[30] but a close look at Job reveals these three words have peculiar relationships to each other.

Ḥokmāh is used in parallel with *bînāh* 9 times.

Bînāh is used in parallel with *dā'at* 10 times.

A belief in synonymy would lead one to expect a similar number of parallels between *ḥokmāh* and *dā'at*. In fact, Job has none.

Why this seeming anomaly?

The answer is that the words have different meanings *in* Job. *Dā'at* is, roughly, experiential knowledge, the "wisdom" we humans possess. Both God and mankind have a *bînāh* ("understanding") appropriate to their experience, but real Wisdom, *hokmāh*, is possessed by God alone. Hence the disquisition in Job 28 in which various elements in creation deny having it. Job 28:28 concludes: "The fear of God is the beginning of Wisdom," a sentiment echoed, with meaningful variations, in Psalm 111:10, Proverbs 1:6; 9:10; 15:33.

Pursuing Wisdom into the Book of Proverbs provides an immediate surprise. That commodity is so much more widely available in Proverbs that one wonders if the author/compilers of both books are dealing with the same concept. It's hard to say. Proverbs certainly, and Job probably, grew to their present form over a long period of time. Do we read them synchronically or diachronically?

Another peculiar aspect of Proverbs' "Wisdom" is its continual advice to young men to avoid the loose woman. This is not, cannot be, merely referring to the common prostitute. In context, it makes more sense to suggest that the woman in question is that well-known camp follower of Alexander the Great, *sophia*. Greek philosophy, with its promise of the Good, the True, and the Beautiful, must have been seductive to young Israelites whose God was . . . where?

On the other hand, we know that some words have restricted meanings, e.g., *bārā'*. This is the verb by which God called the world into being. We translate it "create," of course, but our word fits the Hebrew like Goliath's undershorts on David. *Homo faber*; only God creates.

Another example of the same kind, far less well-known, is the verb *bārah*. We translate "flee," but a run through the concordance shows that the verb means "flight to escape legal jurisdiction," as opposed to, say, "flight from a military defeat." David "flees" from King Saul; Amos "flees" from Beth El (his native country on my reading).[31] Jonah tries to "flee" from God—a futile effort, as Jonah would have known if he'd taken the trouble to read Psalm 139:7ff. first.

Still other cases in which the proper understanding of a single word makes a world of difference are Genesis 3:16 and Psalm 8:5. In the psalm, standard translations agree that God has made humans "little lower than the angels" or, as the New Jewish Publication Society Tanach prefers, "divine," preserving the ambiguity of the Hebrew *'elōhîm*.[32] It seems to me, though, that a better translation would be "has diminished [*Hifil* of *h-s-r*, "to lack"] mankind but little from," implying a higher human status before the Fall.

This nicety might not matter much to those whose interests in Scripture are purely literary. But no one, I think, can escape the import of Genesis 3:16. Here, as the various translations triumphantly tell us, women will want to have children despite the newly decreed pain involved in the birth process. They will crave the attention of their husbands, but the husbands will "rule," "master," or "lord it over" their wives, depending on which translation you favor.

I disagree. As some of the early rabbis clearly saw, the context here is sexual, not domestic. It says nothing about who will be Tarzan and who Jane; rather it implies that now, after the Fall, women's sexual satisfaction will have to wait upon their husbands' slower and mono-orgasmic capabilities. A better translation, I submit, is "regulate."

Semantic field study offers yet another tool for arriving at meanings for individual items. If Hebrew words lack true synonyms, the same cannot be said as certainly of antonyms. We can define some words in a field, as distinct from others, by the terms each pairs off with as presumed opposites. For example, two closely related terms from the field "proper behavior" are ṣaddiq ("righteous") and ḥāsîd ("pious or saintly person"). Back in 1907, the Brown-Driver-Briggs lexicon noted that the Bible uses rāšā' as the opposite of ṣaddiq but never as the opposite of ḥāsîd.[33]

The Bible has lots of words in it, most of which deserve the same kind of consideration indicated here. Treated thus, each word becomes a raindrop, containing its own world of meanings and associations and leading God alone knows where. Admittedly, studying Scripture in this way inhibits the appreciation of the Bible as literature. This is not my intention. I ask only that in our haste to encompass the whole, we do not stint on the naming of parts.

Notes

1. George Steiner, "The Good Books," review of *The Literary Guide to the Bible*, ed. Robert Alter and Frank Kermode (Cambridge: Harvard University Press, 1987), in *The New Yorker*, 11 January 1988, pp. 94ff.

2. Clive Staples Lewis, "The Literary Impact of the Authorized Version," in *They Asked for a Paper* (London: Bles, 1962), p. 46.

3. Clive Staples Lewis, *Reflections on the Psalms* (New York: Harcourt, Brace, 1958), p. 1.

4. Northrop Frye, *The Great Code: The Bible and Literature* (New York: Harcourt, Brace, 1982), p. 4.

5. Edward Sapir, *Language* (New York: Harcourt, Brace, 1921), p. 120; quoted in Stephen Ullmann, *Semantics* (New York: Harper & Row, 1979), p. 236.

6. Friederich Nietzsche, *Beyond Good and Evil* (New York: Vintage Press, 1966), sec. 52, pp. 65f.

7. Stanley Ned Rosenbaum, "It Gains a Lot in Translation," in *Teaching the Bible as Literature*, ed. Barry Olshen and Yael Feldman (Washington, D.C.: MLA, forthcoming).

8. The connection was drawn for me many years ago by my friend and classmate Michael Fishbane, now professor of Near Eastern and Judaic Studies at Brandeis University.

9. Nahum Glatzer, *The Judaic Tradition* (Boston: Beacon Press, 1969), p. 425.

10. Frye, *The Great Code*, p. xiv.

11. Sam says: "Why, to think of it, we're in the same tale still! It's going on. Don't the great tales never end?" J. R. R. Tolkien, *The Two Towers* (Boston: Houghton Mifflin, 1966), p. 321.

12. This argument is far from over. Gordon Wenham, "B'tûlāh, a Girl of Marriageable Age," *Vetus Testamentum* 22 (1972): 326–48, asserts that *b'tulah* encompasses the meaning, "a girl of marriageable age," but was never meant to mean "virgin." T. Wadsworth, "Is there a Hebrew Word for Virgin? *Bethulah* in the Old Testament," *Restoration Quarterly* 23 (1980): 161–71, thinks otherwise.

13. James Barr, *The Semantics of Biblical Language* (Oxford: Clarendon Press, 1961), p. 269 and elsewhere.

14. Sapir, *Language*, p. 213.

15. James Davila, "Qoheleth and Northern Hebrew," forthcoming. Professor Davila kindly shared a manuscript copy with me. A more general and justifiably cautious treatment of the subject is W. Randall Garr, *Dialect Geography of Syria-Palestine* (Philadelphia: University of Pennsylvania Press, 1985).

16. S. N. Rosenbaum, "A Northern Amos Revisited: Two Philological Suggestions," *Hebrew Studies* 18 (1977): 132–45.

17. F. Max Muller, *Chips from a German Workshop* (New York: Scribner, 1872–1900), esp. vol. 4.

18. Eduard Meyer was convinced monotheism could be deduced from the austere life of the Wahhabi, while Alois Musil championed *Manners and Customs of the Rwala Beduins* (New York: American Geographical Society, 1928).

19. Stephen Ullmann, *The Principles of Semantics* (Glasgow: Oxford University Press, 1951), p. 151.

20. Ullmann, *Semantics*, pp. 141f., enlists Dr. Johnson, Macaulay, Michael Breal, and Leonard Bloomfield. He and I also rely on F. de Saussure, Jost Trier, Eugene Nida, Nelson Goodman, and U. M. D. Cassuto, all of whom warn against "synonomizing."

21. E.g., Abraham ibn Ezra (twelfth century) cited in George Buchanan Gray, *The Forms of Hebrew Poetry* (New York: Ktav, 1969), pp. 17ff.

22. All English equivalents are provisional translations.

23. S. N. Rosenbaum, "The Concept 'Antagonist' in Hebrew Psalmography: A Semantic Field Study" (Ph. D. diss., Brandeis University, 1974).

24. Lewis, *Reflections*, p. 67.

25. Othmar Keel, *Feinde und Gottesleugner: Studien zum Image der Widersacher in den Individuelen Psalmen* (Stuttgart: Verlag Kathelisches Bibelwerk, 1969).

26. Solomon Mandelkern, *Concordantiae Hebraicae atque Chaldaicae* (Tel Aviv: Schocken Books, 1967). Now, also, Abraham Even-Shoshan, *A New Commentary of the Old Testament* (Jerusalem: Kiryat-Sepher, 1983).

27. S. N. Rosenbaum, "Israelite Homicide Law and the Term 'Enmity' in Gen. 3:15," *Journal of Law and Religion* 2 (1984): 145–51.

28. Namely mine. My introduction to and love of Job were the results of a graduate class I had with Nahum N. Glatzer. His book *The Dimensions of Job* (New York: Schocken Books, 1969) is an excellent anthology of modern commentary on Job.

29. Bishop Robert Lowth, *De sacra poesie Hebraorum praelectiones academicae Oxonii habitae* (Oxford, 1753); the extent and meaning of "parallelism" has been a topic of controversy ever since.

30. Two fine modern treatments are: James Kugel, *The Idea of Biblical Poetry* (New Haven: Yale University Press, 1981), and Robert Alter, *The Art of Biblical Poetry* (New York: Basic Books, 1985).

31. S.N. Rosenbaum, *Amos of Israel* (Macon, Ga.: Mercer University Press, forthcoming).

32. *Tanach: A New Translation of the Holy Scriptures* (Philadelphia: Jewish Publication Society of America, 1985).

33. Francis Brown, Samuel Rolles Driver, and Charles A. Briggs, *Hebrew and Chaldee Lexicon* (Oxford: Clarendon Press, 1907), p. 957; though still useful, there are more up-to-date lexica available.

From Garden to City:
Closure in the Bible

Diane T. Edwards

University of Victoria

> The thing that hath been, it is that which shall be; and that which
> is done is that which shall be done: and there is no new thing
> under the sun.
> —Ecclesiastes 7:8

> Better is the end of a thing than the beginning thereof.
> —Ecclesiastes 1:9

CONCEPTS of literary unity have not usually been tried out on the Bible as a whole: multiple authorship, three original languages, and several thousand years of composition would appear to defeat any arguments for unity which go beyond the Bible's individual books. Yet, while the authors of the various texts could not have written out of a belief that they were contributing to a collection of unified documents, the redactors of the Bible were very much aware of the need to arrange their materials in a particular order (or particular orders), and did so not from whim but from a sound understanding of how a text's interpretation would be affected and assisted by its location among other related texts. Much of whatever unity we perceive in our reading of the Bible derives primarily from the arrangement of the texts, pronounced intertextual patterns of repetition, both verbal and thematic, and the sense of closure that these devices create.

The feeling that a text is finished, that there is nothing more to explain and that all our expectations have been satisfied or deflected, creates, at least partly, what is meant by an experience of closure.[1] Applying this to a biblical text, however, may appear to be self-contradictory since these texts are always implicitly pointing beyond themselves, and their sequence, while not arbitrary, is also not predetermined by their individual contents. A further consideration arises when we realize that the sequence of books in the Hebrew Scriptures is not the same as that of the Old Testament in the Christian Bible. While both begin with Genesis, the Hebrew Scriptures conclude with the books of the Chronicles, not with the brief text of Malachi. As a further complication, the Septuagint, or Greek Bible, maintains yet another sequence, ending with the prophetic and sometimes apocalyptic Ezekiel and Daniel.

There are sound literary reasons (besides historical ones, which need not concern us here) for each of these sequences, which all rely on delayed fulfillment of expectations created by their common beginning. The creation narratives in Genesis 1 and 2, while they differ in kind as well as in content, together establish a sense of order and relationship among nature, man, and God.[2] With the expulsion of man and nature from this relationship arises the expectation of his eventual return, if not to the exact place, at least to a restored position in some version of that place. Such an expectation may derive in part from our experience of the cyclical patterns of the natural world and from our tenacity in our unwillingness to abandon hope. The repetitions found in nature are reflected in Genesis 1 and its ordered, repetitive patterning of creation, which is also described as consisting of a forward movement in time.[3] Yet repetition can never be an exact duplication of what went before, an observation which led Kierkegaard to question whether a genuine repetition is possible and to conclude that the only true repetition is eternity.[4] Repetition is, for him, a characteristic of the spiritual realm which provides a person with "the blessed certainty of the instant," causing happiness, whereas its counterpart, recollection, causes sadness.[5] Repetition looks forward; recollection, backward. Thus the "true repetition" of eternity unites movement and change with stasis.

Time, begun in Genesis 1, zooms in for a closeup in the garden of Genesis 2 and 3. There, immortality is forfeited by Adam's fall: the possibility of not dying is removed, replaced by the urgency which accompanies a knowledge of death.[6] Time, which now brings him ever closer to death, separates man ever further from Eden. There is no way to get back to the garden, and recollection of it is virtually nonexistent in the Hebrew Scriptures. Ezekiel compares the greatness of Egypt to a cedar unequaled by any: "it was the envy of every tree in Eden, in the garden of God" (Ezek. 31:9),[7] and Deutero-Isaiah writes of God's turning the desolation of Zion "into an Eden, her wasteland into the garden of Yahweh" (Isa. 51:3). But such descriptions look to the present or the future rather than lament the past, and nowhere is there an indication that history will return to its beginnings. Indeed, it cannot. As William A. McClung has so clearly stated:

> The problems of transposing the model of Eden to the other end of history are many, and they turn principally upon memory; Eden cannot be new, and to regain it as it was is only to acknowledge the failure of history—the stasis that lies at the end of the progression must be paradise but not the same Paradise from which knowledge of good and evil was excluded.[8]

We should be aware of the extent to which our sense of biblical unity can be attributed to this Janus-like view, since so much of the Bible looks backwards and forwards at once as it recollects events in Israel's history and hopes for restoration. Northrop Frye has shown this pattern of promise, apostasy and enslavement, and redemption to be the central narrative structure of the Bible, repeated with variations which advance the story while constantly recollecting it.[9] As a kind of incremental repetition, his schema also contributes to our desire for closure within the narrative, a final repetition which satisfies our sense of an ending and includes within it all the previous repetitions. The authors who recorded the promises made to Abraham, Moses, and David create the expectation of the fulfillment of those promises before the "story" is ended. There is in each case a resulting suspense created as the hero leaves his home (and recollecting that home becomes an ongoing element of the narrative) and anticipates a new home which will be for others as well as for himself (thus repeating the hope created by the promises). The books of the Bible thus engage in "building time"[10] by their use of both recollection and repetition to emphasize and also transcend the limits of their present tense.

In his *Confessions*, Augustine questions how past and future exist and how the present has no length except by comparison and measurement:

> Would anyone deny that the future is as yet not existent? But in the mind there is already an expectation of the future. Would anyone deny that the past no longer exists? Yet still there is in the mind a memory of the past. Would anyone deny that the present time lacks extension, since it is but a point that passes on? Yet the attention endures, and by it that which is to be passes on its way to being no more.[11]

History was not cyclical for Augustine, and even as what will be merges into what was, so to him the city of the New Jerusalem "has been coming down from heaven since its beginning" and at the same time is on an earthly pilgrimage to its destination.[12] Augustine elsewhere interprets the six-day Creation as a parallel to six stages of human history, concluding that we now live in the sixth and final epoch which began with the coming of Christ and will be followed by a rest, a sabbath which will be not evening but perpetual day.[13] In all these contexts, past and future are seen to merge into an anticipated state which will recollect the past and repeat it in a new way.

The emphasis on observing the sabbath is always strong in the Hebrew Scriptures, although the reason for its observance varies in an instructive way. In Genesis, and again when the Law is proclaimed to

Moses in Exodus, the sabbath is proclaimed as a recollection and perpetual repetition of God's rest from creating the world. When, however, the Law is reiterated in Deuteronomy, the reason for a sabbath rest changes: there, the sabbath is a commemoration not of creation but of God's deliverance of his people out of Egypt (Deut. 5:15). The narrative pattern is henceforth firmly established as recuperative: it consists of work, slavery, and exile followed by deliverance, freedom, and a sabbath rest. Delivery out of Egypt is equated with God's rest after the work of creation. The repetition of plagues visited upon Pharaoh recalls the repetition of Genesis 1; in both instances, God's power is shown operative on nature for the benefit of his people. That each narrative ends with a release from work (God's in Genesis, the Hebrews' in Exodus) initiates an incremental pattern that overlies both individual books and the Bible as a whole.

Genesis itself affords an example of this. Its opening chapter, as we have noted, is the first statement of the pattern of work followed by rest. The text ends with the story of Joseph, which offers another example of the same recuperative pattern. Joseph, having been sold into slavery, and later imprisoned, rises to power in Pharaoh's household because God is with him.[14] His deliverance from prison leads to the release of "a numerous people" from famine, and the Israelites prosper in Goshen. In a narrative in which God does not figure prominently as a main character, it is noteworthy that he is deliberately given the credit for saving his people: "God sent me before you to make sure that your race would have survivors in the land."[15] The closure of Genesis is, however, incomplete. With the death of Jacob, Joseph's brothers wonder whether they will be forced into slavery. Joseph reassures them, but their worry already anticipates what will become reality in the opening chapter of Exodus. And, when Joseph anticipates his own death, he exacts a promise that his bones will be taken out of Egypt "when God remembers you with kindness."[16] Such an ending resists closure since its "last allusions are to beginnings or to unstable events,"[17] and indicates that the recuperation is not permanent.

The opening verses of Exodus reenforce the idea that the pattern is beginning again. The Israelites are increasing in numbers and prospering, and, as the serpent entered Eden and disrupted its harmony, so immediately there appears a new king in Egypt who is ignorant of Joseph's redemption of the people from famine and who enslaves the sons of Israel. The narrative elaborates on their enslavement, beginning with the proclamation of death to all the sons of the Hebrews, a variation of the pattern which surfaced throughout Genesis as the usurping of the privileges of the first-born by younger siblings.[18] This is connected to recuperative techniques, as it forces a reversal in order to progress. Implied in the preferral of younger to older children is a favoring of youth and newness to age and experience, of those who are lowly to those who are exalted, of the more recent members of the genealogical series to the older ones. Younger sons are, therefore, thematically linked to the end of creation, the sabbath rest, and deliverance from slavery all at the same time. Genesis ended with the death of Joseph, the next to the youngest of Jacob's twelve sons; Exodus begins with the birth of Moses, the great prophet and liberator, himself a second son (he is three years younger than Aaron). The lesson these sons teach is that God can frustrate wicked schemes and turn them to good: from betrayal comes prosperity and from slavery comes deliverance into the promised land.

As Joseph Margolis has argued, "the theory of reading cannot fail to be committed at once to both *cloture* and *ouverture*."[19] These ancient texts are also committed to both, for even as one narrative path closes, it opens in another direction. The five books of the Pentateuch continue their narrative into the Early Prophets even as they form a unit in themselves. Deuteronomy closes this unity with the death of Moses, an event which would in many narrative structures signal a strong closure. But there is with Moses' death the unfinished business of claiming the land of Canaan, an act which was refused to Moses but promised to his successor, Joshua. The recuperative pattern of rest following slavery and deliverance is incomplete even as Moses' grave has never been found, an odd comment in a series of narratives which have been careful to record such locations as the bones of Joseph and the tomb of Rachel.

Deuteronomy, then, recapitulates and seals off the Pentateuch and opens the way for the sequence which begins with Joshua and continues through the Book of Kings. In the Greek and Christian Bibles, Kings is followed by Chronicles; in the Hebrew Bible, by the Later Prophets (Isaiah, Jeremiah, Ezekiel, and The Twelve). From this point on, the versions must be treated separately. Each continues to rely on the established pattern of recuperation, repeating it to create expectation and delay a final closure while granting partial closure along the way. The Hebrew Bible ends with Chronicles, preceded by Ezra-Nehemiah. There is a deliberate rearrangement of the chronological sequence here, since Ezra-Nehemiah ought to follow rather than precede Chronicles. Its contents continue the history narrated in Chronicles, and the opening verses of Ezra repeat the closing verses of Chronicles. Why, then, the reversal of their order? Some early manuscripts preserve the chronological sequence, making the current ordering seem even more calculated.

Ending with Chronicles, however, creates a sense of final closure which is impossible with Ezra-Nehemiah. On the one hand, Chronicles is a recollection of the whole of the Bible, much as Deuteronomy had been in the Pentateuch. It begins with genealogies going back to Adam and rehearses the history of Israel, paying particular attention to the Temple and its worship, and ending with the destruction of the Temple and the deportation into Babylon. There is a structural coherence in beginning with man in a new environment (Adam) and ending with man leaving his home as its spiritual center, the Temple, crashes down behind him. The closure would appear to be final when the Chronicler writes:

> This is how the word of Yahweh was fulfilled that he spoke through Jeremiah, "Until this land has enjoyed its sabbath rest, until seventy years have gone by, it will keep sabbath throughout the days of its desolation." [2 Chron. 36:21]

The recuperative pattern reemerges, as a detailing of history once again culminates in a sabbath rest. But there is a new twist here: the sabbath rest does not, as previously, signal rest from labor and deliverance from slavery but a deportation and a period of sojourn in a foreign land. In fact, the text of Jeremiah does not refer to the seventy years of the sabbath (Jer. 25:11 and 29:10); the Chronicler has picked this detail up from Leviticus:

> Then the land will observe its sabbaths indeed, lying desolate there, while you are in the land of your enemies. Then indeed the land will rest and observe its sabbaths. And as it lies desolate it will rest, as it never did on your sabbaths when you lived in it. [Lev. 26:34]

It appears that the land itself cries out for a sabbath rest which has been denied it by the people who have set themselves against God: God shall remember his covenant and he shall remember the land as the people atone for their sins in the land of their enemies (Lev. 26:42–43). The Chronicler deliberately applies this Levitical curse to the period of the Babylonian Captivity to show the importance of the sabbath and the consequences of its neglect. The pattern of recuperation has been violated by the people themselves, and so it will continue without them for a space of seventy years. The exile in fact lasted only fifty years, but seventy here suggests various possibilities of symbolic reading. The intensity of the neglect of the sabbath is reflected in the number 70, since 7 × 10 magnifies the sabbath (7) in terms of the Law which establishes its observance (10). It is also possible that the author means the seventy years to refer not to the return from exile but to the completion of the second Temple around twenty years later, at which time the recovery would be complete.

Were the text of Chronicles to end with the sabbath of desolation, closure would be tragic and dismal. But, while seventy years may be a lifetime, it is not permanent: the exiles, as the Chronicler knew, did return from Babylon. Because the last verses of Chronicles constitute the opening of Ezra, he could have deferred them, ending the text of Chronicles with a curse. That he chose not to do so is one reason that Chronicles is such a fitting end to the Hebrew Scriptures. The years of exile are silently and swiftly passed over and the narrative continues, without missing a beat: "And in the first year of Cyrus, king of Persia, to fulfill the word of Yahweh that was spoken through Jeremiah, Yahweh roused the spirit of Cyrus king of Persia." Details of the exile are skipped over entirely, for the emphasis of Chronicles was on the Temple and the community of faith, represented by the Davidic kingdom. God had promised (in a passage unique to Chronicles) that "now and for the future I have chosen and consecrated this house for my name to be there forever; my eyes and my heart will be there forever" (2 Chron. 9:16). The author returns to this theme at the end of Chronicles because it is more important than the chastisement of the exiles. The final verse creates a strong closure not only for Chronicles but also for the whole canon of Hebrew Scripture:

> "Thus speaks Cyrus king of Persia, 'Yahweh, the God of heaven, has given me all the kingdoms of the earth; he has ordered me to build him a Temple in Jerusalem, in Judah. Whoever there is among you of all his people, may his God be with him! Let him go up.'" [2 Chron. 36:23]

The call to return to Jerusalem and rebuild the Temple seals off the cycle begun in Genesis: the sabbath of the exile has ended, to be followed by another period of work and creation. The returning Hebrews anticipate it will end in the celebrating of a new Jerusalem in which they will have built a new temple. Their expectation does not weaken the experience of closure because Cyrus's edict has a ring of timelessness to it: it ends with a blessing on God's people and a call to return to their home, an ongoing hope of Israel in all of history.

When we turn to the Christian Bible, we find that Chronicles has been restored to its historical position before Ezra and Nehemiah. The reason for this is readily apparent: the redactors saw the return from exile as yet another instance of God's deliverance of his people, but for them this deliverance was not final but a further repetition of the recuperative pattern which had yet to be completed. Instead, the Scriptures were arranged so that the Prophets rather than the Writings closed the Hebrew Scriptures. This meant ending with the brief text of Malachi, a work that defies closure because it ends with a promise and a warning, two narrative devices which indicate continuity rather than completion. The prophet announces that God will send his messenger (*Malachi* means "my messenger") before the day of the Lord, at which time God "will suddenly enter his Temple" (3:1). By the end of the text, the messenger has been identified as Elijah the prophet (though this is generally regarded as a later addition). In the final verse, we read that "he shall turn the hearts of fathers towards their children and the hearts of children towards their fathers, lest I come and strike the land with a curse." The force of this last phrase is the equivalent of Herbert's "I struck the board, and cried, 'No more,'" the line occurring at the *beginning* of his poem "The Collar." Herbert's line raises the expectation of finding out how the speaker obtains relief from his anger: it grabs our attention by its abruptness and vigor. Malachi's ending has a similar effect except for the noticeable fact that nothing follows it: the text simply stops. One can scarcely imagine any work, much less a work (or collection of works) devoted to revealing God's pattern of restoration, intentionally ending this way. It is as if we have come to the end of a chapter which generates suspense and makes us want to read on.

In the Christian Bible, Malachi is followed by the four Gospels, all of which recollect the promise of Elijah's return. Matthew's recollection comes well into his text (11:10 and 17:12), but he has taken great pains to establish before then the continuity of his story with the Hebrew Scriptures. He begins his Gospel with a genealogy going back to Abraham and placing Jesus firmly in the line of David. Mark's Gospel, which is probably the oldest, immediately connects its narrative to the promise given in Malachi and indicates it has been fulfilled in John the Baptist (1:2–4). Luke explains the prophecy through the words of Jesus himself, who indicates the connection between Elijah and John the Baptist (7:26–27). By explicitly recollecting the words of Malachi, each synoptic writer indicated that for him the Hebrew Scriptures were not closed, or at least that the recuperative pattern which they had established had not ceased to operate.

John's Gospel, as might be expected, operates on a somewhat different principle. Its prologue (1:1–18) utilizes principles of recollection and repetition in the Kierkegaardian sense in which eternity is the only true repetition. Recollection is like discarded clothing which no longer fits; repetition is like an imperishable garment.[20] John's prologue recollects all history, not from Abraham or even Adam, but from before creation. His opening words, "in the beginning," imply that all of sacred history must now be rewritten because of the Incarnation. And he assumes, insofar as it is possible, an eternal perspective from which all repetitions of God's restorative pattern culminate in and are subsumed by the Word made flesh.

After the prologue, the narrative proper opens by questioning the relationship of John the Baptist to Elijah, though their equation here is less direct than in the synoptics. Nevertheless, the link to past Scriptures is made plain. John's Gospel, having indicated in its prologue that the story of creation must now be reconsidered, continues by recounting the first week in the "new" creation brought by Jesus. This day-by-day account culminates in the wedding at Cana on the seventh day, signifying that the "new" sabbath ends with a marriage feast at which Jesus provides the wine. This proves to be an eschatological statement when compared with the marriage of the Lamb later described in Revelation (19:8–9), at which time all repetitions will cease as eternity becomes the only reality.

All the Gospels include a promise of Jesus' return and an end to the repetition in time of God's pattern of restoration, thereby anticipating the closure provided in Revelation. Before discussing that closure, however, it will be useful to examine closure in the Septuagint. This Greek text consists of the books of the Hebrew Bible (with some variations) plus the additional Deutero-canonical books used by Jews of the Dispersion and accepted by the early church. In this Bible, the order of books is a mixture of the sequences found in the Hebrew and Christian Bibles. Like the Christian Bible, it places the prophetic books last, but its final book is not Malachi but Daniel. In the Hebrew Bible, Daniel precedes Ezra-Nehemiah and Chronicles; in the Septuagint, those final two books occur in the earlier historical half. By ending with Daniel, the Greek Bible announces its closure with a strong apocalyptic finale. Daniel is handed a sealed book to be kept "until the time of the End" (12:14). The canon of the Greek Scriptures is simultaneously sealed off, a parallel that a reader or listener could not ignore as the book (or scroll) is finished. Daniel is told to "go away and rest" (12:13) even as the readers or audience may feel that the command applies to them as well. The "rest" is reminiscent of the sabbath rest as it ends a period of struggle and anticipates a new creation in which "of those who lie sleeping in the dust of the earth many will awake, some to everlasting life, some to shame and everlasting disgrace" (12:2).

Unfortunately, this strong closure is disrupted in the Septuagint by the addition of an extra chapter, the Deutero-canonical text of Bel and the Dragon, which would have been better placed *before* Daniel, as is the other Deutero-canonical portion of Daniel, the story of Susanna and the Elders. The story of Bel is a humorous attack on idolatry in which Daniel proves the falsity of the idol called Bel. While, like the story of Susanna, it illustrates Daniel's wisdom, it is simply out of place at the end of the Septuagint. If Daniel really ought to conclude at chapter 12, then the closure of the Septuagint is as strong as that of the Hebrew Bible: both anticipate a deliverance from their enemies and the beginning of a new period of restoration.

The Christian Bible owes much of its closure to the Septuagint. The parallels between Revelation and Daniel are numerous and apparent, and it is not my intention to rehearse them here. Revelation can be considered independently as the book which seals off all the rest, not just in its final verses but in its entirety. It looks backward over all of human history and places it in a larger context of spiritual warfare fought for eternal stakes. More specifically, it is the ultimate rehearsal of what has here been referred to as the recuperative pattern of the Bible. It combines the repetitions of the return from exile and rest from labor, and indicates that the movement toward final closure has not been circular but linear. Repetition in a narrative has cumulative force so that the latter repetitions are stronger than the first, and there can never be a return to the beginning.[21] Thus it is quite incorrect to argue that Revelation restores humankind to its lost paradise: it is a long way back to the garden, and we cannot retrace our steps to find it again.

Nor do we really wish to: the association of Eden with a garden of earthly delights is not implicit in its description in Genesis. In fact, Philo described it only as "a dense place full of all kinds of trees," which symbolically represented the wisdom (*sophia*) by which the rational soul could praise its Creator.[22] In contrast, Revelation presents our ultimate goal not as a garden but as a city, "the new Jerusalem, coming down from God out of heaven, as beautiful as a bride all dressed for her husband" (21:2). How did this movement come about? A city of today hardly seems a desirable prototype of the messianic kingdom. And cities in the Bible do not reap praise from God or the prophets: one need only recall Babel, Babylon, Sodom, Nineveh, Rome, and even Jerusalem to realize that cities do not generally represent either obedience to God or spiritual vitality. Yet Revelation portrays our destination as a "new Jerusalem," a city solid enough to be measured, complete with gates and a wall. Jacques Ellul has argued that the city, because of its innate nature, belongs to man, not to God, and is, biblically, an allegory for sin.[23] But he goes on to state that God "adopted" the city so that he could get "a foothold in man's world."[24] Ellul says this occurred when God allowed David and Solomon to build a temple in Jerusalem, thereby using the city as an outlet through which man could receive forgiveness.

But cities existed well before Jerusalem, and the idea of the city may have existed even in Eden. Philo argues that, before creating the material world, God first formed its pattern or image in his mind, much as a city planner imagines how a city will be constructed before it is built:

> We must suppose that, when He was minded to found the one great city [i.e., the material world], He conceived beforehand the models of its parts, and that out of these He constituted and brought to completion a world discernible only by the mind, and then, with that for a pattern, the world which our senses can perceive.[25]

Philo later refers to Adam as not only our forefather but also "the only citizen of the world" living under the constitution of divine law, and he was preceded in this megalopolis by spiritual citizens, some incorporeal, others, such as the stars, visible to him.[26] The archetypal city, therefore, existed before God created Eden. This conflicts with Ellul's view of the city as a product and a symbol of humankind's separation from God, for it regards the city as a particular expression of the general pattern formed by God himself.

The city as presented in Revelation combines both these views: Babylon is personified as the whore of sin and separation, while Jerusalem becomes the bride who embodies the community of the faithful. This is the distinction which Augustine emphasizes when he writes of the two cities:

> We see then that the two cities were created by two kinds of love: the earthly city was created by self-love reaching the point of contempt for God, the Heavenly City by the love of God carried as far as contempt of self. In fact, the earthly city glories in itself, the Heavenly City glories in the Lord.[27]

The heavenly Jerusalem will overcome Babylon, the usurper will be usurped once and for all as the angel of Revelation announces: "Babylon the Great has fallen" and will be mourned by all the worldly nations while heaven celebrates her downfall (18:2–20). The fall of Babylon, the defeat of one's enemies, signals a strong closure in itself, but its effect is even more forceful when it is seen as the final repetition of the pattern in which the younger succeed over the elder. The pattern began with the rivalry between Cain and Abel, caused because Abel was preferred by God (Gen. 4:4–5). In other words, if "city" is used in Augustine's sense noted above, Abel belonged to the heavenly city, Cain to the earthly. The second-born son belongs to the spiritual, while the first belongs to the animal nature. Paul argues this when he almost impatiently tries to explain how the Resurrection will occur: "first the one with the soul, not the spirit, and after that, the one with the spirit. The first man, being from earth, is earthly by nature; the second man is from heaven" (1 Cor. 15:46–47).

Paul is, of course, referring not to Cain and Abel but to Adam and Christ, but Cain and Abel represent a microcosmic repetition of the pattern which in the Christian Bible finds its largest statement in Christ's being the second Adam. Typologically, Cain and Adam are the same person, as are Abel and Christ. Like Adam, Cain is driven out from his home, and we immediately learn that "he became builder of a town," and named that town after his son, Enoch (Gen. 4:17). Thus he belongs to the earthly city which "glories in itself." Abel could not found a city for the same reason that Jesus had no place to lay his head: citizens of the heavenly city are pilgrims who have no permanent home on earth.

Earlier, the preferral of the second-born was linked to the recuperative pattern of deliverance and rest since the youngest, like the seventh day of creation, came last and were usually the channel through which the promise was secured. The sabbath was observed as a commemoration of God's resting on the seventh day and also of God's deliverance of his people through the Passover and the Exodus.[28] It can now be seen that the New Jerusalem in Revelation fulfills the same expectations. Its descent ushers in the perpetual sabbath and the final deliverance from death through the triumph of the Lamb. Eden was described as an earthly site, and man was fashioned from the earth to live there. God did not live in Eden. Thus it would not suit our sense of closure if our eternal home turned out to be Eden again. In the heavenly city, "God lives among men" and "the world of the past is gone" (Rev. 21:3, 4).

Still, one might ask, why not have a heavenly garden rather than a heavenly city? Why not destroy all earthly cities and restore people to a luxuriant park? Quite apart from theological considerations, the literary genius of the Bible could not allow this. The more aspects of a narrative that are sealed off at its end, the stronger is our sense of closure. The more elements which are brought into a final repetition, the more satisfied are our expectations. The less that is left out, the more sound is the resolution. To end with a garden rather than a city would be to ignore the way human history has traveled since Cain founded the first city. It would produce an ending with a surprise twist: the history of God's people would have been a game with no ultimate meaning. All their kings and kingdoms, the building and rebuilding of the Temple, the cry of the prophets calling cities to repentence, would be evidence of ridiculous ideals now seen to be devoid of meaning if the garden were our goal all along. God would seem to have had a hidden agenda, and Jesus' weeping over Jerusalem would have been crocodile tears. There is a more unsettling aspect of this as well: if we end near where we began (since, as was noted earlier, no two repetitions can ever be exactly identical), what would convince us that we were not just beginning again, and that this beginning implied endless repetitions of the same sort? Such an ending to the Bible would be similar to the anticlosural force of Sisyphus rolling his rock.

But the emblem of the heavenly city closes the pattern of sacred history which has from the beginning been that of a growing community. Eve is created because Adam was lonely; Adam and Eve are told to multiply; Abraham's descendants are to number as many as the stars in heaven; Jesus' followers are sent out to "make disciples of all nations." Many of the parables and miracles associated with the kingdom of heaven also imply growth.[29] Thus our expectation is for expansion and magnitude, and we are more prepared for a closure of hyperbole and extravagance than one of understatement and simplicity. The redactors of both the Hebrew and the Christian Bibles sensed this: the call to rebuild the Temple (in 2 Chronicles) and the call to "come through the gates into the city" of the New Jerusalem (Rev. 22:14) are not different in kind, only in degree. The heavenly city is built of precious gems, gold, and pearls, materials found on earth but assuredly not the common materials of building. The city is more like a work of art by Faberge than an ancient Eastern town.[30] This artistic aspect of the city is the final repetition of man's love of beautiful things and their ability to help him transcend his limitations. Again, it was Cain's descendants who began the arts of music and metalworking (Gen. 4:21–22), and love of craftmanship and precision is found in the descriptions of Aaron's vestments (Exod. 28), the temple Solomon built (2 Chron. 3–4), and the temple in Ezekiel's vision (Ezek. 40–42). In the New Jerusalem, everything is subsumed under the kingship of the Lamb: the nations will enter "bringing their treasure and their wealth" with them (Rev. 21:26). Only in a vision of the city redeemed can humanity find its purpose and its destination.

Throughout the last few chapters of Revelation one hears, as it were, a series of doors shutting along a hallway in anticipation of the final closing of the huge door at the end, much as the unfortunate foolish virgins heard it close from outside (Matt. 25:11). The heavenly city has no temple "since the Lord God Almighty and the Lamb were themselves the temple" (Rev. 21:22), the temple of the Body of Christ in which God permanently meets man. The sun and moon created in the first chapter of the Bible are no longer present, since

God is radiant in the midst of the city. Now, unlike Eden, which the serpent freely entered, "nothing unclean may come into it" (21:27); the possibility of dying has become an impossibility, and the curse of pain and sadness no longer exists (21:4). The tree of life may now be tasted (22:14) and the second Adam, Christ, has won the bride.[31]

The author of Revelation, while transported by the power and beauty of his apocalyptic vision, never lost control of his writing. Because his vision was written down immediately, rather than transmitted orally for a period, his literary self-consciousness was acute. His writing in the first person gives an urgency and an immediacy to his writing even after many centuries, while his sense of the nature of a text is incisive and skilled. He ends his document with a series of references to writing and to books, and ultimately announces that his book, and, by extension, the entire canon of Scripture, is indisputably closed. His book declares its own closure so strongly that the reader never wishes to doubt it. The sequence begins when the servants of the Lamb have his name "written on their foreheads" (22:4). They will see him "face to face" and there will be no need for an author to write of the heavenly city once all the redeemed are in it. We are not told who will do the writing, but can infer it will be God himself because he has marked people since the beginning: Cain is given a mark of the earthly city, the law is written in the hearts of the just, and God's servants are frequently given new names. Next we read that the angel confirms that all we have just read "is sure and will come true," and a blessing is pronounced on all who treasure its message (22:6–7). In a direct allusion to the ending of Daniel, the author then reveals that his book is not to be kept a secret, and, finally, the closure itself is proclaimed:

If anyone adds to [the prophecies in this book], God will add to him every plague mentioned in the book; if anyone cuts anything out of the prophecies in this book, God will cut off his share of the tree of life and of the holy city, which are described in the book. [22:18–19]

By bringing together the tree of life, the holy city, and the book, the author has united the entire Bible from Genesis through to the end of his own book. He finishes with two more glosses on this: a repetition that Jesus will soon return and a prayer that his grace abide until he does. The final "Amen" is the most appropriate ending there could be: it is both a declaration of fact and a strong closural word.

Referring to the closural pattern of Scripture as recuperative indicates its inherently comic nature. The closure is strongest when it is perceived as leaving the narrative at a higher point than its beginning.

The sense is similar to that of recovery, but "to recuperate" is preferred because it is most frequently intransitive, with emphasis on getting better, while "to recover" usually means to get something back. Those biblical books which end with a sense of recuperation achieve a strong closure, though not always a complete one: Genesis and Deuteronomy both seal off a narrative, though their closures are not as strong as those of Daniel 12 and Chronicles. These last two close more forcefully because in them the recuperation is regarded as transcending a particular moment of history and suggesting a perpetual repetition of the people's return to their true homeland. Revelation reenforces this home as the destination of the spiritual pilgrimage on which the second-born children have been traveling since the days of Adam. Awaiting them is the sabbath rest in the heavenly city at the marriage of which they are a part. The community begun with Adam and Eve finds its resolution not in a garden with two inhabitants and a subtle serpent but in a city with a crowd impossible to number and into which no deceitful thing can enter.[32] Human cities, arts, and history are subsumed into the heavenly city. God does not say that Alpha and Omega are the same but declares that he is both beginning and end; he announces that he will make all creation new (21:5) and adds that "it is already done." In time, these things are not yet perceived, but in eternity they are already true and completed. Thus the recuperative nature of the Bible finds it strongest closure here in a vision which excludes nothing but evil; the image of the heavenly city is so inviting that we do not regret the loss of the garden.

Notes

1. Many of Barbara Herrnstein Smith's comments on closure in poetry may readily be applied to prose; see her *Poetic Closure: A Study of How Poems End* (Chicago: University of Chicago Press, 1968).

2. Robert Alter, *The Art of Biblical Narrative* (New York: Basic Books, 1981), pp. 141–47.

3. However, Philo, in his *Legum allegoria*, argues that the world could not have been created in time at all since time is determined by the sun's movements, and the sun was formed after the world was made (1.2).

4. Soren Kierkegaard, *Repetition: An Essay in Experimental Psychology*, trans. Walter Lowrie (Princeton: Princeton University Press, 1946), p. xxii.

5. Ibid., p. 4.

6. Augustine contrasts this state with that of man in the Heavenly City, in which it will be impossible for him to die. *City of God*, trans. H. Bettenson (Harmondsworth: Penguin Books, 1986), 22.30.

7. Quotations are taken from the Jerusalem Bible.

8. William A. McClung, *The Architecture of Paradise: Survivals of Eden and Jerusalem* (Berkeley: University of California Press, 1983), p. 18.

9. Northrop Frye, *The Great Code: The Bible and Literature* (New York: Harcourt Brace Jovanovich, 1982), pp. 169ff.

10. Bruce Kawin, *Telling It Again and Again: Repetition in Literature and Film* (Ithaca: Cornell University Press, 1972), p. 34.

11. Augustine, *Confessions*, 11.28, trans. F. J. Sheed (New York: Sheed & Ward, 1943), p. 284.

12. Augustine, *City of God*, 20.17 and 19.17.

13. Ibid., 22.30. The writer of Hebrews had also referred to a final sabbath rest awaiting the people of God (Heb. 4:9).

14. Genesis 39:2, 3, and 21.

15. Genesis 50:20 and 45:7.

16. Genesis 50:25.

17. Smith, *Poetic Closure*, p. 210. Smith is considering failures of closure, not intentionally forestalled closures as we have here.

18. Abel is preferred to Cain, Isaac to Ishmael, Jacob to Esau, Rachel to Leah, Perez to Zerah, and Joseph to his brothers.

19. Joseph Margolis, "Opening the Closure, and Vice Versa," *Bucknell Review* 30 (1987): 36.

20. Kierkegaard, *Repetition*, p. 4.

21. Even in the case of a work such as Joyce's *Finnegans Wake*, the apparently circular nature of the narrative cannot erase from our minds what we have already read, and even if we dare to begin it again, the experience can never be identical to that of our previous reading.

22. Philo, *Questions and Answers on Genesis*, trans. Ralph Marcus (Cambridge: Harvard University Press, 1961), p. 4.

23. Jacques Ellul, *The Meaning of the City* (Grand Rapids, Mich.: Eerdmans, 1970), p. 56.

24. Ibid., p. 101.

25. Philo, *De opificio mundi*, 1.19, trans. F. H. Colson (Cambridge: Harvard University Press, 1962), p. 17.

26. Ibid., 1.142–44.

27. Augustine, *City of God*, 14.28.

28. Northrop Frye is absolutely right when he states that, thematically, the only thing that happens in the Bible is the Exodus (*The Great Code*, p. 171).

29. Such as the parables of the sower, the mustard seed, and the yeast (in Matthew 13), the parable of the talents (Matthew 25), the miracle at Cana and the miracle of the multiplication of loaves and fishes (John 2 and 6).

30. Yeats's "Sailing to Byzantium" uses the same symbol of inorganic art to stand for eternity.

31. In the apocryphal Gospel of Nicodemus, Adam is led by the right hand out of hell by Christ himself, thus forever ending the struggle between first and second sons.

32. John Bunyan wrote that the image of a city is preferred to that of a spouse, woman, or temple because it indicates how numerous the people will be, how it will traffic with the nations which come to it for grace and life, and how strong it will be in protecting its inhabitants. *The Holy City* (Oxford: Clarendon Press, 1987), pp. 80–81.

Voiceprints, Male and Female

Paradise and Paradox

Deeanne Westbrook

Portland State University

Needing us greatly, even in our disgrace,
Guide us, for gladly do we leave this place
For our own land and wished-for banishment.
 —Karl Shapiro, "Adam and Eve"

IN his discussion of the Jacob stories, Harold Bloom says of the Yahwist that he is "pragmatically the author-of-authors, in that his authority and originality constitute a difference that has made a difference."[1] With his customary astuteness, Bloom has identified something crucial, yet largely unacknowledged, in the Yahwist's narratives, a something which he has named the "uncanny" or "antithetical" elements. I take Bloom to mean that the Yahwist's narratives, like many of the greatest works of literature, refuse to resolve antithetical components coexisting within them. The total effect of such elements is to leave a text with rich ambiguity and meanings, but without a message, stubbornly refusing to take on *a* meaning, despite numerous "strong misreadings" by later authors.

In regard to the Yahwist's stories of the Creation and the Fall in the second and third chapters of Genesis, a matter contributing to their uncanniness is the fact that they are inherently ironic. The irony resides, in part, in the genre. Frazer[2] and recently Frye have pointed out that the creation story is related to a class of ironic folk tales that, as Frye says, relate how humans had immortality "nearly in [their] grasp, but [were] cheated out of it by malicious or frightened deities."[3] In keeping with this class of sardonic tales, the tone of the Yahwistic narrative *sounds*, as Bloom says, "rather matter-of-fact,"[4] and Frye calls the tale's tone "casual," saying, "it is hard to hear in its casual cadences what St. Paul heard in it, the iron clang of a gate shut forever on human hopes."[5]

In fact, the ironic disjunction between the tone and subject matter is only one manifestation of the unresolved antitheses the narrative encompasses. Failure or refusal to acknowledge such antitheses results quite naturally in Paul's "misreading." As a rule, readers—especially of sacred texts—do not bring to their task that ability to which John Keats referred as "Negative Capability," that is, the abil-

121

ity to be "in uncertainties, Mysteries, doubts, without any irritable reaching after fact & reason."[6] On the contrary, one quite naturally seeks certainty in the sacred message. That oracles received from God or the gods are often ironic is unlikely to change a reader's tendency to reach after "fact & reason."

The essay that follows will explore some of the unresolved antitheses contained in the brief narrative of the Creation and Fall, the text that "made a difference," that, indeed, did much to shape the world in which Western humanity continues to live as if in exile. In the process, something of the rich ambiguity of the text and the world view of the ancient author will become apparent, as well as the danger of making easy pronouncements about the text's meaning.

THE TREE OF EXPERIENCE IN THE GARDEN OF INNOCENCE

The tree of the knowledge of good and evil, one of the two wonderful trees growing in Eden, is out of place. We are so used to accepting it as a growth native to the primeval garden that we are unlikely to recognize that its proper soil is the weedy, rock-strewn earth of fallen nature. To plant the tree conspicuously in the exact center of the garden-world is to give that world an order that can only be discerned as it arranges itself around the tree. Like Wallace Stevens's jar placed in Tennessee, the Yahwist's tree imposes its own order on its surroundings; like the jar, the tree takes "dominion everywhere"; and as the jar is "like nothing else in Tennessee," so the tree is like nothing else in Eden.

The tree's anomalous nature is apparent when it is contrasted with the logically indigenous tree, the tree of life.[7] The tree of life appears native in such a setting because of its likeness to other plants of immortality and the worlds in which they grow (Idun's tree of youth in Asgard, for example, or the golden apple tree of the Hesperides) and because within biblical literature the tree of life finds a home in the "new earth" of Revelation (22:2).[8] John of Patmos apparently recognized that the tree of the knowledge of good and evil would have been thematically aberrant in the New Jerusalem, just as it is in the Garden of Eden. However, the Yahwist's more complex, more intriguing, world of antitheses requires such vegetation, while the simplicity of restored perfection explicitly rejects it. Between the Yahwist's scene and John's lies the difference between the sublime and the beautiful, the dynamic, terrifying, and uncontained, as opposed to the static, stable, and patterned.[9]

At the heart of the Yahwist's garden, then, are the two trees which, in some ways, are polar opposites. They may be called the tree of life and the tree of death, for example, or the tree of innocence and the tree of experience. Thus the benefits derived from their fruits are mutually exclusive. Like the Wife of Bath, the Yahwist offers one or the other of the desirable effects, but not both. And yet the trees are not merely opposites, for each tree represents an aspect of the transcendent and ultimately unknowable and ironic divine. God, the text suggests, can unify within his immensity the irreconcilable polarities of the created world. He is both immortal *and* wise, knowing good and evil; humanity must choose one or the other. If humanity can have only one divine attribute, the Yahwist's God seems to prefer immortality rather than knowledge of good and evil, although the preference is by no means clear, as we shall see.

Yet the mere presence of the two trees, side by side at the center of the human realm, creates a tension which pervades the small perfection of the garden. They cannot be ignored or overlooked; they cannot be forgotten; they cannot be understood. The forbidden fruit is a bit like Bluebeard's locked room; and the psychology of Yahweh, too, is similar to Bluebeard's. After Bluebeard has shown his new bride around his castle, he brings her to the one locked room. But Bluebeard, after telling her she may never enter that room, shows her where the key to it is kept. Then he leaves her alone with the locked room and the key. In a sense, Adam and Eve, too, are left alone with a mystery and the key to that mystery. In each case dire consequences result from the woman's curiosity, and yet in each case the outcome, despite the warning, must be seen as inevitable. Thus the apparent freedom of choice exists in tension with the inevitable outcome (the Yahwist, after all, is writing from the perspective of the fallen realm).

The antitheses connected with the two trees are further multiplied by the fact that each is misnamed. The tree of life can be enjoyed, as it seems, only within the garden where the processes of human life (and all that the term implies) are impossible. In the stable perfection of the garden no one is born, grows, learns, gains experience, mothers or fathers children, and dies. Simple arithmetic teaches that generation and immortality are incompatible; no one *lives* with the tree of life.

At the same time the death-bearing tree is implicitly a tree of life, for the eating of its fruit has the effect of propelling the first couple into the world of generation. Further, the tree of the knowledge of good and evil bears a name (and hence a nature) that cannot even be understood by those who must decide whether or not to eat its fruit.

INNOCENCE AND ETHICAL CHOICE

This matter leads to one of the greatest ironies in all of literature, an

irony every bit as bitter as that which mocks the life and career of
Oedipus. Eve, born without ethical knowledge, abides in a place in
which she is forced to make not only for herself, but for all humankind, an ethical decision, having to choose, moreover, between the
conflicting claims of God and the serpent—both of which, as it turns
out, are true and yet not quite true.

God warns the man not to eat the fruit, saying unambiguously that if
he does he will die—that same day: "of the tree of the knowledge of
good and evil you shall not eat, for in the day that you eat of it you
shall die" (Gen. 2:17). If one takes the tale at face value, the notion of
death, like the concepts good and evil, must surely be meaninglesss to
this just-created innocent. In any case, the serpent in its subtlety asks
Eve what God has said concerning the fruit of the trees: "Did God
say, 'You shall not eat of any tree of the garden'?" (Gen. 3:1). And
Eve explains, quoting God, or what she has been told God said: "We
may eat of the fruit of the trees of the garden; but God said, 'You shall
not eat of the fruit of the tree which is in the midst of the garden,
neither shall you touch it, lest you die'" (Gen. 3:3). The serpent,
however, gives her another truth, telling her that she will not die, but
become "like God, knowing good and evil" (Gen. 3:4–5). That the
serpent is telling a sort of truth becomes apparent later, when God
affirms the effect of the fruit, not on the woman, but on the man:
"Behold, *the man* has become as one of us, knowing good and evil"
(Gen. 3:22, emphasis added). In banishing the couple from the garden, and barring the way to the tree of life, God also verifies the subtle, figurative truth of what he has warned, that the couple will die—
eventually. Neither the tension between figurative and literal truth
and falsehood nor the complex, ambiguous interplay between them is
mitigated in the narrative. Has Eve been told only the truth? Only
lies? Or some curious shifting truth that is a lie and lie that is a truth?
The matter is one which rests unresolved in the enigmatic irony of the
text.

BREATH AND DUST

The agonistic relationship between the two trees at the center of the
garden, and their curious misnaming, serves as a reflective surface for
the same pair of antitheses—life and death—embodied in the figures
of God and the woman. Adam stands between them, at once the field
of combat, their joint victim, and ultimately the hero of the tale. There
is a dramatically complex moment in the narrative when the antitheses approach each other and ironically reverse their polar qualities,
the process occurring so quickly that one is left nearly speechless; only

in the silence the man speaks, calling the woman's name Eve, "because she was the mother of all living" (Gen. 3:20). To understand
the drama and dynamics of this moment, it is necessary to go back to
the beginning of the agon, to God's first act: "then the Lord God
formed man of dust from the ground, and breathed into his nostrils
the breath of life; and the man became a living being" (Gen. 2:7).

At first there are only God and dust—the earth from which nearly
all living things are crafted (woman, the helper, is the one exception, a
matter to which I shall return). The fact that the lifeless dust exists
with God from the beginning suggests its ontological necessity to the
divine acts of creation. The reasons why this is so appear to lie in the
submerged text of the Yahwist's account, in the images which tell
their own story, in the title Adam gives the woman ("mother of all
living," a standard epithet for the earth goddess), and in the name of
the man (Adam—*adam*) and its nearness to the word for ground or
earth (*adamah*), a feminine noun. In the beginning there is the lifeless
dust (the earth) and there is the vital, life-creating craftsman God, who
breathes life into the inert clay. Adam is born from the coming
together of the principles of life and death—God and the ground, the
displaced and disgraced goddess, the "mother of all living." He thus
embodies the crucial struggle being waged at the moment of beginning between the antitheses of male and female, god and goddess,
spirit and matter, life and death. His bodily dust, infused with the
divine breath, is quite simply a "battle ground," and the balance of
power between the opposing forces is delicate indeed.

The standard setting for the ancient earth goddess is her garden
(representative of the vegetation to which she gives life), with its symbolic tree of life (Asherah), the vegetal aspect of the goddess herself.[10]
As his second act, therefore, God plants the garden in Eden, thus
revealing himself, rather than the goddess, to be the life force of the
sacred garden of immortality, for, the Yahwist explains, "out of the
ground *the Lord God made to grow* every tree that is pleasant to the sight
and good for food, the tree of life also in the midst of the garden, and
the tree of the knowledge of good and evil" (Gen. 2:9, emphasis
added). It is here that God puts the man—into this setting which, in
the picture language of the narrative, is at once delightful and dangerous, vital and deadly. Readers of the narrative, seeing the scene from a
divine perspective, watch as the small, newly made man of breathing
clay is set down in a world organized around the two wonderful trees,
their branches perhaps intertwined, presenting to his innocent eyes, if
he could recognize it, his own image in the agonistic forces from which
he is made.

As God sets the man down in his garden-world, he speaks for the first time: "You may freely eat of every tree of the garden; but of the tree of the knowledge of good and evil you shall not eat, for in the day that you eat of it you shall die" (Gen. 2:17). The Yahwist's genius for the dramatic and stunning detail is apparent here. One is tempted to see the small, perhaps still-wet clay ears of the man perceiving and conducting to his dawning consciousness, as his first thought, the danger of the tree and the possibility of his own death. In his isolation and vulnerability, the man is at this moment Everyman, every small earthly human forced to entertain for the first time the humbling notion of his or her own nonbeing.

The man's delicate poise at the center of conflict is immediately jeopardized, for the Yahwist has God speak a second time: "It is not good that the man should be alone" (Gen. 2:18). God's solution to the man's ontological isolation is, of course, to make the instrument of the man's fall, ironically called "a helper fit for him" (Gen. 2:18). Andrew Marvell, feeling perhaps how ominous God's pronouncement is, would exclude the woman from his own garden: "Two paradises 'twere in one / To live in Paradise alone" ("The Garden").

We cannot say, of course, whether the Yahwist knew the pun in Sumerian, where "living" (Eve) and "rib" are homophones,[11] but if he did, the irony is intensified here as the principle of his own mortality is removed from the man in the form of the bone whose name meant "living" as well as "rib" to make "a helper" who will lead him to death. One is tempted to see in the removal of the woman a mitigating of the dust principle within the man. Perhaps he becomes more of the nature of "breath," but the suggestion of the pun is that the "living" bone or life is removed, thus nudging the man at the very moment of the woman's inception toward death.[12] The woman, so far as one knows, is not infused with the divine breath. In any case, the man here apparently suffers a first, symbolic death, as he is put into a deep sleep and his feminine aspect is removed and given separate existence. The woman who will subsequently be given the title of the goddess, the "mother of all living," is born out of the very matter of which she consists—the dust from which the man was crafted. Thus a chain of existence is forged: The ground (adamah) gives existence to the man (adam, ish) who gives birth to the woman (ishshah), "because she was taken out of man" (ish), later to be known as Eve ("living," hence "the mother of all living"), who in her goddess form is the earth or ground (adamah). The chain already contains implicitly the conditions of God's curse, "You are dust, and to dust you shall return" (Gen. 3:19). Seen in this light, the "one flesh" to which the Yahwist refers is the common material—dust—from which both spring.

The Yahwist allows the man only a moment of relief from his existential isolation, a relief touchingly apparent in the man's eloquent welcoming of the woman: "This at last is bone of my bones and flesh of my flesh" (Gen. 2:23). For the space of a heartbeat, the man gazes at the reformulation of his own dust and loves her without fear or guilt. Almost immediately, however, the terrible fragility of the situation is revealed when the Yahwist introduces the ironic wisdom of the serpent: "Now the serpent was more subtle than any other wild creature the Lord God had made" (Gen. 3:1).

God's and the man's absence from the temptation leaves the scene to the woman, the serpent, and the tree of the knowledge of good and evil. It is just this configuration of images which in another context would have suggested the richness and promise of life: the goddess in her garden of immortality; her serpent of wisdom and rebirth, capable of endlessly renewing itself by sloughing its skin; and, finally her tree of life, whose fruit was bestowed with the goddess's blessing of eternity.

THE MESSAGE OF THE IMAGES

Joseph Campbell argues that in making use of the one-forbidden-thing motif the story of the Fall becomes one of a class of tales in which a protective taboo is violated and a hero subjected to danger in order that humanity may be released from oppression. He says: "One could reread the episode in the garden from such a point of view and find that it was not God but Adam and Eve to whom we owe the great world of the realities of life."[13] Such a reading might lead to doctrines of the Fortunate Fall, implicit in the words of Paul: "God has consigned all men to disobedience, that he may have mercy upon all" (Rom. 11:32).

The fact that both possibilities—fortune and misfortune—can be seen in the Fall suggests, Campbell argues, "that the mythic imagery ...bears a message of its own" that may be at odds with "the one verbalized in the discourse of the text." Why this is true Campbell ascribes to the fact that the narrative is "a carrier of symbols borrowed from the deep past, which is of many tongues."[14]

Perhaps it is possible to be more precise, if not more accurate. The images borrowed from the past (of the goddess, her serpent, and the mystical tree of life and wisdom) present an image complex which, for a culture in which it arises, is metaphoric of existence seen as cyclic, in which the turning of the seasons, the waxing and waning of the moon, seedtime and harvest, day and night, birth and death, all follow each other naturally, predictably, controlled by the great goddess who is at once the womb and tomb of all that lives. Included in the goddess's cycles of existence, of course, are the human generations which ebb and flow in their turn.

The Yahwist's culture, however, had its own view of existence which, by contrast with the cycles of the goddess, was largely linear. Unlike the religion of the agrarian Canaanites, synchronized with the cycles of nature, Israelite religion required that God be a god of history, a linear, purposive, and progressive history—the frame within which God manipulated nature, events, and peoples in accord with his own world drama from beginning to middle to end.[15] To a people with such a linear, historical orientation, the competing agrarian idea of endless, causeless, effectless cycles may lead to a sense of life as absurd, in which all is "vanity" or "in vain."[16] At the same time, though, the symbols "from the deep past" may offer an image of peace and stability which becomes especially attractive at moments of crisis or despair.

Thus, on the one hand, the message of the images is nostalgic and appealing—a call for rest and the promise of permanence, without struggle and toil. On the other hand, though, the message can be deeply repugnant, presenting a stifling womblike world where achievement is impossible, whose pleasures must pall long before "eternity" has elapsed. The folklorist's motto, "Be careful what you wish for, because you're likely to get it," applies to the desire for the seeming perfection of the garden-world; the Yahwist, wisely, cannot remove humanity from it fast enough.

In some ways, then, the Yahwist's narrative is a tale of competing myth systems—one paradisiacal, mystic, cyclic, and eternal; the other earthly, practical, linear, and timed. To choose the opportunities and vicissitudes of the latter is to choose Yahweh and his world, the world manipulated by the God of history, and thus give the victory to him; to reject the former is to find the goddess and her mode of existence inappropriate to the human condition.

And yet for every choice there is a price; for every gain, a loss. Somewhere in the past calling us with its unrealized potential is the alternative we did not choose, shining in the glow of what might have been. For Western humanity, that "other," lost possibility of the garden of delights is always there in our collective past, nonthreatening now because we have traveled our road of choice too far—indeed one step along it was sufficient. We cannot return, and so we can safely dream of returning. T. S. Eliot captured the message of the images of Eden and their poignant appeal in the opening lines of his *Four Quartets*:

> What might have been is an abstraction
> Remaining a perpetual possibility
> Only in a world of speculation.
> What might have been and what has been
> Point to one end, which is always present.
> Footfalls echo in the memory
> Down the passage which we did not take
> towards the door we never opened
> Into the rose-garden.

And so the rose garden—our first garden, Eden, all the might-have-beens—calls us, and we regret its loss; the Fall was unfortunate. From our perspective in the world of time and process, we long for the still point, for rest, peace, innocence, eternity. Eliot ends his poem with an expression of the symbolic search we make:

> We shall not cease from exploration
> And the end of all our exploring
> Will be to arrive where we started
> And know the place for the first time.

And then? Eliot says, "And all shall be well and / All manner of thing shall be well." The poet, it seems, speaks for a majority of Western humanity. No fall can be deemed fortunate, we may feel, which has exacted so great a price in human suffering: estrangement, sin, guilt, toil, sorrow, disease, death—all the "evils" of existence.

There are others, though, who read another message in the images of paradise. If one could return, as Eliot imagines, would one find indeed that all manner of thing was well? Perhaps not. There is a suggestive episode in the *Odyssey* which reveals something altogether different. Writing within the heroic tradition of Greece, with its likewise linear world view, Homer brings his protagonist, Odysseus, to Ogygia ("navel"), the island realm of the goddess Calypso. Ogygia is very much like Adam's garden; it is a world of peace and plenty, timeless and serene, under the control of a representative of the ancient goddess. Odysseus arrives on the island as the sole survivor of Ithaca's contingent to the Trojan War, having come there after thirteen years of war and wandering and the assorted horrors associated therewith. Calypso takes Odysseus in and cares for him, and he remains with her for some seven years. In the structure of the epic, however, the first glimpse one has of the great hero is as he sits on the shore of Ogygia, looking toward what he hopes is home, weeping. Sent to rescue him from the goddess, Hermes hears her side of the relationship. She says, "I fed him, loved him, sang that he should not die nor grow old, ever, in all the days to come."[17] Paraphrased only slightly, Calypso's words might have been spoken by God, telling of his care of the man and the woman: "I fed them, loved them, arranged that they should not die nor grow old, ever, in all the days to come." In both versions of the speech a certain parental relationship is implicit; both imply the care of childlike beings. What interests me about Odysseus is his uncompromising rejection of this "perfect world," where Calypso plays the roles of both God and Eve in the Genesis story.

Forced to let Odysseus resume his quest for Ithaca and Penelope, his wife, Calypso tries to understand. She says that if Odysseus could see into the future and know what lies in store for him, he would remain with her. After acknowledging that Penelope "would seem a shade" before Calypso's beauty, that aging and death are natural at home, and that his bride has no doubt changed in the twenty years he has been away, Odysseus asserts that, nevertheless, he longs for his home in the world and will endure any hardship to return: "Let the trial come."[18] If asked, Odysseus might have responded similarly to Karl Shapiro's Adam, "Gladly do I leave this place for my own land and wished-for banishment."

From such a perspective, the expulsion from the garden must be seen as a release from prison, a freeing of humans who long for meaningful toil, growth, challenge, and change in a world of generation and time.

PARADISE AND PARADOX

Some sense of the paradoxical meanings of the Yahwist's narrative is captured in James Joyce's pun on the phrase "fortunate fall" (*felix culpa*): "Oh phoenix culprit!" It is a phrase whose rich irony plays notions of falling and rising, sin and redemption, death and life, against each other, holding them unresolved in a perpetual dance of signs. It is an appropriate emblem for the Yahwist's narrative of the Creation and Fall. As the tale builds to a climax, its signs become increasingly ambiguous. The woman, the serpent, and the tree of the knowledge of good and evil—all on the side of death—have existed in agonistic relationship with God and life. The three have been brought together nonchalantly enough, and nonchalantly too have won the day and the man without contest. As God's three curses fall like hammer blows first on the serpent, then on the woman, and finally on the man, the human world as its residents know it gradually, inexorably takes form. The serpent becomes the legless, poisonous snake of earthly gardens, cursed to eat dust and to remain the enemy of man; the cycle of generation is inaugurated as the woman is cursed to suffer pain in childbirth and to feel desire for her husband; patterns of dominance and submission within the patriarchal family come into being, as does unending toil.

All these consequences from the forbidden fruit begin to reveal the truth of the tree of the knowledge of good and evil: it is itself a tree of life, of human life in the world. God's final curse on Adam is the sentence of death: "In the sweat of your face you shall eat bread till you return to the ground, for out of it you were taken; you are dust, and to dust you shall return" (Gen. 3:19).

As the grand, sententious, yet simple, message falls, the reader may react with horror. Like Cain, we may want to cry that our punishment is greater than we can bear. Certainly it exceeds the crime. Yet Adam's reaction is interesting. Having heard that he is dust and shall return to dust, he does not cringe or protest; instead he utters a counter message, audaciously seizing a kind of power by naming, actually renaming, the woman—Eve, "living." This, according to the Yahwist, was the word uttered in the terrible silence following God's irrevocable judgment, an announcement of life breathed into air that still reverberated with the divine sentence of death.

Thus at the climax of the Yahwist's tale of the origins of human mortality and suffering, God's and the woman's associations are dramatically and ironically reversed. Just as the tree of the knowledge of good and evil has been revealed as the tree not of death but of human life, so now God is associated with dust, the death principle, as the agent and creator of death. And at the same time, the renamed woman—Eve ("living")—is associated with life as the agent and procreator of "all living." As the mother of all living, each thing in the garden is her child—the plants, the animals, even the man.

The world of the "mother of all living" is a world of procreation rather than creation, and in the new world of generation and consciousness sexuality—"nakedness"—is, to borrow a phrase from Dylan Thomas, "the force that through the green fuse drives the flower" and the "green age" of the first couple. In sexuality, in other words, lies the principle of *life*—as that term has been redefined in the narrative.

In keeping with the reversed polarities of God and the woman, God's first act following the sentence of death is to kill some of the animals of the garden from whose skins he will fashion garments to cover the now-significant nakedness. The slain animals "redeem" the mortal, yet living, humans, existing under God's sentence of death as the woman begins her work of producing life in the human world outside the garden.

And so the Yahwist's narrative of the Creation and Fall ends, as it began, in paradox. With this closing, he presents a last image of God, the Creator, the living breath, repelled by the nakedness of the man and the woman whom he has made, slaughtering some of his creatures, perhaps rinsing their blood from his hands in the bright river of life, skinning them with primitive tools, fashioning a crude awl or needle and stitching carefully the rustic garments to hide the organs by which, now, all new life will be generated. We imagine that Adam and Eve—"dust" and "living"—watch, as we do, in surprise and fascination.

Notes

1. Harold Bloom, "From J to K, or The Uncanniness of the Yahwist," in *The Bible and the Narrative Tradition*, ed. Frank McConnell (New York: Oxford University Press, 1986), p. 20.

2. James George Frazer, *Folklore in the Old Testament: Studies in Comparative Religion, Legend, and Law* (New York: Hart, 1975), pp. 1–32.

3. Northrop Frye, *Creation and Recreation* (Toronto: University of Toronto Press, 1980), p. 43.

4. Bloom, "From J to K," p. 23.

5. Frye, *Creation and Recreation*, p. 43.

6. John Keats, *Letters*, ed. Maurice Buxton Forman, 4th ed., rev. (New York: Oxford University Press, 1952), p. 71.

7. Joseph Campbell, *The Masks of God: Occidental Mythology* (New York: Viking Press, 1964), draws attention to the fact that in other myth systems the two trees are one tree: "The Tree of Knowledge is itself the Tree of Life." The knowledge associated with the typical tree of life is of the mystical, magical, or archane sort that provides the recipient practical religious knowledge. Odin's "death" on Yggdrasil gained him knowledge of charms for healing, warding off danger, defeating enemies, and so forth. Campbell calls the separation of functions and meanings in Genesis an aspect of "mythic dissociation," by which "God and his world, immortality and mortality, are set apart" (p. 106).

8. Biblical citations are from The New Oxford Annotated Bible with the Apocrypha, Revised Standard Version, ed. Herbert G. May and Bruce M. Metzger (New York: Oxford University Press, 1973).

9. Harold Bloom, *The Breaking of the Vessels* (Chicago: University of Chicago Press, 1982), referring to this quality of the Yahwist, calls him "perhaps the greatest master of the literary Sublime in what has become Western tradition" (p. 50).

10. Campbell, *The Masks of God*, pp. 13–15. The same name (Asherah) is give to both the goddess and her sacred tree, her vegetal aspect. Robert Graves and Raphael Patai, *Hebrew Myths: The Book of Genesis* (New York: McGraw-Hill, 1966), have noted the popularity in biblical times of the goddess and her sacred tree: "goddesses were well known to Hebrews . . . who worshipped in the groves of the Goddess Asherah" (p. 26).

11. James S. Ackerman et al., *Teaching the Old Testament in English Classes* (Bloomington: Indiana University Press, 1973), p. 43.

12. William Irwin Thompson, *The Time Falling Bodies Take to Light: Mythology, Sexuality, and the*

Origins of Culture (New York: St. Martin's Press, 1981), recalls the popular tradition which finds that in his desire for a mate Adam fell long before "the fall": "In the division into sexuality in Hebrew mythology, a great theme of division is being announced which will echo on down throughout history" (p. 23).

13. Campbell, *The Masks of God*, p. 110.

14. Ibid., p. 110.

15. Herbert N. Schneidau, *Sacred Discontent: The Bible and Western Tradition* (Berkeley: University of California Press, 1977), points to the contrast between "the Hebrew habit of finding their God active in history, as against the pagan conception of the divine immanent in nature" (p. 174); and Robert Alter, *The Art of Biblical Narrative* (New York: Basic Books, 1981), notices how closely tied to history the biblical narratives are, arguing that they produce "an imaginative reenactment of the historical event" (p. 41).

16. The weary, yet wonderful, opening poem of Ecclesiastes suggests the sense of absurdity which the cyclic vision of existence produces in the Western, linear-minded individual. It is a horrifying, meaningless world in which there is, and can be, "nothing new under the sun."

17. Homer, *The Odyssey*, trans. Robert Fitzgerald (Garden City, N.Y.: Anchor Books, 1963), p. 85.

18. Ibid., p. 87.

Contemporary Biblical Literary Criticism: The Objective Phallacy

Esther Fuchs
University of Arizona

THE recent proliferation of literary approaches to the biblical narrative confirms that in regard to biblical women, *plus ça change plus c'est la même chose.* The dominant critical trends in the field manifest a disconcerting degree of what Catherine MacKinnon, in another context, calls "aperspectivity": an objective, neutral posture of male-centered scholarship.[1] There is a stunning resemblance between the objective posturing of contemporary Bible critics and the aperspectivity which is one of the master tropes of biblical discourse. Just as the biblical narrator presents the power relations between men and women as divinely ordained, so do androcentric critics write about biblical men and women with an air of unperturbed disinterestedness. Just as patriarchal ideology is taken for granted by the biblical narrator, so does it remain unchallenged in the works of most contemporary rhetorical and literary critics. By assuming a "nonpartisan" stance, biblical critics end up legitimizing the marginalization of biblical women and the relentless focus on male-oriented concerns. The aperspectival stance of most biblical literary critics reencodes biblical sexual politics which seek to universalize and absolutize the dominance of women by men. Though most literary critics agree that the biblical narrative is androcentric, they rarely allow this fact to interfere with their analytical procedures. Coupled with a scriptural vision which ignores the ideological nature of biblical literature in general, contemporary biblical criticism reendorses biblical sexual politics.

In a classical analysis of the biblical narrative, Erich Auerbach insists on the latter's prescriptive nature, a feature that often eludes contemporary critics. Unlike Greek epic, Auerbach notes, the biblical narrative lays "claim to absolute authority: . . . If the text of the biblical narrative, then, is so greatly in need of interpretation on the basis of its own content, its claim to absolute authority forces it still further in the same direction. Far from seeking, like Homer, merely to make us forget our own reality for a few hours, it seeks to overcome our reality: we are to fit our own life into its world, feel ourselves to be elements in its structure of universal history. . . . Everything else that happens in the world can only be conceived as an element in this sequence."[2] In their attempts to show how artful, how intricate, how ironic, how carefully crafted the biblical narrative is, contemporary critics ignore the prescriptive aspect that is in many ways its most obvious characteristic.

Substituting for the search for Truth an indefatigable search for Beauty (often understood to mean textual complexity), the modern critic does not, in essence, abandon the scriptural approach which accepts rather than questions biblical ideology. The desired analogy Moshe Greenberg, for example, draws between the traditional exegete and the modern critic assumes that the modern reader is male and urges this reader to subjugate his concerns to the designs of the biblical text: "As the religious person approaches the text open to God's call, so must the interpreter come 'all ears' to hear what the text is saying. He [sic] must subjugate his habits of thought and expression to the words before him and become actively passive—full of initiatives to heighten his receptivity."[3] Since "receptivity" and the reader's self-subjugation to the biblical text are the order of the day in what is known today as rhetorical or literary criticism of the Bible, it is not surprising that most if not all contemporary analyses of the biblical narrative have failed to question the latter's patriarchal prescriptions. For one thing, that would mean criticizing an ancient text, which "good" historians cannot afford to do. For another, this would mean allowing the reader's habits of thought to interfere with the poetic designs of the text, which a good poetician is not supposed to do. The only thing the "good" reader of the biblical text is enjoined to do, then, is to marvel at the text's complexity and wisdom. The "good" reader, who in recent theoretical articulations of biblical literary criticism is invariably male, must not bring "his" own concerns into the process of deciphering and enjoying the biblical text. As a good obedient son, the contemporary literary critic is not supposed to question the Bible's claim to authority and its interpretation of human history and destiny. A peculiar collusion thus emerges between the procedures of traditional religious readings of the Bible and contemporary rhetorical/literary readings.

For all of the controversy sparked by the modern procedures of biblical literary criticism, the fact remains that the deviations from traditional rules of reading the biblical text have not been so great after all. For the fundamental disposition of the modern reader is to paraphrase and exfoliate the original text. Whether primarily aesthetic or hermeneutic, modern literary criticism of the Bible remains by and large paraphrastic. The absence of a critical perspective in contemporary criticism of the Bible delegitimizes a priori any attempt to

question the Bible's patriarchal ideology, which sanctions the dominance of men over women. Bracketed as irrelevant, the prescriptive
character of the biblical narrative is sidestepped by the poeticians who
do not cease to find new ways to glorify its poetic ingenuity. What
traditionalists like James Kugel denounce as the "unmediated encounter between Modern Man and Ancient Text"[4] is in fact mediated
by the assumption that the reader is a man and that the encounter
consists in the son's acceptance of the father's word.

The rare critic who does acknowledge that the biblical narrative is
fundamentally ideological tends to ignore the patriarchal aspect of
this ideology. Meir Sternberg, for example, focusing exclusively on the
Bible's theistic ideology interprets most of its poetic principles as
strategies in "justifying the ways of God to Man."[5] Sternberg's aperspectival approach, which much as the omniscient stance of the biblical narrator lays an implicit claim to absolute truth, postulates an ideal
androcentric reader. The ideal reader's sensitivity to gaps, repetition,
shifting perspectives, and other literary subtleties can only be matched
by *his* obliviousness to the androcentric premises that bind him to
the text. It should not surprise us, for example, that his theory of
"gapping" which invites the androcentric reader to fill the gaps does
not recognize as a gap the suppression of a female perspectivity. In his
discussion of the story of David and Bathsheba in 2 Samuel 11, the
only gaps that seem to be legitimate have to do with what one or
another male character does, thinks, wants, and with what the male
narrator tells the male reader.[6] The marginalization of Bathsheba is
for Sternberg a nonquestion. "Between the Truth" sought by the
androcentric critic and the "Whole Truth" often hidden by the patriarchal narrator, the female character is dismissed, and the female
reader made invisible.

Just as Bathsheba gets lost in Sternberg's system of gaps, so is
Rebekah lost in "the movement from divergence to convergence"
(*PBN*, p. 136), which is primarily concerned with the perspectives of
the male characters involved in the narrative. In a similar fashion
Dinah's rape is subsumed under the broader concern with the "delicate balance" between the points of view of Dinah's brothers and
father and the points of view of her male rapist and his father (*PBN*,
p. 445).

Needless to say, Dinah in Genesis 34 and Bathsheba in 2 Samuel
11 are already peripheral characters. By construing the antagonistic
relationship of male characters as the fundamental frame of his analysis, Sternberg validates and contributes to the marginalization of the
female characters.

Though he presents his questions as neutral, objective responses to the informational gaps of the text, Sternberg's questions are often based on androcentric presuppositions. In his discussion of the rape of Dinah, for example, he argues without explaining his own axiological priorities that rape is less heinous a crime than murder. "The trouble is," he states, "that mass slaughter will not balance against rape according to conventional normative scales" (*PBN*, p. 445). Just what these "conventional scales" are, when, how, by whom and to whom they have become normative, is not made clear. Glossed over is the fundamental question of the narratee. The implicit assumption is that the same "conventional scales" are normative, both in biblical and in modern times, to male and female alike. We are expected to believe that the narrator performs a feat of manipulative artistry in order to balance out Shechem's murder and the revenge of Dinah's brothers. The objectification of Dinah, the informational gaps about her perspective, her motivations, and her response to her own rape, are problems that remain untouched. Despite the hair-splitting analysis to which almost every single verse in Genesis 34 is subjected, the entire first verse describing Dinah as a subject who "goes out" on her own "to see the daughters of the land" (*PBN*, p. 446) is presented without commentary. Because she does not fulfill a function in the male-centered scheme of things, the female character is discarded. Sternberg refers to Dinah only when and if she illuminates in some fashion her brothers' conduct. The androcentric obsession with the male parties forecloses otherwise interesting informational gaps that could have pointed up the investments of the Bible's patriarchal ideology. Thus, for example, one might ask, Why rape? Is it mere coincidence that Dinah, the first and only Israelite daughter, is presented as a rape victim who is subsequently disqualified from becoming a licit heiress to her father and a tribal leader as do her brothers? One can also ask, of course, Why is Dinah, the rape victim, silenced by the narrator? Why are we not told what she feels about Shechem or, for that matter, about her brothers? These questions are no longer possible within the male-centered bipolar scheme erected by Sternberg. If gaps are by definition those empty spaces that the phallocentric critic is expected to penetrate and fill with the help of his logos, then it is also up to him, one assumes, to decide what qualifies as a gap and what does not.

In a similar vein, Sternberg all but eliminates Bathsheba from what he calls "the David and Bathsheba story" (*PBN*, p. 188). While he dedicates considerable space to the question "does Uriah know about his wife's infidelity and pregnancy?", Sternberg does not explain why he judges Bathsheba's actions as "infidelity." Surely this is not a term suggested by the text. The fact is that the text is peculiarly silent about Bathsheba's motivations and responses to David's actions.

This, however, does not seem to represent a problem or a gap for Sternberg. While he seems to think that what Joab or the servant think or mean are urgent problems of specific as well as heuristic value, he ignores the obvious gap concerning the presentation of Bathsheba. What the female character thinks or knows belongs to the category of nonquestions, and trying to understand the ideology behind the reticent presentation of female characters amounts to what Sternberg calls "illegitimate gap-filling." The theoretical law set down by the critic invalidates any attempt to question the marginalization of Bathsheba. "Illegitimate gap-filling is one launched and sustained by the reader's subjective concerns . . . rather than by the text's own norms and directives" (*PBN*, p. 188). But are not Sternberg's numerous questions about what Uriah knows inspired by an androcentric subjectivity? Are not the many questions about what the husband knows motivated by a set of male-centered anxieties and preoccupations? After all, there is nothing in the text indicating that what the husband knows about his wife is more important than what the wife knows about her husband. Nowhere in his analysis does Sternberg explain why Uriah's awareness is more important than Bathsheba's. Sternberg judges Bathsheba's actions as "infidelity" (*PBN*, p. 201), but is this definition justified by the text? The concept of infidelity entails a voluntary crime. But the extent to which Bathsheba was coerced into adultery by the king is a question left open. It is in fact one of the most interesting gaps in the narrative: Did Bathsheba object? Could she object? What did *she* know? Sternberg's failure to consider these questions as gaps leaves serious gaps in his own theory of the biblical narrative.

By ignoring the ideological problem posed by stories of rape and adultery, by ignoring the patriarchal implications of the way in which the woman in the text is silenced, the modern androcentric critic reinscribes biblical sexual politics. The poeticist reinscription of patriarchal ideology is made possible by combining on the one hand an aperspectival stance and on the other a submissive stance vis-à-vis the text. The ideological identification of father-text and the obedient son results in the latter's adjusting his voice to that of the biblical narrator, which according to Sternberg projects itself as the "voice of the one and indivisible truth" (*PBN*, p. 128). The choral harmony of the authoritative narrators and the "objective" critics reencodes the silence about woman's oppression.

The aperspectival poeticist approach to the biblical narrative excludes questions about gender which consequently renders the Bible's patriarchal ideology invisible. The fundamental premise in contemporary biblical poeticism is that it is possible to articulate rules about the way in which the biblical narrative "behaves" regardless of its male voice. Dialogue, characterization, point of view, gaps, repetition, and omission are discussed in a neutral "objective" fashion as if the ideology of male supremacy has nothing to do with the construction of these elements. The godlike gaze of the critic seems unperturbed by the interactions of patriarchal ideology and poetics—poetics seems to be "outside" the vexing presence of *this* kind of ideology. Promulgating the poetic rules by which the biblical narrative allegedly operates, the modern androcentric critic imitates the biblical omniscient narrator whose prescriptive interpretations of reality preclude women from the sphere of consciousness and will.

One of the most important premises of current poeticist approaches is that the biblical narrative is not didactic. Thus, for example, the repetition of certain motifs and what Robert Alter brilliantly identifies as type-scenes have been interpreted as poetic strategies aimed mainly at heightening the aesthetic pleasure of the audience: "The only plausible hypothesis, then, is that these intriguing instances of recurrent sequences of motif reflect a literary convention which, like other narrative conventions, enabled the teller of the tale to orient his listeners, to give them intricate clues as to where the tale was going, how it differed delightfully or ingeniously or profoundly from other similar tales."[7] The ingenuity, delight, and profundity marking the permutations of various annunciation type-scenes are to be enjoyed by the modern audience at least to the same degree that they have been appreciated by the ancient audience. A careful reading of Alter's analysis reveals the collusions of aesthetic bliss and the ancient *and* contemporary concern with the male protagonist. Though, as its name suggests, the annunciation type-scene is at least equally interested in the fate of a prospective mother as it is with the son, Alter interprets it as a foreshadowing mechanism alluding to the fate of the son as a male adult. Similarly, in his discussion of the betrothal type-scene, which by its very name suggests a measure of heterosexual reciprocity, Alter focuses on the function of the type-scene as foreshadowing the future of the groom.[8] With the groom as protagonist, the bride cannot help but be consigned to the periphery, signaling a mere stage in the multiphased evolution of the male protagonist. Alter speaks of the "archetypal expressiveness" of the betrothal type-scene as he explains that the foreign land to which the groom travels "is chiefly a geographical correlative for the sheer female otherness of the prospective wife," and, as he points out, the "well in the oasis" is "obviously a symbol of fertility, and in all likelihood, also a female symbol"(*ABN*, p. 52). Does this mean that femaleness is by definition other? That female otherness is a universal archetype or a biblical convention? These questions are neither raised nor answered. What is clear is that Alter perceives the adventures of the groom as central to the betrothal type-scene, for it is in the latter that the future exploits of the groom are foreshadowed. While the entire convention of the type-scene is interpreted as an ingenious literary means by which the narrator presents the groom's story, the bride becomes willy-nilly a point of reference in the male-centered frame. The bride shrinks in the course of the analysis from a full-fledged character to a stage on the groom's road to adulthood, to a symbol of fertility, and in the case of Rachel to an object of the groom's desire, to a womb. "If the well of the betrothal scene is in general associated with woman and fertility, it is particularly appropriate that this one should be blocked by an obstacle, for Jacob will obtain the woman he wants only through great labor, against resistance" (*ABN*, p. 55). Rachel's desire for Jacob and for sons, Rachel's labor against resistance, are not discussed in this context. The preoccupation with the groom eclipses the bride's significance.

To enjoy as an archetypal motif what Alter calls the "sheer female otherness" of the mother or the bride presupposes an androcentric vision continuous with biblical definitions of femininity. To construe as aesthetic ingenuity type-scenes that progressively write female characters out of existence reveals a poeticist viewpoint that remains oblivious to the political and didactic aspects of the biblical type-scene. To say that the problem does not exist uses aestheticism and aperspectivity as excuses for modern patriarchalism in knowledge-producing communities.

That modern poeticism ends up validating biblical definitions of womanhood becomes evident in works whose declared object of inquiry is women. In *Women Recounted* James Williams mystifies the problematic marginalizations of women as symptomatic of a poetic construction he calls "the arche-mother": "The arche-mother performs symbolic functions as the progenitress [*sic*], the object of love and inspiration, and agent of change for the hero, enabling him to move successfully into the world or actually determining his destiny. In these functions, especially as mediatrix between world and hero, her acts and character are reminiscent of the mythical feminine."[9]

The poetic construct of the arche-mother is used as an explanation/justification for the subordinate roles played by female characters. Williams associates the arche-mother with the "mythical feminine" with the same ease that Alter refers to woman's archetypal otherness in the betrothal type-scene. Just what this "mythical feminine" is remains unexplained; it is assumed that we all know what this mysterious concept is. Williams writes as if Simone de Beauvoir, Kate

Millet, and Mary Ellmann never existed, and as if the mythical feminine has not been exposed as one of the most oppressive stereotypes of
the androcentric canon.[10] Williams describes the arche-mother as the
male hero's "object of love" or "agent of change" without bothering
to problematize these terms. The auxiliary role of many female characters is thus naturalized and neutralized as the obvious result of a
transhistorical truth embodied by the arche-mother. What Sternberg
does by dismissal, Williams does by mystification. Though their
methods differ, the result remains the same, for both reinscribe
woman as other. The symbolic interpretation of biblical womanhood
diffuses the ideological problems and risks repeating the less sophisticated apologetic work of, for example, John H. Otwell and Leonard
Swidler.[11]

To a considerable degree, biblical patriarchalism continues to inspire the most dominant literary approaches to the Hebrew Bible.
While the biblical narrator marginalizes women, the contemporary
critic takes this marginalization for granted or mystifies it. Just as the
biblical narrator lays claim to absolute truth so does the modern
androcentric critic endorse this claim through his aperspectival posturing. Man is a self-evident point of reference in both biblical literature and in modern scholarly discourse about this literature. Worse,
contemporary criticism suppresses woman as character and reader
even more than the original text tends to do.[12]

If the Bible has been understood as a prescriptive compilation of
documents, modern biblical scholarship presents itself as a descriptive
and neutral venture. The apparent transparency of contemporary
literary approaches to the biblical narrative risks reinscribing what I
call elsewhere biblical sexual politics.[13] The continued obliviousness
of contemporary scholars to the implications of biblical sexual politics
risks as well turning what we understand today as literary biblical
scholarship into a secular form of obedient reinscription of attitudes
that have long become untenable.

Notes

1. "Feminism not only challenges masculine partiality, but questions the universality
imperative itself. Aperspectivity is revealed as a strategy of male hegemony." Catherine A.
MacKinnon, "Feminism, Marxism, Method, and the State: An Agenda for Theory," *Feminist
Theory: A Critique of Ideology*, ed. Nannerl O. Keohane, Michelle Z. Rosaldo, and Barbara C.
Gelpi (Chicago: University of Chicago Press, 1981), p. 23.

2. Erich Auerbach, *Mimesis: The Representation of Reality in Western Literature*, trans. Willard
Trask (Garden City, N.Y.: Doubleday, 1953), pp. 12–13.

3. Moshe Greenberg, "The Vision of Jerusalem in Ezekiel 8–11: A Holistic Interpretation,"

in *The Divine Helmsman: Studies on God's Control of Human Events, Presented to Lou H. Silberman*, ed. James L. Crenshaw and Samuel Sandmel (New York: Ktav, 1980), pp. 145–46.

4. James Kugel, "On the Bible as Literature," *Prooftexts* 2 (1982): 332.

5. Meir Sternberg, *The Poetics of Biblical Narrative: Ideological Literature and the Drama of Reading* (Bloomington: Indiana University Press, 1985), p. 482; see esp. pp. 84–128. Hereafter, *PBN*, cited parenthetically in the text.

6. "Between the Truth and the Whole Truth" is Sternberg's title for chapter 7, pp. 230–63, in which he discusses ambiguity and temporary versus permanent gaps.

7. Robert Alter, "How Convention Helps Us Read: The Case of the Bible's Annunciation Type-Scene," *Prooftexts* 3 (1983): 128.

8. Robert Alter, *The Art of Biblical Narrative* (New York: Basic Books, 1981), pp. 47–62. Hereafter, *ABN*, cited parenthetically in the text.

9. James G. Williams, *Women Recounted: Narrative Thinking and the God of Israel* (Sheffield: Almond Press, 1982), p. 113.

10. See Simone de Beauvoir, *The Second Sex*, trans. and ed. H. M. Parshley (New York: Knopf, 1952); Mary Ellmann, *Thinking about Women* (New York: Harcourt Brace Jovanovich, 1968); Kate Millet, *Sexual Politics* (New York: Ballantine, 1969).

11. It is instructive to compare William's treatment of biblical women with John H. Otwell's *And Sarah Laughed: The Status of Woman in the Old Testament* (Philadelphia: Westminster Press, 1977). Otwell, too, tends to emphasize the "positive" in woman's alleged role as mediatrix between God and the people of Israel. See also Leonard Swidler, *Biblical Affirmations of Woman* (Philadelphia: Westminster Press, 1979). Swidler's taxonomies appear to give us an inclusive picture of biblical women by considering "negative," "positive," and "ambivalent" images of women. For a critique of Swidler, see Bernadette J. Brooten, "Early Christian Women and Their Cultural Context: Issues of Method in Historical Reconstruction," *Feminist Perspectives on Biblical Scholarship*, ed. Adela Y. Collins (Chico, Calif.: Scholars Press, 1985), pp. 73–77.

12. On the traditional androcentric interpretation of biblical texts, see Phyllis Trible, *God and the Rhetoric of Sexuality* (Philadelphia: Fortress Press, 1978). How subsequent readings of the Hebrew Bible have further marginalized biblical women is exemplified in Mieke Bal's *Lethal Love: Feminist Literary Readings of Biblical Love Stories* (Bloomington: Indiana University Press, 1987).

13. Esther Fuchs, "The Literary Characterization of Mothers and Sexual Politics in the Hebrew Bible," in *Feminist Perspectives on Biblical Scholarship*, ed. Collins, pp. 117–36. See also my forthcoming book, *Sexual Politics in the Biblical Narrative: Toward a Feminist Hermeneutic of the Hebrew Bible* (Bloomington: Indiana University Press, forthcoming).

Old Testament Women as Tricksters

Ann W. Engar

University of Utah

IN the *Odyssey* Homer's portrayal of Odysseus as the ideal Greek hero includes admiration for Odysseus' deceit. Ancient Greeks seemed to have prized the ability to outwit another, to best an opponent in a battle of minds. Odysseus (and his grandfather Autolycus) are early examples of the trickster and exemplify Greek glorification of intellect.

The heroes in the Bible, however, are primarily men of spirit, of faith and obedience rather than intelligence. Adam, Noah, Daniel—none of these could be called tricksters. Abraham and Isaac do make feeble and unsuccessful attempts at trickery in trying to pass their wives off as their sisters to King Abimelech (Gen. 20, 26).[1] The closest figure in the Bible to exhibit the cleverness of Odysseus is Jacob, who wrestles with the Lord and follows divine instructions to amass a fortune based on striped and spotted sheep. More often the trickster is female. While a few of the tricksters, like Delilah, are presented as evil, many are good women and examples for their people. Rebekah, Jacob's mother, is perhaps the most prominent trickster, though Lot's daughters, Leah, Tamar, Ruth, Esther, and many of the women in the Old Testament use trickery.

One could easily dismiss their trickery with socioeconomic interpretations, such as women in low status only able to bring about their wills through trickery or early examples of the stereotypical association of women with deceit. But the issue of trickery is more complex here. First is the matter of intelligence. In each case the woman exhibits greater understanding of the needs of her family or her nation than the man does. Second is the matter of faith. Though deceit has connotations of wrong doing, the trickery of each woman is seemingly blessed by God and brings about his will. The women, then, more closely at times understand God's purposes than do their male counterparts. Their use of trickery is also not demeaning since they are carrying out God's will and often employ heroes like Jacob as their assistants. Third is the matter of sexuality. The trickery sometimes involves either sexual intercourse, the marriage relationship, or the production of children. These women are not passive sexual objects, but through trickery actively enter into the determination of when and with whom they have sex and bear children.

Although many scholars have written on these women individually, none has traced the trickster figure throughout the Old Testament. The purpose of my study is to examine the woman as trickster figure in the Old Testament and to determine its ramifications in the complicated association of deceit, piety, and sexuality.

Rebekah, the second of the great matriarchs of the Hebrews, stands far above the other patriarch's wives in her completeness. The beautiful and much beloved matriarch Sarah has the figure of Hagar shadowing her. She herself cannot conceive and so another woman must be brought in to stand as mother of Abraham's children. Even after Isaac is born, Sarah feels threatened by Hagar and Ishmael. Similarly, Leah and Rachel together make the Hebrew matriarch of their generation: Rachel, the beautiful and most loved wife, is barren for many years. Leah, the first wife, lacks the beauty and desirability of Rachel but, unlike Rachel, she is fertile. In the baby wars of the Jacob story, Leah and Rachel also each have their shadow figures in the persons of their maids Bilhah and Zilpah.[2] Clearly, to the Hebrews completeness of female personality demands both support of husband and ability to reproduce.

Rebekah alone of the patriarch's wives has no shadow figure. She is much loved by Isaac and, though she does not give birth for twenty years, never needs the complement of another woman. What, then, is the personality and character of this complete woman who is nevertheless a trickster?

Rebekah first appears as a very beautiful virgin who hospitably gives water to Abraham's servant and his camels (Gen. 24:15–21). She submits to the servant's bedecking her with a gold nostril ring and two bracelets. After telling him that her family has room to lodge him, she runs home to tell the story of her adventures to her mother and brother. She does not shrink in fear of the stranger. Though Laban and the mother have ultimate authority over Rebekah and want her to stay with them for ten days before leaving with Abraham's servant, they let her decide whether she should tarry or go immediately. She emphatically and succinctly states she will go and leaves soon after (Gen. 24:54–60).

In her first meeting with Isaac, she is again a woman of action. She sees Isaac first, jumps down from her camel to ask the servant who he is and veils her face. Then in a few pithy statements her marriage relationship with Isaac is presented: "Isaac led Rebekah into his tent and made her his wife; and he loved her. And so Isaac was consoled for the loss of his mother" (Gen. 24:67). The last verse is particularly interesting—in what sense does a wife take the place of a mother and does a husband need her to? Does Rebekah fill Isaac's loneliness and need for tenderness, or does she become a strong mother figure to him?

Isaac himself is an interesting figure. His rather sketchy story bridges the more complete portrayals of the heroic Abraham and Jacob. In comparison to them, Isaac seems weak—he follows his father to the point of being sacrificed, marries the girl his father chooses for him, pretends Rebekah is his sister when he comes into a foreign land, and leaves Abimelech's land when told. The only active role he takes is in blessing his sons and digging wells. The other things we know of him are that in old age he is blind and that he likes venison. Rebekah both contrasts with and complements this man. She is the partner of vision, the one who can judge the characters of her sons and see who can best lead the family. She is the one who understands God's will for her children and brings it about.

Rebekah's closeness to Yahweh is not present at first. She is in some sense a "foreign" woman in that her mother is an Aramean and her father, though Abram's and Sarah's sibling, was still an idol worshiper. Even so, she becomes a faithful follower of Yahweh. When she remains barren for twenty years, Isaac prays on her behalf and she immediately conceives. When the twins struggle within her womb, she complains, "If this is the way of it, why go on living?" and then goes to consult Yahweh, who speaks directly to her, a woman (Gen. 25:20–23). She herself is bitterly disappointed when Esau marries a Hittite.

In her adult life she retains her independence. Though her husband favors the elder son because Esau is a hunter and provides his father with wild game, Rebekah prefers Jacob. Her independence and love for Jacob turn to trickery when she hears Isaac promise to give Esau a blessing. The author attempts to confer respectability on her fraud by Yahweh's speech to the uncomfortably pregnant Rebekah. Yahweh has told her that her younger son shall rule her elder. This prophecy is one source of her affection for her younger son.

The story of the deception has two curious aspects. First is Isaac's behavior. He clearly doubts whether the disguised Jacob is Esau. As a blind man would, he asks Jacob who he is after Jacob has said, "Father, I am here." He listens to Jacob's voice and recognizes it as Jacob's. He questions how Esau could have hunted and prepared the dish so quickly. Jacob replies that "Yahweh put it in my path," a statement that is more true than Isaac knows. Isaac then wants to touch Jacob and, in order to smell him, asks him to kiss him. Would a man so dependent on his senses other than sight not have developed an acute sense of touch which could distinguish between animal fur and human hair and an acute sense of taste which could distinguish between goat meat and venison? Why does Isaac, despite his doubts, bless Jacob rather than calling both sons before him to clear up the confusion? Does he in any sense consent to the deception? Isaac trembles when he discovers that Esau has not received the blessing. Does he tremble solely because Esau has not received the blessing or because he realizes that Yahweh has achieved his ends in spite of Jacob's own wishes? At any rate Isaac never reproaches Rebekah or Jacob for the deception.

Another curious aspect is that Rebekah does not seem to have shared the revelation she received at the boys' birth with her husband. Nor do we read of her trying to persuade him to favor the son whom God favors. She does not leave it up to Isaac or to fate to ensure that Jacob's destiny, as decreed by Yahweh, will come to pass. By her trick she consciously forms herself as God's instrument to make Jacob the significant son.

Rebekah's manipulation of Isaac indeed has proved so successful that, when she hears Esau threatening Jacob's life, she tells Isaac she is worried that Jacob will take a wife from one of the Canaanite daughters of Heth: "if Jacob take a wife of the daughters of Heth . . . what good shall my life do me?" (Gen. 27:46). In this way she gets Isaac to send Jacob away to Padanaram, to her brother's house, to seek a wife safely away from the wrath of Esau. John Gammie has suggested that Rebekah is punished for her deceit because she is deprived of her son's presence,[3] but Jacob's absence is her own idea. Again Rebekah's actions lead Isaac to provide an inheritance for Israel—safety from internal conflict and self-destruction and a new posterity to continue the race.

Rebekah's courageous independence in preserving God's chosen leads to no condemnation of her as a manipulating, deceptive woman, even by Paul, whose general opinion of women is not high. In fact, assuming Paul is the author of or inspiration for the Epistle to the Romans, he praises her and uses her family as proof that only God chooses those who are to be his people (Rom. 9:10–13).

The Yahwistic author of chapters 29 and 30 of Genesis is clearly interested in the idea of trickery and delights in the trickery when the results are favorable to the survival of the Hebrews. As Duncan Macdonald notes, this author "liked Rebekah and even Jacob as Thackeray liked Becky Sharpe and as Galsworthy liked all the multitude of figures in his *Forsyte Saga.*"[4] Not only is Rebekah a trickster, but so is her son Jacob, her brother Laban, and her nieces Leah and Rachel. Following his mother's advice, Jacob flees the tense situation with Esau and travels to Haran, where he falls in love with his cousin Rachel. Laban requires Jacob to work for him for seven years to win Rachel's hand. After the seven years Laban gives a banquet but "when night came he took his daughter Leah and brought her to Jacob, and he slept with her" (Gen. 29:23).

In this case the originator of the trickery, as the subject in the preceding sentence reveals, is Laban. And it is Laban that Jacob blames in the morning: "What is this you have done to me? Did I not work for you to win Rachel? Why then have you tricked me?" (Gen. 29:25). Although Laban originates the scheme, Leah must carry it through. She must act the part of Rachel through the night and face Jacob's wrath and her own humiliation in the morning. Like the trickster, she gambles and acts boldly. Probably because Leah is "tender-eyed" (Gen. 29:17), she agrees to the deception because her marriage prospects are poor (if she had been a good catch, Laban would not have had to deceive someone into marrying her). Yahweh rewards Leah, though not with Jacob's love which she so desires. There is no record of Jacob reproaching her, however, and from the number of times she conceives, it is impossible to believe that he loathes her. Her real reward comes from God who repeatedly hears and favors Leah with a fruitful womb. Through her son Levi come the priests of Israel, and through her son Judah come Israel's most powerful kings. Leah may not have the creative intelligence of Rebekah, but her disguising herself as her sister makes her the fit consort of the man who disguised himself as his brother, all for the sake of the continuance of Israel's line according to God's choice.

Rachel, too, is a trickster, and her trickery continues the theme of the trickster being tricked. Just as Leah deceived the deceiver Jacob, so Rachel deceives her crafty father Laban. When Jacob's family departs from Laban's house, Rachel steals the household idols (Gen. 32:34–35). Laban arrives in a rage and demands his idols, which Rachel has hidden in the camel's litter, which she is sitting on. When Laban comes to tear the tent apart, Rachel excuses herself from rising by claiming to be menstruating. Laban never recovers his idols.

This scene shows, too, the humor that abounds in the stories of the trickster, humor often directed at the trickster herself or himself. Though we seldom think of the Old Testament in terms of humor, Toni Craven, J. K. Kohn and L. Davidsohn, and others have pointed out that there is much humor in it and that humor may have been a

conventional narrative technique.⁵ Very often that humor is connected to the story of a trickster: not only the humor of Rachel pretending to be menstruating, but also Jacob dressed in animal skins
pretending to be his brother, Lot's daughters being so concerned
about the imminent destruction of the world that they get themselves
with child by their father, Boaz's surprise and trembling at seeing
Ruth lying on the threshing floor, and Judith's prayer before she cuts
off Holofernes' head. Part of trickery is the element of the game, and
the trickster stories are comedies with successful outcomes. Yet the
game involves outrageous daring, and the outrageousness—the
heroine's or hero's willingness to go to extremes, to become the fool—
often creates laughter. So, too, is laughter created at the success of the
trick.

Rachel's trickery is an exception to the general rule that early
female trickery in the Old Testament most often involves dynastic
inheritance, the primary concern of women in a patriarchal society
(though the trick does involve the inheritance of idols). The story that
demonstrates most intensely the Hebrew concentration on continuing
the race is the story of Lot's daughters. Having fled the destruction of
Sodom and Gomorrah, these women fear their father's line will die
out. They trick their father by plying him with drink, sleeping with
him and becoming pregnant by him. Their trickery is not direct
seduction, yet Athalya Brenner has suggested that there is some taint
to their act since they remain anonymous and because their progeny
become the ancestors of the Moabites, enemies to the Hebrews (*IW*,
p. 111). In this interpretation the daughters, with their apocalyptic
visions, are seen as fools and the laughter their acts inspire is derisive.
William Cole, on the other hand, says that the namelessness of the
daughters "suggests that the heroism and initiative lay with their
father,"⁶ a view hard to support since Lot is in a drunken stupor.
These women's fears have root in their experience with the destruction of Sodom; their love for their father is real and commendable, and
Harold Fisch has seen in their story a structural precursor to the gentler tale of their descendant, the Moabite Ruth, who is likewise concerned about the continuance of the Hebrew line and who is named as
an ancestor of Jesus.⁷
The story of Tamar and Judah weaves together a number of the
themes we have previously seen in the trickster stories: the foreign
woman being adopted into Hebrew society, the woman seeing the
importance of continuing the race, taking steps to ensure it, and tricking the deceiver. In this story, however, the seduction is overt: Tamar

disguises herself as a prostitute to trick Judah into sleeping with her when he has failed to marry her to his third son and thus continue his oldest son's line (Gen. 38). Judah himself is a trickster. In the previous chapter (Gen. 37), he has persuaded his brothers to sell Joseph into slavery (as a more humane act than killing him or leaving him to die) and has helped his brothers dip Joseph's coat in blood and present it to their father as if Joseph had been devoured by wild beasts. With Tamar it is Judah's turn to be tricked, but her trick is a righteous one—while his is questionable. She not only receives her due when she becomes the mother of twins, but through one of the twins, Perez, she becomes an ancestor of David and of Jesus. Thus, the foreign woman, acting courageously and desperately when her father-in-law has wrongly deprived her of the security of male heirs, is rewarded by becoming one of the founding mothers of what becomes the greatest of the Twelve Tribes.

That her sexuality and deceit mingle with piety is clear from the original Hebrew: though Judah refers to her by the word for a common prostitute, *zona*, she terms herself a *qades* or hierodule or hallowed one, a word often used for temple prostitutes of the Canaanite religions (*IW*, p. 78). She sees herself as sacrificing for her new god Yahweh to continue the Hebrew line. Robert Alter and other commentators have claimed that one of the purposes of the Judah-Tamar story is to contrast Judah's lax sexuality with Joseph's chastity in the scenes with Potiphar's wife in the next chapter of Genesis.[8] The story also strongly contrasts Tamar's sexuality as devotion to the Hebrew race with Potiphar's wife's lust.

As with the stories of Odysseus in which Odysseus arouses in his listeners a longing for Odysseus, creating fictions in order to heighten or recreate reality, Tamar, too, creates a fiction which hints to Judah of the reality which should and is to be. When Judah asks what pledge she requires of him after their night together, she asks for his seal, his cord, and his stick. Each symbolizes his leadership and inheritance: the seal by which he authorizes actions, the cord by which generations are bound, and the stick with which he guides his flocks. In asking for these pledges, she is demanding, on an unconscious level at least, his authority and his lineage.

The story of Ruth, who marries Boaz, a descendant of Judah and Tamar, has many similarities to their story. Brenner has identified three "types" of women which converge in Ruth's story—the hero's mother, the foreign woman, and the temptress (*IW*, p. 90)—but not the trickster. Again a foreign widow is concerned about continuing the Hebrew line and uses trickery to bring the man into accord. Ruth, following Naomi's plan, anoints and dresses herself. She waits until

Boaz, full of food and drink, lies down on the threshing floor. Then she turns back the covering at his feet and lies there until he awakens in the middle of the night. She explains his "right of redemption" over her, and after arrangements are made, they soon marry. Ruth, like Tamar, has picked a time of fruition (shearing time for Tamar, harvesting for Ruth) to use tricks to make herself fruitful.

Boaz has known who Ruth is and what his responsibility as a relative of Naomi's husband is, but it is Ruth and Naomi who take charge to provide security for themselves. Ruth's actions, though seductive, have what the Hebrews would judge as just intent. Fisch has called her story a typical "bed-trick" tale (*IW*, p. 432), and Leonard Swidler points up that the Hebrews used "feet" as a euphemism for genitals.[9] Yet other scholars soften their judgment of her. The author of the Book of Ruth does not infer that Ruth's actions intend to compromise Boaz. Also, Ruth is obeying her mother-in-law and demonstrating her love for a woman rather than a man, an act which Brenner claims breaks the enmity-between-women tradition of the shadow stories (*IW*, p. 98). Unlike Tamar, Ruth receives not only the reward of a son but also the security of a husband. She too is mentioned as an ancestor of Jesus in Matthew's genealogy.

Aside from Ruth, most of the female tricksters outside of Genesis are less concerned with marriage, children, and trickery within a family and more concerned with political intrigue against Israel's enemies. As Israel becomes a nation rather than just a family and often a weak and subject nation at that, it often derives its power from the politically weakest elements within its society: its women.

Trickery is practiced by the women who surround and nurture Moses, the greatest Israelite leader. In the cases of Shiphrah, Puah, Jochebed, and Miriam, the trickery is not played out on their own families but against the enemy, the Egyptians. Their trickery does not involve dynastic inheritance but the survival of a subject people. Pharaoh commands the Hebrew midwives Shiphrah and Puah to kill every male Hebrew born. The midwives, however, fear God more than Pharaoh and spare the boys. When Pharaoh calls them to account, they roguishly answer, "The Hebrew women are not like Egyptian women. They are hardy, and they give birth before the midwife reaches them" (Exod. 1:19). Evidently the midwives are not punished too harshly for their bold deceit since, we are told, Yahweh granted them descendants (Exod. 1:21).

Moses' mother and sister use similarly desperate yet ironic trickery to preserve Moses' life. Pharaoh commands all newborn Hebrew boys to be thrown into the river; Jochebed puts Moses in a basket and floats it at the river's edge (Exod. 1:22). Pharaoh's daughter finds the baby and needs a nurse for it; Miriam volunteers to get a nurse and gets the baby's own mother. Pharaoh's daughter names the baby Moses "because, she said, I drew him out of the water" (Exod. 2:10). In this case, the humor created by the trickery comes not from the extremes to which the trickster is willing to go but from the enemy getting literally what he asks for and receiving what he does not want.

The story of the woman of Tekoa (2 Sam. 14) operates on somewhat the same level as the frauds of Odysseus and Tamar: the woman of Tekoa as a trickster creates fiction to heighten reality. Under the direction of Joab, the woman of Tekoa pretends to be in mourning and complains to King David that her son's life is endangered. Though her surviving son has killed his brother, she does not want him punished because that will leave her without heirs and leave her husband without anyone to carry on his name. Her fictitious story brings the ruling from David that her son will not be harmed. Then the woman drops her disguise and boldly asks the king why he does not bring home his own son Absalom, who has been in exile since killing his brother Amnon. David sees through the trick but also recognizes the concern of his people that there will be no heir to the throne of Israel and no peaceful succession. He then allows Absalom to return, though he refuses to see him. The woman of Tekoa, like Leah, operates under the direction of a man, but the risk and rhetorical skill are hers. Brenner extols the woman of Tekoa's wisdom:

> This "wise" woman can be commissioned to manipulate a person to act the way she wants him to. She achieves that by enlisting the person's cooperation instead of arousing his anger or animosity. She can be counted on for sensing undercurrents of emotions and opinions, and for utilizing them. [*IW*, p. 35]

In David's case the woman of Tekoa senses that the best course is to convince him intellectually. Given the explosive situation, an emotional appeal would only have worsened Absalom's chances. But, by putting David into the role of objective judge, she makes it so that he can judge his own family's problems impartially.

In the later stories of female tricksters—Rahab, Jael, Judith, and Esther—the women remain daring, but the authors tend to emphasize their sexuality, their physical deeds, or their beauty more than their intelligence. This change in emphasis may have its source in the diminished authority and power which women in later Jewish society had. In these cases the image of the female trickster at times merges with that of the temptress, a more demeaning and morally questionable role.

Although Rahab is a prostitute, her trickery involves intelligence and faith rather than sexuality. The author emphasizes her sexual status because Joshua's men capitalize on it. They go to her because they will not attract attention at a harlot's house, where many men circumspect about their identities might go. She hides Joshua's spies from the king of Jericho's men and lies to the king's men in saying that the spies have fled in the opposite direction (Josh. 2:1–24). She, too, is a foreign woman who has nonetheless come to believe in Yahweh. Her faith in his power to support the Israelites motivates her to save Joshua's men and to extract a promise from them to spare her and her family from the destruction of Jericho. The Israelites are to know her home by the scarlet cord she hangs from her window. Her story thus has similarities to the story of the destruction of the firstborn in Egypt when the Hebrews save their children by putting blood as a sign over their doors.

Though Rahab is a foreigner, her trickery does assist in the Israelite victory over the enemy, and her motivation in fearing Yahweh and wanting to save her family exemplifies Hebrew ideals. It is, then, no surprise that she, too, is an ancestor of David and Jesus. Swidler has speculated that Matthew, in his genealogy of Christ, sees a pattern of sexually "irregular" women (including Tamar, Rahab, and Ruth) as playing crucial roles in the history of the chosen people: Tamar with the founding of the Twelve Tribes, Rahab with the gaining of the promised land, and Ruth as founding the house of David (*BAW*, p. 244). Seen from the perspective of her own culture, however, Rahab would be a traitor who betrays her own people to strangers. The irony of the story is that a shrewd prostitute sees more clearly the power of the Israelites than the king of her own city does (*IW*, p. 80).

Jael's racial heritage is not clear, but she is the wife of Heber the Kenite, who is at peace with Jabin, king of Hazor. Deborah at the same time was a judge in Israel, which had been suffering military oppression for twenty years. Deborah marches into battle with Barak against Sisera, Jabin's commander-in-chief. Before the battle Deborah predicts that "Yahweh will deliver Sisera into the hands of a woman" (Judg. 4:9). The woman is not the great, intelligent leader Deborah, as expected, but the lowly Jael, who breaks the code of hospitality by driving a tent peg through Sisera's temple as he rests in her tent.

Jael's story is full of symbolic and ironic gestures. Like a mother, she provides milk—the food of children—to Sisera and tucks him in bed. Yet Sisera is the enemy who for twenty years has committed outrages against the wives, mothers, and little children of Israel. Jael's final blow to Sisera's temple is a blow for mothers and children, a blow with a tent peg which is symbolic of home and family life.

Swidler has concluded that because Jael's "deceitful" and "cowardly" deed is "at variance with the ethical principles of truthfulness, etc., elsewhere in the Hebrew Bible," it "clearly reflects an earlier stage of ethical development and as such offers little for emulation" (*BAW*, p. 112). Yet the Jael story clearly fits the trickster pattern of both early and later Old Testament stories in which the supreme value is social preservation and community. Certainly Deborah's song celebrates Jael's deed, which resulted in forty years of peace for Israel, and contrasts her daring with the "shaken and self-deluding Canaanite ladies."[10] Jael puts the needs of the Hebrew community above considerations of conventional morality: her initiative and energy within her own sphere are admirable. The mood of the story, however, does not rejoice in Jael's intelligence or craftiness, but that by using a woman Yahweh "humbled Jabin the king of Canaan before the Israelites" (Judg. 4:23). It is not the intelligent leader Deborah who brings final victory against Sisera but Jael, who relies on physical action and instincts (Judg. 5:28–30).

A widow like Tamar and Ruth, Judith saves her people by killing the enemy leader Holofernes. Surrounded by Assyrians and suffering from a water shortage, the people of Bethulia have vowed to surrender if Yahweh does not relieve them in five days. Judith upbraids the town elders for putting Yahweh to the test, prays to him for help, and bedecks herself in costly clothing and jewelry. She goes to the enemy camp and ironically uses the truth to trick the Assyrians. She claims to be disheartened by the wickedness and weakness of her people and so begs to be allowed to help the Assyrians. She will pray daily to discover when her people are so weakened by sin that God will allow them to be defeated. Then she will tell Holofernes when to attack.

Though Judith's wisdom and eloquence are mentioned a few times, over and over her beauty is trumpeted: the Assyrians "were immensely impressed by her beauty and impressed with the Israelites because of her. 'Who could despise a people having women like this?' they kept saying" (Jth. 10:19). Holofernes feels he will be a laughingstock if he does not seduce her. She attends a banquet in his tent and "enchants" him so that he gets more drunk than he has ever been. Holofernes collapses "wine-sodden" on his bed; Judith does indeed pray—but for strength for herself—and chops off his head (Jth. 12:20). When Judith returns home, she is praised for her courage and her faith. Her song of victory, though, does not emphasize her cunning—it is her "face" which "seduced" Holofernes (Jth. 13:19). And, as with Jael, the fact that Yahweh has used a lowly woman to triumph is heralded: "This is the head of Holofernes, general-in-chief of the Assyrian army . . . The Lord has struck him down by the hand of a woman!" (Jth. 13:20).

Swidler has said that "the moral of the Book of Judith is not that women are good creatures of God, but rather that God is so great that he can bring good out of evil; not that women are to be valued greatly, but rather that God is so great that he can humble Israel's enemies through the lowliest of instruments" (*BAW*, p. 114). Though there are antifeminist undertones in the Book of Judith, especially in the harping on her beauty as a sexual weapon, Swidler undervalues the celebration of Judith as a preserver of her community, as a bold and faithful follower of Yahweh: "God grant you to be always held in honour, and rewarded with blessings, since you did not consider your own life when our nation was brought to its knees, but warded off our ruin, walking undeterred before our God" (Jth. 13:20).

Esther's story is very similar to Judith's, though the enemy is now Haman and her own husband rather than a general. She, too, combines piousness and sensuality. She dresses herself in sorrowful mourning and covers her head with ashes and dung while praying to Yahweh for three days. Then she arrays herself in full splendor and delicately walks into the king's chamber uninvited. Esther is "rosy with the full flush of her beauty," her face radiates "joy and love; but her heart shrank with fear." She faints in the king's presence, and God softens the king's heart so that he does not condemn her to death. She flatters him, "My lord, you looked to me like an angel of God, and my heart was moved with fear of your majesty. For you are a figure of wonder, my lord, and your face is full or graciousness" (Esther 5:16–19). With a beautiful, adoring female languishing in his arms, the king is conquered and offers Esther half his kingdom. She has, after all, given him the greatest flattery of all in risking her life to see him. She cleverly asks only for his and Haman's attendance at a banquet.

Since Ahaseurus likely spent the night with her after such a scene, perhaps coincidently—or perhaps arranged by Esther—the king reads that night how Mordecai had saved his life from an assassination plot. Haman is then forced to lead Mordecai in honor through the city square rather than hanging him from the gallows as planned. Then Esther uses her dinner party to expose Haman as the persecutor of her people. Until this time (and for nine years) she has concealed her Jewish heritage. Esther's trickery thus consists in using her beauty and flattery to manipulate her husband and in playing on Haman's greed for power and recognition to bring about his downfall. Her deception of Haman is a play on the theme of the deceiver deceived. Haman has manipulated the king and concealed the truth about Mordecai; now he himself is deceived by the appearance of honor in being asked to the queen's table and is brought down.

Esther then appeals to the king to revoke Haman's order to exterminate the Jews and is given the right to write in the king's name and seal letters with his seal. As Judith was given Holofernes' property, Esther is given Haman's house. Esther in no way is condemned for her manipulation. Ahaseurus calls her "the blameless partner of our majesty" (8:11). But neither is she exalted for her intelligence, nor do we hear how wisely she counseled and manipulated her husband later as, say, Rebekah does. The rest of the book praises Mordecai, "a power in the palace," "next in rank to King Ahaseurus" (9:4). In Esther's case, then, beauty is the weapon of a woman's trickery aimed at a foreign enemy who threatens extermination of the Jews. Though her actions take courage and intelligence, the author of the text chooses to emphasize the power and responsibility of her uncle Mordecai, who had implored her to save her people but had no part in the actual plan.

Swidler concludes that the fact that in both the Esther and Judith stories the heroines are "women indicates not that women were often heroines or highly thought of in Jewish society at that time, but just the opposite, that women were not heroines or highly thought of in that society; otherwise the stories would not have been interesting or worth telling" (*BAW*, p. 117). But could not the same be said of the stories of the hero—that they were exceptions rather than the norm (the definition of a hero)? Swidler again undervalues the role models these stories are presenting; women may have been second-class citizens, yet those who act cunningly and courageously to save their people are praised.

Many of the admirable women of the Old Testament thus combine trickery and deception with their faith. The earlier women like Rebekah and Tamar at the tribal stage of society use trickery against their own family members to ensure the succession of God's chosen line. Later women like Rahab and Judith, at the stage when Israel has become a nation, use trickery against Israel's enemies to defend it. These women deceive not for personal pleasure or profit but with sacred intent as preservers of their people. None of the authors of these stories condemns the tricksters for their craftiness: whatever is good for the survival of Israel is acceptable (though, of course, when women like Delilah and Jezebel use the same tactics against Israel on behalf of their own countries or values, they are branded as evil). Indeed, as Brenner notes in her discussion of Ruth and Tamar:

> The storytellers relish rather than moralize. Women who risk whatever little social status they have, and possibly their lives, in order to perpetuate the continuity of Judahite leader stock display a rare kind of courage. . . .The authors celebrate the matriarch's achievement to such an extent that the dubious means she employs are considered tokens of her resourcefulness and determination. [*IW*, p. 108]

A number of the authors also use trickery as a device for creating humor in their narratives. The humor thus also mitigates the moral judgment against the means the trickster uses. It is clear, as Eugene Fisher has commented, that "the ancient mind enjoyed the interplay of wit."[11] At times the humor is at the expense of the trickster because of the extremes to which she goes in carrying out her plans. At other times the humor is directed at the deceived, often because he himself has been a deceiver. And, as A. Thimme has noted about the story of Jacob and Esau, "there is no feeling of moral indignation at such roguery, because laughter at the success of the trick displaces all moral resentment."[12]

The Old Testament for the Hebrews was a record of the dealings of Yahweh with his people. But these stories were also told and retold to help teach Hebrews who they were and how they should behave. If the Old Testament is looked at as a collection of tales of Hebrew heroes and heroines, what did Hebrew women learn from these examples of tricksters? They learned that although women held little power and authority in society, they were intelligent and could take bold action to ensure their own security as mothers in Israel or to save their people from long years of war and subjugation. Their wisdom and courage were valued. Hebrew women also learned the importance of faith in Yahweh, especially because many of these heroines were originally foreign idol worshipers.

Besides the themes of the deceiver deceived and the foreign women, the trickster stories also often include the theme of recognition—women helping men to recognize the will of the Lord—as in Isaac's recognition of Jacob as his true heir and Judah's recognition of his responsibility to Tamar. Also, in later stories especially, the trickster role often weds the view of women as temptresses who use their beauty and seductive power along with their intelligence and eloquence to overcome their enemies. Curiously, with the exception of the Tamar and Ruth stories, these tricksters/temptresses are not concerned with the begetting or birthright of children, as earlier tricksters were. Their concern is to use sexuality as a weapon against warrior enemies who are full of their own masculinity. When the female tricksters become temptresses, there is less delight in their cunning and more of a threatening undertone—women are seen as dangerous creatures.

What finally happens to the tricksters? Trickery ends happily for all of the trickster heroines: they conceive, live in peace with their families and within Israel, and become ancestors of Jesus Christ.

Notes

1. All scriptural references are taken from The Jerusalem Bible, gen. ed., Alexander Jones (Garden City, N.Y.: Doubleday, 1966).

2. See Athalya Brenner, *The Israelite Woman: Social Role and Literary Type in Biblical Narrative* (Sheffield: Journal for the Study of the Old Testament Press, 1985), pp. 89, 92–93. Hereafter, *IW*, cited parenthetically in the text.

3. John Gammie, *Encounter with the Text*, ed. Martin J. Buss (Philadelphia: Fortress Press, 1979), pp. 118–19.

4. Duncan B. Macdonald, *The Hebrew Literary Genius* (Princeton: Princeton University Press, 1933), p. 216.

5. See Toni Craven, *Artistry and Faith in the Book of Judith* (Chico, Calif.: Scholars Press, 1983), pp. 113–16, and J. K. Kohn and L. Davidsohn, in *Judisches Lexikon*, vol. 2, ed. George Herlitz and Bruno Kirschner (Berlin: Judischer Verlag, 1978), col. 1687.

6. William Graham Cole, *Sex and Love in the Bible* (New York: Association Press, 1959), p. 393.

7. Harold Fisch, "Ruth and the Structure of Covenant History," *Vetus Testamentum* 32 (1982): 427–32.

8. Robert Alter, *The Art of Biblical Narrative* (New York: Basic Books, 1981), p. 10.

9. Leonard Swidler, *Biblical Affirmations of Woman* (Philadelphia: Westminster Press, 1979), p. 119. Hereafter, *BAW*, cited parenthetically in the text.

10. Alan J. Hauser, "Judges 5: Parataxis in Hebrew Poetry," *Journal of Biblical Literature* 99 (1980): 40–41.

11. Eugene J. Fisher, "Divine Comedy: Humor in the Bible," *Religious Education* 72 (1977): 571–78.

12. A. Thimme, *Das Marchen*, p. 56, as quoted in Hermann Gunkel, *What Remains of the Old Testament and Other Essays*, trans. A. K. Dallas (New York: Macmillan, 1928), p. 184.

Fathers and Daughters:
Two Biblical Narratives

Hebrew College, Boston
Brandeis University

THE actions of the biblical individual are rooted in situation rather than in character. We do not find in the Hebrew Bible a "characterization" that serves as the source and explanation of action. By contrast, Odysseus is never at a loss; regardless of his circumstances, he remains Odysseus. The Bible has no equivalent to such a "character." Biblical protagonists are not labeled "cunning," "wise," or "foolish"—as are the protagonists in the Greek epic. Thus the Greek epic interposes the elements of character between the individual and his actions, and we therefore know what to expect of him. In the biblical narrative, this is a gap left open. We know that Laban is not honest, but we come to infer this from his actions, not from a prior characterization of him. Moreover, biblical individuals are thrown into situations that have no precedents. The situations are new, and the protagonists must react to them as new. They may do right or do wrong in the sight of the Lord, but in the course of human interrelations they act as free and undetermined agents. This also means that they are free of any expectations *we* might have for them, expectations stemming from any "characterization."

A further quality in the actions of the biblical individual stems from the *indeterminacy* in man's fate. Greek tragedy is played out against the background of iron destiny. But since there is nothing in biblical narrative corresponding to Greek *moira*, the biblical individual hovers in the indefinite *facticity* of his situation—as reflected in his exile (Jacob), or his having to flee as a fugitive (David), or in a generally tragic dimension (Saul; Jephthah and his daughter). Some individuals experience humiliation and fear as they oscillate between biblical blessing and curse.

Passion is linked to a series of trials—involving uprootedness and doubt—whereby the individual gains insight into God's design and the individual's role in the God-governed world. (This is a vital part of the process whereby the biblical protagonist is individuated in his role.) Purposiveness in general is perceived as God's design for man and the world. That purpose is not superseded by notions of "nature" and "natural law" (as it was for Greek thinkers). There is no sense of time as the image of eternity (as in Plato's *Timaeus*). Instead, the biblical view sees time as the dimension wherein God's purpose is manifested—and, as far as man is concerned, that purpose is perceived by him when in a situation of trial. Thus there is a direct line between purpose and perception: it is through trial that the perception comes to be shared by man and the purpose is revealed.

The biblical narrative is epic in its scope and structure, thus making it comparable to all epics as such. Yet it is unique in the dialectical nature of its drama. Although the biblical individual is free to choose—and his freedom is central to his makeup—that freedom is enclosed within a universe of divine design. Here, then, is the basis for the tension (and its resolution) which constitutes the story of the chosen one: the Bible is the narrative of the growth of the individual in the sight of the Lord. (There is no comparable growth in the Greek hero).

Thus the biblical narrative asserts man's capacity to choose and his spiritual autonomy, while acknowledging a divine design wherein certain individuals are chosen to fulfill purposes not of their choosing. (In Oedipus, for example, this seeming contradiction is resolved by the hero's character: the fates have ordained...but his character confirms...). The biblical narrative thus presents its own interplay of freedom and foreknowledge—although the biblical protagonist continues to exercise his will, satisfying his appetite and indulging his passion, while fully initiated into his designated role in the history of his time (as in the David and Bathsheba story). Yet action and purpose do not always coincide, and protagonists are not always aware of their intended role in the wider scheme of things (e.g., Hagar and Sarah).

The biblical protagonist is marked both by his timelessness and his immediacy to our own experience. This enables the biblical narrative to present a gallery of characters with whom we can identify, characters who never are merely remote paradigms; indeed, their closeness toeveryday consciousness serves to focus their individuality and to make a generalized imitation impossible. The biblical protagonist, therefore, is never presented as mythic (even if the Bible gives us a myth of man).

As in many of the ancient texts, the protagonist's individuality is often entailed in his or her name. One thinks, here, of the Homeric epithets. It is a sign of the higher level of individuation in the Hebrew Bible that it does not use epithets but has the protagonist's individuality expressed *within* the name itself. This is brought to its culmination in Exodus 3:14, where God names himself to Moses; and although one can hardly think of God as a protagonist in the ordinary sense, his uniqueness is acknowledged in the fact that, unlike all other protagonists, God is self-naming ("I am that I am").

Human protagonists, more often, are "named" when they are given a new name by God, the naming coming as a result of their unique experience and selection in the role of the chosen. Thus Jacob wrestles with the angel and is then told what his new name is: "Thy name shall be called no more Jacob, but Israel; for thou hast striven with God" (Gen. 32:29). "Israel" means, literally, "he will strive with God." In a similar vein, Abram and Sarai are renamed Abraham and Sarah by God when they embark upon their historic mission as progenitors of nations (Gen. 17:5, 15). The ambiguity of their situation (a post-menopausal ninety-year-old mother and a one-hundred-year-old father) is reflected in the name of their promised son: Isaac (Itzhak, meaning "he will laugh"). What is of special significance for the purposes of this paper is the fact that God designates Sarah as coparticipant in the covenant (Gen. 17:16).

Can the female protagonist be regarded as biblical protagonist in the fullest sense? I suggest that there are four aspects typifying the biblical protagonist—promise, trial, dialogue, and exile—and women such as Eve, Sarah, Hagar, Miriam, and others meet and fulfill these aspects. I shall argue that the woman is part of the divine scheme, thereby paralleling the major male protagonists (even to the point of having a flaw).

To begin with, woman is centrally involved in the birth of the chosen one—not as a passive birth mother but as a problematic figure actively concerned in trial. There is, for example, the barrenness of women such as Sarah, Rebekah, Rachel, and Hannah, the eventual mother of Samson. Further, there is the woman as initiator of events: from Eve through Sarah and Esther, women have shaped sacred history through word and deed. In addition, the Hebrew Bible is studded with images of wise women who changed the course of events: from Sarah to Deborah, Abigail, and the wise woman of Tekoa (2 Sam. 14). For this paper, however, I shall discuss only two women (Dinah and the daughter of Jephthah) and the unique experiences they respectively undergo (rape and sacrifice).

The story of Dinah, Jacob's daughter, raises any number of questions. And the application of the concepts of narrative poetics (in regard to biblical texts in general) has uncovered a world of ambiguities and hitherto hidden meanings. The problem of authorial intention in the choice of "showing" or "telling" techniques reflects aesthetic and/ or rhetorical considerations. Although Dinah's story appears in Genesis 34, we may read the story in that limited context or in a wider one (33:18 to 35:8), such that we have a different "text," different questions, and different answers. How shall we come to terms with the father's silence (34:5)? Was this due to simple prudence, as the extended reading would suggest (35:5)?

The story embraces two acts of violence: the rape of Dinah and the slaughter of all the males of Shechem. Can we equate these acts so that the slaughter is a just retribution for the rape? Are the brothers to be regarded as one group, or shall we isolate Simeon and Levi from the others, not only as the two who perpetrated the slaughter, but as the two who were especially unwilling to compromise their sister's honor in exchange for better relations with the lords of the land? How are we to interpret Jacob's curse of the two (49:5–7)? Shall we judge Jacob in terms of intention or outcome? Who are the moral heroes of the story—the two vengeful brothers or Jacob, who acts with prudence because he fears reprisal?

Both Isaac and Jacob—true to the tradition of endogamy—went to Mesopotamia to get a wife from within the larger clan. With the sons of Jacob, there are intimations of change and possible relations with the local Canaanites. (Both Joseph and Moses in effect married outside the faith, taking Egyptian wives.) All this should color our reading of Genesis 34. Samuel Sandmel has suggested that there are two distinct layers in the story: the earlier account involving the love story of Shechem and Dinah; and the account of the marriage negotiations conducted between the local people and the clan of Jacob. The second layer introduces the rape episode to justify the act of slaughter on the part of the sons of Jacob. Thus verses 2, 5, 13, the last part of 27 and verse 31 are to be seen as later additions.[1]

A more subtle interpretation is offered by Meir Sternberg.[2] To begin with, verse 1 states that Dinah is the daughter of Leah (not of his beloved Rachel). Would that fact detract from her importance in the eyes of Jacob? Further, does Jacob relate to the marriage negotiations as the basis for peace or as a danger to the endogamous clan? Although it was Jacob's only daughter who was defiled, he keeps silent until his sons return from the fields. What is the meaning of his silence? By verse 31, it is the brothers who occupy the proprietary place (vis-à-vis Dinah) once held by the father. Verse 34:7 sees the rape of Dinah as an offense against Israel (Jacob's other name); but it is also the sons who take offense, and by 34:13 it is the sons who respond to Shechem's conciliatory plea rather than Jacob (even though it is Jacob, as titular head, who is being addressed). They pretend to accept the marriage offer, but with the proviso that every male of Shechem be circumcised as a mark of their conversion. Verse 13 says the sons of Jacob spoke "with guile"; does this mean that they intended to reject the offer of intermarriage between the two groups and that no conversion would atone for their sister's rape?

Deuteronomy 22:28–29 (applying, admittedly, to a later age) stipulates that if a man rapes an unbetrothed virgin, he must pay her father fifty shekels and he must marry her "and may not put her away all his days." Assuming that the same rule applied in the era of Jacob, and that the men of Shechem underwent conversion willingly, there could be no bar to the marriage and honor would be preserved for all concerned. As for Shechem, he certainly is presented as having fallen in love with Dinah (Gen. 34:3) and as wanting more than anything to do right by her. He pleads with Jacob and his sons: "Let me find favor in your eyes, and what ye shall say unto me I will give" (34:11). Are we to recognize the obduracy of Dinah's brothers, who refuse to sell their defiled sister for money? There are two basic facts to be noted here: first, Dinah is not consulted as to her wishes in the matter. Second, as a defiled woman she is doomed to a life of disgrace if she is returned home unmarried, while as the wife of the converted Shechem she would have some status.

Sternberg's interpretation ennobles the brothers' motives, despite the words "with guile" that precede their insincere acceptance of the offer of intermarriage. They appear to be talking cool "business"— the conversion of the Hivites in exchange for Dinah's marriage to Shechem—but their real motive is a thoroughgoing vengeance. Does the rape justify the deceit and the massacre? The mass slaughter of innocent men, women, and children is followed by vicious looting, carried out by the other sons of Jacob. To Sternberg, however, Simeon and Levi emerge as heroes, since they kill the offender(s) and recover their sister—even though the willing circumcision is taken by Sternberg as another part of the punishment for rape—and Simeon's and Levi's implacable bloodthirst is taken as their rejection of "material-ism," their espousal of "idealism," and the two themselves as "the most intricate, colorful, and attractive characters in the story" (*PBN*, p. 473).

Jacob reproaches the two for making him "odious unto the inhabi-tants of the land," and he expresses the fear that other groups may unite to destroy him and his house (Gen. 34:30). To Sternberg, this reveals Jacob to be the least sympathetic character in the story, Jacob's argument sounding shabby in the "Bible's court of con-science" (*PBN*, p. 474). That "court of conscience," presumably, is expressed by the closing words to chapter 34, the brother's rejoinder:

"Should one deal with our sister as with a harlot?" As I have suggested, it is anything but harlotry that is involved here (one need not rape a harlot; and Shechem was ready to make amends as far as anyone could). Nevertheless, Sternberg takes the brothers' words as the voice of idealism (since they averted the insidious threat posed by exogamy) as against Jacob's selfishness and the instinct for mere survival. In Sternberg's view, whoever would have closed his eyes to the rape and would have accepted compensation (even if such compensation be in accordance with the eventual prescription in Deuteronomy 22!) would have been as complicitous in "making a whore of Dinah" as the rapist himself (*PBN*, p. 475).

What we have is a story based on confrontation: between Dinah and Shechem, between Jacob and his sons, and between the sons of Jacob and the Hivites. What is the fabula, here, and what is the narrative? What is the central theme: the rape and retaliation? the problem of retaining a national identity despite the threat of assimilation? the unremitting rage that can use deceit as its instrument? or the broader theme of action versus inaction? These are questions about the intent and the coherence of the text—and these can be decided only after the boundaries of the text have been delineated. Should the story of Dinah be seen as an independent tale in the Jacob cycle? Yet the containment of that story in chapter 34 may be unwarranted from the standpoint of narrative structure, and it may be more illuminating to see chapter 34 as an integral part of the 33:18-to-35:8 passage.

From that perspective, Jacob's silence is not diffidence or cowardice but the understandable caution of a man who has bought a parcel of land amidst a region of strangers and has at last settled into peace after years of uncertainty. Having spent twenty years elsewhere, he has returned to Canaan, faces his (till then presumed hostile) brother Esau, and manages to emerge as a lord in his own right. (The moving meeting with the wronged brother precedes the story of Dinah.)

The prelude (33:18–20) says: "And Jacob came in peace to the city of Shechem, which is in the land of Canaan, when he came from Paddan-aram; and encamped before the city. And he bought the parcel of ground, where he had spread his tent, at the hand of the children of Hamor, Shechem's father, for a hundred pieces of money. And he erected there an altar, and called it El-elohe-Israel." This brings up a number of points: 1) The phrase "in peace" is a translation of the single word *shalem*. I am inclined to agree with Nisan Ararat, who identifies it with a place such as Shiloh, the city of the holy tabernacle in Canaan.[3] 2) Jacob's purchase of the land indicates his desire to settle there permanently. 3) Setting up an altar, Jacob is at last coming into his own, a fulfillment of the promise and vow in Genesis

28:11–22. All this sheds additional light on Jacob and his motives. Surrounded by the deceitful Hivites (who have Dinah in their possession) and his unruly sons, the cautious Jacob appears as anything but the unsympathetic character that Sternberg makes him out to be.

There is a further ambiguity in the closing verse of 34: "And they said: 'Should one deal with our sister as with a harlot?'" A more accurate, if cruder, translation is: "And they said: 'Should he turn our sister to the likes of a harlot?'" If the brothers are addressing Jacob, the "he" refers to Shechem. But if they are talking amongst themselves, the "he" can also refer to Jacob and reflect their resentment at his willingness to sell their sister for money and material gifts.

According to the Hebrew ordering, the Dinah story ends with the first eight verses of chapter 35. This epilogue begins with God's command to Jacob to go to Beth-el to build an altar and reside there. It is the same Beth-el mentioned in chapter 28, connected with promise, exile, epiphany, and dialogue. Jacob calls upon the members of his house to rid themselves of all pagan gods and paraphernalia. There is some ambiguity in 35:5. "And they journeyed; and a terror of God was upon the cities that were round about them, and they did not pursue after the sons of Jacob." Is this to be linked to the purification of Jacob's camp and the building of the altar? Or shall we assume that it was the slaughter after the Dinah episode that prevented the neighboring tribes from pursuing the sons of Jacob?

The actions of Simeon and Levi have their full effect on Jacob many years later. He is dying, and he calls his children together to foretell their future and to bless them. Clearly, their earlier actions are what turn his blessing into a curse: "Simeon and Levi are brethren; weapons of violence their kinship. Let my soul not come into their council; unto their assembly let my glory not be united; for in their anger they slew men, and in their self-will they houghed oxen. Cursed be their anger, for it was fierce, and their wrath, for it was cruel; I will divide them in Jacob, and scatter them in Israel" (49:5–7).

I have discussed three readings of the Dinah story: Sandmel's, Sternberg's, and my own. The first of these addresses the incongruities and contradictions in the text and seeks to resolve them by reconstructing the story as a combination of independent narratives: thus the rape episode was supposedly introduced to justify the massacre. The second reading is the most controversial of the three, pitting the self-interested caution of Jacob against the vengeance demanded by the brothers, thus presenting a standoff between a prudential and a formalistic morality. The third reading extends the text at both ends, providing a broader historical biblical context within which to set the story, making Jacob the main protagonist and vindicating his motives.

The story of Israel as presented in the Hebrew Bible includes not only secular chronicle but myth, folklore, and providential history. The redactors of the material were interpreters, their choice and arrangement of the material being guided by a clear telos. Following the Exodus from Egypt, and prior to the establishing of the kingdom, the Book of Judges depicts the settlement of the land. The process of settlement is tainted by chaos. Unity amongst the tribes is rare. The reign of an oppressor generally gives rise to a man (or woman: Deborah) who brings some respite for a time. The individual stories in Judges follow a conventional story frame:

a) the children of Israel do that which is evil in the sight of the Lord;
b) God gives them over into the hands of a hostile nation;
c) the children of Israel cry unto the Lord;
d) God sends a deliverer, and
e) the land has some rest—typically for forty years.

The story frame is not uniform; each story is individual, although there is a typical interplay of strength and cunning, integrity and corruption. Some of the stories have no theological "message," although all involve some ethical dilemma(s). The stories are told for their value as moral models or for their nationalistic significance (underlining the calamities inevitably befalling a land without a unifying ruler).

Jephthah and his daughter make a unique story (thus illustrating the heterogeneous nature of Judges). Yet the story is steeped in universal qualities: Jephthah is a self-made man, the son of his father's "other woman"; through cunning, integrity, intelligence, fortitude, and the will to power, he reverses his fate and becomes the leader of his people. He is a diplomat, a prototheologian, a historian; but he is brought down by a rash oath, and he must sacrifice his only daughter, whom he loves, to fulfill the oath.

The inviolability of an oath is declared in Numbers 30:2–5 and Deuteronomy 23:22–25. In both places, that inviolability is asserted by God. As to Jephthah's oath: "And Jephthah vowed a vow unto the Lord, and said: 'If thou wilt indeed deliver the children of Ammon into my hand, then it shall be, that whatsoever cometh forth of the doors of my house to meet me, when I return in peace from the children of Ammon, it shall be the Lord's, and I will offer it up for a burnt-offering'" (Judg. 11:30–32).

As we know, it is his only child who comes out to meet him, with timbrels and dancing. Seeing her, he realizes the catastrophe he has inflicted upon himself. At this juncture, his daughter (whose name is not mentioned) becomes the heroine of the tale (Judg. 11:34–40). In a way, we have at least three stories in this short passage, each bearing an ethical message, from the simple and immediate to the timeless and sublime: first, there is the story of Jephthah's reversal of fortune, from outcast to leader; then there is the tragic tale of his vow; and then there is the daughter's story, and it is she who gives the entire episode its mythic dimension.

The reversal of one's lot, due to deep conviction, is a frequent motif in the biblical narrative. The protagonist often begins in a position that is the diametric opposite to his or her designated place in the divine scheme: thus the barren woman shall give birth to the chosen one, as in the stories of Sarah, Rebekah, Rachel, Hannah, and others; the handmaid Hagar, sent to her death in the desert, becomes the mother of a nation. Similarly in the case of Jephthah, there is a reversal of fortune in the fact that the banished son of the "other woman" will become the leader of the Gileadites. As a leader he seeks peace, but failing in this search he takes to war and wins.

His eventual fall is another reversal, reminiscent of the typical *peripeteia* in Greek tragedy. Indeed, the sort of vow Jephthah makes is to be found in Greek drama, where it is invariably the expression of the protagonist's hubris. Further, there is a typical irony in the fact that neither Jephthah's brothers nor the Ammonites could vanquish him, but that it is his beloved daughter who brings him down. When he realizes what he has done, and tears his clothes in grief, he undergoes the typical *anagnorisis*, the full realization on the part of a man who has made himself the measure of things. The moral message is more intense for the fact that he is the firstborn (although in the biblical pattern the firstborn is not necessarily the chosen one). Yet through his own action he makes himself the head of his clan. His flaw (the Greek *hamartia*) is therefore tragic in essence. Had everything ended with this second story, there would have been enough in it for an interesting drama according to the traditional Aristotelian precepts.

Here the third story begins. (Yet another story, as a subtext, will be elucidated later.) Here the voice of the daughter is heard, but first there is the "preparation" by Jephthah:

> And Jephthah came to Mizpah unto his house, and behold, his daughter came out to meet him with timbrels and with dances; and she was his only child; beside her he had neither son nor daughter. And it came to pass, when he saw her, that he rent his clothes, and said: "Alas my daughter! thou hast brought me very low, and thou art become my troubler; for I have opened my mouth unto the Lord, and I cannot go back." [Judg. 11:34–35]

It would be instructive to compare her words to those of the Greek Iphigeneia. Jephthah's daughter says:

"My father, thou hast opened thy mouth unto the Lord; do unto me according to that which hath proceeded out of thy mouth; forasmuch as the Lord hath taken vengeance for thine enemies, even of the children of Ammon." And she said unto her father: "Let this thing be done for me: let me alone two months, that I may depart and go down upon the mountains, and bewail my virginity, I and my companions." And he said: "Go." And he sent her away for two months; and she departed, she and her companions, and bewailed her virginity upon the mountains. And it came to pass at the end of two months, that she returned unto her father, who did with her according to his vow which he had vowed; and she had not known man. And it was a custom in Israel, that the daughters of Israel went yearly to lament the daughter of Jephthah the Gileadite four days in a year. [11:36–40]

How shall we come to terms with all this? Northrop Frye seeks to explain the sacrifice in terms of something like a transcultural archetype. Thus he speaks of Jephthah's daughter in terms of "her virginity, which made her an untouched and hence acceptable sacrificial figure, and the fact that she became the center of a local female cult, doubtless originally on the principle mentioned earlier that virgin goddesses, like Artemis, are often the protectors of childbirth."[4] Perhaps this approach raises more questions than it provides answers for.

A reading of a different nature is offered by Robert Alter. He points out that the story may have been read for its etiological value as a way of explaining the origin of a cult obliquely referred to in verse 40 (i.e., the four-day retreat practiced yearly by Israelite women). It may well be that there was a local pagan cult of a Persephone-like goddess whose origins had been forgotten, and then the story of Jephthah's daughter was invented in order to account for the existence of the cult (as well as to justify its existence). As Alter reminds us, such etiological tales are "essential elements of many artfully complex and symbolically resonant stories in the Hebrew Bible."[5] He goes on to argue that the reduction of the story to something like a primitive folk tradition [e.g., Persephone, Artemis] is an act of condescension. Instead, he places the story within the great chain of narratives from Joshua to 2 Kings. He sees it as a tale about "vow-taking," not only on the part of Jephthah but also on the part of the Gileadites, as well as Jephthah's brothers and others. In addition, there is much dialogue used to delineate political relations, nuances of character, and attitude (Alter, p. 20). The story of Jephthah, therefore, is to be seen as interconnected with the political theme of Judges. Thus the vow is to be seen as a political act and understood for its political consequences. As Alter says, Jephthah shows himself to be a tough and effective military leader. "But the vow, together with his inflexible adherence to carrying it out, is a fatal flaw, and it is not surprising that after his personal catastrophe he should preside as leader over a bloody civil war (chap. 12) in which tens of thousands of fellow Israelites perish at the hands of his army" (Alter, p. 21).

In my discussion of the Dinah story I ended with a presentation of my own view, based on an extended text. Here, too, I shall refer to an extended text—my purpose being to discuss the Hebrew word *nahalah*, which means "property," "estate," "inheritance," or "heritage." Jephthah's story concerns property rights, birthrights, and land ownership—and, implicitly, about the right of a woman to inherit property. I see *nahalah* as the key word in the text. In Judges 11:2, the legitimate sons of Gilead drive Jephthah out, saying: "Thou shalt not inherit in our father's house," and the word *nahalah* appears in its three-letter root, *nhl*, in the phrase "Thou shalt not inherit" (*Lo tin'hal*). The banished Jephthah, son of Gilead and a harlot, is a man without property, without *nahalah*. We may assume that when he returns as chieftain and leader his rights are reinstated and he becomes a man of means.

As we saw, Alter focuses attention on the element of dialogic confrontation here as a way of delineating political claims. Land is the basis of his conflict with the Ammonites, for when Jephthah asks their king the reason for their attack, the answer is: "Because Israel took away my land, when he came out of Egypt" (Judg. 11:13). With all this before us, we can now see an added meaning in Jephthah's words to his daughter, "Alas my daughter! thou hast brought me very low" (11:35). That is, he might be referring not only to his personal tragedy but also to his vision of the future: the death of his daughter means that no child of his will inherit his property but that the brothers who banished him will be his hated inheritors.

According to biblical law, women can inherit, and the inheritance passes to a daughter if there is no son. God instructs Moses: "If a man die, and have no son, then ye shall cause his inheritance to pass unto his daughter. And if he have no daughter, then ye shall give his inheritance unto his brethren" (Num. 27:8–9). And according to Numbers 36:6–9 a daughter is instructed to marry into her father's tribe so that the property she inherits will not go out of the tribe. With his daughter's death, therefore, he loses not only his one direct inheritor but also his chance of establishing a legitimate place for himself (after his death) by having his property become the patrimony of the tribe as a whole.

From what we have seen of biblical narrative, woman has a definite legal status—a fact almost unique in the ancient world. Yet all biblical protagonists, male and female, are moored in their humanity, their vulnerability and mortality. This is part of the complex interplay between divine design and human purposiveness. Accordingly, woman in the Hebrew biblical narrative is not confined to a mere place in genealogical reports and chronicles (as has been claimed). Rather, she is a central dramatized persona, being both a part of the narrative fabric and a wearer of it. The multiple possibilities of interpretation reflect this.

Notes

Biblical quotations are taken from *The Holy Scriptures* according to the Masoretic Text (Philadelphia: Jewish Publication Society of America, 1955).

1. Samuel Sandmel, *The Hebrew Scriptures* (New York: Oxford University Press, 1978), pp. 365–66.

2. Meir Sternberg, *The Poetics of Biblical Narrative: Ideological Literature and the Drama of Reading* (Bloomington: Indiana University Press, 1985), pp. 445–75. Hereafter, *PBN*, cited parenthetically in the text.

3. Nisan Ararat, "Reading According to the 'Seder' in the Biblical Narrative: To Balance the Reading of the Dinah Episode" (in Hebrew), *Ha-Sifrut*, No. 27 (1978), p. 16 n.13.

4. Northrop Frye, *The Great Code: The Bible and Literature* (New York: Harcourt Brace Jovanovich, 1983), p. 185.

5. *The Literary Guide to the Bible*, ed. Robert Alter and Frank Kermode (Cambridge: Harvard University Press, 1987), p. 17. Hereafter, Alter (referring to his introduction), and cited parenthetically in the text.

The Trickster Tricked:
Strategies of Deception and Survival
in the David Narrative

Raymond-Jean Frontain
University of Tennessee

ABRAHAM Cowley was not the first editor of the David narrative perplexed by a particularly troublesome incident in the story. In composing *Davideis*, his unfinished epic poem on the life and deeds of King David, the seventeenth-century poet puzzled over the purpose of the scene in 1 Samuel 20 in which Jonathan connives with his friend to plot the changing course of Saul's attitude toward his young rival. The friends agree that Jonathan should seek proof of either his father's hatred of or affection for the shepherd turned princely son-in-law, and then repair to David's hiding place in the countryside where, under pretext of archery practice, he would either alert David to flee the murderously jealous king's rage or assure him of a safe return to court. Here is the denouement of the episode:

> Next morning, Jonathan went out into the fields to meet David at the appointed time, taking a young boy with him. He said to the boy, "Run and find the arrows; I am going to shoot." The boy ran on, and he shot the arrows over his head. When the boy reached the place where Jonathan's arrows had fallen, Jonathan called out after him, "Look, the arrows are beyond you. Hurry! No time to lose! Make haste!" The boy gathered up the arrows and brought them to his master; but only Jonathan and David knew what this meant; the boy knew nothing. Jonathan handed his weapons to the boy and told him to take them back to the city. When the boy had gone, David got up from behind the mound and bowed humbly three times. Then they kissed one another and shed tears together.[1]

The device of the arrows "was a Subtlety that I cannot for my Life comprehend," Cowley protested in pious confusion, "for since he went to *David*, and talk'd to him himself, what needed all that politick Trouble of the shooting?"[2]

What indeed? Curiously, there is a similar episode in 2 Samuel 11 in which the narrator again details the "politick Trouble" taken by a character when a more directly relayed message would seem more pragmatic and efficient. Anxious to countermand Uriah's possible testimony to his own adultery with the soldier's wife, David privately orders his field commander, Joab, to place Uriah in the front line of battle, where he must inevitably be killed. Uriah does indeed die, along with a number of other soldiers, while storming an enemy city's walls after being ordered to use a procedure that past experience has taught Israel's chieftans is foolhardy. Is it to forestall the king's protests over the losses incurred that Joab instructs the messenger to report Uriah's death only after describing the army's strategic blunder? Or is he, as Meir Sternberg suggests, using the messenger to "bait . . . a seriocomic trap for the king," one designed to expose David's willingness to let his personal interests undermine the good of the nation?[3] David's rage is effectively quelled, but the reader is left to question the exact nature of Joab's actions on the battlefield: Did he callously sacrifice the other soldiers in order to make Uriah's death look more natural? Or does he shrewdly use Uriah's death to distract attention from his own military miscalculation, adroitly turning David's personal vendetta to his own advantage? More troubling in this instance is the extent of David's understanding. Does he accept Joab's implied excuse that so many others had to be sacrificed to ensure Uriah's death, so preoccupied is he with covering up his adultery with Bathsheba? Or does he see through Joab's device and tacitly go along with the commander's fiction as a way of maintaining his own?

The narrator does not observe in 2 Samuel 11 as he did in 1 Samuel 20 that "only David and Joab knew what the message from the field meant, the person carrying the message from Joab did not." But clearly the messenger plays the same role within the narrative as the servant boy who chased Jonathan's arrows. Both are unwitting actors in a continuing drama of multiple deceptions, the depth of which is shadowed by their naive and uncomprehending participation in schemes the full value of which has at least been suggested to the reader. After uncovering Saul's true feelings for David, Jonathan plots a new deception to be able to reveal that truth; the son's deception counteracts the father's dangerous duplicity. Likewise, Joab turns against David the very kind of deception that the king is using to defend himself against possible scandal. Whether deliberately committed or not, Joab's strategic mistake on the battlefield is meant to cover David's in the bedroom. The servant boy and the field messenger blithely pass (or facilitate the passing of) messages, the full import of which they do not understand, dramatizing the limitations of men's knowledge, as well as how easily those limitations may be manipulated by other men for devious, self-serving purposes. Ironically, it was none other than naive and ever-loyal Uriah who carried David's sealed instructions to Joab in the first place, the pathetically oblivious bearer of his own death warrant.

Jonathan and David's "politick Trouble" with the arrows, like David's and Joab's surreptitious and ambivalent messages, are part of the drama of lies, feints, and repeated instances of deception that is enacted within 1 and 2 Samuel, and the opening chapters of 1 Kings. Initially such actions ensure a beleaguered David's survival against overwhelming odds and place him within a tradition of other Israelite heroes—most notably Abram and Jacob—who survive by their wits. David is, in the early part of his story at least, a hero of the "absolute comic,"[4] a trickster figure capable of feigning madness, of fatally deceiving a family of priests, and of luring a giant to his death, in order to ensure his own survival and that of his race; he is a representative of the irrepressible life force. But, significantly, after his political position is consolidated and his survival is ensured, the deception he practices changes in character; he risks becoming the ruthless ruler that Yahweh warned the Israelites against when they foolishly pleaded for a king, the beleaguer and no longer the beleaguered. As though as a check to his power, figures arise within the narrative whose purpose it is to trick the trickster himself. First Joab in the episode already mentioned, but later and more obviously Nathan, whose parable of the man with one ewe sheep slyly turns David's conscience against him after his treacherous treatment of Uriah. Deception quickly becomes the currency of the narrative's economy. David's sons and retainers continue his practices of deception, but exaggerate and distort them. Amnon lures his stepsister Tamar to his room and rapes her, and then is himself fatally tricked by her brother, Absalom. Absalom, frustrated by his dependence upon his father politically, repeatedly deceives David, only to be himself betrayed, first by David's "mole" Hushai, and then by ruthless Joab. And finally Joab—in some ways David's evil genius—is basely repaid for his serviceable treacheries after David's death, in a scenario that had been concocted by the dying king himself, thus putting an end to the cycle. Moving from the comedy of limited human perception to the tragedy of the same, David's story is finally that of the trickster who is himself justly tricked.

THE DIFFICULTY OF SEEING CLEARLY

The opening scene of 1 Samuel suggests the all-too-human difficulty of recognizing the nature of others and of interpreting their motives correctly.[5] Coming upon a solitary woman in the tent of the ark whom he observes for a long time to be moving her lips without speaking, the priest Eli concludes that she must be drunk and soundly rebukes her. Hannah explains, however, that rather than having poured out drink, she has been "pouring out my heart before the Lord . . . speaking out of the fullness of my grief and misery" because, although married many years, she is as yet childless (1 Sam. 1:14–16). The narrative does not go on to report whether Eli displayed either shame or embarrassment to discover how badly he had misjudged the woman, simply that he blessed her and that she later successfully conceived and gave birth to the judge and prophet whose name is assigned to the two scrolls that contain the early history of the Israelite monarchy.

Restraining Samuel's impulse to anoint the oldest son of Jesse who, tall and strong, seems a likely replacement for the rejected king, Saul, the Lord tells him: "Take no account of it if he is handsome and tall; I reject him. The Lord does not see as man sees; men judge by appearances but the Lord judges by the heart" (1 Sam. 16:7). The narrative does not specify what the Lord sees in Eliab's heart that demands that he be rejected, nor can it. The ways of God are inscrutable, and repeatedly men stumble to interpret what he means. As a boy, Samuel is confused by God's call in the night and must be taught how to hear it (1 Sam. 3); as a man, Saul's misunderstanding the Lord's instructions regarding the disposition of the defeated Amalekites results in the spirit passing from him to David (1 Sam. 15). More seriously, lacking the Lord's ability to see into the human heart, men are condemned to judge by appearances. If Eli misjudges Hannah, and Samuel mistakes Eliab—and they are men of the Lord—then how much more difficult is it for others to assess the complete situation! Advancing to meet the Israelite champion on the battlefield, for example, Goliath is enraged by the slight he thinks is being paid him: "and he looked David up and down and had nothing but contempt for this handsome lad with his ruddy cheeks and bright eyes" (1 Sam. 17:41). Appearances are not only deceiving, but as the outcome of Goliath's duel with David shows, mistaking them can even be fatal.

The drama that is played out in 1 and 2 Samuel might be called the drama of "reading." Men and events must be assessed and interpreted insofar as men's limited means permit. In some instances, careful proceeding allows a certain success. Frustrated by the plague that has afflicted their population since the captured ark of the Israelites has been in their possession, for example, the Philistine priests and soothsayers instruct their nation's leaders to place the ark in a wagon drawn by "two milch-cows which have never been yoked . . . and let it go where it will. Watch it: if it goes up towards its own territory to Beth-shemesh, then it is the Lord who has done us this great injury; but if not, then we shall know that his hand has not touched us, but we have been the victims of chance" (1 Sam. 6:7–9). The cows and wagon, of course, move directly across the border into Hebrew territory "and halted there. . . . The five princes of the Philistines watched all this, and returned to Ekron the same day" (1 Sam. 6:14–16).

Such instances of careful study and experimentation confirming a tentative interpretation, however, are rare. More often men strain to know, as David does when he attempts to "read" the news of the approaching runners who carry messages from the battlefield:

> David was sitting between the two gates when the watchman went up to the roof of the gatehouse by the wall and, looking out, saw a man running alone. The watchman called to the king and told him. "If he is alone," said the king, "then he has news." The man came nearer and nearer. Then the watchman saw another man running. He called down to the gate-keeper and said, "Look, there is another man running alone." The king said, "He too brings news." The watchman said, "I see by the way he runs that the first runner is Ahimaaz son of Zadok." The king said, "He is a good fellow and shall earn the reward for good news." [2 Sam. 18:24–28]

The scene is an emblem to be deciphered. An unaccompanied runner is most probably a messenger and not a survivor from the battlefield making his way home. The runner's style gradually offers a clue as to his identity, and that identification arouses a particular expectation. The Philistine princes who actively probe events for their meaning are rewarded by confirmation of their suspicions. But how much more often in 1 and 2 Samuel is a character rendered passive, as David is in this scene. With experience bearing down upon him, he is condemned to sift through the few grains of information that events supply, attempting to extrapolate some meaning or meager significance from them.

And how painful is it to learn to "read" events and men. Not knowing the overpowering love that David yet feels for his rebellious son, Absalom, Ahimaaz is eager to bear the news that the king's enemies have been routed and the rebellion been put down. Joab, ever perceptive and politically astute, knows that David cares more for his son than for victory, and attempts to dissuade him. Yet, even though a Cushite messenger has already been dispatched, Joab is worn down by Ahimaaz's pleading and permits him to follow after the first messenger. Ahimaaz ironically outstrips the other runner and is the first to greet David, but when questioned about the fate of Absalom, equivocates, leaving the Cushite to deliver the very news that Ahimaaz had so eagerly sought to bear. What does Ahimaaz read in David's face that suddenly allows him to understand the full import of the information he holds? The scene approaches the sublimity and horror of Greek tragedy as four characters, possessing different degrees of knowledge, interact. Like the messengers discussed earlier, the Cushite does not know and never understands the nature of the drama in which he participates. Ahimaaz, however, must suddenly learn the full irony of his situation: the news that he was so eager to carry, thinking that it would bring his beloved king joy, is actually the source of David's greatest sorrow. David, on the other hand, eagerly leans forward to hear the very words that he would rather not hear; like Saul visiting the Witch of Endor, he learns exactly what he does not want to know. In the irony of his situation, David is brother to Oedipus, commanding that he be told the very news that will most pain him. Finally, Joab—the only one of the four who sees and understands the full significance of his knowledge—fails to control how the news will be released. David's cry of grief for his son's death, as Faulkner well understood, holds within it the unbearable sorrow and pain that issues from knowledge. The tragedy of human existence as represented in the David story is that knowledge can be as destructive as blindness.

TRICKERY, THE BEST DEFENSE AGAINST TREACHERY

Appearances are deceptive, and the individual must learn to read other men and events if he is to survive, even if the knowledge he gains is itself tragic. The danger of not scrutinizing appearances, however, is compounded by the possibility of treacherous deception on the part of another. Only he can see into the human heart, the Lord tells Samuel; alert men must attempt to chart the course of another person's actual disposition. And when faced with the possibility of treachery, men quickly learn that their only defense is, paradoxically, further trickery.

David is traditionally considered to be Israel's greatest king in part because he best satisfies the type of hero whose guileful stratagems enable him to triumph against dangerous deceit. Like Abram or Isaac, who unchivalrically pretend that their wives are only their sisters when passing through hostile territory to avoid being murdered by rulers who covet the beautiful foreign women (Gen. 12:10–20; 20:1–18; 26), David has no reluctance to assume undignified or unappealing roles in order to survive.[6] He feigns madness to pass unmolested through the territory of enemy king Achish of Gath (1 Sam. 21:10–15). Later he deceives the same Achish, even as he protects David against the wrath of Saul, as to whom he leads raiding parties against, craftily leaving no witnesses who might testify to his slaughter of the Philistines who have befriended him (1 Sam. 27:7–12).[7] David resembles other patriarchs in this regard as well, entering the world of Saul's court an inexperienced but hopeful young lover who is duped, very much as Jacob was, by his crafty future father-in-law in dealing for a prospective bride. Like Laban, Saul substitutes another daughter for the promised one, demanding that the hero perform outrageous labors to win her; and true to his fairy-tale-hero status, David, like Jacob, outtricks his trickster father-in-law by succeeding at the seemingly impossible task (David delivers twice the stipulated number of Philistine foreskins just as Jacob outwitted Laban in the matter of the brindled livestock; compare 1 Sam. 18:20–27 with Gen. 29:15–30, 30:25–43). What is more, the wife won by each is clearly her new husband's equal in planning duplicitous strategies to ensure their survival, Rachel conniving in Jacob's escape from her father's camp by stealing Laban's household gods, hiding them under her skirts, and feigning menstrual discomfiture to prevent their being found by Laban's search party (Gen. 31:19–35), while Michal stage-manages one of David's close escapes from Saul by lowering him from a window and then claiming to her father's messengers that the household god she has covered with a blanket is really her husband too ill to leave bed and answer Saul's summons; she lies again in justifying her trick to her angry father once it has been exposed (1 Sam. 19:11–17).[8] Finally, like Joseph whose ruse of planting a cup in Benjamin's sack, only to accuse him of theft, provokes a moving recognition among his once-treacherous brothers which ends in a loving reconciliation (Gen. 44–45), David twice secretly appropriates and then publicly displays possessions of Saul in scenes which result in the vengeful king's confession of his past treachery and in a tearful, if short lived, reconciliation with David (1 Sam. 24:1–22; 26:1–26).[9] This witty resourcefulness and genius for survival in a hostile and threatening environment contributes much to the reader's sense of David's greatness.

And never before were such skills so desperately needed. Like Jacob who flew the wrath of his brother only to be deceived by the maternal uncle from whom he sought refuge, and like Joseph who was betrayed first by the stratagems of his jealous brothers and then by those of Potiphar's wife, David escapes the frying pan only to fall into the fire when, fleeing the treachery of his supposed friends and countrymen, he must walk a delicate balance among his nation's enemies who agree to protect him from Saul. Unlike Jacob and Joseph, however, David's life throughout 1 Samuel is seriously in danger. The Samuel narrative vividly dramatizes Saul, who should be grateful to David for delivering Israel from the threat of Goliath, cunningly plotting

David's destruction by sending him off to battle the Philistines under pretext of securing a dowry worthy of a king's daughter:

> Saul said to David, "Here is my elder daughter Merab; I will give her to you in marriage, but in return you must serve me valiantly and fight the Lord's battles." For Saul meant David to meet his end at the hands of the Philistines and not himself. . . . But Michal, Saul's other daughter, fell in love with David, and when Saul was told of this, he saw that it suited his plans. He said to himself, "I will give her to him; let her be the bait that lures him to his death at the hands of the Philistines." [1 Sam. 18:17–24]

In case the reader has not seen through the pious and patriotic mask that Saul wears to cover his vengeful and murderous feelings, the narrator adds one last time, "Saul was counting on David's death at the hands of the Philistines" (18:25).[10]

Saul, however, quickly learns the worth of his adversary and resorts to less subtle maneuvers. When Saul realizes that David "by himself is crafty enough to outwit me" (1 Sam. 23:23), his hatred surfaces, and thrice he attempts to kill David with a spear. David is several times forced to flee the court, escaping once—as has been seen—with the help of Jonathan (whose "politick" device of the three arrows symbolically parallels Saul's murderous use of the three spears), and a second time with that of Michal. But even in retreat David is not safe. Saul openly pursues him with an army, and he is ever in danger of being betrayed by the folk among whom he takes refuge, narrowly escaping being betrayed to Saul by the people of Keilah (1 Sam. 23:1–13). Ultimately driven out of the country, David survives among the enemies of the Israelites only by tricking them into believing that "he had won such a bad name among his own people . . . that he would remain his [Achish's] subject all his life" (1 Sam. 27:11–12). David, thus, survives by gingerly negotiating between the countrymen who have betrayed him and the enemies who have befriended him, slaying the allies of his host and secretly delivering the Israelites from danger of attack even while pretending to raid the Israelites to the delight of the Philistines. But it is impossible for even a master trickster to sustain this double deception for very long. When David is expected to join Achish in an assault on the Jews, the only thing which prevents his bluff from being called is the fear of Achish's allies that David will betray them in battle (1 Sam. 29:1–11). Excused from having to join the battle on either side, David is left free to maintain whatever pose he wants. The reader, however, cannot help but wonder if the mistrustful Philistines had not finally suspected that beleaguered David was devising a strategy to escape from being pushed to the unthinkable extreme of attacking his own people, a strategy by which he could have further tricked the enemy that was unknowingly helping him trick the friends who had betrayed him!

Like the cat that always lands on its feet, David is wiley and unfailingly resourceful, inevitably escaping even the closest of calls. He has a trick for all seasons. Whereas other biblical characters are celebrated for a single influential trick (left-handed Ehud for the assassination of fat Aglon, Jael and Judith for their seductive disposings of enemy chieftans, widowed Tamar and Ruth for successfully ensuring the continuance of their family lines, the brothers of Dinah for avenging their sister's rape, wise Daniel for delivering Susannah from the perjurous elders, etc.), only one other character in Hebrew Scripture approaches David for the sheer number of his tricks—Jacob—and his story is told in ten chapters, David's in one and a half scrolls. Thus, in Hebrew narrative where tricksters abound, David may be called the "Trickster's Trickster." Countering every threat, parrying every thrust, he is the ideal hero for a small nation surrounded by larger, militarily overpowering countries, his narrative serving as psychological reenforcement to the ever beleaguered Jews by asserting that one can survive by brains when deficient in brawn.[11]

And lest it seem that in its celebration of David's acute perception and effective formulation of strategy, the narrative loses sight of the horror of a world in which treachery can only be met by trickery, let us recall the deception that David practices upon Ahimelech of Nob in escaping Saul's murderous reach, and the tragic consequences of that deception's success. Recognizing David as the slayer of Goliath and assuming him still to be a favorite of the king, Ahimelech is disturbed only that so important a personage should be traveling unattended and without provisions. David lies, claiming to be on such urgent business for the king that his departure could have brooked no delay. Generous Ahimelech, eager to serve both his king and the deliverer of his nation, easily accepts David's excuse and provides him with sacred bread from the sanctuary and with the sword of Goliath which had been entrusted to the priests's keeping (1 Sam. 21:1–9). The narrative continues to focus on David's escape, following him to Gath where he successfully practices his first deception on Achish, and finally to the caves of Adullam where like Robin Hood he collects a band of outcasts who will loyally serve him in his defense against the mad machinations of Saul. The incident at Nob appears to be but one of the several tricks practiced in the successive stages of David's escape.

But not quite. Just when David seems in the clear and his deception of Ahimelech to be forgotten, the narrative suddenly shifts to Saul's camp where Doeg the Edomite, who had silently observed David's exchange with the priest at Nob, reports on it to an angry Saul. An ingenuous Ahimelech is questioned and judged by the king:

> Then Saul said to him, "Why have you and the son of Jesse plotted against me? You gave him food and the sword too, and consulted God on his behalf; and now he has risen against me and is at this moment lying in wait for me." "And who among all your servants," answered Ahimelech, "is like David, a man to be trusted, the king's son-in-law, appointed to your staff and holding an honourable place in your household? Have I on this occasion done something profane in consulting God on his behalf? God forbid! I trust that my lord the king will not accuse me or my family; for I know nothing whatever about it." But the king said, "Ahimelech, you must die, you and all your family." He then turned to the bodyguard attending him and said, "Go and kill the priests of the Lord; for they are in league with David, and, though they knew that he was a fugitive, they did not tell me." [1 Sam. 22:13–17]

The narrative concludes with a description of the massacre of eighty-five priests, along with their families and households. Only one son of Ahimelech escapes to join David in exile. Hearing Abiathar's report of Saul's revenge, David makes a chilling admission. "'When Doeg the Edomite was there that day, I knew that he would inform Saul. I have gambled with the lives of all your father's family'" (1 Sam. 22:22), he tells the sole survivor. A cold comfort.

The scene is as rich in irony as any other thus far analyzed. Ahimelech, on the one hand, is incapable of suspecting David; "a man to be trusted," he persists in calling the person who has so craftily deceived him. Saul, on the other hand, is brutally certain of treachery on the part of the one man whom the narrative makes clear is without duplicity. Ahimelech and all who are associated with him pay the price of both his trusting to appearances and Saul's inability to do so even when they are truthful. Unlike the other messengers discussed so far, Doeg the Edomite fully understands the meaning of the deception that he witnesses, and it is his understanding which hastens Ahimelech's tragedy to its end. And David, who takes the survivor Abiathar into his inner circle, must live with the knowledge of the consequences his deception has had for others. Is it memory of Saul's hasty misjudgment of Ahimelech that comes to mind when later, as king, David adjudicates between the conflicting protests of Ziba and Mephibosheth and gives each the benefit of the doubt? (2 Sam. 16, 19).

Appearances are deceiving, treachery can only be met with trickery, but even this defense can be means of yet further betrayal.

"You are the man!": The Trickster Tricked

The incident narrated in the first sixteen verses of 2 Samuel foreshadows the change in David's character and fortunes which occurs once, with Saul and Jonathan dead, he need no longer fear the former's persecution and ascends the throne as Saul's successor. The narrative has already established that Saul fell upon his sword to avoid being taken captive in battle (1 Sam. 31:4), yet the Amalekite who brings news of Saul's death to David claims to have dispatched Saul himself and as proof presents Saul's crown to David. The scene is ambiguous. Has the narrative's redactor compiled two conflicting versions of Saul's death, as earlier he presented two conflicting accounts of David's presentation to Saul, and refused to mediate between them? Or, more importantly thematically, is the Amalekite—like Falstaff upon the death of Hotspur—attempting to claim credit for a deed he did not do, in hopes of claiming a reward? If the latter, then the narrative continues the motif of the messenger who does not understand the full import of the message he bears. Just as Ahimaaz has no intimation of David's love for Absalom, his rebellious son, the Amalekite cannot fathom David's regard for Saul, his pursuer yet his surrogate father and the Lord's anointed. His only reward for supposedly killing David's supposed enemy is death itself. This is the fate of the trickster whose deception is practiced, not to ensure his own or his nation's survival, but for self-aggrandizement: he is himself tricked, oftentimes fatally, either by the very irony of his circumstances or by a greater trickster whose role in the narrative seems to be to check the first trickster's abuse of deception's power.[12]

The division between 1 and 2 Samuel is effected as much by the metamorphosis of David from beleaguered to beleaguerer, as by the death of Saul and ascension of David to the throne. Within the larger historical cycle, the narrative makes clear, David's transformation simply fulfills the prophetic warning given by the Lord to his people through Samuel when they asked for a king to guide them:

> "This will be the sort of king who will govern you," he said. "He will take your sons and make them serve in his chariots and with his cavalry. . . . He will take your daughters for perfumers, cooks, and confectioners, and will seize the best of your cornfields, vineyards, and olive-yards, and give them to his lackeys. . . . He will take a tenth of your flocks, and you yourselves will become his slaves. When that day comes, you will cry out against the king whom you have chosen; but it will be too late, the Lord will not answer you." [1 Sam. 8:11–18]

Thus, David grows to abuse his kingly power just as surely as Saul had. But within his personal cycle of development, David's continued trickery—once his survival is assured—becomes the very kind of treachery he originally had to defend himself against in others. Basically, while his actions do not necessarily change, their significance is altered by his change in social rank and power. This shift necessarily colors the reader's response to him as well. Readers sympathetic to his deceptive tactics when performed in the interest of survival can only feel threatened to witness his exercising similar strategies against those who are now as vulnerable to a king's power as he himself once was. The employment of such tactics against the people he is bound to protect causes him to grow momentarily as vile as Saul, who originally persecuted him. The balance of power is restored by the ruses of those who trick him just as surely as he used to outwit Saul with the help of Jonathan and Michal.

The incident which most clearly reflects this change in David's character occurs in 2 Samuel 11–12.[13] Israel is once again at war, and while Joab commands the army in the field, David "remained in Jerusalem" where he engages in adultery with Bathsheba, the beautiful wife of one of his soldiers. When their liaison results in Bathsheba's pregnancy, David hastily summons Uriah to the palace where he tries to persuade the warrior to sleep with his wife and, then, presumably trick him into later believing himself responsible for Bathsheba's pregnancy once it is publicly disclosed. His attempts recall Saul's stratagems so many years before to entice David into a marriage contract in hopes that David would be killed while attempting to obtain the seemingly impossible dowry of 100 Philistine foreskins (1 Sam. 18). A black comedy is played out as the success of David's plan is repeatedly postponed by the pious responses of his victim. Uriah refuses to violate the religious codes that govern a soldier's behavior in wartime even though he is encouraged to do so by his commander-in-chief who is also, ironically, the Lord's anointed. Earlier David has similarly frustrated Saul's plan by refusing, ingenuously enough, to believe that a man of his humble origins could be considered a worthy son-in-law to the king. But whereas Saul's scheme was finally foiled by David's success in the field, David's plot against Uriah is only too successful.

The significance of this repetition of situation is clear. In turning against another innocent man the same stratagem that Saul had once used against him, David reverses his role, employing just as effectively to ensure Uriah's destruction the wit that he had previously used to guarantee his own survival. But whereas David had later dramatized to Saul the injustice of the king's persecuting him, and thus secured Saul's repentance, David's deceit against hapless Uriah eliminates his rival, and his abuse of power can only be checked by the stratagem of

a new figure in the narrative, the prophet Nathan. In recounting for
the king the tale of a wealthy man who owns "large flocks and herds"
but who appropriates the "one little ewe lamb" of a poor man in his
village to save the expense of slaughtering one of his own for a guest's
dinner, Nathan deviously holds a mirror up to David which reveals
the horror of his treachery against Uriah. "'You are the man,'"
Nathan reveals in response to David's outrage at the injustice perpetrated by the rich man. The prophet's parable tricks the trickster and
leads him to repentance just as surely as David had secured Saul's by
first stealing and then publicly revealing the spear and water jug from
Saul's sleeping camp (1 Sam. 26:1–25; cf. 1 Sam. 24:1–22).[14]

Shrewd Nathan's subtle manipulation of David delights the reader.
Justice has been served, but with a neat and efficient reverse parallelism that can be deemed "poetic" both in terms of the character's
psychology and of the narrative's structure. David's growing passivity
in 2 Samuel, however, as he is increasingly manipulated through stratagem and deceit by others, can only cause the reader unease. For
after Nathan reveals to David the injustice of his abusing Uriah,
David appears less frequently as the clever actor on whom the narrative's spotlight shines, and more regularly as the dupe of a host of
other trickster characters whose antics claim center stage, nearly
pushing David off to the wing. Only occasionally is their tricking for
David's own good, as when Joab—in a maneuver which recalls
Nathan's device of the subversive parable—prompts the Tekoite
woman in a petition, the circumstances of which mirror a particular
difficulty which David has refused to resolve. "'May I add one more
word, your Majesty?'" she pleads after David has delivered his judgment in her case, only to tell the startled king how "'Out of your own
mouth . . . you condemn yourself.'" David recognizes the hand of
Joab in the stage-managing of this little drama, is grateful for his
lieutenant's subtle urging, and resolves his inner conflict by following
his own advice (2 Sam. 14:1–20). Of greater consequence is the
byzantine court drama enacted by his sons which perversely mirrors
the pattern of David's own worst trick. It is as though, in abusing his
power as Trickster, David unintentionally begins the spinning of a web
of deception that is extended by his lust-, ambition-, and revenge-
driven sons so far beyond the bounds of David's intention that he is
nearly trapped in it himself.

Following David's repentance for his adultery with Bathsheba and
for the murder of Uriah, the narrative shifts to the story of Amnon and
Tamar. Amnon desires his stepsister just as badly as David had lusted
for Bathsheba, and is more devious, even, in obtaining her. Jonadab,
whom the narrative describes as "a very shrewd man" (2 Sam. 13:3),
devises a strategy in which, by feigning illness to secure the

sympathetic but naive cooperation of his father, Amnon is promised that his unsuspecting half sister will visit him privately, when he subsequently rapes her and then publicly humiliates her. Outraged by their father's failure to punish Amnon for his crime, Tamar's full brother Absalom carefully dissimulates his hatred for his older half brother and bides his time until, unsuspected, he may take his revenge. Two years later Absalom tricks David into sending Amnon to what will prove his death (2 Sam. 13:23–27) just as guilefully as Amnon had manipulated his father into sending Tamar to him for violation.[15] In both instances, David is reduced to playing the part of the naive go-between who is tricked into carrying messages the import of which escapes him. The success of his sons' dissimulation reveals a king so preoccupied with administrative duties or so blinded by paternal love that he is no longer capable of discerning the hidden motives of others. Domestic and political chaos may easily reign when Trickster himself is so easily tricked.

For the reader who has grapsed the plot's basic pattern, the direction the narrative must go in seems clear. Saul abused his power in dissembling his jealous hatred of David and in trying to trick his rival to his death and was in turn tricked by David, with the help of Jonathan and Michal. Likewise, when David callously tricked Uriah to his death in order to disguise the fruit of his adultery with Uriah's wife, he was himself tricked by Nathan. Appropriately enough, Amnon has been mortally punished by Absalom's deceptive ploy for the subterfuge by which he satisfied his lust for Tamar. The reader breathlessly waits to see by whose trick Absalom will in turn be repaid for cunningly masking his feelings for Amnon and for stage-managing his brother's death. Such a pattern of revenge achieved through dissembling for a violation or affront which is itself the fruit of deception could conceivably be continued indefinitely. But in a series of maneuvers reminiscent of his father's earlier survivalist tactics, Absalom adroitly defuses the anger and resentment that his violent deception has aroused. First, he enlists Joab's aid in being recalled from exile; Joab's subversive parable, as has been seen, has the proper effect, for no one knows the king's mind as well as he. But what Absalom does not foresee is that David, having learned the painful lesson of letting his son's violence go unchecked, still refuses him access to the court even while permitting his return to Jerusalem. Absalom must devise yet another stratagem in order to get Joab to intercede for him one more time (2 Sam. 14:28–33). All's well that seems to end well, as domestic harmony is restored through Absalom's shrewd maneuver of David through Joab. No one remains who is committed to paying Absalom in kind for his tricks.

But in the Machiavellian world of the court, where kings have wealth to amass and to distribute as well as power to wield and abuse, it seems impossible that men should live humbly and honestly for long. David's forgiveness and reinstatement of Absalom only frees the proud young man to turn his attention from domestic to national affairs. Frustrated by his father's political omnipotence as well as by his longevity, Absalom plots the greatest trick of all, to steal his father's country just as his ancestor Jacob had stolen his brother's birthright:

> He made it a practice to rise early and stand beside the road which runs through the city gate. He would hail every man who had a case to bring before the king for judgement and would ask him what city he came from. When he answered, "I come, sir, from such and such a tribe of Israel," Absalom would say to him, "I can see that you have a very good case, but you will get no hearing from the king." And he would add, "If only I were appointed judge in the land, it would be my business to see that everyone who brought a suit or a claim got justice from me." Whenever a man approached to prostrate himself, Absalom would stretch out his hand, take hold of him and kiss him. By behaving like this to every Israelite who sought out the king's justice, Absalom stole the affections of the Israelites. [2. Sam. 15:2–6]

It is a brilliant performance! By standing democratically at the city gate and enthusiastically embracing weary travelers, Absalom dramatizes David's aloofness in the palace. He coyly plays upon the petitioner's fear of injustice at the moment when he's most vulnerable, just before he goes to meet his judge. The narrative even suggests Absalom's perfect timing as an actor, breaking Absalom's discourse with the directive, "And he would add." One can almost see Absalom pausing to let the weight of his suggestion of David's bias sink in before modestly extending what the frightened petitioner is eager to seize upon as his only hope: "'If only I were appointed judge in the land.'" Little wonder that "by behaving like this to every Israelite who sought out the king's justice, Absalom stole the affections of the Israelites."

Absalom does not stop here, however. Next he secures the counsel of his father's advisor, Ahithophel, whose reputation for shrewdness recalls Jonadab, the mastermind of Tamar's rape and instigator of the earlier domestic insurrection. Then, finally, under pretext of going to worship in Hebron, Absalom dupes his father into permitting him and two–hundred followers to leave the city (2 Sam. 15:7–9). The extent of Absalom's duplicity is indicated not only by David's failing yet once again to question the motives of his son when responding to one of his requests, but by the fact that the two hundred men who accompany Absalom are likewise unaware of the conspiracy into which they are being drawn: "they were invited and went in all innocence, knowing nothing of the affair." How much more devious can a fellow get? David seems finally to have met his match. The reign of Old Trickster seems at an end and that of new trickster beginning when, his forces growing, Absalom takes David by surprise and forces him to flee from his capital.

But, following the narrative's recurring pattern, if Absalom can gain a kingdom through trickery, he can be tricked into losing it as well. His deceptions are to be countenanced as long as they serve simply to restore the domestic balance upset by another's self–serving dissimulation, as in the case of his punishing Amnon's rape of Tamar and of subsequently securing his own return to favor. When, however, they upset the established order solely to promote the trickster's private interest, the threat he offers must be deflected by the stratagem of a more powerful trickster. Curiously, Absalom's civil war is more a battle of tricks than a contest of arms. David recognizes that success will lie in defeating his son less on the battlefield than in the council room, where he understands his most powerful opponent is shrewd Ahithophel. "'Frustrate, O Lord, the counsel of Ahithophel,'" he prays just before meeting Hushai, whom he realizes will be the perfect double agent, pretending loyalty to Absalom in order to slyly undermine Ahithophel's authority (2 Sam. 15:31–37). In a crucial debate over battle strategy, Hushai does persuade Absalom to do the opposite of what Ahithophel wisely counsels. What follows deserves to be quoted in full:

> Hushai told Zadok and Abiathar the priests [who are also secretly in David's employ] all the advice that Ahithophel had given to Absalom and the elders of Israel, and also his own. "Now send quickly to David," he said, "and warn him not to spend the night at the Fords of the Wilderness but to cross the river at once, before a blow can be struck at the king and his followers." Jonathan and Ahimaaz were waiting at En-rogel, and a servant girl would go and tell them what happened and they would pass it on to King David; for they could not risk being seen entering the city. But this time a lad saw them and told Absalom; so the two of them hurried to the house of a man in Bahurim. He had a pit in his courtyard, and they climbed down into it. The man's wife took a covering, spread it over the mouth of the pit and strewed grain over it, and no one was any the wiser. Absalom's servants came to the house and asked the woman, "Where are Ahimaaz and Jonathan?" She answered, "They went beyond the pool." The men searched but could not find them; so they went back to Jerusalem. When they had gone the two climbed out of the pit and went off to report to King David and said, "Over the water at once, make haste!", and they told him Ahithophel's plan against him. So David and all his

company began at once to cross the Jordan; by daybreak there was not one
who had not reached the other bank.

When Ahithophel saw that his advice had not been taken he saddled his
ass, went straight home to his own city, gave his last instructions to his
household, and hanged himself. So he died and was buried in his father's
grave. [2 Sam. 17:15–23]

The passage is an extraordinary recapitulation of the entire narrative. First of all, we meet with the recurring difficulty of "reading" a
person correctly as Absalom mistakes the motives of Hushai just as
surely as he himself had tricked his father earlier as to his own.
Second, comparison of this scene with the earlier one in which a messenger was used to warn David of the need to flee approaching danger
suggests just how serious the implications of the widening circle of
deception have become. Jonathan, who sent his message through the
servant who collected his arrows, has been replaced by Hushai, who
tells Zadok and Abiathar, who tell a servant girl to warn Ahimaaz and
a new Jonathan, who with the help of the woman of Bahurim carry
the message to David. The simple number of people involved in the
deceit is staggering. Third, as in the Ahimelech episode, a servant
loyal to David's pursuer witnesses a significant scene and reports it to
his master. But here the narrative moves too quickly to establish
whether the "lad" who "saw" Jonathan and Ahimaaz enter the town
understood—as Doeg the Edomite had—the significance of what he
has seen, or whether his betrayal of David's party is naive and unin-
tentional. Witness to a drama of multiple deceptions, the reader is
himself unable to distinguish among conflicting levels of knowledge
and experiences a frustration similar to that of the characters who can
only guess at who among them knows exactly what. Finally, the narrow escape of Jonathan and Ahimaaz through the quick thinking of
the woman of Bahurim suggests something of the Chinese box-like
effect of deception itself. If Hushai's messengers had been captured
and made to speak, Hushai's duplicity would have been revealed and
his life, not to mention David's, lost. Instead, the woman's dodge protects the threatened messengers, allowing Hushai's deception to succeed in preserving David from the devious assault of Absalom: her
trick saves the trickster (Hushai) of the trickster (Absalom) who
threatens Trickster himself (David)!

This is the crucial moment in the civil war, as well as the entire
narrative, in which both the threatening and the protective values of
trickery can be seen, the latter neatly canceling out the former. Significantly, shrewd Ahithophel—sensing that he has been outmaneu-
vered by Hushai—withdraws from Absalom's circle and calmly com-

mits suicide. His shrewdness allows him to understand that there is no place in the world for a trickster who has been outtricked.[16]

CONCLUSION

In a world where men's knowledge is already dangerously limited, the Israelites's clamoring for a king can only have tragic consequences. Appointing a king may provide the Israelites with the kind of centralized rule that seems to make other nations function more effectively, but a king's perspective must always be inferior to Yahweh's. The ultimate impossibility of David's accurately discerning human motives is dramatized in the two scenes concerning Ziba and his master Mephibosheth while David is in exile from Jerusalem. Fleeing the city at the approach of Absalom's rebel forces, David is met by Ziba, a onetime servant of Saul who now waits upon Saul's surviving heir, lame Mephibosheth, whom David has protected in deference to the memory of Jonathan. Ziba heaps provisions upon the exhausted king:

> "The asses are for the king's family to ride on, the bread and the summer fruit are for the servants to eat, and the wine for anyone who becomes exhausted in the wilderness." The king asked, "Where is your master's grandson?" "He is staying in Jerusalem," said Ziba, "for he thought that the Israelites might now restore him to his grandfather's throne." The king said to Ziba, "You shall have everything that belongs to Mephibosheth." Ziba said, "I am your humble servant, sir; may I continue to stand well with you." [2 Sam. 16:1–4]

But when David returns to Jerusalem victorious after the defeat of Absalom, he is met at the Jordan by a strange assortment of place seekers and fence menders who are anxious about their position with the reinstated king. Among them is Ziba, who appeared "with his fifteen sons and twenty servants. They rushed into the Jordan *under the king's eyes* and crossed to and fro conveying his household *in order to win* his favour" (19:17; emphasis added). But, the narrative continues:

> Saul's grandson Mephibosheth also went down to meet the king. He had not dressed his feet, combed his beard or washed his clothes, from the day the king went out until he returned victorious. When he came from Jerusalem to meet the king, David said to him, "Why did you not go with me, Mephibosheth?" He answered, "Sir, my servant deceived me; I did intend to harness my ass and ride with the king (for I am lame), but his stories set your majesty against me. Your majesty is like the angel of God; you must do what you think right." [2 Sam. 19:24–30]

Did Ziba tell the truth about Mephibosheth, or did he cunningly take advantage of the lame man's handicap to supplant him in David's favor? Is Mephibosheth as poignantly concerned for the king's welfare as he appears to be, or is his earnestness a carefully staged drama designed to win back his confiscated estates? Significantly, the narrative does not, as in the case of Hushai's and Ahithophel's conflicting advice to Absalom, make clear to the reader whose version is to be trusted and whose is not. Nor, as in the opening scene of 1 Samuel, does the narrative supply the reader with the superior perspective that corrects a faulty human one from within the story—in this case, David's. Rather, David is presented as too exhausted by feuds, civil war, and petty jealousies to attempt to find out the truth.[17]

Only the Lord sees fully—in time, in space, and even in the darkened interior of the human heart. The disintegration of certainty when one relies upon fallible human judgment in the face of duplicitous human behavior is poignantly dramatized in the final episode of David's life. Adonijah, presuming that he is heir to his dying father's throne, has alienated the prophet Nathan:

> Then Nathan said to Bathsheba, the mother of Solomon, "Have you not heard that Adonijah son of Haggith has become king, all unknown to our lord David? Now come, let me advise you what to do for your own safety and for the safety of your son Solomon. Go in and see King David and say to him, 'Did not your majesty swear to me, your servant, that my son Solomon should succeed you as king; that it was he who should sit on your throne? Why then has Adonijah become king?' Then while you are still speaking there with the king, I will follow you in and tell the whole story."
> [1 Kings 1:11–14]

Bathsheba artfully embroiders the speech that Nathan has given her, Nathan times his entrance perfectly, and the result of their drama is that David has Solomon's succession publicly proclaimed.

Whereas the first two kings of Israel were chosen by divine guidance, Samuel carefully following divine commands even when they appeared self-defeating, the narrative is at pains to emphasize the role of human duplicity in the selection of David's successor. It is a brilliant scene in a narrative of many such brilliant scenes. Nathan once again stage-manages David's public admission, but without the narrative's earlier assurance that what he says is true. Had David made such a promise earlier, or is Nathan concerned that in the reign of Adonijah old men such as himself will be pushed aside? Bathsheba, whose first appearance in the story was as the vulnerable prey to David's carnal appetite and whose feeling at being sexually possessed and whose possible complicity in or shock at her husband's murder are never recorded, here commands the scene; she adds the very words to the speech that Nathan taught her that will convince David, namely that he swore to her "by the Lord God" (v. 17). And, as in so many scenes before, David's face registers neither ignorance nor complicity. The narrative gives no indication of what he knows or even suspects. Are Nathan and Bathsheba taking advantage of the befuddlement of the senile old man who lies under blankets on his couch all day, and who requires the warmth of virgin Abishag to counteract the hardening of his arteries? Or, as David slips in and out of consciousness, does the old fox dream of one last trick to play upon his enemies, allowing Nathan and Bathsheba to think themselves in control because he recognizes that Adonijah will not carry out his wishes concerning Joab and Shimei, whereas Solomon will? Has the throne been saved or stolen through Nathan's stratagem? Is the trickster being tricked one last time, or is he carefully allowing others to think they are tricking him because it suits a private purpose?

The narrative will not tell.[18] It remains as opaque for the reader as human motives often are within the world of the story.

Notes

1. 1 Samuel 20:35–40. I use the text and translation established in The New English Bible with the Apocrypha (New York: Oxford University Press, 1970). For conveniency's sake, I refer to the people governed by Saul and David as the Israelites rather than attempt to distinguish what group was governed at what time.

2. *The Complete Works in Verse and Prose of Abraham Cowley*, ed. Alexander B. Grosart, 2 vols. (1881; reprint ed., New York: AMS Press, 1967), 2:76, n. 37. Cowley's poetic recasting is one of the most astute interpretations of the David narrative available; his poet's eye allows him an insight into the workings of the narrative that I have found in few other commentaries. As the most sophisticated narrative of the ancient world, the Books of Samuel have elicited voluminous commentary and discussion, but generally my thinking about their meaning and operations has been most stimulated by the following: Robert Alter, *The Art of Biblical Narrative* (New York: Basic Books, 1981); Charles Conroy, *Absalom Absalom! Narrative and Language in 2 Sam. 13–20* (Rome: Biblical Institute Press, 1978); J. P. Fokkelman, *Narrative Art and Poetry in the Books of Samuel*. Vol. 1: *King David* (Assen: Van Gorcum, 1981); Kenneth R. R. Gros Louis, "The Difficulty of Ruling Well: King David of Israel," *Semeia* 8 (1977): 15–33; Meir Sternberg, *The Poetics of Biblical Narrative: Ideological Literature and the Drama of Reading* (Bloomington: Indiana University Press, 1985); and Jan Wojcik, "Discriminations against David's Tragedy in Ancient Jewish and Christian Literature," in *The David Myth in Western Literature*, ed. R.-J. Frontain and J. Wojcik (West Lafayette, Ind.: Purdue University Press, 1980), pp. 12–35.

3. Sternberg, *Poetics of Biblical Narrative*, p. 215.

4. The term is Edith Kern's although she discusses Jacob and not David as a comic trickster. See *The Absolute Comic* (New York: Columbia University Press, 1980), p. 124. Cowley, to his credit, is sensitive to David's strategies for survival, referring to the "Arts" that David uses at Achis's court (*Davideis*, 3. 52) and that Michal uses to help David escape her father's murderous designs in such terms as "just Deceit," "a virtuous Lie," and "good dissembling tears" (1. 575–77).

5. Jan Wojcik analyzes the conflict between Eli's "uninformed, realistic perspective" and the narrator's informed, moral one (which he sometimes shares with Yahweh), and the thematic significance that this opening scene has for the Books of Samuel in general, in "Discriminations against David's Tragedy," pp. 13–15. See Peter D. Miscall's discussion of the importance of Eli's "blindness" in terms of the reader's perspective in *I Samuel: A Literary Reading* (Bloomington: Indiana University Press, 1986), p. 13.

6. The motif of survival through trickery is so important that after delivering it once in the stories of the Patriarchs (and in the prominent position immediately following the Lord's covenant with Abram by which the Jewish race is promised that it shall flourish), the Book of Genesis repeats it twice. Modern readers have been as puzzled by these incidents as Cowley was by the "Subtlety" of Jonathan's stratagem with the arrows. Gerhard von Rad, for example, actually calls the first episode "offensive" and admits that its purpose is finally obscure to him; see *Genesis: A Commentary* (London: SCM Press, 1976), p. 170. Samuel Sandmel, on the other hand, sees the storytellers as encouraging Jewish readers to be as shrewd as their ancestors were, and as offering "advance retaliation" against the Egyptians who will later enslave the Israelites; see *The Enjoyment of Scripture* (New York: Oxford University Press, 1978), p. 85. As Jan Wojcik notes, in each retelling the enemy grows wiser, more respectful of the Jews, and so less threatening to Jewish readers; changes in the outcome of each episode work to confirm the Jews' confidence in their ability to deceive and so to master a physically stronger enemy. (As It Is Written: A Poetics of Biblical Narrative, unpublished manuscript, pp. 116–21).

7. Joel Rosenberg is one of the few commentators who recognize "David's genius under adversity" in the episode of Gath; see his "1 and 2 Samuel," in *The Literary Guide to the Bible*, ed. Robert Alter and Frank Kermode (Cambridge: Harvard University Press, 1987), p. 133. The editors of The New Oxford Annotated Bible with the Apocrypha, expanded edition (New York: Oxford University Press, 1977), on the other hand, note that "If David really became loyal to the Philistines, then he was a traitor to his own people; if he was not loyal to the Philistines, then he was a deceiver—so the dilemma is posed." They resolve the issue by reverting to laws of behavior not implied by this specific text: "Perhaps [David] . . . was uncertain, and waited for God's guidance. From the standpoint of Biblical theology, it was God's will that he should return and become king of Judah first, and then of all Israel" (p. 368, commentary).

8. As Robert Alter has shown, one of the essential characteristics of biblical narrative is "the repeated use of narrative analogy, through which one part of the text provides oblique commentary on another" (*Art of Biblical Narrative*, p. 21; see pp. 180–81). Alter anticipates the parallel that I draw between Michal's stratagem in 1 Samuel 19 and Rachel's in Genesis 31 (see p. 120). Similarly, David M. Gunn lists four parallels between David and Jacob, only the third of which applies to the theme under examination here; see *The Story of King David: Genre and Interpretation* (Sheffield: Journal for the Study of the Old Testament Press, 1978), p. 27. David's prominence in the long line of biblical survivalist tricksters is made most clear, I think, by the Samuel author's paralleling the incidents of his early career with the central incidents of the life of that earlier Hebrew survivor and trickster extraordinaire, Jacob. On Rachel as trickster, see Genesis 30:8, in which she tricks her sister Leah and so names her son Naphtah ("tricks").

9. The narrative emphasizes the craftiness of both maneuvers. In the first, David is "concealed" in the very cave that Saul selects in order to have privacy as he relieves himself, and "stealthily" cuts off a piece of Saul's cloak; the situation is given to him and he simply improvises upon it. In the second, however, he deliberately sneaks into Saul's camp. His ability to avoid physical confrontation with Saul is ingenious. Twice he turns potential tragedy to comedy, the narrative deflating Saul's threat in the first episode by placing him in an unkingly scatological position, and in the second by the Keystone-cops-like inefficiency of Saul's guards and their surprise upon learning that they have been tricked.

10. David is forced Hamlet-like to maneuver in a treacherous court where, Claudius-like, Saul masks his hatred of his rival. On Shakespeare's possible use of the David story as an

analogue to *Hamlet*, see Gene Edward Veith, "'Wait upon the Lord': David, *Hamlet*, and the Problem of Revenge," in *The David Myth*, pp. 70–83. David's feigning madness before Achish anticipates for Veith Hamlet's putting on an "antic disposition" before Claudius.

One might deduce that David learns to read trickery (and trickily) from Saul and Jonathan. I analyze Saul's tricks in my text above, but note the additional possibility that he is paid for his tricks not only by David but by Samuel, some readers concluding that Samuel's delay in 1 Samuel 13 and his challenge to Saul's interpretation of Yahweh's prohibition in 1 Samuel 15 are ploys to undercut Saul's political authority. With his armour-bearer, Jonathan is guided by the Lord to approach an enemy encampment by climbing up a cliff and emerging as though from the rocks, catching the camp's guard by surprise; the enemy panics, thinking that the Israelites have hidden themselves in foxholes from which they are now emerging in a surprise assault (1 Sam. 14:1–23). Jonathan later twice saves David from Saul's anger by advising him to hide (1 Sam. 19:1–7 and 20:35–40), thus proving himself a worthy tactician. A final possible teacher from whose instruction David profits is Abigail, whose shrewd move to intercept David before he can destroy Nabal and his household not only saves her people but keeps David from acting rashly (1 Sam. 25).

11. Because a small nation and ever threatened by larger and more powerful neighbors, the Israelites were historically forced to maneuver in a treacherous world and, consequently, relied more upon brains than upon brawn for survival. Disguise and deception were divinely inspired tactics which ensured survival, as when the Lord inspires David to hide in a mulberry thicket until he hears the Lord's signal, and then to fall upon the Philistines which the Lord will lead to him (2 Sam. 5:22–25). The greatest of Israel's heroes are physically her least likely; in a pattern of twinning, it is always the weaker or younger member of the pair who achieves success. As David's introductory scene with Goliath attests, he is a man of wit and strategy moreso than of strength and arms.

12. The historical problem of reading David's character stems, I believe, primarily from readers' difficulty with him in the dual role of survivalist trickster in 1 Samuel and as self-serving trickster who deserves to be himself tricked in 2 Samuel. As the victor over Goliath, the sovereign over the two kingdoms, the founder of Israel's royal line, the conqueror of the holy city of Jerusalem, and the author of the holy Psalms, David is Israel's greatest king. For Christians, in addition, he is the ancestor and a type of Jesus, as well as the model of Christian repentance; as John Donne says, "*David* was not onely a cleare Prophet of Christ himselfe, but a Prophet of every particular Christian; He foretels what I, what any shall doe, and suffer and say." But David is also responsible for the deaths of the innocent priests of Nob, is the robber baron of the hills of Carmel, and the adulterer with Bathsheba and murderer of Uriah. As T. R. Henn protests, the David story "is great literature, but it is not a moral story"; see *The Bible as Literature* (New York: Oxford University Press, 1970), p. 204. Earliest readers, as Jan Wojcik points out ("Discriminations against David's Tragedy"), uniformly sought to avert their eyes from the naked moral realism of David's tragedy. In the eighteenth century, an attempt to have his story censored happily provoked Christopher Smart to write "A Song to David" in the biblical hero's defense. As recently as 1933, a president of the Society of Biblical Literature and Exegesis protested the tendency of most later writers to "deliberately ignore most of his crimes and faults" and to focus on his virtues; see J. M. P. Smith, "The Character of David," *Journal of Biblical Literature* 52 (1933): 1–11. In *The King David Report* (1973), East German novelist Stefan Heym makes witty use of what K. Gros Louis calls in another context the "contradictions" in David's character ("Difficulty of Ruling Well," p. 17).

13. There is a general consensus that the shift in David's character takes place at this point, but readers discuss it in different terms. See, for example, R. A. Carlson, *David the Chosen King: A Traditio-Historical Approach to the Second Book of Samuel* (Stockholm: Almquist & Wiksell, 1964), who describes the story of David before his encounter with Bathsheba as "David under the Blessing" and after as "David under the Curse."

14. Fokkelman, *Narrative Art and Poetry*, pp. 76–82, offers an excellent analysis of Nathan's process of entrapment.

15. Both Fokkelman (*Narrative Art*, pp. 110–16) and Conroy (*Absalom Absalom!*, pp. 18–19, 90–92) are sensitive to patterns of repetition and reversal in these chapters.

16. Again, Fokkelman (*Narrative Art*, pp. 203–31, esp. 223–28) is the most astute commentator on this scene, as he analyzes its "concentric composition" and Hushai's role as a double agent in terms of the "concealment/appearance opposition" of the narrative in which "duality is either real or unreal" according to the context. I would add that while the narrative provocatively mentions that Jonathan and Ahimaaz escape to the house "of a man in Bahurim," it is the man's wife who assures their survival. Is she, like Abigail in 1 Samuel 25, acting counter to her husband's wishes or perhaps even oblivious to what they might be? The possibility of trickery on the domestic level makes the incident even richer.

The death of Absalom at the hands of Joab in express violation of David's command that his son not be harmed makes for a subplot in which "the trickster tricked" theme is played out in terms of the most violent destruction. In 2 Samuel 2:17–23, Joab's brother Asahel is killed by Abner after attempting to deceive him. In 3:22–27, Joab treacherously avenges his brother's death, ironically accusing Abner of deceit. Likewise, in 20:8–13, Joab treacherously murders Amasa, who had replaced him in David's counsel. Angry that Joab has killed both Amasa and Absalom, but unable to move against him in life, David plots a final trick on his deathbed, arranging for Joab's violent demise after he himself is dead (1 Kings 2:28–35). Appropriately, Joab—who is incapable of respecting his own promises and who is the perpetrator of so much cold-blooded violence—is himself betrayed and cold-bloodedly killed. His murder when hanging from the sacred horns in the temple parallels Absalom's when hanging from the tree by his hair. On David's deathbed equivocation regarding his enemies, see Gunn, *Story of David*, p. 107.

17. Fokkelman (*Narrative Art*, pp. 23–40) suggests that David falls for Ziba's deception both in haste of judgment and in gratitude for his material support at a time of crisis. Gunn astutely observes that there is "a delicate irony in the possibility that in 16:1–4 Ziba's gesture of generosity to the dispossessed David may be no less devious than David's to the dispossessed Mephibosheth" in making a place for him earlier at court (*Story of David*, p. 97). Sternberg, *Poetics of Biblical Narrative*, p. 255, likewise suggests that David's generosity to Mephibosheth was possibly a ploy to keep his political rival under his eyes. Ziba's deception of David would then be a trick that ironically repays David for having tricked Mephibosheth.

18. Fokkelman (*Narrative Art*, p. 354) suggests that the reader cannot discern from the text if Nathan and Bathsheba are manipulating the issue of succession, but Alter (*Art of Biblical Narrative*, pp. 98–100) and Gunn (*Story of David*, pp. 105–6) analyze Nathan as the stage manger of the episode. In view of the pattern that I have tried to highlight in this essay, I think it inevitable that Nathan and Bathsheba at least be seen as *attempting* to manipulate David.

Dream Interpreters in Exile:
Joseph, Daniel, and Sigmund (Solomon)

Ken Frieden
Emory University

THE biblical Joseph and Daniel have much in common with Sigmund Freud, for all three experienced the powerlessness of exile and later attained the power they lacked by interpreting dreams. Unable to control historical destiny, exilic Jews have characteristically reinterpreted events, texts, and dreams; the interpretive successes of Joseph, Daniel, and Sigmund at once reflect and defy the Jewish condition. Although Freud made every effort to distance himself from his ancient forerunners, *The Interpretation of Dreams* indirectly responds to them.

While many adepts at dream interpretation appear in the Bible, in the Talmud, in the *Sefer Chassidim*, and in other Judaic sources, Joseph, Daniel, and Sigmund have special significance. Joseph is sold into slavery by his jealous brothers, and yet saves them and the Jewish people after he gains authority in Egypt. In the Book of Daniel, Nebuchadnezzar exiles the Jews to Babylonia, and yet Daniel achieves such importance that he can influence both individual lives and Israel's collective future. Finally Sigmund Freud, also known by his Hebrew name Shlomo (or Solomon), emerges from obscurity to create an international movement. Beneath the subtle manipulation of signs and symbols, this triumvirate reveals an underlying relationship between power and interpretation.

Exile is a central theme in the Hebrew Bible, as it has been in recent Zionist thought. Especially since the fall of the Second Temple in 70 C.E., Jews have perceived themselves as a people in exile. The manifest reality of slavery and weakness has, however, been at odds with the belief that God benevolently guides the Jewish fate. Thus an intolerable discrepancy—between the promised divine covenant and the actual historical decline—inspired a vital tradition of commentary. Interpretation recreated history, and made everything seem possible; even the harshest poverty took on meaning, within a prophetic cycle of exile and return. In short, through biblical commentary and Talmudic debate, the Jewish people sought to transcend suffering and remain spiritually strong.

Leslie Fiedler has written shrewdly on the Jew as a "master of dreams." This is what Joseph's brothers call him—a *ba'al ha-chalomot*, a master of dreams or dreamer. At one point, Fiedler cites Juvenal, who, "describing the endless varieties of goods on sale in Rome . . . remarks that 'for a few pennies' one can buy any dream his heart desires 'from the Jews.' *From the Jews!*"[1] Fiedler briefly speculates on what it means for Jews to have been chronically perceived as peddlers of dreams. Bereft of land and natural resources, Jews in the Diaspora have apparently learned a kind of alchemy, transforming dreams (or texts) into interpretations, and interpretations into power.

Joseph begins as a dreamer who wanders the fields wearing a "coat of many colors" (*ketonet passim*, Gen. 37:3). He loses his way; then his brothers strip him of his special garment and throw him into a pit. Afterwards, they sell him to Ishmaelite traders who are headed for Egypt. In spite of his initial powerlessness, Joseph rises to become Pharaoh's influential adviser.

Both a dreamer and an interpreter of dreams, Joseph is the quintessential Jewish figure who attains strength from a position of utter weakness. He initially tells this dream to his brothers: "Behold, we were binding sheaves in the field, and behold, my sheaf arose and stood upright, and . . . your sheaves surrounded mine and bowed down to my sheaf" (Gen. 37:7). Psychoanalysts might view Joseph's dream as an expression of his ambition, but ancient dream interpreters customarily predicted the future through dreams. Consequently, Joseph's brothers are uneasy with the prospect his dream suggests. They mock him, saying "Shall you rule over us?" This disbelieving, rhetorical question later proves to be an interpretive prophecy, when the brothers indeed come before Joseph and bow down to him (Gen. 42:6). Their taunting language returns to haunt them.

When Joseph has his second dream, his brothers envy him, whereas his father Jacob takes its meaning more seriously and "guarded the matter" (Gen. 37:11). The second dream also suggests Joseph's special status: "Behold, I have again dreamt a dream; and behold, the sun, the moon, and eleven stars are bowing down to me" (Gen. 37:9). Jacob now interprets the dream, employing the form of a question as did Joseph's brothers: "Shall I, your mother, and your brothers come to bow down to you to the earth?" (Gen. 37:10). Although Jacob phrases this prophetic interpretation as a question, he is more willing to consider it possible than are Joseph's envious brothers. In his youth, then, Joseph is a dreamer, not an interpreter of dreams; his family members act as the interpreters.

Joseph's extraordinary rise to power occurs only after he has gone into exile. Experienced as a dreamer, Joseph begins to serve as an interpreter of dreams as well. When he has been imprisoned on the incriminating testimony of Potiphar's wife, he comes into the company of Pharaoh's cupbearer and baker. Both of Pharaoh's servants

> dreamed a dream, each man his dream on a certain night, and each man according to the interpretation of his dream. . . . Joseph came to them in the morning and saw that they were sad. And he asked Pharaoh's officers . . . "Why do you look so ill today?" And they said to him: "We have dreamed a dream and there is no interpreter of it." And Joseph said to them: "Do not interpretations belong to God? Tell me." [Gen. 40:5–8]

Joseph's self-assurance might be called either hubris or *chutzpah*. If "interpretations belong to God," why should Pharaoh's servants tell their dreams to Joseph? What authorizes him to act as God's mouthpiece? Regardless of such questions, the narrative assures that Joseph will triumph as an interpreter.

Joseph's ascent occurs only after he spends two years in prison, when Pharaoh has a dream which none of his wise men can interpret (Gen. 41:1–8) and Pharaoh's cupbearer belatedly recalls Joseph's interpretive abilities. The cupbearer tells Pharaoh that he and the baker "dreamed a dream on a certain night. . . ; [Joseph] interpreted to each man according to his dream. And it came to pass, as he interpreted to us, so it was" (Gen. 41:11–13). Here the plot thickens. What does it mean for the cupbearer to say, "as he interpreted to us, so it was"?

These words suggest two basic, and diametrically opposed, meanings. Their more obvious sense is that the interpretation accurately predicts what is destined to occur. Presumably the dreams signify imminent future events which Joseph successfully foretells. Yet rabbinic sources uncover a second level of meaning and contest the notion that a dream's prophetic meaning inheres in it. Instead, they indicate that the meaning of a dream *follows* its interpretation; interpretations can even produce meanings and cause events which were not predestined. One Talmudic opinion metaphorically asserts that "all dreams follow the mouth." This saying itself takes on diverse meanings in the mouths of interpreters. It is associated with an account of Rabbi Bana'ah, who had a dream and went to learn its meaning from twenty-four dream interpreters in Jerusalem. All of them gave different interpretations "and all of them were fulfilled."[2]

The Midrash to the Joseph narrative tells another story that illustrates the potential influence of interpretation over a dream's meaning:

A certain woman went to R. Eliezer and said to him: "I saw in my dream that the second story of my house was split." He said to her: "You will conceive a male child"; she went away and so it was. A second time she dreamed this and went to R. Eliezer, who told her: "You will give birth to a male child"; and so it was. A third time she had the same dream and came to him again but did not find him. She said to his students: "I saw in my dream that the second story of my house was split." They said to her: "You will bury your husband," and so it was. [Some time later,] R. Eliezer heard a voice of wailing and said to them: "What is this?" They told him the story, and he said to them: "You have killed a man, for is it not written, 'As he interpreted to us, so it was'?" R. Jochanan said: "All follows the interpretation."[3]

This tale characterizes one rabbinic approach to dream interpretation and may even help to explain the rabbis' associative manner of interpreting Scripture. Although not all commentaries are valid, any convincing interpretation may become significant, at least through its influence on hearers and readers. From one rabbinic standpoint, reading and interpretation are potential weapons, not means to escape from the social or political realm.

There is a direct link between Joseph's calling and the exilic condition. Only by being sold into slavery in Egypt is Joseph able to emerge as a potent interpreter of dreams. For only after being imprisoned can he victoriously interpret the dreams of his fellow prisoners and of Pharaoh. And only when Pharaoh accepts his interpretation does Joseph become a powerful leader. Exile promotes interpretation, which restores power. One way to deal with weakness is to reconceive past and future events.

The Book of Daniel in many ways alludes to the Joseph narrative.[4] Like Joseph, Daniel begins his success story in exile. The book opens by describing a moment of collective defeat: "In the third year of the reign of King Jehoiakim of Judah, King Nebuchadnezzar of Babylon came to Jerusalem and besieged it. And the Lord gave King Jehoiakim of Judah into his hand" (Dan. 1:1–2). At the time of the destruction of the First Temple in 586 B.C.E., Nebuchadnezzar plunders Jerusalem; part of his loot is Daniel, who is then taught Babylonian languages and literature. Perhaps Nebuchadnezzar anticipates a need for translators, or perhaps he merely wishes to enlarge his retinue of wise counselors. As it turns out, he educates the prophet of his own destruction.

The strongest echoes of Genesis in the Book of Daniel occur when King Nebuchadnezzar, like Pharaoh, has a disturbing dream: "in the second year of Nebuchadnezzar's reign, Nebuchadnezzar dreamed dreams, and his spirit was troubled" (Dan. 2:1). Here "his spirit was troubled" (*titpa'em rucho*) echoes a nearly identical and semantically indistinguishable phrase, *tipa'em rucho*, in Genesis 41. Troubled by dreams, both Pharaoh and King Nebuchadnezzar request interpretations from their wise men and are disappointed. Subsequently, both rulers learn of a Hebrew slave who performs dream interpretations. Both of them immediately accept the interpretation they receive and grant the interpreter immense power.

Through its language, the Daniel story underscores the conflict between human and divine strength. At several points in the story, for instance, a hand beyond human hands spells out the destruction to come. At the start of the Book of Daniel, the narrative explains that God gave King Jehoiakim of Judah into Nebuchadnezzar's hand (*b'yado*). The literal rendering of *yad* is "hand"; translators ordinarily interpret the verse to mean that God delivered Jerusalem into Nebuchadnezzar's *power*. The metaphor returns several times in the subsequent tale, for this story dramatizes the battle between opposing hands, between opposing modes of power. Nebuchadnezzar may be the strongest king on earth, yet this text asserts that he is impotent against the "hand" of God. In Nebuchadnezzar's initial dream, as retold by Daniel,

> "You, O King, did watch, and behold, a great image. This image, which was mighty and of surpassing brightness, stood before you, and its form was awesome. The head of the image was of fine gold, its breast and arms of silver, its belly and thighs of bronze, its legs of iron, and its feet part iron and part clay. As you watched, a stone was hewn out, *not by hands*, and struck the image on its feet of iron and clay and crushed them. Then the iron, clay, bronze, silver, and gold were crushed, and became like chaff of the summer threshing floors; and the wind carried them away, so that no trace of them could be found." [Dan. 2:31–35; emphasis added]

Nebuchadnezzar's dream image is destroyed by a stone that is cut out "not by hands," but by some mysterious, superhuman force (which Homer might have called by the name *daimon*). Again, the image of a hand suggests power, and the description of an action undertaken "not by hands" implies that divine guidance is at work.

Later, Nebuchadnezzar tries to improve on his dream by building a statue of solid gold. When three children of Israel refuse to bow down to Nebuchadnezzar's golden statue, the king threatens to throw them into a furnace; "and who is the god," he rages, "that will deliver you from my hands (*min-yadai*)?" (Dan. 3:15). Daniel's friends answer that their God will deliver them from Nebuchadnezzar's hand. A transcendent force challenges human will when God's hand appears to annul Nebuchadnezzar's power.

Belshazzar, one of Nebuchadnezzar's successors, also learns of his doom when it is spelled out by a supernatural hand. During a blas-phemous debauch, in which he desecrates the vessels that Nebuchad-nezzar had plundered from the Temple, Belshazzar suddenly becomes terrified: "In the same hour, the figure of a hand in human form appeared" (Dan. 5:5). This enigmatic hand produces the proverbial "writing on the wall" which Daniel interprets as a prophecy of the king's destruction. Again, a hand that transcends the visible world points the way, and the interpreter claims to decipher the message by means of his special relationship to its divine source.

After passing through an apprenticeship in exile, Joseph and Daniel learn the ways of interpretation. Ostensibly weak, these interpreters nevertheless write the Jewish people into a new position of strength. Pharaoh and Nebuchadnezzar exert immense control over the waking world, but they cannot fully master the realms of imagination, dream, and sleep. Prophecy appears to be at work, and Jewish interpreters claim to grasp an otherwise ineffable power.

Sigmund Freud did not agree that higher powers are at work in dreams; he maintained that they arise from deeper processes of the mind. Nonetheless, as a dream interpreter he stood very much in the line of Joseph and Daniel. In *The Interpretation of Dreams*, Freud rejects Joseph's intuitive methods, yet he admits that he identifies with him.[5] His analogous position is most evident in one of his own dreams, which reveals even more than he was willing to acknowledge.

On about 6 January 1898, Freud reported what may be termed "the Passover dream." Here, as in the stories of Joseph and Daniel, Freud's activity as dreamer and interpreter is associated with his ex-ilic condition. Although Freud was an assimilated Viennese physi-cian, he was aware of his marginal position as a Jew and was sensitive to the current anti-Semitism. By analyzing Freud's Passover dream in ways that Freud himself neglects, we discover that it aptly sums up the cyclical history of Jewish servitude and liberation, exile and redemption.

The Interpretation of Dreams explains the immediate source of Freud's dream: a play by the Zionist leader Theodor Herzl, entitled *The New Ghetto*, which Freud was among the first to see in Vienna, possibly on 5 January 1898. Freud indirectly expounds this play's intellectual content when he writes that it induced the dream's manifestly Zionist "concern for the future of children, to whom one cannot give a father-land; concern about educating them so that they may become inde-pendent [*freizügig*]" (*Td* 427/*ID* 478). Like Joseph and Daniel in Egypt and Babylonia, Freud and Herzl in Austria anticipated poten-tial threats to future generations. Moreover, Freud's dream and commentary, like the interpretive activities of Joseph and Daniel, respond to weakness.

The dream has its setting in Rome. Despite this specific geographical location, Freud's imagination alludes to several episodes from Jewish history. His report of the dream begins with a crisis situation:

> As a result of certain events in the city of Rome, it is necessary to evacuate the children, which also takes place. The scene is then in front of a gateway, a double door in the ancient style (the Porta Romana in Siena, as I am already aware during the dream). I sit on the edge of a fountain and am very dejected, close to tears. A female person—an attendant or nun—brings the two boys out and delivers them to their father, who was not myself. The older of the two is clearly my eldest; I do not see the face of the other one. The woman who brought out the boy requests a kiss from him in parting. She is remarkable for having a red nose. The boy refuses her the kiss, but while reaching out his hand in parting says [to his Christian attendant]: *Auf Geseres*, and to both of us (or to one of us): *Auf Ungeseres*. I have the notion that the latter signifies a preference. [*Td* 426/*ID* 478]

Freud's initial association to this dream is Herzl's play. His second association is a biblical psalm, which Freud himself cites: "By the waters of Babylon, we sat down and wept." This is one of the most famous expressions of exilic emotion in Hebrew Scripture, drawn from Luther's translation of the first verse of Psalm 137. It also resonates with the Book of Daniel, which similarly takes place after the fall of Jerusalem and during the Babylonian captivity.

The most obscure moment in Freud's dream involves his invented words *Auf Geseres* and *Auf Ungeseres*. His eldest son employs these words rather than the expected words of parting, *Auf Wiedersehen*. Freud wishes to show that, despite their superficial meaninglessness, these phrases actually bear significant messages from the unconscious. Freud's own rather forced interpretation relates the dream to technical questions concerning his psychological theories. In view of the initial scene of exile and Freud's associations to the Zionist leader Herzl and to Psalm 137, however, the dream may also be understood as searching for a solution to the so-called Jewish question.

To grasp the Passover dream's significance, we should recall that Freud was himself raised with the assistance of a Christian governess, and that before his marriage he considered (and decided against) conversion to Christianity. Freud's dream confronts the tense Jewish-Christian relations in fin de siècle Vienna by placing him in a state of crisis and his sons in custody of a Christian attendant. The dream enacts Freud's response to this scenario, which more broadly refers to the disadvantaged standing of Jews in Europe.

Freud's further associations bring the Judaic background to the fore. Freud indicates that the "nonsense" words *Auf Geseres* and *Auf Ungeseres* accoustically remind him of a central symbol of the Exodus from Egypt, unleavened bread (*ungesäuertes Brot*). "During their hasty departure from *Egypt*," Freud emphasizes, "the children of Israel did not have time to let their dough rise, and to this day, in memory of this, eat unleavened bread at Easter-time" (*Td* 427/*ID* 479). First a note about language. Freud never uses a Judaic term for "Passover" (Hebrew *pesach* or German *Passah*), but rather employs the euphemism "at Easter-time." Despite this disguise, his association of the dream with Passover evidently alludes to Jewish exile. Passover is the holiday during which Jews reexperience the Egyptian servitude and bondage under a "new king," before liberation by Moses. Freud's dream alludes to the exilic condition of Daniel in Babylonia and of Joseph in Egypt, and recalls their successes as interpreters. His numerous verbal associations to this dream may be summarized as follows:

	Auf Geseres	*Auf Ungeseres*
Aramaic/ Hebrew	*gezeres* (decrees)	Non-
Yiddish	*gezeres* (decrees, misfortunes)	
Viennese German	*machen (ein) Geseres* (to make a fuss)	
German	*gesäuertes Brot* (leavened bread)	*ungesäuertes Brot* (unleavened bread)

One of Freud's unconscious wishes, expressed indirectly by his dream, was to alleviate the modern Jewish exile. The language of Freud's dream report reveals a further link to Judaic experience. Freud recognizes that the mysterious word *Geseres* comes to him by way of Yiddish, following Aramaic and Hebrew sources. He writes that he has received information from rabbinic scholars who told him that the word *Geseres* signifies "imposed sufferings, doom" (*Td* 427/*ID* 478). More accurately, it refers to anti-Semitic decrees, pronouncements against the Jews. The most familiar anti-Jewish decrees in Europe were motivated by "blood libels," in turn associated with the celebration of Passover. In 1421, for instance, the Jews were expelled from Vienna after being accused of ritual murder; this was called the "Wiener Geserah."[6] Freud occasionally claimed that he had forgotten the Hebrew he learned as a child, yet he recognizes that the *Geseres* and *Ungeseres* in his dream have their roots in Hebrew and Yiddish.

Given the linguistic associations, then, Freud's dream verbally imposes counterdecrees on the Christian attendant, while it revokes such decrees in relation to himself. In the dream, his son's words *Auf Geseres* and *Auf Ungeseres* suggest this fuller meaning: "Upon you— nun—*Geseres*, decrees and misfortune. Upon you—father—*Ungeseres*, the annulment of decrees and misfortune." Reversing the familiar anti-Semitic decrees, Freud's son affirms Judaic traditions by employing a phrase that resonates with Hebrew, Aramaic, and Yiddish. Once again, language is the medium of Jewish self-assertion. The dream places Freud's eldest son in a position to establish his continuity with Judaic traditions, recalling the Passover ritual with its references to harsh decrees and its four traditional questions ascribed to four sons.[7] The verb *gazar* actually occurs in the Passover Haggadah, which was the one Jewish ritual maintained in the Vienna home of Freud's parents.[8] Hence the Passover dream suggests the resolution of a problem, the future of Freud's children. In the midst of difficulties, like those caused by the Viennese anti-Semitism of Karl Lueger after 1897, Freud's eldest son can respond with an indirect affirmation of Judaism.[9]

Freudian psychoanalysis provides methods which uncover hidden meaning beneath the surface of our experiences; it presupposes that appearances are deceptive. Interpretation acts as a mode of power, capable of undermining and overcoming the manifest reality. Hence Freud's implicit answer to weakness and exile was interpretation, which potentially redefined the roles. As we have seen in the stories of Joseph and Daniel, even a captive slave can rise to prominence if granted the authority to interpret dreams. Incidentally, in Freudian practice the dream text plays much the same role as does Scripture in rabbinic thought. Freud himself comments that, in general, he treats the dream "as a holy text."[10]

While Freud for the most part chose assimilation as his answer to the "Jewish question," he never denied that he was Jewish, and sometimes even proudly asserted his difference.[11] His residual malaise, a discomfort over the Jewish condition, was most evident in his uneasy relationship to Rome. Freud postponed his planned trip to Rome for many years and was painfully ambivalent toward its cultural wealth, because he could not forget the anti-Semitic decrees promulgated by the Romans. One scholar has even referred to this ambivalence as Freud's "Rome neurosis."[12] When Freud finally reached Rome, the famed and feared center of the Christian world, he visited the most highly charged monument for a Jew who is aware of his collective history: the Arch of Titus. This monument commemorates the triumphal march of Titus in 70 C.E., leading the Jews out of the fallen Jerusalem and into slavery. After visiting the site, Freud sent a picture postcard on which he expressed his sentiments to his friend Karl Abraham:

"Der Jude übersteht's!"

which means

"The Jew withstands it!"

"It" is the history of exile. Freud defiantly boasts that he has succeeded in withstanding the many decrees against the Jews.

Separated by centuries, Joseph, Daniel, and Sigmund (Solomon) were all dream interpreters in exile. All of them experienced weakness, and all found a way to assert themselves. Freud survived his struggle against a position of impotence, in part, by unconsciously allying himself with his ancient forerunners Joseph and Daniel. Even when Freud disavowed his precursors and strained to assert his independence, he attested to their continuing authority. If *they* were able to rise to power by interpreting dreams, so could he. And so he did. Freud was far closer to the biblical tradition of dream interpretation than he cared or even dared to admit.

Notes

This paper, presented to the Religion Department of Florida State University on 11 March 1988, contains a synopsis of some central motifs in my book *Freud's Dream of Interpretation* (Albany: State University of New York Press, 1990). A shorter version formed part of the session on the Bible as literature at the College English Association Convention in April 1988. I have slightly modified existing translations of the Bible, the Talmud, the Midrash, and Freud's works on the basis of the original sources. Abbreviations for Freud's works refer to: *GW*—Sigmund Freud, *Gesammelte Werke*, 18 vols. (London: Imago, 1940–68); *ID*—Sigmund Freud, *The Interpretation of Dreams*, trans. James Strachey (New York: Avon, 1965); *SE*—*The Standard Edition of the Complete Psychological Works of Sigmund Freud*, 24 vols., ed. James Strachey (London: Hogarth Press, 1953–74); *Td*—Sigmund Frued, *Die Traumdeutung*, in the *Studienausgabe*, vol. 2, ed. Alexander Mitscherlich, Angela Richards, and James Strachey (Frankfurt: S. Fischer, 1972).

1. See Leslie A. Fiedler's "Master of Dreams: The Jew in a Gentile World," in *To the Gentiles* (New York: Stein & Day, 1972), p. 176.

2. The Babylonian Talmud, Berakhot 55b–56a.

3. Bereshit Rabbah 89:8. This translation is based on the second critical edition of Chanoch Albeck, *Bereshit Rabbah* (Jerusalem: Wahrman Books, 1965). An English translation is contained in *Midrash Rabbah*, 3d ed., ed. and trans. H. Freedman and Maurice Simon (London: Soncino, 1983), 2:825.

4. Concerning the story of Daniel as a rewriting of the Joseph story, see Shemaryahu Talmon, "Daniel," in *The Literary Guide to the Bible*, ed. Robert Alter and Frank Kermode (Cambridge: Harvard University Press, 1987), pp. 350–52.

5. See *Td* 117–18, 466n/*ID* 129, 522n. On Freud's identification with Joseph, see Leonard Shengold, "Freud and Joseph," in *Freud and His Self-Analysis*, ed. Mark Kanzer and Jules Glenn (New York: Aronson, 1979), pp. 67–86, and William J. McGrath, *Freud's Discovery of Psychoanalysis: The Politics of Hysteria* (Ithaca: Cornell University Press, 1986), chap. 1.

6. See *The New Standard Jewish Encyclopedia*, ed. Cecil Roth and Geoffrey Wigoder (Jerusalem: Massada, 1970), entry "Vienna," p. 1924.

7. Another relevant association might be the tenth plague inflicted upon the Egyptians, the plague of the firstborn (Exod. 11:4–5), which followed the Egyptian decrees against male children (Exod. 1:16,22).

8. Later in life, Freud's children became members of Zionist youth organizations.

9. For pertinent analyses of Freud's dream, see Peter Loewenberg's "A Hidden Zionist Theme in Freud's 'My Son, the Myops . . .' Dream," *Journal of the History of Ideas* 31 (1970): 129–32, and compare Avner Falk's "Freud and Herzl," *Contemporary Psychoanalysis* 14 (1978): 357–87.

10. Freud writes that "what according to the opinion of other authors is supposed to be an arbitrary improvisation, hurriedly brought together in the embarrassment of the moment, this we treated as a holy text" (*Td* 492–93/*ID* 552).

11. Freud discusses his relationship to Judaism in his address to the B'nai Brith Society (*GW* 17: 51–53/*SE* 20:273–74). Among other passages, see Freud's *Autobiographical Study* (*GW* 14:33–35/*SE* 19:7–9), his letter to the *Jüdische Presszentrale Zürich* (*GW* 14:556/*SE* 19:291), and his prefaces to the Hebrew editions of *Introductory Lectures on Psychoanalysis* and *Totem and Taboo*.

12. See Carl E. Schorske, *Fin-de-Siècle Vienna: Politics and Culture* (New York: Knopf, 1980), pp. 189–93.

Charts of Biblical Texts

Genesis According to Michelangelo

Aaron Lichtenstein
The City University of New York

THE Sistine ceiling remains a revelation that is hardly to be matched; these paintings are like the thunderous manifestations of a new force compared to the works of the preceding generations." So wrote the art historian Heinrich Wolfflin in his *Die Klassische Kunst* (1899) about Michelangelo's rendition of the biblical creation still visible in Rome.[1]

Do these powerful artistic statements emerge directly from the artist's Bible-reading? Michelangelo's own testimony, in a letter to Giovan Francesco Fattuci dated December 1523, indicates that he was granted a commission to "make whatever I wanted, whatever would please me there."[2] Beyond this, we can deduce Michelangelo's readiness to rely on his reading from the way he shaped an earlier work, his sculptured *Moses* of 1516. The artist placed a pair of stubby horns on Moses' head because of what he read in his own Bible, the Vulgate, for Exodus 34:29:

> Cumque descenderet Moyses de monte Sinai tenebat duas tabulas testimonii, et ignorabat quod cornuta esset facies sua ex consortio sermonis Domini. Videntes autem Aaron et filii Israel cornutam Moysi faciem, timuerunt prope accedere.

The Biblica Vulgata here conveys that the countenance of Moses was horned or that he had sprouted horns. On the other hand, the original text translates into, "the skin of Moses' face shone," or "Moses' countenance radiated," or "the flesh of Moses' face flashed lights." The common visual expression for this effect is the halo, painted around the heads of angelic figures. But the *Moses* by Michelangelo has horns as a result of what the artist read, or was taught to read, in his Latin Bible—of which he was an avid student.[3]

Among the panels of the Sistine Chapel, the creation of Adam stands out in its power and artistry. What are the sources that projected onto the inner eye of Michelangelo that vision of *Creazione Umana* which he transferred to fresco? If the artist had limited himself to the account in Genesis, the *Creation of Man* would not have turned out as it did. Either Adam would have appeared emerging from the ground at God's behest, in exact parallel to the *Creation of Eve* panel, or God would have been shown puffing the spirit of life into Adam. For the Genesis account reads, "God created man dust from the earth, and He blew into his nostrils a living soul" (2 : 7). Where then did Michelangelo get the idea of God having made man, not with his breath, but with his touch? As seen in *Creazione Umana*, God's finger is close to Adam's, but clearly the fingers are not touching. This leaves us with two alternatives: to think of the fingers either as already having met or as about to meet. The first alternative is not tenable. The sweep of God's cloak and the direction in which his entourage is facing indicate that God is still advancing, not that he is retreating after having touched Adam into being. But the second alternative carries with it this puzzle: If God is still advancing and the fingers have not touched, how is it that Adam is depicted as already having been created?[4]

Our thesis is that in rendering the *Creazione Umana* as he did, Michelangelo was influenced by the first chapter of Jeremiah. This section tells how God elected and inspired Jeremiah with a touch of his hand. It includes mention of Jeremiah's birth, for which the term "creation" is used; thus Michelangelo might easily have associated the "beginning" of Jeremiah with the beginning of man. Jeremiah 1 : 4 reads:

> The word of God came to me saying, "Before I created you in the womb I knew you; and before you were born I sanctified you; I made you a prophet unto the nations." And I said, "Woe, Lord God! Behold I know not how to speak, for I am but a boy." And God said, "Do not say, 'I am but a boy,' for wherever I shall send you, you will go; and whatever I shall command you, you will speak. . . . ." Then god extended His hand and He touched it to my mouth. God said to me, "Behold I have put My words into your mouth."

The parallel between the election of Jeremiah and the creation of man suggests a new interpretation of the *Creazione Umana*. What Michelangelo meant to portray here may be the creation of man's soul, that is, the introduction of the human spirit into Adam's body which has already been brought into existence. In Jeremiah's case it was with a touch of his hand that God filled the prophet with spirituality; just so Michelangelo has God inject the human soul into Adam with a touch of his finger. This implies that two distinct acts of creation were involved in the emergence of Adam. Michelangelo's source for this approach would have been the Genesis verse: "God created man dust from the earth, and [then] He blew into his nostrils a living soul." This verse portrays the infusion of Adam's soul coming later and apart from the creation of his body. Michelangelo mingled the Jeremiah source with the Genesis source in arriving at his visualization of the *Creazione Umana*, and if one would have asked the artist to indicate which moment of biblical history he had captured in fresco, his answer would have been, after "God made man dust from the earth," and just before "He blew into his nostrils a living soul." The duality of body and soul was not a concept unfamiliar to Michelangelo. On the contrary, he felt at home with the idea and believed in it. That this is so we can deduce from the *en passant* fashion in which Michelangelo cites the duality concept in a sonnet dedicated to Tommaso de' Cavalieri:

> Veggo nel tuo bel viso, Signor mio,
> Quel che narrar mal puossi in questa vita:
> L'anima, della carne ancor vestita,
> Con esso e' gia' pui' volte ascesa a Dio.[5]

> I see in your goodly face, my lord,
> What hardly can be said of existence:
> The soul still clothed by the body,
> So accompanied ascends verily unto God.

We began our analysis of *Creazione Umana* by raising the following problem: since the fingers of God and Adam have not yet met, by what acceptable device does Michelangelo show Adam as already existing? This problem can now be solved, for Adam's body can be shown since it has previously been created. What *Creazione Umana* depicts is not the physical creation of the human species, but the creation of the humanity in man. This new understanding is not distant from that offered in 1553 by Ascanio Condivi, Michelangelo's confidant, that God is shown with his arm and hand outstretched, as if imparting to Adam wisdom as to what is right and wrong.[6] The expression on the face of Adam is uninspired, even dull. The body is that of a beautiful, powerful adult, but the facial expression lacks vitality and has a passive quality. Vitality, wisdom, and spirituality are exactly the elements which God, by his touch, is about to introduce into the body of Adam.

Scrutiny of a detail may further substantiate our contention. In *Creazione Umana* Michelangelo shows Adam clearly uncircumcised. The artist is known to have given attention to such details. For example, David is sculptured distinctly circumcised, after the fashion of Jewish men. However, in the *Creation of Eve* the artist presents us with a circumcised Adam! Furthermore, Michelangelo has seemingly drawn special attention to the male organ in *Creazione Umana*. Adam's

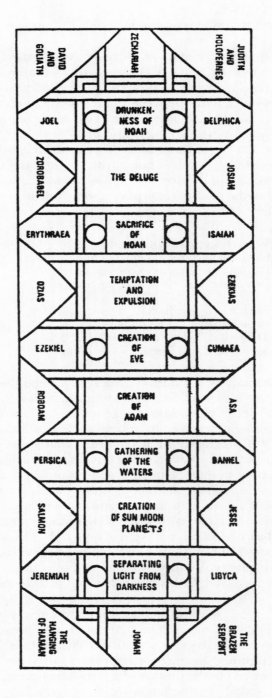

Figure 1. Ceiling of the Sistine Chapel, 1508–1512

slouching position is such that the male organ appears at the approximately center of the figure. The lines of the arms, legs, and torso lend further emphasis to this part of Adam's body. What is more, Adam's position is essentially the same as that of the drunken, exposed Noah, and surely in the *Drunkenness of Noah* Michelangelo intended to illustrate the verse, "he became uncovered in his tent; and Ham, the father of Canaan, saw the nakedness of his father" (Gen. 9:12). Why should the artist wish to draw our attention to Adam's organ? Michelangelo may be calling attention to the fact that he was rendering Adam uncircumcised in *Creazione Umana*. In biblical terms, circumcision implies sanctification of the body and the introduction of spirituality into flesh. As a student of the Bible, Michelangelo was undoubtedly aware of this connotation, evident in verses such as: "God will circumcise your heart and the hearts of your children, so that you can love God" (Deut. 30:6). And "Circumcise yourselves for God, remove the foreskins of your hearts" (Jer. 4:4).[7] In rendering Adam uncircumcised, the artist may be suggesting that the Adam before us is body without soul, man prior to his being invested with spirituality; that the inauguration of the human spirit, not the physical creation of man, is the subject of the panel. Thus, in the *Creation of Eve*, where the presence of spirituality is not in question, Adam is seen circumcised.[8]

Our thesis carries with it some significance for establishing the unity of the Sistine ceiling histories. To force the nine histories into a unified theme is not an easy task. Some consider the upper four panels a unit in that they depict moments of moral crisis: sin, punishment, thanksgiving; and the lower four panels, which concern creation, are seen as having Genesis as the only unifying factor.[9] This interpretation is weak in that it burdens the *Creation of Eve*, the odd middle panel, with serving as transition from the creation group (there is the element of creation in the Eve panel) to the morality group. The domestic nature of the Eve panel supposedly qualifies it for association with the morality group, or perhaps the artist sees woman as central to all moral issues. This interpretation is hardly convincing. Then, too, such an understanding of the *Capella Sistina* unity implies that Michelangelo arbitrarily divided the center strip of the ceiling between two subjects, and that he established such a division not on the sound basis of a visual or technical separation, but on purely intellectual and informational grounds.

However, if we grant that the subject of *Creazione Umana* is the creation of Adam's soul, we can view the ceiling not as divided between two groups of panels, but in a single progression as follows: First the artist presents God in three wondrous acts of creation. The point is to underline the unlimited power of God, or his Godliness. Next the artist shows God imparting of his Godliness to Adam. The remaining scenes demonstrate what man—coupled with Eve[10]—makes of his spirituality, how he invites misery through sin and immorality, but how, on occasion, he will treat his God-given soul to an act of thanksgiving. The misarrangement of the *Sacrifice of Noah*, which surprisingly precedes the *Deluge* scene, seems to convey that the artist intended the sequence to have a climax. This break from the Bible's chronology yields a subgroup comprising the large *Deluge*, flanked by the small *Drunkenness of Noah* and *Sacrifice of Noah*. Humankind's continuing moral vacillation may have been Michelangelo's parting idea, then.

But Condivi terms the seventh scene the *Sacrifice of Abel and Cain*, not the *Sacrifice of Noah*. Scholars dismiss Condivi's identification out of hand, as does Charles Seymour with a glib, "Condivi did not know the true subject."[11] This is an astounding accusation to make, directed as it is to the man who learned whatever he knew about the ceiling from the artist himself, even if the writing came thirty years later. Secondly, the internal evidence sustains Condivi. The foreground has Abel the shepherd preparing the sacrifice of "the firstlings of his flock and the fat thereof," assisted by three comrades. The middle ground shows Cain or his assistant with stalks "bringing the fruit of the ground as offering." The background then has a venerable Adam and Eve presiding over the sacrificial fire, disputing with or about the rejected Cain, "who was very wroth" (Gen. 4:1–5). But nothing about the portrayal corresponds to details that Michelangelo would have read in Genesis 8 regarding Noah's sacrifice. Finally, by entitling this scene the *Sacrifice of Abel and Cain*, the nine visual histories follow biblical chronology, reasserting our finding that Michelangelo was directed by his Bible-reading in his portrayals of biblical subjects.

It was shortly before Michelangelo's time that, in England, another example of art based on text emerged: the Ellesmere illuminated *Canterbury Tales* manuscript, preserved today at the Huntington Library in California. Alongside the *Canterbury Tales* text, some unknown artist or artists had expertly provided visual expression for Chaucer's storytelling characters. In the most recent study of the Ellesmere miniatures, Martin Stevens has judged the manuscript as reflecting a purposeful intent to represent visually the character nuances in the tales. That is, a rendition impulsed by what the words conjured for the mind's eye of the artist. This, in opposition to a rendition that would amount to a gloss of the text.[12] In Italy as in England, in sacred art as in secular, in massive form as in miniature, painting from narrative is a phenomenon whose time had come.

Notes

1. See P. Murray's translation, *Classical Art* (London: Phaidon, 1968), p. 51.

2. Translated in Robert J. Clements, *Michelangelo—A Self-Portrait* (New York: New York University Press, 1968), p. 50.

3. Acknowledgments are due to Dr. David Fink and Professor Joshua Finkel for helpful discussions on this point. See Ruth Mellinkoff, *The Horned Moses in Medieval Art and Thought* (Berkeley: University of California Press, 1970).

4. Also untenable is a third alternative: that God is shown as he is about to create, but that Adam is shown as just having been created. Such a disunified presentation cannot be imputed to the artist. Of course, in the *Drunkenness of Noah* Michelangelo does present Noah in his intoxicated state and also, anachronistically, places him outside the door planting his vineyard. Here this is an acceptable device, for the two Noahs are on different visual planes and are not interacting. The same point applies to the double exposure in the *Expulsion from Eden* panel, where Adam and Eve are displayed first eating of the forbidden fruit and then, on the second half of the divided plane, leaving the Garden of Eden. But in the *Creation of Man*, there must be an interaction between God and man, and Michelangelo places them on the same plane. The dynamic tension so powerfully evident in the near-touch of the fingers confirms that the figures of God and Adam are unified in terms of time and visual plane. See Robert J. Clements, "Eye, Mind, and Hand in Michelangelo's Poetry," *PMLA* (Sept. 1975): 324–36.

5. Michelangelo Buonarroti, Sonnet No. 64, in *Rime* (Milano: Rizzoli, 1954); my translation. The parallel between Jeremiah's election and *Creazione Umana* is not exact: Jeremiah is touched on the lip, Adam on the finger. Perhaps it was a consideration of composition which moved the artist to avoid placing God's hand to Adam's mouth, just as it was probably an artistic consideration which prompted Michelangelo to draw on the Jeremiah source instead of staying with the original Genesis picture of God breathing a soul into Adam. Or perhaps Michelangelo felt that a juxtaposition of fingers better characterizes Adam's whole being as about to take on aspects of God's essential being, whereas in Jeremiah's case a hand-to-mouth action best depicts the initiation of a prophetic message, "Behold I have put my words in your mouth."

6. *Vita di Michelangelo*, trans. A. S. Wohl and cited in Charles Seymour, *Michelangelo: The Sistine Chapel Ceiling* (New York: Norton, 1972), p. 116. Regarding a further detail, I received the following in a letter from Professor Herbert Basser (Toronto): "The Finger of God in early Christian writers implies the Holy Spirit. So in St. Irenaeus (J. P. Smith, editor), 'Proof of the Apostolic Teaching,' *Ancient Christian Writers*. London: Longmans Green & Co., 1952, chapter 26 and notes." Seymour too (*Michelangelo*, p. 93) associates the finger with the deepest elements of church tradition, and he cites Augustine's "De spiritu et littera," wherein the finger of God is identified with the Holy Spirit. But Condivi, whose account may have been dictated by Michelangelo, does not mention this idea.

7. Recent efforts at reconstructing the Chapel as it looked in 1500, and as Michelangelo would have seen it, indicate that one of a half-dozen wall paintings illustrated the circumcision of Moses' son Eliezer, under a *titulus* reading: OSERVATIO ANTIQUE REGENERATIONIS A MOISE PER CIRCONCISIONEM. See Seymour, *Michelangelo*, pp. 95, 71.

8. Talmudic tradition has it that Adam emerged circumcised; see "Ethics of Rabbi Nathan," The Babylonian Talmud, chap. 2; also that Adam was created resembling a twenty-year-old man. Michelangelo's Adam is strikingly close to twenty, but it is unlikely that Michelangelo had access, even indirectly, to Talmudic sources. See François Secret, "Notes sur les hébraïsants chrétiens de la Renaissance," *Sefarad* 22 (1962): 107–27.

9. Whether the panels are to be viewed top-to-bottom or bottom-to-top is the subject of scholarly debate.

10. In our view we need not attribute to the Eve panel an important transitional role, a role

difficult to assign to one of the small-sized panels. For us the Eve panel serves solely to depict the entrance of woman onto the world stage.

11. Seymour, *Michelangelo*, p. 117. For a different interpretation see: Esther Gordon Dotson, "An Augustinian Interpretation of Michelangelo's Sistine Ceiling," *The Art Bulletin* 61 (1979): 223–56.

12. Martin Stevens, "The Ellesmere Miniatures as Illustrations of Chaucer's *Canterbury Tales*," *Studies in Iconography* 7–8 (1981–82): 113–34: "The illustrations of the Ellesmere MS. are very much ahead of the times in their effort to provide a direct visual representation of the literary personages that they portray . . . a surprisingly close reading of the text proper, making every effort to reflect the details that Chaucer provided and thus creating individual portraits rather than types" (p. 113). The Huntington dates the Ellesmere manuscript ca. 1400, the Chaucer Society ca. 1420, and by 1500 its first owner had died.

Redactional Structuring in the Joseph Story: Genesis 37–50

Gary A. Rendsburg
Cornell University

THE trend in biblical criticism in recent years has been toward treating large sections of the Hebrew Bible as unified wholes. For when all is said and done, no matter which school of source criticism one adheres to, we are still left with the Hebrew text as we have it. Instead of dividing up the text into its microscopic parts, scholars have been pulling back the lens and viewing the text as a macroscopic whole. The biblical book which started the move to fragmentation, the Book of Genesis, has not been immune from this trend.

Several important studies should be mentioned here at the outset. In 1975 Michael Fishbane published a seminal article on the Jacob cycle (25:19–35:22),[1] in which he showed that the various stories concerning the third patriarch are all duplicates of one another, aligned in chiastic order. That is to say, the first and last episodes share the same motifs and concerns, as do the second and next-to-last episodes, etc. Moreover, the relationship between these matching units is highlighted by a series of shared vocabulary items, or theme-words.

In 1980 Jack M. Sasson wrote a similar work on the primeval history (1:1–11:9).[2] Here, too, there are matching units, again sharing related themes and various theme-words. In this instance, the individual units are not in chiastic structure, rather in parallel columns. Thus, the first and sixth episodes are paired, the second and seventh, the third and eighth, the fourth and ninth, the fifth and tenth. Sasson referred to the literary schema used by the compiler as "redactional structuring" (a term which is borrowed herein) and noted that "the episodes culled from Hebraic traditions of early history were conceived in two matching sequences."[3]

The groundwork for redactional structuring in a third portion of Genesis had actually been laid years earlier by Umberto Cassuto.[4] This savant noted that the Abraham cycle (12:1–22:19) also consisted of a series of episodes which, to a great extent, duplicate and parallel each other, again in chiastic order. Cassuto did not live to complete his work on Genesis, so there is no way to determine if he also would have noted theme-words linking the paired units. Nahum M. Sarna had noticed, apparently independently of Cassuto, some of the same structure.[5] He did point out shared vocabulary items, at least for the two *lek lĕkā* ("go forth") stories, the call at Haran (12:1–9) and the Akedah (22:1–19).

Once it was determined that the first three cycles of Genesis contain a purposeful literary structure, the search for such a pattern in the one remaining cycle, the Joseph story, became an obvious task. The Joseph story, by all accounts, is the most unified narrative in Genesis, perhaps in the entire Bible. As great a source critic as Gerhard von Rad described it as "an organically constructed narrative,"[6] and Sarna spoke of its "unparalleled continuity of narrative."[7]

Accordingly, if Sasson, Cassuto, and Fishbane are correct about the literary structures of the first three cycles in Genesis, it should not be surprising to find a similar system operating in the Joseph story. This holds not only for the chapters dealing with Joseph directly, but for the material in which he is absent or nominally present as well. I refer, of course, to the interruptions of 38:1–30 and 49:1–28. The Judah and Tamar episode and Jacob's testament are interludes which break up the telling of the Joseph story, but they nevertheless have been skillfully worked into the redactional plan of the cycle.

The structure of the Joseph story is as follows:

A   Joseph and his brothers, Jacob and Joseph part (37:1–36)

B   Interlude: Joseph not present (38:1–30)

C   Reversal: Joseph guilty, Potiphar's wife innocent (39:1–23)

D   Joseph hero of Egypt (40:1–41:57)

E   Two trips to Egypt (42:1–43:34)

F   Final test (44:1–34)

F′   Conclusion of test (45:1–28)

E′   Two tellings of migration to Egypt (46:1–47:12)

D′   Joseph hero of Egypt (47:13–27)

C′   Reversal: Ephraim firstborn, Manasseh secondborn (47:28–48:22)

B′   Interlude: Joseph nominally present (49:1–28)

A′   Joseph and his brothers, Jacob and Joseph part (49:29–50:26)

    The cycle builds through six episodes, A–F, leading to the climax of the tale, and then concludes with six parallel episodes, F′–A′. The structure is a chiastic one, just as Cassuto proposed for the Abraham cycle and as Fishbane demonstrated for the Jacob cycle.[8] The themes and motifs of the first half of the cycle are repeated or echoed in the second half. Moreover, just as Fishbane showed in the Jacob cycle, the relationship between any two matching units is cemented by the inclusion of shared vocabulary items, or theme-words.

    These theme-words can be of several types. The most obvious are those where the same word is used in matching episodes. Others are different words or, to use more precise grammatical terminology, different inflections, from the same root. Some theme-words can be like-sounding words which derive from separate roots, and still others may be merely similar in meaning or share a similar connotation. What links all of these variations is the ability to connect, if the writer or compiler has achieved his goal, the different units of the cycle.

    Let us progress to a unit-by-unit discussion where all of this is more clearly seen.

A Joseph and his brothers, Jacob and Joseph part (37:1–36)

A′ Joseph and his brothers, Jacob and Joseph part (49:29–50:26)

    Unit A establishes the major conflict of the tale, the conflict between Joseph and his brothers. This conflict will not be fully resolved until the story's end, unit A′. The action of A is repeated in A′ in two major ways. In both sections Joseph is alone with his brothers, their father Jacob not part of the scene. Also, in A father and son part due to the faked death of the latter, and in A′ father and son part due to the actual death of the former.

    Twelve theme-words link the episodes still further:

    1)   In 37:1 we read that Jacob lived *bĕ'ereṣ mĕgûrê 'ābîw* "in the

land of his father's sojourning"; and in 49:29 the patriarch instructs Joseph *qibrû 'ôtî 'el 'ăbôtāy* "bury me with my fathers."

2) *bĕ'ereṣ kĕnā'an* "in the land of Canaan" occurs in 37:1; and *'arṣāh kĕnā'an* "to the land of Canaan" occurs in 50:13.

3) The word *rā'āh* "evil" appears three times in each unit, in 37:2, 37:20, 37:33, and in 50:15, 50:17, 50:20.

4) *'ăbîhem* "their father" is also prominent in both A and A', occurring in 37:2, 37:4, 37:12, 37:32, and in 49:28, 50:15.

5) In 37:4 we read *wayyir'û 'ehāw* "his brothers saw"; and in 50:15 we have *wayyir'û 'ăhê yôsēp* "Joseph's brothers saw."

6) The verbal root *dbr* "speak" is used in A in 37:4 and commonly in A' in 49:28, 50:4 (bis), 50:17, 50:21.

7) In 37:7, 37:9, 37:10, the Hištaph'el (Št) of *hwh* "prostrate"[9] is used in Joseph's dreams to illustrate his brothers' obeisance; this reverberates with *wayyipĕlû lĕpānāw* "they [his brothers] fell before him [Joseph]" in 50:18.

8) *wayyelĕkû (gam) 'ehāw* "his brothers went" occurs in 37:12 and 50:18.

9) A local man assists Joseph in 37:15–17 and the local Canaanites witness Joseph's and his entourage's mourning in 50:11.

10) The verbal root *nkl* in the Hithpa'el "plot" is used in 37:18, and the nonrelated but assonant root *klkl* "sustain" is used in 50:21.

11) Similarly, the verbal root *nkr* "recognize" is predicated of Jacob in 37:32–33, and Joseph reports Jacob's use of *karîtî* "I dug" from the nonrelated but assonant root *krh* in 50:5.

12) The root *'bl* "mourn" is used in connection with Jacob's mourning for Joseph in 37:34–35, and in 50:10–11 in connection with Joseph's mourning for Jacob.

B Interlude: Joseph not present (38:1–30)

B' Interlude: Joseph nominally present (49:1–28)

It hardly takes deep analysis into the Joseph story to realize that B is a unit with no direct relationship to the general story line. Joseph is nowhere mentioned, and although there are connections between B and A and C,[10] the narrative is complete without 38:1–30. That this chapter is an interlude has not only been recognized by modern scholars,[11] but by Rashi and Ibn Ezra centuries ago.

Although it has been worked into the story a bit more directly, B' is also an interlude. It interrupts the narrative, as a comparison of 48:21–22 and 49:29 demonstrates. Joseph is only nominally present, unlike C' and A' where he dominates. 49:1–27 is clearly an independent poem. Donald B. Redford has astutely noted that it is set in Canaan,[12] and in this sense it is a fitting parallel to 38:1–30 which deals with Judah's life in Canaan. The Egyptian flavor which characterizes the Joseph story throughout is lacking in both units.[13]

The Judah and Tamar episode and the Testament of Jacob might seem too different—beyond their role as interludes and their setting in Canaan—to have themes and theme-words linking them in any meaningful way. But such is not the case, for as the following list indicates, there are surprisingly more such items shared by B and B' than by any other matching units in the cycle.

Since the only common material in B and B' is that concerning Judah, it is appropriate to begin looking at Jacob's words to his fourth son in 49:8–12. These verses are filled with cruxes, but scholars in the last several decades have begun to solve many of them by reading them as references to the Judah and Tamar episode. From the works of Edwin Good,[14] Calum Carmichael,[15] and James Ackerman[16] the following tie-ins may be cited.

1) The key to seeing the blessing of Judah as a reference to 38:1–30 is the similarity between *šîlôh*, traditionally rendered "Shiloh," in 49:10, and *šēlāh* "Shelah" in 38:5, 38:11, 38:14, 38:26.[17]

2) The *šēbeṭ* "sceptre" shall not depart from Judah in 49:10, just as Judah's *maṭṭeh* "staff" was handed to Tamar in 38:18 and used as evidence against him in 38:25.

3) A sexual connotation can certainly be read into *mĕḥôqēq mibbēn*

raglāw "the staff between his legs" in 49:10, and allied to Judah's visiting a prostitute in 38:15–19.

4) *‘îrôh* "his donkey" in 49:11, evokes *‘ēr* "Er," Judah's first son, in 38:3, 38:6, 38:7.

5) Similarly, *bĕnî ’ătônô* "son of the she-ass" in 49:11, brings to mind *’ônān* "Onan," Judah's second son in 38:4, 38:8, 38:9.

6) *śôrēqāh* "vine, stock" in 49:11, alludes to the valley of Soreq, which recalls Timnah in 38:12–13.[18]

Other links between the blessing to Judah and his earlier escapades may also be pointed out.

7) The verbal root *swr* in the Qal "depart" appears in 49:10; and in the Hiph‘il "remove" it occurs in 38:14, 38:19.

8) *yābō’* "he comes" in 49:10, suggests *wayyābō’* "he came" in 38:18.

9) *sûtôh* "his robe" in 49:11 is not etymologically related to *kissĕtāh* "she covered" in 38:15, but they share three consonants, sound alike, and both convey the idea of clothing.

10) The root *lbš* "clothe" appears in both 49:11 and 38:19.

The few verses spoken to Judah thus contain ten theme-words which link B′ with Judah's history in B. But the blessings to the other sons also contain similar expressions to those in 38:1–30.

11) *bĕkôr* "firstborn" occurs in 49:3 and 38:6.

12) *’ônî* "my vigor" in 49:3 might also suggest *’ônān* "Onan" in 38:4, 38:8, 38:9.

13) The word *‘āz* "strong, fierce" is used in 49:3, 49:7; and in 38:17, 38:20 we have *‘izzîm* "goats."

14) *wayyēṭ* is used in 49:15 and in 38:16 meaning "he bent, he turned"; and it also occurs in 38:1 meaning "he pitched."

15) In 49:17 we read *‘ălê derek* "by the road"; and in 38:16 we have *’el hadderek* "by the road."

16) The alliteration *gād gĕdûd yĕgûdennû* "Gad shall be raided by raiders" in 49:19, suggests the important *gĕdî* "kid" in 38:17, 38:20, 38:23.

17) *yāgud* "he shall raid" in 49:19, evokes *wayyuggad* "it was told" in 38:24.

In sum, there are seventeen theme-words which highlight the parallel status of 38:1–30 and 49:1–28. As a comparison with other matching units in the Joseph story will determine, seventeen such parallels is an unusually high number. Perhaps because the Judah and Tamar tale and the Testament of Jacob are so dissimilar, the need was felt for more shared words and ideas than is customary. That is to say, A and A′ and the other matching units are similar enough in action not to require that many theme-words. B and B′ are less homogeneous, however, and thus the redactor has ensured their correspondence through a veritable plethora of theme-words. Commentators have usually dismissed the two pericopes as interludes, which is here not denied, but they should also be recognized as the balancing second and penultimate sections in the Joseph story.[19]

C Reversal: Joseph guilty, Potiphar's wife innocent (39:1–23)

C′ Reversal: Ephraim firstborn, Manasseh secondborn (47:28–48:22)

In the first of these pericopes, a switch of positions finds Joseph, who is innocent, found guilty, and Potiphar's wife, who in actuality is guilty, found innocent. In the second episode, Ephraim, who actually is the secondborn, is declared the firstborn, and Manasseh, who naturally is the firstborn, is reduced to the secondborn. In both instances, Joseph's superior is ultimately responsible for the reversal, whether it be his master Potiphar or his father Jacob. In each case the action centers around the bed. This is explicit in C′ where Jacob lies in bed (*miṭṭāh* in 47:31) and Joseph is beside him, and implicit in C where Potiphar's wife presumably is in bed or has the bed in mind and Joseph is beside her.

A series of theme-words links the two units.

1) The verbal root *brk* "bless" is important in both units, occurring in 39:5 (bis) and in 48:3, 48:15, 48:16, 48:20 (bis).

2) *wayĕmā'ēn wayyō'mer* "he resisted and said" appears in 39:8; and the same words with the subject *'ābîw* "his father" interposed occur in 48:19.

3) In 39:4 we read *wayyimṣā' yôsēp ḥēn bĕ'ênāw* "Joseph found favor in his eyes"; and in 47:29 we have *'im nā' māṣā'tî ḥēn bĕ'ênekā* "if I have found favor in your eyes."

4) The word *ḥesed* "favor" is used in both 39:21 and 47:29.

5) The verbal root *škb* "lie" is prominent in C, occurring four times in 39:7–14, and it reverberates in C' in 47:30.

6) *yād* "hand" in its various forms is extremely common and very important in C, occurring nine times. It is equally important in C' since the reversal results from Jacob's crossed hands and because it is used in Joseph's swearing to Jacob; see 47:29, 48:14, 48:17 (bis).

7) The method of swearing in 47:29 involves the sexual organs,[20] and clearly Potiphar's wife has sexual intercourse in mind in 39:7, 39:12.

8) *leḥem*, literally "bread" but figuratively "wife,"[21] occurs in 39:6; and *bêt lāḥem* "Bethlehem (house of bread)" occurs in 48:7.

D Joseph hero of Egypt (40:1–41:57)

D' Joseph hero of Egypt (47:13–27)

Twice during the Joseph story we have episodes which describe how Joseph saves Egypt from famine and becomes a national hero. It is clear that these units, one relatively long and one relatively short, are parallel. The following theme-words highlight the correspondence.

1) The word *rā'āb* "famine" occurs ubiquitously in D and in D' in 47:13 (bis), 47:20.

2) The word *leḥem* "bread" is used twice in D in 41:54–55, and commonly in D'.

3) *(wĕ)tālāh* "he hung, he will hang" occurs in 40:19, 40:22, and *wattēlah* "languished" appears in 47:13.

4) The verbal root *šbr* "buy/sell grain" is used in 41:56–57 and in 47:14; the noun *šeber* "grain" also occurs in 47:14.

5) *qāneh* "stalk" appears in 41:5, 41:22; and the verbal root *qnh* "buy" occurs in 47:19, 47:22, 47:23.

6) *'ārîm* "cities" is used in 41:48 and 47:21.

7) *'ereṣ miṣrayim* "the land of Egypt," or simply *hā'āreṣ* "the land," are exceedingly common in D and D'; the latter also uses *'ădāmāh* "land" and various forms.

8) The root *ḥmš* in the sense of dividing the land into fifths occurs in 41:34 and 47:24, 47:26.

E Two trips to Egypt (42:1–43:34)

E' Two tellings of migration to Egypt (46:1–47:12)

As the Joseph story progresses there follows the account of the brothers' two trips to Egypt. In the first trip they go merely to acquire food and in the second trip they return with Benjamin in order to free Simeon. Parallel to the two journeys are two tellings of how Jacob's family migrates to Egypt and settles in Goshen. The first account is comprised mainly of a genealogical list and the second describes the presentation of Jacob and his sons before Pharaoh. Furthermore, the first trip to Egypt in E and the second telling of the eventual migration to Egypt in E' are both centered on economic concerns. Similarly, the second trip in E and the first telling in E' are both centered on family concerns. Accordingly, even within the greater chiastic structure of the entire Joseph story, there is a minichiasm built into these two matching units.

Various items link the two units.

1) In 42:1–2 *rĕdû* "go down" and *miṣrayim* "Egypt" are collocated; in 46:3 we read *mērĕdāh miṣraymāh* "from going down to Egypt."

2)   The brothers present themselves as *'ăbādekā* "your servants" to Joseph in 42:10, 42:11, 42:13, and use the same term in speaking to Pharaoh in 46:34, 47:3, 47:4 (bis).

3)   Judah has a prominent role in 43:3–10, and he appears in 46:28 as well.

4)   The verbal root *šlḥ* "send" is used in connection with Jacob sending his sons led by Judah to Egypt in 43:4–5, and in 46:28 when he sends Judah ahead to pave the way.

5)   *lô' tir'û pānay* "you shall not see my face" are Joseph's words quoted to Jacob in 43:5; and *rĕ'ôtî 'et pānekā* "I have seen your face" are Jacob's words to Joseph in 46:30.

6)   Similarly, *ha'ôd 'ăbîkem ḥay* "is your father still alive?" are Joseph's words quoted to Jacob in 43:7; and *kî 'ôdĕkā ḥāy* "that you are still alive" are Jacob's words to Joseph in 46:30.

F Final test (44:1–34)

F' Conclusion of test (45:1–28)

Standing at the middle of the Joseph story are the units leading up to the cycle's denouement and the denouement itself. The former is highlighted by Judah's famous speech, unsurpassed in Scripture for the sympathy and suffering, emotion and pathos it stirs. Indeed it moves Joseph to tears and to disclose his true identity, actions which dominate the latter unit.

F and F' are further connected by the following theme-words.

1)   The verbal root *mhr* "hasten" occurs in 44:11 and in 45:9, 45:13.

2)   *pî* "mouth of" occurs in the sense of the mouth of the bag in 44:1, 44:2, 44:8, and in the sense of a human mouth in 45:12, 45:21.

3)   Benjamin is essential to F, mentioned specifically in 44:12 and alluded to as the youngest brother throughout Judah's speech in 44:18–34; he is also notable in F' in 45:12, 45:14, 45:22.

4) The verbal root *šlḥ* "send" appears in F in 44:3 and commonly, six times to be exact, in F'.

5) The verbal root *yrd* "descend" is common in F, occurring seven times, and appears in F' in 45:9, 45:13.

6) Judah describes Jacob's reaction to Joseph's absence and presumed death in 44:28 *ṭārōp ṭōrāp* "he must have been torn to pieces"; Joseph lets his brothers know that he knows the true story in 45:5 *mĕkartem 'ōtî* "you sold me."

The foregoing dissection of Genesis 37–50 demonstrates that a systematic editorial pattern is operative in the Joseph story. A series of units builds toward a climax, then follows a second series where matching units in reverse order bring the story to resolution and fulfillment. The two sequences A–F and F'–A' are hinged at a pivot point standing smack in the center of the cycle, 45:1–4, where Joseph reveals himself to his brothers.[22] Everything in A through F (with the possible exception of the interlude in B) has been structured to lead us to this climax, with Joseph in the position of power whereby he can exact playful revenge on his brothers. From F through A (again with the possible exception of the interlude in B) all is resolved. Jacob's family migrates to Egypt and settles in Goshen, famine strikes, yet Joseph sustains the people, Joseph's children receive Jacob's blessing, Jacob breathes his last breath, and Joseph too dies, having lived the fullest of lives as indicated by his 110-year lifespan.[23] Our redactor has done his job remarkably well, even to the very last word of Genesis, *bĕmiṣrāyim* "in Egypt," a fitting conclusion to the Joseph story which also neatly sets the scene for the Book of Exodus.[24]

The shared theme-words cement the parallelism of the respective units. It is obvious that an occasional example among the dozens listed above may be coincidental, especially when we are dealing with a fairly common verb, e.g., *šlḥ* "send," which links both E and E and F and F (in each case as point 4 in the lists above). However, the cumulative weight of the evidence suggests that the theme-words have been specifically selected by the redactor to link the units of the cycle. Moreover, my sense is that, with few exceptions, the redactor intended the various theme-words to operate collectively. They connect the matched units as a group, not just as single words.

The recognition of the literary structure of the Joseph story has important ramifications for both redaction criticism and source criticism. The results of my study impact on the traditional methods of each of these approaches, as the following examples will illustrate. A glance at any standard commentary on Genesis will reveal that most scholars believe that the Joseph story in its final form is an expanded version of an originally shorter tale. That is to say, various secondary passages have been added, for one reason or another, to the essential story. However, the literary structure of the cycle I am proposing invalidates these suggestions. Four examples may be put forward.

First, the reference to the unnamed stranger who assists Joseph in his search for his brothers in 37:15–17 is admittedly most peculiar. Both von Rad and Redford have labeled this passage "secondary,"[25] but a closer look reveals that is is integral. It is needed to counterbalance the reference to the local Canaanites in 50:11. Redford also considers the latter verse secondary,[26] but it is odd that both "secondary" additions are among the points which cement the bond between A and A (point 9 in the appropriate list above).

A second example is especially illustrative. Many scholars have been puzzled by the reference to Rachel's death and burial in 48:7. John Skinner wrote, "The notice . . . is very loosely connected with what precedes."[27] Von Rad stated, "The reference to Rachel's death has no recognizable relation to what follows or precedes."[28] Robert Davidson opined, "This brief note about the death and burial of Rachel (see 35:16–20) is poorly related to the context. . . . What is not clear is why it appears at this point in Jacob's speech to Joseph."[29] And finally Bruce Vawter called it "a seemingly pointless reference to Rachel's death and burial."[30] August Dillmann was less concerned about the notice as a whole, stating that "the absence of any apparent motive prevents our regarding the verse as a mere gloss," but he did note that "the words *hw' byt lhm* are out of place in Jacob's mouth, and are a late addition."[31] Admittedly this is correct, for one would not expect to see such a gloss (see Genesis 14 for many more examples) in direct speech. But by paying heed to the use of *lehem* in C in 39:6, where it is pregnant with meaning, we are able to uncover the redactor's reason for including *bêt lāhem* in C in 48:7 (see point 8 in the appropriate list above). Such an important word from C needed to be reverberated in C, and the inclusion of Bethlehem, no matter how out of place, was a way of accomplishing that task.

My third example deals with an entire unit, namely D, the fifteen verses which describe the implementation of Joseph's agrarian reforms in Egypt. Redford considered the entire section "extraneous to the plot of the Joseph Story,"[32] but attention to redactional structuring indicates that this pericope is needed to counterbalance unit D and thus should be considered an integral part of the cycle.

My final example of a redactional problem which may be alleviated by paying heed to the literary structure outlined above is the case of 46:6–27, the list of Jacob's descendants. E. A. Speiser considered these verses to be "intrusive in the present narrative,"[33] and Davidson has similarly contended that "the list has obviously been inserted into the narrative at this point; verse 28 being the natural continuation of verse 5."[34] One cannot deny that the genealogical material interrupts the flow of the narrative, but the literary schema I have presented explains why the list is placed where it is. Since there are *two* journeys which the brothers make in E, there needs to be *two* descriptions of the final migration to Egypt in E'. Since there was only one actual migration by Jacob's family, the compiler could give only one account, namely 46:28–47:12. But to balance the two actual journeys of 42:1– 43:34,[35] the redactor incorporated a brief notice about a theophany discussing the descent (46:1–5) followed by a long genealogy describing the extent of the family which settled in Egypt (46:6–27).

These four examples sufficiently demonstrate the lesson to be learned here. Exegetes should be careful in their use of the term "secondary" and should take note of the artistic manner in which *all* portions of a particular story operate together.[36]

The implications of the literary structure of the Joseph story for source criticism are also crucial. The establishment of a basic unity in a large section of narrative in the Torah by necessity leads to a discussion of the Documentary Hypothesis. Now it is true that the resence of a literary structure in the Joseph story does not a priori militate against the conclusions of the JEDP Theory.[37] Fishbane, for example, in his treatment of the Jacob cycle, wrote, "This is not to side-step 'documentary' issues. For it is clear that the Jacob Cycle has been composed from numerous traditions. It is, however, the point of this paper to see what was 'done' with these traditions."[38] In other words, it is possible that the compiler of the Joseph story or the Jacob cycle merely took the J, E, and P materials and edited them in a manner to produce the corresponding sections.

Cassuto took a more negative view toward the Documentary Hypothesis in his discussion of redactional structuring in the Abraham cycle. He concluded, "The perfected form of this sturcture does not support the view espoused by most modern exegetes, who regard the text as an accidental product of the combination of a number of fragments from various sources. . . . This theory and the problem of the sources of the narratives in general we shall discuss later."[39] Unfortunately, the author's death prevented him from completing this task, though a few pertinent sentences may be culled from the commentary on 12:1–13:5 which survived. But even these statements do not speak to the specific point of how the cycle's unity contradicts the JEDP Theory. Thus it is difficult to predict what route Cassuto would have used.

This does not mean that Cassuto's basic assumption is incorrect. Notwithstanding my statement above that redactional unity need not a priori invalidate the JEDP Theory, when one considers the evidence of the theme-words, the failings of this traditional approach to source criticism become readily apparent. That is to say, as the examples below will illustrate, if source X uses theme-words a, b, c, d, e, etc., and source Y uses the same items, it becomes clearer and clearer that we must see one hand behind the authorship of the Joseph story and not multiple hands.

Let us use units D and D' as our first illustration. The former is usually ascribed to the Elohist and the latter to the Yahwist. If this is so, however, then we must posit the question as to why $r\bar{a}'\bar{a}b$, $lehem$, tlh, $\check{s}br$, qnh, $'\bar{a}r\hat{i}m$, $'eres$ $misrayim$, and $hm\check{s}$ are used in 40:1–41:57, presumably by one author, and then again in 47:13–27, presumably by another author (the items listed are points 1 through 8 in the discussion of C and C' above).

Similarly, most of unit A, especially the first twenty verses, is customarily assigned to the Yahwist, whereas most of unit A', especially from verse 15 on, is typically ascribed to the Elohist. Again we ask: how is it then that presumably one author uses $r\bar{a}'\bar{a}h$, $'\bar{a}b\hat{i}hem$, $wayyir'\hat{u}$ $'eh\bar{a}w$, dbr, the Hištaph'el of hwh, $wayyel\check{e}k\hat{u}$ $'eh\bar{a}w$, and nkl, and that presumably another author uses $r\bar{a}'\bar{a}h$, $'\bar{a}b\hat{i}hem$, $wayyir'\hat{u}$ $'\check{a}h\hat{e}$ $y\hat{o}s\bar{e}p$, dbr, $wayyipp\check{e}l\hat{u}$ $l\check{e}p\bar{a}n\bar{a}w$, $wayyel\check{e}k\hat{u}$ gam $'eh\bar{a}w$, and $klkl$ (these are points 3 through 8 and point 10 in the discussion of A and A' above).

I could continue to multiply such examples from among the various units which comprise the Joseph story, but the point is already clear. I contend that there is more source unity in the Joseph story than is generally assumed and I have no problems claiming that one hand is responsible for the whole narrative. The evidence, especially when the total picture is properly assessed, leads me to conclude that the standard division of the Joseph story into J, E, and P strands should be discarded.[40] This method of source criticism is a method of an earlier age, predominantly of the nineteenth century. If new approaches to the text, such as literary criticism of the type advanced here[41] and as pursued by other scholars as well,[42] deem the Documentary Hypothesis unreasonable and invalid, then source critics will have to rethink earlier conclusions and start anew.

Obviously, I would not go so far as to claim that one individual authored all of the Joseph story's constituent parts. It is quite probable that the genealogical list in 46:6–27 and the Testament of Jacob in 49:1–28 once existed independently, to cite two instances. However, I would hasten to add that the distinction many scholars make between "author" and "redactor/compiler" is a modern one. It is more than likely that an ancient reader would not have recognized this distinction and that to him the individual responsible for the whole of Genesis 37–50 was its single author.

One thing remains certain: the Joseph story, already a masterly woven plot filled with emotion and suspense, is built from a well-conceived blueprint expertly executed by the individual responsible for this classic tale.

At the outset I noted that the Joseph story is the most unified of the four major cycles in Genesis, and I quoted several authorities to that effect. This conclusion has been borne out thoroughly, highlighted through theme-words shared by matching units. Standing at the center is the pivot point, the focus of the entire narrative, Joseph's disclosure to his brothers. The story begins with only Joseph and his brothers present (A) and ends the same way (A). It is therefore fitting that the midway point should include only these very characters. Recognition of the chiastic structure, the theme-words, and the pivot point, placed on top of what is already a masterly constructed story filled with emotion and suspense, permits us to reaffirm what earlier readers have already discovered: that the Joseph story is truly *aḥsana al-qaṣaṣi* "the most beautiful of narratives."[43]

Notes

1. Michael Fishbane, "Composition and Structure in the Jacob Cycle (Gen. 25:19–35:22)," *Journal of Jewish Studies* 26 (1975): 15–38. A slightly altered version of this article appears as chap. 3 in Michael Fishbane, *Text and Texture* (New York: Schocken Books, 1979), pp. 40–62.

2. Jack M. Sasson, "The 'Tower of Babel' as a Clue to the Redactional Structuring of the Primeval History (Gen. 1–11:9)," in Gary A. Rendsburg et al., eds., *The Bible World: Essays in Honor of Cyrus H. Gordon* (New York: Ktav, 1980), pp. 211–19.

3. Ibid., p. 218.

4. Umberto Cassuto, *From Noah to Abraham* (Jerusalem: Magnes, 1964), p. 296.

5. Nahum M. Sarna, *Understanding Genesis* (New York: Schocken Books, 1966), pp. 160–61.

6. Gerhard von Rad, *Genesis* (Philadelphia: Westminster Press, 1961), p. 342.

7. Sarna, *Understanding Genesis*, p. 211.

8. The technical name for such a literary structure is "palistrophe," which appears to have been introduced into the scholarly literature by Sean E. McEvenue, *The Narrative Style of the Priestly Writer* (Rome: Pontifical Biblical Institute, 1971), pp. 157–58. Additional examples of such structures may be found in J. P. Fokkelman, *Narrative Art in Genesis* (Assen: Van Gorcum, 1975). See also the sources cited by Fishbane, "Composition and Structure," p. 19, nn. 21–26; and Joann Dewey, *Markan Public Debate* (Chico, Calif.: Scholars Press, 1980), pp. 34–35, 206–7, nn. 125–53. Many more suggestions may be found in the essays in John W. Welch, ed., *Chiasmus*

in Antiquity (Hildesheim: Gerstenberg, 1981), but as even a brief look at this volume will indicate, many of these posited chiasms lack perfect symmetry.

9. For this grammatical analysis of *hištaḥăwāh*, etc., see Cyrus H. Gordon, *Ugaritic Textbook* (Rome: Pontifical Biblical Institute, 1967), p. 395.

10. The first to note such nexuses were R. Yohanan, R. Lazar, and R. Samuel bar Nahman, whose comments in Bereshit Rabbah 85:2 are most insightful. From the medieval period see the comments of Rashi at Genesis 39:1 and of Ibn Ezra at Genesis 38:1. Among modern scholars see Umberto Cassuto, "The Story of Judah and Tamar," in *Biblical and Oriental Studies* (Jerusalem: Magnes Press, 1973), pp. 30–31 (Hebrew original 1929); Benno Jacob, *Das erste Buch der Tora: Genesis* (Berlin: Schocken Books, 1934), p. 724; Donald B. Redford, *A Study of the Biblical Story of Joseph* (Leiden: Brill, 1970), p. 18; John Emerton, "Some Problems in Genesis XXXVIII," *Vetus Testamentum* 25 (1975): 347; Judah Goldin, "The Youngest Son or Where Does Genesis 38 Belong," *Journal of Biblical Literature* 96 (1977): 28–29; and Robert Alter, *The Art of Biblical Narrative* (New York: Basic Books, 1981), pp. 6–10.

11. See, for example, von Rad, *Genesis*, p. 351; Robert Davidson, *Genesis 12–50* (Cambridge: Cambridge University Press, 1979), p. 224; and E. A. Speiser, *Genesis* (Garden City, N.Y.: Doubleday, 1964), p. 299.

12. Redford, *Story of Joseph*, p. 25. See also Bruce Vawter, "The Canaanite Background of Genesis 49," *Catholic Biblical Quarterly* 17 (1955): 1–18; and J. Coppens, "La Bénédiction de Jacob," in *Volume du Congrès Strasbourg*, Supplements to *Vetus Testamentum* 4 (Leiden: Brill, 1957), pp. 97–115.

13. On the Egyptian coloring of the Joseph story, see most importantly J. Vergote, *Joseph en Égypte* (Louvain: Publications Universitaires, 1959); Redford, *Story of Joseph*, pp. 187–243; and Sarna, *Understanding Genesis*, pp. 211–37.

14. Edwin M. Good, "The 'Blessing' on Judah, Gen. 49:8–12," *Journal of Biblical Literature* 82 (1963): 427–32.

15. Calum M. Carmichael, "Some Sayings in Genesis 49," *Journal of Biblical Literature* 88 (1969): 439–41.

16. James S. Ackerman, "Joseph, Judah and Jacob," in Kenneth R. R. Gros Louis, ed., *Literary Interpretations of Biblical Narratives* (Nashville, Tenn.: Abingdon Press, 1982), 2:111.

17. A possible connection between Shiloh and Shelah has been noted earlier by Arnold B. Ehrlich, *Randglossen zur hebräischen Bibel* (Leipzig: Hinrichs, 1908), 1:246; Walter Schröder, "Gen. 49:10, Versuch einer Erklärung," *Zeitschrift für die alttestamentliche Wissenschaft* 29 (1909): 194–95; John Skinner, *Genesis* (Edinburgh: Clark, 1910), pp. 520, 524; and Jacob, *Genesis*, p. 907. This interpretation may already have been in the minds of the translator of Targum Yonatan which reads *z'yr bnwy* "his youngest son," and Qimhi and other medieval exegetes who accept this understanding of Masoretic *šylh*.

18. This point is made only by Ackerman, "Joseph," p. 111, who states unequivocally that Timnah "is located in the valley of Sorek ('vineyard')." Ackerman has in mind the Timnah of Judges 14:1, though actually the Timnah of 38:12–13 is probably another Timnah, higher in the Judean hills. See Skinner, *Genesis*, p. 453; S. R. Driver, *The Book of Genesis* (London: Westminster, 1910), p. 329; Jacob, *Genesis*, p. 714; von Rad, *Genesis* , p. 354; and Davidson, *Genesis*, p. 228. But this does not mean that the *śôrēqāh*/Timnah parallel between B and B′ fails. The Hebrew reader, not conscious to identify every geographic locale specifically, might easily have thought of the Timnah of 38:12–13 as the Timnah in the Soreq Valley. We may even ask whether it is relevant that two of Samson's loves are his unnamed fiancée of Timnah (Judges 14) and Delilah of the Soreq Valley (Judges 16).

19. As such, units B and B′ of the Joseph story are similar to units B and B′ of the Jacob cycle which also act as interludes. See Fishbane, "Composition and Structure," p. 24.

20. On this point see Meir Malul, "More on *paḥad yiṣḥāq* (Genesis XXXI 42, 53) and the Oath by the Thigh," *Vetus Testamentum* 35 (1985): 192–200; and Meir Malul, "Touching the

Sexual Organs as an Oath Ceremony in an Akkadian Letter," *Vetus Testamentum* 37 (1987): 491–92.

21. For this understanding of *lehem*, obvious from a comparison with 39:9, one must consult the medieval Jewish exegetes (Rashi, Ibn Ezra, Qimhi, and others) who derive their knowledge ultimately from Bereshit Rabbah 86:6 and Targum Yerushalmi to Genesis 39:6. None of the modern commentators, save Jacob, *Genesis*, p. 728, mentions this. For another example of *lehem* = "wife, woman," see Exodus 2:20; see also Shabbat 62b and Ketubot 13a in the Talmud.

22. Fishbane, "Composition and Structure," p. 32, has found a similar pivot point, which he calls "the archetechtonic pivot," in the Jacob cycle at 30:22–25.

23. On this as the ideal age limit in ancient Egypt, see J. M. A. Janssen, "On the Ideal Lifetime of an Egyptian," *Oudheidkundige Mededeelingen uit het Rijksmuseum van Oudheden te Leiden* 31 (1950): 33–44; and Sarna, *Understanding Genesis*, p. 226.

24. This point has been duly noted by Skinner, *Genesis*, p. 540; Jacob, *Genesis*, p. 945; and Speiser, *Genesis*, p. 378.

25. Von Rad, *Genesis*, p. 347; and Redford, *Story of Joseph*, p. 145.

26. Redford, *Story of Joseph*, p. 246.

27. Skinner, *Genesis*, pp. 504–5.

28. Von Rad, *Genesis*, p. 410.

29. Davidson, *Genesis*, p. 294.

30. Bruce Vawter, *On Genesis* (Garden City, N.Y.: Doubleday, 1977), p. 452.

31. August Dillmann, *Genesis* (Edinburgh: Clark, 1897), 2:437–38.

32. Redford, *Story of Joseph*, p. 180.

33. Speiser, *Genesis*, p. 347.

34. Davidson, *Genesis*, p. 279.

35. As Redford notes, duplicate episodes are a major literary feature of the Joseph story (*Story of Joseph*, pp. 74–75).

36. I should state here that a literary symmetry of the Joseph story has also been advanced by George W. Coats, *From Canaan to Egypt* (Washington: Catholic Biblical Association, 1976), pp. 7–55 (an expansion of his earlier article "Redactional Unity in Genesis 37–50," *Journal of Biblical Literature* 93 [1974]: 15–21). I make no attempt to dovetail my analysis with Coats's, for we differ on one major point. The basis for my study is the finished product, i.e., all of chapters 37–50. Coats, on the other hand, limits himself to 37, 39:1–47:27, considering 38 "not an intrinsic element in the Joseph story" and 47:28–50:26 to be "a framework narrative" and thus exclusive of "the primary structure of the Joseph story" (see *From Canaan to Egypt*, p. 8, n. 3).

The entire cycle has been treated from a literary perspective by Donald A. Seybold, "Paradox and Symmetry in the Joseph Narrative," in Kenneth R. R. Gros Louis, ed., *Literary Interpretations of Biblical Narrative* (Nashville, Tenn.: Abingdon Press, 1974), 1:59–73. I accept many of Seybold's conclusions as well as the entire thrust of his article. It should be pointed out that his study upsets none of my conclusions nor does my study contradict any of his.

37. The JEDP Theory remains the most popular appraoch to source criticism among biblical scholars. J stands for the Yahwist, E stands for the Elohist, D stands for the Deuteronomist, and P stands for the Priest. These hypothesized strands generally are dated respectively to the 900s, 800s, 600s, and 400s B.C.E. A recent popular exposition of the theory may be found in R. E. Friedman, *Who Wrote the Bible?* (New York: Summit, 1987).

38. Fishbane, "Composition and Structure," p. 26, n. 39.

39. Cassuto, *From Noah to Abraham*, p. 294.

40. See the oft-cited article by R. N. Whybray, "The Joseph Story and Pentateuchal Criticism," *Vetus Testamentum* 18 (1968): 522–28; and the recent treatment by Adele Berlin, *Poetics and Interpretation of Biblical Narrative* (Sheffield: Almond Press, 1983), pp. 113–21.

41. For a more extensive treatment, incorporating all of the Book of Genesis, see Gary A. Rendsburg, *The Redaction of Genesis* (Winona Lake, Minn.: Eisenbrauns, 1986).

42. See most importantly Meir Sternberg, *The Poetics of Biblical Narrative: Ideological Literature and the Drama of Reading* (Bloomington: Indiana University Press, 1985).

43. Qur'an 12:4. I hasten to add that a similar chiastic pattern has been uncovered in the Sura of Joseph in the Qur'an by Mustansir Mir, "The Qur'anic Story of Joseph: Plot, Themes, and Characters," *The Muslim World* 76 (1986): 1–15. See also Gary A. Rendsburg, "Literary Structures in the Qur'anic and Biblical Stories of Joseph," *The Muslim World* (forthcoming).

"Enemies Round About":
Disintegrative Structure in the Book of Judges

Alexander Globe
University of British Columbia

THE period of Israelite history described in the Book of Judges coincided with a time of general upheaval in the eastern Mediterranean about the year 1200 B.C.E., when the politically organized, culturally developed, and literate Mycenean, Hittite, and Canaanite societies collapsed, to be replaced by less culturally developed, nonwriting Greeks, Phrygians, and Israelites.[1] Despite the disruptions, ample archeological and literary evidence suggests continued cultural exchange between the Mediterranean and Near Eastern peoples.[2] Samson has long been recognized as a folk hero in the style of Mycenean Heracles, while Jephthah and Agamemnon both sacrifice virgin daughters for the national cause.[3] Like the legends of the heroic age in Greece, the traditions of the biblical judges circulated orally for several centuries before being committed to writing. The originally self-contained, independently transmitted prose narratives about Ehud, Gideon, Jephthah, and Samson, as well as the poem in Judges 5, retain many traits of oral literature, including type-scenes, stereotype plots, episodes arranged in rings, and the run-on paratactic style.[4]

When these episodes were incorporated into the Book of Judges, a "writerly" style took over, adapting some of the oral features but overwhelming others. The Deuteronomistic theological assessment in chapters 2:6–3:6 sees the age as marked by continuing apostasy that leads to the disintegration of Israel. This prologue provides the model for the discursive frames in which the individual episodes of chapters 3:7–16:31 are set, drawing cause-and-effect connections between them, and imposing an artificial sense of chronological coherence and national unity. The first and last five chapters are usually stigmatized as afterthoughts tacked on by a later editor. Judges 1 begins without a general statement and at first sight seems a hopeless jumble of conquest notices. But its arrangement of tribes parallels the order of the episodes in chapters 3–16, and its bias is clearly Judean. The southernmost Judah comes first, triumphing unequivocally in Judges 1:1–20 and 3:7–11. As the texts move northward through Ephraim and Manasseh to the Galilean tribes, failure enters then dominates. A second geographical arrangement of the episodes is based on the location of Israel's enemies. From this perspective, the book falls into two sections (chapters 3–9 and 10–21), each spiraling clockwise from the northeast to the northwest, then ending at the center of the nation. Both cycles begin with an ideal situation which degenerates—quickly in the second cycle—into chaos. Ephraim, a synonym for the later northern kingdom of Israel, is at the center of the maelstrom. Only this tribe appears out of geographical sequence, focusing the anarchy in the last five chapters, where a new refrain runs, "In those days there was no king in Israel; every man did what was right in his own eyes." Finally, the material is arranged in six rings, the first and last sections setting Judah's successes beside northern deterioration, the second and penultimate sections providing another contrasting frame, and so on through a total of six pairs until the central episode of Gideon throws two Deuteronomistic themes into relief—illicit marriages to non-Israelites and the worship of idols. In its present form, Judges is a structural and thematic unity written by a single author, arguing not only for the necessity of a king, but elliptically for the Judean monarchy.

THE WRITERLY STRUCTURE OF THE DEUTERONOMISTIC CORE OF JUDGES

Most scholarly treatments see Judges 2:6–16:31 as the core of the book, with older, often orally based episodes set into an evaluative framework whose ideas are based on an abstract theological introduction in chapters 2:6–3:6. Here the author carefully outlines his evaluation of the age. This work is part of the theological history of Israel stretching from the time of Moses as presented in Deuteronomy, through the Books of Joshua and Judges, to the monarchy, which is founded in 1–2 Samuel then shattered in 1–2 Kings. This large project has been assigned to the "Deuteronomist," an author or school whose ideas, turns of phrase, and occasional style of incremental repetition derive from the Book of Deuteronomy.[5] Foremost among his beliefs is God's demand for absolute obedience to the Law of Moses as recorded in Deuteronomy. Yahweh is to be worshiped as the sole Israelite deity. As a corollary, other gods are not to be revered, their images and altars are to be destroyed, and marriage with people of other religions is to be avoided (Deut. 5:9; 7:2–4; Josh. 23:12–13). Obedience to these precepts results in the successful settlement of

Canaan, while disobedience leads to dispossession (Deut. 28; 2 Kings 17:7–41).

In the Deuteronomistic introduction of Judges 2:6–3:6, the Israelites turn to gods other than Yahweh after the death of Joshua and his generation. In anger, God delivers them into the hands of their enemies. Although he sends them judges who free them, they continue to worship foreign gods. Consequently, God determines to allow the original inhabitants and other plunderers power to test Israel's obedience to him. The prologue ends with the Israelites ominously unable to withstand temptation: they marry Canaanites and serve their gods. The cyclical departures from Deuteronomistic godliness lead to the collapse of the nation that should be devoted to Yahweh.

This introduction provides the language for an abstract theological framework starting and ending the episodes devoted to the six major judges: Othniel (formula in Judges 3:7–9 + 10b–11), Ehud (formula in 3:12–15 + 30), Deborah/Barak (4:1–3 + 4:24 + 5:31b), Gideon (6:1–2a + 6:6–10 + 6:34a + 8:28 + 8:32, where the account of Gideon ends), Jephthah (10:6–16 + 11:29a + 11:33b + 12:7), and Samson (13:1 + 13:25 + 14:6a + 14:19a + 15:14b + 15:20 + 16:31b). Not only do the shorter accounts come first (with 5, 19, 55, 97, 60, and 96 verses respectively), but the theological framework, fully developed for Othniel, becomes generally shorter and shorter until it is a mere vestige in the Samson cycle, with 4.5, 5, 5, 10, 14, and 7 verses, or 90, 26, 9, 10, 23, and 7 percent of the total text.

These circumstantial narratives fall into six main parts. 1) A stereotype description of wickedness invariably begins with the same phrase—"And [again] the sons of Israel did evil in the eyes of Yahweh"—repeated from Judges 2:11 and recurring as a condemnation of 25 Israelite and Judean monarchs in 1–2 Kings.[6] A Deuteronomistic condemnation of continuing apostasy thus strikes the reader at the start of every episode. Only the narratives about Othniel and Jephthah specify the nature of the evil, using the language of the introduction to describe the worship of foreign gods and Yahweh's consequent anger (Judges 3:7–8; 10:6–7; cf. 2:11–14, 17, 19–20). 2) Next Yahweh delivers Israel to a specific enemy, and the people languish for a specific number of years (see Table 1). 3) Another formulaic notice (missing from the Samson saga) describes the Israelites' cry for help, and (apart from Jephthah) God's sending of a deliverer. 4) The Spirit seizes Othniel, Gideon, Jephthah, and Samson (Judges 3:10; 6:34; 11:29; 13:25; 14:6, 19; 15:14). 5) The description of the deeds of the individual judges reverts to the non-Deuteronomistic language of the different traditions as they came to the author. 6) After a mechanical note about the enemy's defeat, the first four narratives end with the land resting in peace for a number of years, while the last two narratives record the length of the judgeship (see Table 1). Death notices are provided for Othniel, Gideon, Jephthah, and Samson.

For the five minor judges, Tola, Jair, Ibzan, Elon, and Abdon (Judges 10:1–5; 12:8–15), a different frame begins "After . . . [arose] . . .judged Israel," and finishes by noting the time judged, his death, and his burial. This formula is adapted from the Deuteronomistic frames for the monarchs in 1–2 Kings, with their initial statements about the accession and length of reign, and their concluding notices about the ruler's death, burial, and successor (e.g., 2 Kings 15:1–7, 32–38; 16:1–20). Naturally the language changes for the two types of ruler, but the notions of chronology and orderly succession underlie both formulas.

The chronology outlined in Table 1 is artificial, but its patterns reenforce the book's central themes. The length of time that the land rests or the judges rule falls into three main groups, 40 or 80 years for the first four judges, approximately half that (22 and 23 years) for the sixth and seventh judges, then (leaving aside Samson's 20 years) less than half again (6, 7, 10 and 8 years) for the eighth through the eleventh judges. The ratio of peace to oppression also shifts dramatically. The first four judges enjoy five times, about four times, two times, then almost six times as many years of peace as years of servitude. The ratio inverts for Jephthah and Samson, who enjoy only a third or a half as many years of peace as oppression. The Deuteronomistic view of the age, expressed in these numbers, the renewed apostasy introducing each episode, and the pessimistic evaluation in Judges 2:6–3:6, leaves an impression of increasing disintegration.

PATTERNS OF GEOGRAPHICAL ORGANIZATION IN THE BOOK OF JUDGES

A modern book or essay would start with the Deuteronomistic thesis in chapters 2–3. The potpourri of conquest traditions in chapter 1 has led most scholars of the last century to stigmatize it as a late addition to the book, with verses 10–15, 21, 27–28 and 29 pillaged from Joshua 15:13–19, 63; 17:11–13; and 16:10. Yet the first chapter of Judges has the historical function of explaining how Canaanite gods remained easily accessible to the Israelites. Furthermore, the chapter is arranged schematically, with the cities in groups of twelve or seven, and the tribes ordered geographically from south to north. Since the episodes in chapters 3–16 appear in a similar sequence, the chapter is an integral part of the final version of the book, announcing one of its

Table 1: The Deuteronomistic Chronology of the Age of the Judges

Judge	Years of oppression	Years the land rests	Years judged	Death notice
1 Othniel*	8 (Judges 3:8)	40 (3:11)		Death only (3:11)
2 Ehud*	18 (3:14)	80 (3:30)		Not noted
3 Deborah*	20 (4:3)	40 (5:31)		Not noted
4 Gideon*	7 (6:1)	40 (8:28)		Death, burial (8:32)
5 [Abimelech]			[ruled 3] (9:22)	Killed (9:53–57)
6 Tola			23 (10:2)	Death, burial (10:2)
7 Jair			22 (10:3)	Death, burial (10:5)
8 Jephthah*	18 (10:8)		6 (12:7)	Death, burial (12:7)
9 Ibzan			7 (12:9)	Death, burial (12:10)
10 Elon			10 (12:11)	Death, burial (12:12)
11 Abdon			8 (12:14)	Death, burial (12:15)
12 Samson*	40 (13:1)		20 (15:20, 16:31)	Death, burial (16:31)

*The exploits of these six judges are set in the formulaic Deuteronomistic framework.

important structures. In verse 1, the Israelites ask, "Who shall go up first for us against the Canaanites, to fight against them?" The rest of chapter 1 records the progress of these battles from south to north, led by Judah since God has "given the land into his hand" (Judges 1:2). The other tribes fail to emulate Judah's triumphs, so that this passage concludes in chapter 2:1–5 with another condemnation of the age expressed in Deuteronomistic language. An angel chastizes the Israelites for making covenants with the Canaanites and letting their shrines stand. As a consequence, Yahweh stops driving out the Canaanites and promises that their gods will become snares. Although the Israelites weep, they continue to worship Yahweh.

The first tribes listed in Judges 1 are the southernmost Judah and Simeon, settlers of the territory that was the traditional entrance of the Israelites from east of the Jordan (see Table 2). They succeed in all they do, winning eleven cities and districts (twelve if the hill country in verse 9 is counted). The only other tribe mentioned as winning any territory is Joseph, who destroys Bethel, a city in the tribal allotment of Ephraim, whose fall was attributed to Joshua, an Ephraimite by birth (Josh. 8:17; 12:16; Num. 13:8, 16). This twelvefold success is appropriate, given both the twelve-tribe structure of Israel and the total of twelve judges presented in chapters 3–16. The southern bias of the first chapter could not be more obvious: almost single-handedly, Judah routs the Canaanites from Bezek in Manasseh (just south of Mount Gilboa) all the way south to the Negeb bordering the Sinai desert. The victories include two important Davidic cities: Hebron, where the Judeans anointed David as king (2 Sam. 2:1–4), and Jerusalem, the stronghold which he conquered and made his capital.

The Judean slant continues in verse 21, where Benjamin does not capture Jerusalem. By contrast, the source of this note in Joshua 15:63 attributes the failure to Judah, which represents the historical reality until David. Whereas Joshua speaks of Judah's inability to conquer ("could not"), Judges insinuates Benjamin's unwillingness ("did not").[7] The same shift of motivation occurs between the notes on Manasseh in Joshua 17:11–13 and Judges 1:27–28. One city is also dropped to bring the number of settlements in Judges down to five, corresponding to Manasseh's position as fifth tribe in the list. With Ephraim, the total of towns not taken in verses 21–29 reaches seven, the number that often denotes a complete cycle in the Bible.

Neither Reuben nor Gilead is mentioned, because Joshua 12:1–6 presents Moses as winning that trans-Jordanian territory. In verse 29, Issachar is expected. Ephraim, however, appears, geographically out of place and already mentioned as Joseph in verse 22. This anomaly will be explained at the end of the next paragraph. The list then jumps to the Galilean tribes, proceeding northward through Zebulun, Asher, Naphtali, and Dan. Although the Danite cities in Judges 1:34 lie in its early location adjacent to Ephraim, the tribe moved north in premonarchial times according to Judges 17–18. The late author is here working with the boundaries of his own age rather than ones he considers obsolete. The second part of the list is as schematic as the first. A total of fourteen cities is mentioned; the seventh-named tribe, Asher, fails to deliver seven cities.

The accounts of the judges in chapters 3–16 give the tribal origin of each figure. Leaving aside the unpaired sections, the episodes are arranged in the same sequence as in chapter 1, moving from south to north (see Table 2). First in both sections comes Judah, and to make the connection even clearer the exploits of Othniel are mentioned in both Judges 1:11–15 and 3:7–11. Benjamin is next in both sections, followed by the first unpaired figure, Shamgar, who is given no tribal origin. Ephraim (called by the alternative name of Joseph in Judges 1:22) is represented by Deborah, the prophetess who initiates the action of Judges 4; Naphtalian Barak is not out of geographical order since he merely follows her commands. Next comes Manasseh, Gideon's tribe. Abimelech is not called a judge, and he wreaks havoc at his home town, Shechem. In early sources (such as Joshua 17:7), Shechem is set in Manasseh, but later traditions (such as Joshua 20:7 and 21:21) associate Shechem with Ephraim.[8] Since the author of Judges 1 has the later perspective elsewhere, the placing of Ephraim out of its proper order in Judges 1:29 matches the tribe prejudiciously with the pernicious Abimelech.

The next four judges are unpaired, but they proceed northward from Issachar through trans-Jordanian Gilead until Zebulun is matched on both lists. Ibzan's tribe is uncertain, but it appears to be Zebulun.[9] Northernmost Dan is the last tribe paired in both chapters 1 and 3–16. The only two long narratives in this section concentrate on the increasing disorder that Jephthah and Samson bring with them. Before Dan comes another aberration: Abdon is from Ephraim, which thus appears out of place once in each of two otherwise orderly lists. In addition, Ephraim is the tribe associated with the two blood-chilling narratives following Samson. When it is remembered that Ephraim often appears as a synonym for the northern kingdom of Israel, a further Judean bias seems probable. Whenever it appears, Ephraim is not only out of order but proves disruptive.

PATTERNS OF GEOGRAPHICAL DISINTEGRATION IN JUDGES

An examination of the location of the enemies of Israel suggests an

Table 2: The Geographical Arrangement of Judges 1 and 3–21

Text	Tribe	Cities captured	Text	Judge	Tribe	Enemy	Location
1:1–20	1–2 Judah + Simeon	Won Bezek, Jerusalem, [hills], Negeb, Shephelah, Hebron, Debir, Arad, Hormah, Gaza, Ashkelon, Ekron	3:7–11	1 Othniel	Judah	Aram	NE
1:21	3 Benjamin	Not Jerusalem	3:12–30	2 Ehud	Benjamin	Moab	SE
			3:31	3 Shamgar	?	Philistines	SW
1:22–6	4A Joseph [=Ephraim]	Destroyed Bethel	4:1–5:31	4 Deborah [Barak]	Ephraim [Naphtali]	North Canaan	NW
1:27–8	5 Manasseh	Not Beth-Shean, Taanach, Dor, Ibleam, Megiddo	6:1–8:32	5 Gideon	Manasseh	Midian	CE
1:29	4B Ephraim	Not Gezer	8:33–9:57	Abimelech	[Shechem]	[Manasseh]	C

Reference	Judge	Tribe/Place		Direction
10:1–2	6 Tola	Issachar [+Ephraim]		[NE]
10:3–5	7 Jair	Gilead [=Gad]		[NE]
10:6–12:7	8 Jephthah	Gilead [=Gad]	Ammon	SE
12:8–10	9 Ibzan	Bethlehem [Judah? Zebulun?]		[SW? NW?]
12:11–12	10 Elon	Zebulun		[NW]
12:13–15	11 Abdon	Ephraim		[CW]
13–16	12 Samson	Dan	Philistines	SW
17–18	Micah	Ephraim	Dan	SW-C-NE
19–21	Levite	Ephraim	Benjamin	C

[Reuben, Asher, and Simeon not included]

Reference	Tribe	
1:30	6 Zebulun	*Not* Kitron, Nahalol
1:31–2	7 Asher	*Not* Acco, Sidon, Ahlab, Achzib, Helbah, Aphik, Rehob
1:33	8 Naphtali	*Not* Beth-Shemesh, Beth-Anath
1:34	9 Dan	*Not* Harheres, Aijalon, Shaalbim

[Reuben, Gilead, and Issachar not included]

additional geographical arrangement in chapters 3–21 (see Table 2). Both halves of the book (chapters 3–9 and 10–21) shift from eastern to western adversaries, then end with Israelite antagonists in the center of the nation. The episodes in chapters 3–9 spiral clockwise from the northeast around to the northwest, then home in to the center, where a judge, Gideon, makes an idol and his depraved son leaves a wake of destruction after he has himself declared king of Shechem, a city in Ephraim. In chapter 9, the enemies thus shift from foreigners to an Israelite. The minor judges follow the same pattern, spiraling from the northeast around to the northwest, and ending with Ephraim. Whether the Bethlehem of Judges 12:8 lies in Judah or Zebulun, it does not disturb the design. In the middle of chapters 10–12, Jephthah's rule is marred by civil war initiated by Ephraim. The book ends with three episodes shifting from external enemies in the southwest and northeast to internal disturbances initiated by Ephraimites. In both halves of the book, then, the episodes are ordered to reflect increasing disintegration, reenforcing the Deuteronomistic judgment in chapters 2:6–3:6 that Israel's continuing apostasy had catastrophic internal effects.

The heroic ideal achieved by the first four judges moves to national and personal disintegration by the end of chapter 9. The first two heroes are called "deliverer," or "savior" (*mōshiyaᶜ*, Judges 3:9, 15)— a Hebrew word punning on the names of both Moses and Joshua. Their accomplishments are exemplary, and there is no ironic tension between the Deuteronomistic framework and the episodes. Virtually no detail survives about Othniel's exploits, which are hidden under the Deuteronomistic formulas. As a consequence, he resembles the invincible Joshua, driven by the Spirit, and, given the phrasing of Judges 3:10, winning the battle against an Aramean enemy single-handedly. Ehud embodies Deuteronomistic virtue, and his story follows oral conventions ideally. Once he arises, he has the shrewdness to craft a special sword which he manages to hide until he assassinates King Eglon. He also leads the Israelites to a resounding defeat of the Moabite army. Shamgar's one-verse exploit focuses on Ehud-like cunning, as he slays six hundred Philistines with a simple ox goad. The verb "to deliver" comes from the same root as the noun used of Othniel and Ehud, placing Shamgar's heroism with theirs. The fourth judge, the prophetess Deborah, is equally triumphant in rousing the Israelites who defeat the formidable Canaanites in their nine hundred iron-clad chariots. If there is some irony in the Israelite commander, Barak, doing little more than executing a woman's instructions, that stigma is soon intensified by the victory being sealed by Jael, the woman who kills Sisera after his cowardly flight from the battlefield.

The extensive Gideon saga is another orally based collection of tales that delights in relating how a people reduced to threshing grain in wine presses could defeat the Midianites on their seemingly unconquerable camels. After destroying the altar of Baal in his home town, Gideon drives the invaders away in panic with a mere handful of three hundred men. Their nighttime attack is manipulated to seem like the vanguard of a huge army. But the story does not end in unalloyed triumph. Two Gileadite cities that are afraid of Midianite reprisals have to be punished for not helping Gideon capture the fleeing enemy; civil war almost breaks out when the Ephraimites complain that they were not included in the successful venture; and Gideon himself, whose earlier insistence on signs intimates a latent penchant for idolatry, makes an ephod of gold from the booty. During his lifetime, the Israelites worship this object; after his death, they turn wholeheartedly to Baal-Berith, an ironically non-Yahwistic "Lord of the Covenant." These disparities between Deuteronomistic values and the events of Gideon's life intensify with the sixth figure in the book. At what first appears to be the half-way point of the twelve judges, the ideal disappears with the rise of an "anti-judge." Gideon's son by a Canaanite concubine in Shechem seizes power as a king who "ruled over Israel" (Judges 9:22) illegitimately, like the seceding first ruler of the northern kingdom, Jeroboam I. He slaughters all but one of his seventy stepbrothers, and wreaks havoc in Shechem and Thebez before being killed by a woman who crushes his skull with a millstone. Nowhere are the words "deliverer" or "judge" applied to him. Instead, he leads an attack on Israel from the inside.

The list of minor judges in chapters 10–12 seems to reverse this sense of impending chaos by suggesting an orderly transfer of rule in a land that has finally gained relief from outside attack. The list even circles back on itself, beginning and ending with the territory of Ephraim (Judges 10:2; 12:15). The impression of stability is further reenforced by the stereotype numbers associated with three of the judges: Jair's thirty sons, their thirty donkeys, and their thirty cities; Ibzan's thirty sons, thirty daughters, and thirty daughters-in-law; and Abdon's forty sons, thirty grandsons, and their seventy donkeys. In terms of biblical symbolism, which sees perfection in the number seven, what could sound better than a pair of sevens multiplied by ten? The length of time that these officials hold sway also totals a stereotypical seventy years. Yet almost two-thirds of that time is given over to the first two, Tola and Jair. After Jephthah's tragic six-year rule, Ibzan, Elon, and Abdon all hold sway for just over half as long as either Tola or Jair. Finally, none of these figures leads a party against the still-potent external enemies or the Canaanites who continue to lead Israelites astray within their own borders. Once more, under the surface of an apparently serene text lurk signs of disintegration.

These darker hints find open expression in the exploits of Jephthah. At first dispossessed by his stepbrothers for being the son of a harlot, he is forced into the wilderness as a bandit. Hoping that renewed status among the Gileadites will bring security for his descendants, he agrees to help them defeat Ammon. Yet his victory ends in personal tragedy. A vow he makes before the battle requires him to sacrifice his only child, a daughter. Finally, the tribal jealousies that Gideon was able to smooth over break out into full civil war. Responding to threats, Jephthah mobilizes the Gileadites, who kill 42,000 Ephraimites. Israel is once more torn apart by internal dissensions originating in Ephraim.

The Samson saga presents the most complex orally based narrative in Judges. By the time it is over, Samson has broken all the Nazirite vows in Judges 13:4–5, 7, and 14, by eating honey rendered unclean by touching a dead lion's carcass, by taking part in the wedding "drinking bout,"[10] and by divulging the secret of his strength so that his hair is cut. Another three vows are broken in Judges 14:1–9, where he decides to marry a Philistine and not tell his parents either about killing the lion or where the honey came from. The wedding feast may end with the killing of thirty Philistines, but he loses his bride, and his action is motivated only by spite, which could have been prevented if he had not so willingly told the secret of his riddle. The massacre of a thousand Philistines with a jawbone may be genuinely heroic, but it is necessitated by the Judean's cowardly surrender of their unwanted leader. Although Samson tears the gates off of Gaza and carries them twenty miles after an evening of sexual indulgence, nobody takes advantage of the town's defenselessness to press an attack, as did Ehud. After Delilah dupes him into betraying the Nazirite secret of his strength, his self-imposed death as he kills three thousand Philistines is motivated only by personal revenge for his blindness. The wording of the text does not even permit the dignified explanation that public triumph can be achieved only at the cost of personal sacrifice. Heroic myth, with its raw human appeal and tragic overtones, turns into unenlightened lust and blind temper when set in the Deuteronomistic context.

Far from being afterthoughts clumsily appended to the book the final two episodes intensify the deterioration of society as the Israelites turn farther and farther away from the Deuteronomistic ideal. Judges 17–18 opens in Ephraim, where Micah has an idol cast from a mere fifth of a sum of money consecrated to that purpose. The refrain, "In those days there was no king in Israel; every man did what was good in his own eyes," records the scorn of the Deuteronomist as Micah sets his son in charge of the shrine. This priest is soon replaced by a Levite from Bethlehem in Judah, who, Micah thinks, will bring him greater prosperity. Meanhile, in this age without a king to resolve disputes, the Danites cannot find a home. On a reconnaissance mission, some Danite scouts stay with Micah. The Levite impresses them so much that they steal the idol and priest on their way to reduce Laish in the north, where they settle permanently. Micah has no recourse but to watch, overpowered, as he is robbed. The tone consistently belittles every aspect of this story of the founding of one of the most important sanctuaries in the later northern kingdom. The impious shrine existed only because a vow to Yahweh was broken, and because one tribe plundered another.

Chapters 19–21 are even less savory. The story begins with a lovers' spat that is patched up by an Ephramite Levite going to fetch his Judean concubine back from Bethlehem. On the return to Ephraim, he stays the night at Gibeah in Benjamin, where the townsmen gather at the host's door asking for the same homosexual access to the visitor as occurred at Sodom in Genesis 19. Unlike Lot, who courageously faces the attackers outside the house, the Levite callously throws his concubine outside, where she is raped to death. Calling an assembly of Israelites by hacking the body into twelve pieces, the Levite galvanizes the nation, which attacks Benjamin in revenge, killing all but six hundred men of the tribe. Later regretting the decimation, the Israelites connive to obviate their vow and allow the Benjaminites to procure Israelite wives for the repopulation of their tribe. A disloyal town is raided, and the Israelites allow their virgin daughters to be seized during an annual festival at Shiloh. The story focuses not only on the violence of unbridled emotion, but also on the horrors of using tribal feuds to settle matters of justice. For the author, the age's lack of central monarchial authority leads to anarchy. If the refrain in Judges 17:6, 19:1, and 21:25 suggests that the ambivalent history of the origin of Israel's kingship in 1–2 Samuel is the only acceptable alternative to an age of chaos, these narratives and the first chapter of the book explain why a Judean dynasty is preferable. The ancestors of the northern kingdom proved historically too violent to lead a country righteously.

DISINTEGRATION IN THE RING STRUCTURE OF JUDGES

A final structure of six rings framing a central passage gives overarching coherence to the various parts of the book. In Table 3, the parallel themes in the paired sections are italicized. Ring structures

Table 3: Ring Structure in the Book of Judges

A   Historical Introduction (1:1–2:5). *Judah* is sent first to *battle Canaanites*. A Judean
           wife brings Othniel land with water. The *northern tribes fail to
           displace Canaanites*, whom God leaves as enemies. The weeping
           Israelites *worship Yahweh*.

  B   Theological Introduction (2:6–3:6). Yahweh punishes *apostasy* by delivering
             Israel to *foreigners*. Judges free them, but the Israelites marry
             Canaanites and *worship other gods*.

    C   Othniel of Judah (3:7–11), who had an *Israelite wife, defeats* the king of Aram.

      D   Ehud of Benjamin (3:12–30) has *two messages* for Eglon, king of Moab
             (3:19, 20), who is *killed* by him. With *Ephraimites*, he slays *10,000*
             Moabites at the *Jordan*.

        E   Shamgar (3:31) *kills* 600 Philistines.

          F   Deborah of Ephraim (4:1–5:31), a *prophetess of Yahweh wed to an
                 Israelite*, urges Barak to defeat Sisera. *Jael* drives a tent peg
                 through Sisera's *skull*. Deborah's *Victory ode*.

            G   Gideon of Manasseh (6:1–8:32). Gideon *destroys an altar of Baal*
                 and builds an altar to Yahweh. He *routs Midian*. *Ephraim threatens*
                 to arm, and *Gileadite* cities have to be disciplined. Gideon refuses
                 kingship but *makes an ephod* that leads Israel astray.

          F'   Abimelech of Shechem (8:33–9:57), son of Gideon's *concubine*, uses
                 money of *Baal-Berith* to slay 70 stepbrothers. When Abimelech is
                 made king, Jotham's *parable* prophesies Shechem's ruin and his
                 death. A *woman* crushes his *skull* with a millstone.

        E'   Five minor judges (10:1–5; 12:8–15) *do not battle*.

      D'   Jephthah of Gilead (10:6–12:7), the dispossessed son of a *harlot*, delivers
             two messages to the king of Ammon (11:12–13, 14:28), which are
             ignored. He defeats Ammon, but must *sacrifice* his daughter.
             Gileadites slay *42,000 Ephraimites* at the *Jordan*.

    C'   Samson of Dan (13:1–16:31) has *Philistine wives or harlots*, two of whom
             betray him. Though he *kills* over 4,000 Philistines, Judeans
             surrender him, he dies in Gaza, he wins no Philistine territory,
             and his tribe is forced to migrate.

  B'   Micah of Ephraim and the Danite Migration (17:1–18:31). Micah makes an
             idol out of silver consecrated to Yahweh. God does not stop
             Danite *migrants from stealing the image* and priest.

A'   Benjamin is punished for the outrage at Gibeah in Benjamin (19:1–21:25). An
           Ephraimite's Judean *concubine* is raped to death when he avoids
           Canaanite sexual attack. *Judah* is sent first to *battle against sinful
           Benjamin* (20:18). The defeated tribe get new *brides*.

are commonly used in the Bible to mark differences between the two
halves of a work, the conclusion reversing the state of affairs at the
beginning. The event with greatest thematic significance appears at

the center of the text.[11] In Judges, the Deuteronomistic ideal of the first four figures is replaced by the depravity of the end of the book. Gideon provides the transition from order to chaos.

In the first frame (A and A'), Judah's orderly elimination of Canaanite influence contrasts with northern excesses that jeopardize the existence of the nation. Othniel's Judean wife brings the stability that the dowry of land with water bestows. In the final narrative, the rape of the Ephraimite's Judean concubine, occasioned by Canaanite lust, leads to the decimation of a tribe. The phrasing of Judges 20:18 consciously echoes 1:1–2, but whereas Judah's advance to battle is intended to drive out Canaanites in chapter 1, chapter 20 has Judah attacking an Israelite tribe, attempting to extirpate Canaanite influences that should have been overcome earlier. In the next ring (B, B'), the Deuteronomistic condemnation of the Israelite worship of Canaanite gods is paired with a narrative that illustrates the point concretely. No judge arises in the second passage. Instead, Micah ironically creates a powerless idol out of silver devoted to Yahweh, and Danite marauders steal this worthless image.

The first four judges are also paralleled with sections that intensify this sense of deterioration in the second half of the book. In frame C, Othniel, whose Israelite wife brings him land and who successfully conquers the king of Aram, is paired with Samson, whose Philistine women betray him and who does not conquer any Philistine territory. Frame D turns to Ehud and Jephthah who both relay two messages to a king, but Ehud succeeds in destroying Eglon of Moab, while the Ammonite monarch ignores Jephthah before being defeated on the battlefield. The Ephraimites join with Ehud to slay ten thousand Moabites at the fords of the Jordan, but Jephthah is reduced to killing four times as many Ephraimites in a civil war at the same river. In frame E, Shamgar's heroic slaying of six hundred Philistines outshines the minor judges, who do not fight despite many signs of undesirable foreign influence. The next frame (F) contrasts Deborah, a prophetess of Yahweh, with Abimelech, an Israelite devotee of Baal-Berith. Whereas Deborah rouses Barak to defeat Canaanites, Abimelech declares war on his own, killing his stepbrothers and razing his home town of Shechem. Both narratives end with a woman crushing the skull of a villain—the Canaanite Sisera and the Shechemite Abimelech.

In the seventh section (G), at the center of this structure, stands Gideon. While his early destruction of an altar of Baal and reduction of Midian place him in the company of the previous heroes, he is the first judge to face revolt. Although he calms the Ephraimites, he has to discipline two Gileadite cities that refused to help him capture the fleeing Midianite princes. Even worse, he is the first judge to make an idolatrous image that leads Israel astray. His marriage to a concubine at Shechem is equally disturbing since that city is presented as a center of Baal worship. All the following episodes present at least one of these sins which the Deuteronomistic prologue condemns so roundly. Abimelech, the son of the possibly Canaanite concubine, himself worships Baal. The judge Ibzan weds his sons and daughters outside his clan. Jephthah is the son of a "harlot." The cognate verb of this noun is used in Judges 2:17 and 8:27, 33 to describe idolatrous worship of foreign deities. Samson dallies with three Philistine women, Micah has an idol cast out of silver dedicated to Yahweh, and the Ephraimite of the last story is drawn into the whirlpool of Canaanite sexual practice.

CONCLUSION

Whereas the modern historian, philosopher, or theologian remains most sensitive to sequential arguments, the student of literature knows that several nonsequential rhetorical, thematic, and symbolic patterns can coexist in a complex text. All of the themes and patterns in the Book of Judges cohere to emphasize the author's belief that the era disintegrated because of the Israelite failure to establish a religion uncontaminated by foreign influences. Instead of remaining faithful to Yahweh, the Israelites marry Canaanites and inevitably begin to worship foreign gods. The first chapter contends, as is supported by archaeological and literary records, that the Israelites failed to drive out all Canaanite influence. Judah and Simeon may conquer eleven cities and districts, including important Davidic centers, and Joseph may contribute the one nonsouthern triumph, bringing the tally to a perfect twelve; however, the chapter continues with the failure of the northern tribes to achieve similar victories. The sevenfold failure of Benjamin, Manasseh, and Ephraim, coupled with the fourteenfold failure of the Galilean tribes to subdue the Canaanite populations, points to a southern bias against the ancestors of the northern kingdom, Israel, which was also known as Ephraim. In the arrangement of tribes from south to north in chapters 1 and 3–21, Ephraim is deliberately out of sequence, first paired with the disruptive Abimelech, then providing the anarchic ending of the book. The Deuteronomistic comment in Judges 2:1–5 sums up the theological significance of the first chapter. The nation is chastized for not destroying Canaanite religion and warned that the alien gods will become a snare. The passage ends with the Israelites weeping, but they still turn back to Yahweh.

Judges 2:6–3:6 moves from a short description of the death of Joshua to a generalized Deuteronomistic evaluation of the main features of the age of the judges, which is marked by recurring apostasy. Whether God sends deliverers before or after they are requested (Judges 2:16, 18), the Israelites refuse to turn wholeheartedly to him. In this section, whole nations, not just the cities of chapter 1, are left to test Israel's religious and military powers (Judges 2:21–3:2). Ominously, this prologue ends with the nation marrying with Canaanites and turning from Yahweh to worship other deities.

The disintegration intimated in this prologue colors the rest of the book, with its ring structure heightening the contrast between Judah's victories at the beginning and northern ungodliness at the end. In both halves of the book, two geographical spirals lead to chaos at the center of the nation. The first four judges in chapters 3:7–9:57 present a series of brilliant victories, pushing back the enemies of Israel from the four corners of the world, as Aram, Moab, the Philistines, and northern Canaanites are defeated. The enemies recede in a circle moving clockwise from the northeast, the farthest extreme from the southern tribes with which the book begins. The geographical organization may be intended as a structural parallel to the Deuteronomistic phrases "peoples round about" (Judges 2:12; Deut. 6:14; 13:7; 2 Kings 17:15), and "enemies round about" (Judges 2:14; Deut. 12:10; 25:19; Josh. 23:1). But the sense of triumph does not endure. Israelite apostasy not only resurfaces after each victor's death, but the fifth episode, at the epicenter of the ring structure, is marred by failure. Gideon himself makes an ephod that his contemporaries worship. Worse, the sixth figure, Gideon's son Abimelech, seizes kingship by force and attacks Israel from an Ephraimitic city.

The disintegration increases with the final seven judges. The order hinted at in the clockwise arrangement of minor judges is soon shattered by Jephthah's failure to avert either personal tragedy or civil war with Ephraim. Samson has neither the military success of an Ehud, the prophetic illumination of a Deborah, nor even the support of his tribesmen or neighbors, who hand him over to the enemy. Dan consists of a gang of leaderless predators, stealing an innocent man's shrine and destroying a peaceful settlement. In the final grisly episode, the tribe of Benjamin is almost exterminated by other Israelites. Ephraimites are the central characters of the last five chapters, emphasizing the strong antinorthern bias of the book. Twice earlier in the text, at Judges 1:29 and 12:13–15, Ephraim appears out of the proper geographical order, possibly to suggest its destabilizing influence. The book ends not just with a plea for a king to end the anarchy, but also—recalling the idealization of Judah in chapter 1—with the insinuation that only a Davidic monarch could unite the festering tribes into a great and godly nation.

Notes

1. For historical background, see R. de Vaux, *The Early History of Israel*, vol. 2 (London: Darton, Longman, & Todd, 1978); A. D. H. Mayes, "The Period of the Judges and the Rise of the Monarchy," in *Israelite and Judaean History*, ed. J. H. Hayes (Philadelphia: Westminster Press, 1977), pp. 285–331; N. K. Gottwald, *The Hebrew Bible: A Socio-Literary Introduction* (Philadelphia: Fortress Press, 1985), pp. 230–88 and bibliography on pp. 630–33; *The Harper Atlas of the Bible*, ed. J. B. Pritchard (New York: Harper & Row, 1987); and *The Cambridge Ancient History*, 3d ed., vol. 2, pt. 2, *History of the Middle East and the Aegean Region c. 1380–1100 B.C.*, ed. I. E. S. Edwards (Cambridge: Cambridge University Press, 1975). Hereafter, *CAH* 2.2. For commentaries in English on Judges, see George F. Moore, *A Critical and Exegetical Commentary on Judges*, International Critical Commentary (Edinburgh: Clark, 1895); C. F. Burney, *The Book of Judges with Introduction and Notes*, 2d ed. (London: Rivingtons, 1920); John Gray, ed., *Joshua, Judges and Ruth*, Century Bible, New ed. (London: Nelson, 1967); Robert G. Boling, *Judges: Introduction, Translation, and Commentary*, Anchor Bible (Garden City, N.Y.: Doubleday, 1975); J. Alberto Soggin, *Judges: A Commentary* (Philadelphia: Westminster Press, 1981). See also R. Polzin, *Moses and the Deuteronomist: A Literary Study of the Deuteronomic History* (New York: Seabury Press, 1980), esp. pt. 1, on Deuteronomy, Joshua, Judges. The Revised Standard Version of the Bible is quoted throughout. Conversations about Judges with my colleague, Paul Mosca, have proved illuminating.

2. For a well-illustrated review of the Israelite archeological material, see V. Fritz, "Conquest or Settlement? The Early Iron Age in Palestine," *Biblical Archaeologist* 50 (1987): 84–100. The standard sourcebook of literary analogues is *Ancient Near Eastern Texts Relating to the Old Testament*, 3d ed., ed. J. B. Pritchard (Princeton: Princeton University Press, 1969). On the Aegean connections of the Philistines and other "Sea Peoples," see *CAH* 2.2, pp. 371–88, 508–12; and T. Dothan, *The Philistines and Their Material Culture* (New Haven: Yale University Press, 1982), pp. 21–23, 289–96. On Mycenean borrowings from the Near East, see T. B. L. Webster, *From Mycenae to Homer* (London: Methuen, 1964), pp. 64–90.

3. For many of the parallels between Samson and Heracles, see O. Margalith, "Samson's Foxes," "Samson's Riddle and Samson's Magic Locks," "More Samson Legends," and "The Legends of Samson/Heracles," *Vetus Testamentum* 35 (1985): 224–29; 36 (1986): 225–34, 397–405; 37 (1987): 63–70. Agamemnon sacrificed Iphigeneia for favorable winds to hasten his fleet to Troy: see Aeschylus, *Agamemnon*, ll. 151–55, 223–46, 1372–1576; and Sophocles *Electra*, ll. 530–32. Artemis substitutes a hind for Iphigeneia at the last moment in Euripides, *Iphigeneia in Aulis*, ll. 1581–1601, and *Iphigeneia in Tauris*, ll. 6–9, 27–34. Compare the ram that God gives Abraham in place of Isaac in Genesis 22.

4. The literature on oral composition is now vast. See, for example, G. S. Kirk, *Homer and the Oral Tradition* (Cambridge: Cambridge University Press, 1976); R. C. Culley, *Studies in the Structure of Hebrew Narrative* (Philadelphia: Fortress Press, 1976); *Semeia* 5 (1976); R. Alter on typescenes in *The Art of Biblical Narrative* (New York: Basic Books, 1981), pp. 47–62; J. A. Notopoulos, "Parataxis in Homer: A New Approach to Homeric Literary Criticism," *Transactions of the American Philological Association* 80 (1949): 1–23; and A. J. Hauser, "Judges 5: Parataxis in Hebrew Poetry," *Journal of Biblical Literature* 99 (1980): 23–41.

5. On the Deuteronomist, see Polzin's *Moses and the Deuteronomist*, and the brief survey with

bibliography in N. K. Gottwald, *The Hebrew Bible*, pp. 138–39, 240–47, 296–302, 624, 633–34. The earliest date for the Deuteronomist would be the reign of Josiah (640–609 B.C.E.), but his work is usually placed after the destruction of Judah in 587 B.C.E. Once one has worked through the texts with a concordance, the theory of the Deuteronomistic authorship of Joshua–2 Kings seems irrefutable. Not only are many of the phrases rare outside Deuteronomy–2 Kings, but their combination and concentration is unique in these works. Several pages would be required to list all parallels relevant to Judges.

6. The phrase appears in Judges 2:11; Deut. 4:25; 1 Sam. 15:19; 2 Sam. 12:9; 1 Kings 11:6; 14:22; 15:26, 34; 16:25, 30; 2 Kings 3:2; 8:18, 28; 13:2, 11; 14:24; 15:9, 18, 24, 28; 17:2, 17; 21:2, 20; 23:32, 37; 24:9, 19.

7. See M. Weinfeld, "The Period of the Conquest and of the Judges as Seen by the Earlier and the Late Sources," *Vetus Testamentum* 17 (1967): 94.

8. See R. G. Boling's commentary on Joshua in the Anchor Bible (Garden City, N.Y.: Doubleday, 1982), pp. 408, 412, 475–77.

9. Jewish tradition places Ibzan's home at Bethlehem in Judah, but elsewhere Judges 17:7, 8, 9, and 19:1, 2, and 18 invariably use the phrase, "Bethlehem in Judah." Since the Judean city is not mentioned in Joshua, while the Bethlehem of Zebulun is (Joshua 19:15), several commentaries conclude that Ibzan comes from Zebulun. See Moore, p. 310; Burney, p. 334; and Boling on Judges, pp. 215–16 (all cited in n.1).

10. The Hebrew word usually translated "feast" in Judges 14:10 means "party," or "drinking bout;" see Boling's Anchor Bible (1975) commentary on Judges, pp. 228, 231.

11. Compare the ring structure sketched by D. W. Gooding, "The Composition of the Book of Judges," *Eretz-Israel* 16 (1982): 70*–79*. On ring structures in the Bible, see my forthcoming article on Ruth in a Modern Language Association volume on biblical literature, edited by Y. S. Feldman and B. Olshen; Y. T. Radday, "Chiasmus in Hebrew Biblical Narrative," in J. W. Welch, ed., *Chiasmus in Antiquity* (Hildesheim: Gerstenberg, 1981), pp. 50–117; J. P. Fokkelman, *Narrative Art in Genesis* (Assen: Van Gorcum, 1975), and *Narrative Art and Poetry in the Books of Samuel*, 4 vols. projected (Assen: Van Gorcum, 1981–).

Narrative Control in the Book of Ruth

State University of New York College at Brockport

> Where you go I will go,
> and where you lodge I will lodge;
> your people shall be my people,
> and your God my God;
> where you die I will die,
> and there will I be buried.
> May the Lord do so to me and more also
> if even death parts me from you.

THIS familiar passage that opens the Book of Ruth quickly draws our attention to the daughter-in-law who rejects her right to the protection of her parents' home upon the death of her husband for the uncertain future with her widowed mother-in-law, Naomi. The rich details of the story—Ruth and Orpah fleeing their barren futures in Moab, Ruth gleaning in fields under the favorable eye of Boaz, the wealthy bachelor arranging the marriage at the city gate—so engage us that the craft of the consummate storyteller is disguised.

While the tale initially appears to be about Ruth's faithfulness, the careful reader discovers that like through Shakespeare's Brutus, its meaning is found through Naomi. By using her to advance the plot and seeing much of the story through her eyes, the author subtly shows the biblical theme of self-help: God's plan is unconsciously carried out by the Naomis of this world who think they are only working out their own destiny. A close study of the plot reveals that the narrator keeps Naomi ever present in the story, either through her direct involvement or through Ruth's actions guided by and later reported to her mother-in-law.

The following breakdown of the story into nine major scenes somewhat modifies Werner H. Schmidt's outline.[1] By dividing the Book of Ruth into these components, we can more readily see that the narrator intended that the reader never forgets Naomi from beginning to end. The phrases highlighted below support how deliberately the narrator included her.

1:1–7a   In the exposition, Naomi becomes a widow, though not without hope, since the narrator transfers the parental claim from the dead father to the living mother. Naomi is "left with *her* two children"(v. 3).[2] Naomi is mentioned in six of the first seven verses, whereas Ruth is mentioned only three times—and two of these are as Naomi's daughter-in-law.

1:7b–19a   The rising action begins when Naomi tells Orpah and Ruth to return to their families and ends as Ruth utters the famous "where *you* go . . ." (emphasis added throughout the rest of the outline is mine).

2:19b–22

The scene shifts from Moab to Bethlehem where Naomi who was once known as "the gracious one, the sweet one" is now Mara, "bitter." Not a word is said about changes in Ruth's character or station in life.

2:1–17   Boaz and Ruth first meet in the Bethlehem field at harvest time. Although the text is silent about motivation, surely Naomi knew that her wealthy relative Boaz owned the field into which Ruth went to glean. Finding her favorable, Boaz says to Ruth: "It has been shewed me, all that thou hast done unto thy *mother-in-law* since the death of thine husband" (v. 11).

2:18–23   Ruth tells Naomi of her special treatment by Boaz. "And her *mother-in-law* saw what she had gleaned . . . (v. 18b). And her *mother-in-law* said unto her . . . (v. 19). And *Naomi* said unto her daughter-in-law . . . (v. 20). And *Naomi* said unto Ruth her daughter-in-law . . . (v. 22).

3:1–5   Naomi's plan is for Ruth to meet Boaz. Aware of the kindness of Boaz, Naomi begins to act upon it. "She does not wait for matters to take their course or for God to intervene with a miracle. Instead, she herself moves from being the receiver of calamity to becoming the agent of change and challenge. . . . Now she returns to that need with the power of a plan: When Naomi says, 'My daughter, should I not seek a home for you, that it may be well with you?' Ruth responds: 'All that thou sayest unto me I will do.'"[3]

3:6–18   The nocturnal meeting of Ruth and Boaz on the

threshing floor is followed by Ruth's reports to Naomi. "And when she came to her *mother-in-law* (v. 16). . . . These six measures of barley gave he me; for he said to me, Go not empty unto thy *mother-in-law*" (v. 17).

4:1–12   Naomi and Boaz must have met sometime before the legal proceedings in the gate at which he publicly declares himself for Ruth, for in verse 9 he says: "Ye are witnesses this day, that I have bought all that was Elimelech's and all that was Chilion's and Mahlon's, of *the hand of Naomi*." "The redeemer" withdraws when he discovers that—following the Levirate Law—he must purchase Naomi's land (v. 9) as well as relinquish the land to Ruth's firstborn son.

4:13–17   When Boaz marries Ruth, we learn that "there is a *son born to Naomi*" (v. 17). In the final nine verses of the chapter, Ruth is mentioned once, and then as a daughter-in-law, and Naomi four times.

4:18–22   The tale closes with a list of generations from Pharez down to David. More will be said later about what appears to be a weak denouement to an otherwise aesthetically satisfying story.

If we were to think of this story as primarily being Ruth's, then mentions of Naomi are unnecessarily intrusive. However, given the narrator's emphasis on Naomi's explicit presence throughout the story, Ruth assumes the role of a willing marionette in the hands of a crafty, strong-willed mother-in-law.

Beside what is stated in the narrative, Naomi's presence is also *implicit* throughout in the plot. Two examples should suffice for the many silences about her actions we can only infer from the plot development. First, Naomi is the only one who could have told the Bethlehemites about Ruth's kindness, later mentioned by Boaz (2:11). And she must have settled the sale of her land to Boaz sometime between chapters 3 and 4, before he met Such a One at the gate (4:1–12). Thus, the plot clearly emphasizes Naomi whenever possible, and when Ruth is centerstage she is often identified as Naomi's daughter-in-law rather than as the most important figure in the cosmos of the story.

Equally important to the action, to the events, is the narrator's control of the point of view. Whenever possible, the narrator tells the story from Naomi's perspective, for when Ruth acts we readers often learn of her action in Naomi's presence or through her eyes. In large part, for instance, the rising action is about Naomi's sorrows (1:7b–19a). And likewise, the denouement is about her happiness.

For example, in chapter 2 the narrator repeatedly shows Ruth's actions through Naomi's eyes: "And her mother-in-law saw what she had gleaned..." (v. 18b). "And her mother-in-law said unto her..." (v. 19). "And Naomi said unto her daughter-in-law..." (v. 20). "And Naomi said unto Ruth her daughter-in-law..." (v. 22). Thus Naomi functions at the center of the story. She is offstage only when it would be inappropriate for her to be present, such as in the nocturnal meeting between Ruth and Boaz or at the gathering of men by the city gate; and when she is offstage, the narrator often summarizes events and later presents them through her eyes.

But we can understand at a deeper level how Naomi holds together the Book of Ruth when we approach it from the structuralist premise that form precedes function. "Vladimir Propp, in his foundational study, *Morphology of the Folktale* (2nd. ed. 1968) defined the dramatis personae functionally; as 'actants' the actors are determined by the spheres of action in which they participate" writes Glendon E. Bryce. Bryce adds, "The form of the story, then, is the narrative syntax, that which is found within a narrative but which is presupposed by it. Stories consist of substance and form, but it is the form that produces the narrative and determines its significance."[4]

The remainder of this paper is an application of this approach to the Book of Ruth. Through a study of its form, we can approach the deeper meaning of a story—a meaning whose key is the character of Naomi. Having shown that our attention is fixed on her, I further propose that she is the principal actant of every scene—whether or not she actually appears in it.

David Jobling, writing in *The Sense of Biblical Narrative* about the Book of Samuel, notes that "the theme of *knowledge* of who knows what is going on in the narrative is a very important and also very problematic one."[5] This is also true of the Book of Ruth. Jobling rightfully points out that finding out "who knows what is going on in the narrative" is best revealed through the actantial schema developed by A. Julien Greimas[6] from Vladimir Propp's *Morphology*, a study which focuses on the changed states of characters within a story. Before applying Greimas's narrative theory to the Book of Ruth, we need to review its principles, illustrated in the following schema:

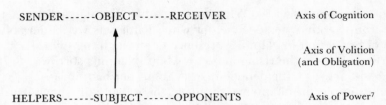

Starting in the upper left corner, the sender helps get the object to the receiver. In turn, the subject—aided by helpers and thwarted by opponents—sets out to win the object. In the right column, the axes deal with the modality of the story, or *why* events occur. The Axis of Cognition and the Axis of Power are actual or known while the Axis of Volition (and Obligation) are virtual or wished for.[8]

Applying this to the Book of Ruth, we have:

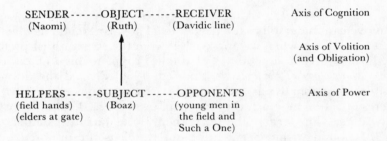

Note in the left side of the schema that the *sender* (Naomi) sets the stage—to get the *object* (Ruth) to the *receiver* (Yahweh or the Davidic line). The *subject* or *protagonist* (Boaz) is aided by various *helpers* (field hands and elders by the city gate) and thwarted by *opponents* (young men in the fields and Such a One).

On the Axis of Cognition modality level, Naomi is the most knowledgeable character in the story: she understands what must happen from the beginning. She directs the daughters-in-law in their thematic roles of dependent, marriageable women, or "objects," to place themselves under male protection upon the deaths of her husband and sons. When Orpah returns to her Moabite family, Naomi is free to direct her attention to Ruth.

Naomi must have known what her return to Bethlehem held for them. The famine over (1:6), she could turn her family's land there to good use. Also, she must have known the Levirate Law as well as the genealogy of her kinfolk: Such a One, her closest relative, preceded the wealthy land-owning bachelor, Boaz. Naomi must have surmised that Such a One was not eager to mar his own family's inheritance (4:6) by buying land that he would lose if Ruth would have a son. I think that Naomi deliberately brought Ruth to Bethlehem where she could be put in the path of Boaz: he alone was willing and able to take a bride, especially when Naomi could add the lure of her land.

The narrator's tour de force is to make Boaz the protagonist in the story while keeping Naomi in our minds. To do this, Boaz must be raised to Naomi's level. Again, Bryce provides the theoretical framework: "At the beginning of the instruction, the disciple, who will become the eventual subject of the action envisaged, is assumed to be in a state of ignorance. [He] must first acquire the competence, the cognition necessary for his eventual performance."[9] In other words, Boaz must be ignorant about Ruth: he only sees her as a widowed relative who "happens" on his field. True, he protects her from the field hands, but the text suggests he does so as a family leader rather than as a lover.

Enter Naomi. Most likely through her Boaz learns about Ruth's past and present condition (2:11). And through Naomi's sale of her land to him, Boaz acquires the means to outwit Such a One. In short, with the continuing help of Naomi, Boaz takes charge. The narrator has gradually shifted the story from one of cognition to one of action, of power—from Naomi to Boaz—yet continues to keep her in our minds. Such a shift does not deny Phyllis Trible's view: "Boaz and Naomi unite as an older generation concerned for the safety of a young woman in an environment of young men."[10]

But there is another level. Our attention is shifted from the sender Naomi to the subject Boaz in the Axis of Volition (and Obligation) modal, the "wished for"; at this level his function goes beyond protecting Ruth to seeking her hand. To overcome the greatest hurdle—the Levirate Law—Boaz and Naomi must join forces behind the scene to give her land to Ruth rather than to the most immediate relative, Such a One. Finally, in the Axis of Power modal, Boaz takes charge from Naomi: to our delight, he outwits the redeemer Such a One by requiring him to buy Naomi's land that would revert to Ruth's firstborn male heir; when the redeemer wisely declines the offer, Boaz and Ruth are free to marry.

By using Bryce's theoretical framework, we can see yet another way in which the narrator keeps Naomi before us. Bryce's comments about the subject/hero, Boaz, apply to her as well. "Thus, not until the Subject is recognized as the hero, a function that takes place at the cognitive level, does he realize the effects of his performance. Even though the subject has overcome the Anti-Subject and restored the situation of lack, he must undergo a final glorifying test before he is given the Object of his quest. These three narrative components on the syntagmatic plane, the qualifying test, the principal test, and the glorifying test, form a narrative isotopy, the common axis of meaning being the struggle of the Subject."[11]

Both Naomi and Boaz pass these tests. Ruth's qualifying test is the death of husband and sons—the threatened end of the family line; her principal test, the marriage and restoration of the family line; and her glorifying test, the recognition of her family line. Likewise, Boaz has three trials: his qualifying tests are to protect Ruth from the young men in the fields and from gossip following the threshing-floor incident; his principal test, with Such a One at the gate; and his glorifying one, the recognition of his lineage. It is important to note that Naomi and Boaz pass the glorifying test together, leading to the triumphant phrase: "There is a son born to Naomi." At the story's end, the sender, object, subject, and receiver are one—thus weaving together its threads to our aesthetic satisfaction.

We could ask, What aesthetic value does the genealogy of the House of Pharez which closes the Book of Ruth add to the story? Some textual critics argue that since these concluding verses are a later addition they can be ignored; however, I think that it culminates the narrative. First, it obviously links Ruth and Boaz to the House of David, thereby strengthening the book's claim as Holy Scripture. But of at least equal importance, the genealogy rounds out Naomi's story. This question of inclusion that initially seems to be about content turns out to be a question of form: we return to the axis of cognition to finally locate the Book of Ruth and its characters in the Davidic line. Not Boaz, but the House of Pharez—the Davidic line—is the receiver. And our delight is increased when we see once again the trickster gets tricked in Scriptures: behind the text is the story of God's will being worked out in history. The seemingly clever Naomi unwittingly has done God's work even though she thinks she is in charge. "And Boaz begat Obed. And Obed begat Jesse, and Jesse begat David" (4:21b–22)—Israel's salvation. Thus on the profound plane of God's will being worked out in time, Naomi truly becomes the sender of Ruth to the House of Pharez.

Notes

1. Werner H. Schmidt, *Old Testament: Introduction*, trans. Matthew J. O'Connell (New York: Crossroad, 1984), p. 315.

2. Phyllis Trible, "A Human Comedy: The Book of Ruth," in *Literary Interpretations of Biblical Narratives*, ed. Kenneth R. R. Gros Louis (Nashville, Tenn.: Abingdon Press, 1982), 2:162.

3. Ibid., pp. 176–77.

4. Glendon E. Bryce, "The Structural Analysis of Didactic Texts," in *Biblical and Near Eastern Studies: Essays in Honor of William Sanford LaSor*, ed. Gary A. Tuttle (Grand Rapids, Mich.: Eerdmans, 1978), p. 109.

5. David Jobling, *The Sense of Biblical Narrative: Three Structural Analyses in the Old Testament* (Sheffield: Journal for the Study of the Old Testament Press, 1978), p. 20.

6. A. Julien Greimas, *Semantique structurale: Recherche de méthode* (Paris: Larousse, 1966), pp. 172–91.

7. Jobling, *Biblical Narrative*, p. 15.

8. Bryce, "Didactic Texts," pp. 112–13.

9. Ibid., p. 112.

10. Trible, "A Human Comedy," p. 175.

11. Bryce, "Didactic Texts," p. 111.

"Samuel, Whear 'Ast Tha Been Sin' I Saw Thee?"

John I. Ades

Southern Illinois University at Edwardsville

THE genesis of this paper represents for me one of the continuing pleasures of university teaching: the situation where a classroom exchange can stimulate a teacher to reexamine more closely a text he may have brushed over too lightly. For years I had remarked (like many others) that the Old Testament has no clear formulation of the nature of afterlife. Then one day in class after we had gone over the seance at En-dor in 1 Samuel 28, a student suddenly raised her hand and asked, "If Samuel is dead but can still be called back by the witch, where has he been?" Where, indeed? "Sheol," I answered. "What's that?" came back the student. Like the Furies, when certain students get onto your case, they are persistent—and rightly so. At that point this paper was inevitable, title and all.

Thinking over the student's question has led me to consider the general problem of afterlife in the Old Testament, and what follows are some observations I have sorted out from scholarly discussion of the subject and from one Old Testament unit, 1 Samuel 28:3–25, which I think clearly brings together several Hebrew beliefs about afterlife.

The Hebrew faith, modern as well as ancient, seems firmly anchored in this world, a view that has been confirmed to me in conversations I have had with a rabbi and with one of my Jewish colleagues. The great normative documents of the Ten Commandments and the discourses of Moses in Deuteronomy—in fact Torah in general— seem to bear this out. The Old Testament has nothing like the conclusion of John's Gospel, where the person of faith is promised "life in his name" (20:31b). In fact Adam is explicitly expelled from Eden "lest he put forth his hand and take also of the tree of life, and eat, and live forever" (Gen. 3:22). Nevertheless, as is almost always the case in any society, the thought of annihilation at death is scarcely tenable (*pace* Lucretius, although even his "atoms" survive), and Hebrew culture is no exception.

Theodore Gaster puts the generally accepted view of Hebrew concerns with afterlife concisely: "The Old Testament offers no formal doctrine concerning the destination and fate of the dead; all that it says on the subject belongs to the domain of popular lore."[1] In this he is undoubtedly correct. But popular lore need not be given the back of the hand; rather it should be examined as potentially suggesting cultural beliefs that may lie outside doctrinaire formulation. I do not know whether Gaster would consider the seance at En-dor "popular lore," but I believe the scene does give clear indications of certain attidudes toward afterlife. A more extreme negative statement about the subject comes from G. W. Caird in his exegesis of the En-dor scene in *The Interpreter's Bible*: "This account of the reappearance of Samuel has often been used by those who wanted to prove that Israel had an early belief in afterlife. There is no justification for this idea. It is true that Sheol is often described as though it were a place of continued existence, but this continued existence is death rather than life."[2] Well, as the famous Danish scholar, Horatio, put it, "There needs no ghost, my lord, come from the grave to tell us this." In Caird's crisp tautology, *all* afterlife is death. Period. End of report. But the fact remains that Samuel reappears in this world in the seance at En-dor, and that says to me that he has some form of continuing existence.

We get a more balanced view from W. O. E. Oesterley: "We find in the Old Testament a mass of antique conceptions regarding life beyond the grave which the Israelites shared with other peoples, and which had been handed down from time immemorial";[3] and from H. H. Rowley, who suggests "it is sometimes maintained that no inklings of a worthwhile afterlife are to be found in the Old Testament. . . . While the differences between the two Testaments are not to be ignored or minimized, it will be seen that the contrast is not so strong as is supposed, and the seeds of every side of New Testament thought are to be found here."[4] Rowley adds a note that Old Testament evidence about funerary and mourning customs provided by archaeology point to a belief in survival after death. An instance relevant to Samuel's burial "in his house in Ramah" (1 Sam. 25:1, so also Joab, 1 Kings 2:34), I would note, is the discovery of lamps and food bowls in graves under house walls in Israelite times, designed presumably to assist the departed in the journey to Sheol.[5] Both may of course be purely symbolic, but we are at least entitled to speculate about the perceived nature of the deceased that after death he could make use of illumination and food. In fact, Oesterley argues that "a consideration of the mourning and burial customs . . . among the Israelites offers perhaps the most instructive illustration of their belief in Immortality [and that] throughout the Old Testament . . . from the foundation of the monarchy there was a 'popular' as well as an 'official' doctrine of Immortality."[6]

I would have been more comfortable with Oesterley's contention, however, had he used "afterlife" instead of "immortality" and thereby escaped any connotation of a positive or blissful state; for whatever the nature of continuing existence in Sheol, the Old Testament makes it abundantly clear that the Hebrews would have echoed Achilles' sentiments: "Let me hear no smooth talk of death from you, Odysseus, light of councils. Better, I say, to break sod as a farm hand for some poor country man . . . than lord it over all the exhausted dead."[7]

But both Oesterley's and especially Rowley's points are given further support by N. J. Tromp in *Primitive Concepts of Death and the Nether World in the Old Testament*, where he shows that the Psalms contain numerous specualtions about afterlife and that the writers are "by no means marginal figures."

> The frequent poetical reflection on the nether world shows that this theme was not a peripheral phenomenon. . . . [The Psalms are] a book of common prayer . . . voic [ing] the daily emotions and the vital anxieties of the Israelite. . . . The Psalms, merely because of their frequent use, must have exerted a great influence on Hebrew thinking. The references to the hereafter in the psalter are extraordinarily numerous and they seem to imply that the people's conceptions of after-life were not so elementary and primitive as is often believed. Even if this range of ideas was not originally popular, it must have become so through the psalter.[8]

Elsewhere Tromp exhaustively examines the word *Sheol* as an index to Hebrew concern with afterlife, concluding that "we can say that the word is used there as soon as the thought of the beyond becomes operative in the Bible. As its occurrence presupposes some degree of reflection on the after-life, it seems in the nature of things that the word 'Sheol' is more frequent in poetical literature (Psalms, Proverbs, Job, Isaiah) than in the historical books."[9] Instances of Tromp's point would be Psalm 49:15: "But God will ransom my soul from the power of Sheol, for he will receive me," and Psalm 16:10: "For thou dost not give me up to Sheol, or let the godly one see the pit." Tromp also cites the divine judgment on Korah's rebellion in Numbers 16:31–33: "the ground split asunder; and the earth opened its mouth and swallowed them up, with their households and all the men that belonged to Korah and all their goods. So they . . . went down alive into Sheol; and the earth closed over them."

I want now to recapitulate the En-dor sequence and then point out the several indications there of the character of afterlife, concluding with a comment on what I consider the skillful literary art of the final paragraph.

The seance at En-dor begins with a notice that Samuel is dead and buried (in his house) in Ramah and sets up the necessary plot detail that Saul had banished all who traffic in necromancy. But when Saul sees the size of the Philistine army arrayed against him at Gilboa and finds that his inquiries for God's advice are met with only silence (rejection), he then asks his servants to find him a female with a "familiar spirit" he can consult for advice. That they have no difficulty whatever in immediately directing him to the *sorcière à En-dor* makes clear that his necromancy policy had not been effective. Being ashamed, however, of violating his own interdiction, Saul dons a disguise, goes in the night with two servants to En-dor, where he directs the medium to call up whoever he names. She balks, knowing that the king has threatened death to practicing necromancers, but being assured by the disguised Saul that no harm will come to her, she agrees to call up Samuel, whose sudden appearance (to her only, if we understand the text) causes her to shriek, "Why have you deceived me?. . . You are Saul!" (1 Sam. 28:12b).

The logic here has long troubled commentators: why should she suddenly recognize the disguised *Saul* when Samuel appears? Among many explanations are these: 1) the encounter was originally with an anonymous ghost, the name "Samuel" being supplied by a later prophetic writer who did not then edit the text accordingly;[10] 2) the witch suddenly recognizes Saul when she *hears the name* Samuel;[11] 3) and most ingenious: "Probably Samuel's voice was simulated by ventriloquism and the speech represented gave the witch an opportunity to avenge herself on Saul for his treatment of her and her fellow magicians."[12] McCarter's view (1, above) is undoubtedly correct, Rust's (3, above) being refuted by the touching generosity of the witch at the end of the chapter.

Saul brushes the recognition aside and asks what she sees. "I see a god (*elohim*) coming up out of the earth!" she replies. "What is his appearance?" demands Saul; and being told he is old and wrapped in a robe, Saul immediately recognizes Samuel, whereupon he prostrates himself in homage. "Why have you disturbed me by bringing me up?" asks an angry Samuel, and Saul replies that the Philistines press him and God will give no advice. Samuel then gives him three pieces of advice, the first of which Saul already knew: 1) God has torn the kingdom away and given it to David because Saul had disobeyed Samuel (read "God") in executing the Amalekite judgment (as reported in 1 Sam. 15); 2) the Philistines will win the impending battle;

and 3) "tomorrow you and your sons shall be with me," that is, in
Sheol. Samuel then disappears and the scene concludes by giving six
verses (more than one-fourth of the entire unit of 22) to the poignant
details of Saul's despair and hunger and the witch's successful insistence that he and his servants eat a meal she furnishes.

Now, what do we learn from this incident about the attributes of
Samuel's continuing existence that point to Hebrew beliefs in afterlife? I list six items with brief comments on each.

First, he can be summoned back to earth by a skilled medium,
which suggests a continuing cultural belief in the efficacy of necromancers despite orthodox proscription. Elsewhere we are told that
God can do likewise: "The LORD . . . brings down to Sheol and raises
up" ("Song of Hannah," 1 Sam. 2:6, which may, of course, be a
purely symbolic way of asserting God's omnipotence).

Second, he is recognizable by certain visual particulars that link
him to his earthly form: his clothing, his countenance, his bearing, his
attitude—all immediately allow Saul to identify him. Unless we are
dealing here with hallucination—always an allowable possibility in
such a scene—then we must conclude on the basis of the text that the
deceased Samuel has yet a being apprehensible by Saul's senses, both
visual and auditory. That is, Samuel has postmortem continuity with
his earthly form beyond what lies buried in Ramah. Here, curiously,
we see the aptness of Rowley's assertion that "the seeds of every side
of New Testament thought" lie in the Old. The Apostles' Creed
states, "I believe . . . in the resurrection of the body"; and the Gospels
insist that while the resurrected Christ is not a resuscitated corpse,
neither is he a disembodied spirit. Samuel is certainly not "resurrected" since he returns to Sheol. The Jewish belief in resurrection,
such as it is, is, except for the very late Book of Daniel, largely post-
biblical. But the "seed" is there, as Rowley suggests.

Third, he comes up out of the ground, which means that Sheol is
some kind of habitable enclosure below the surface of the earth (i.e.,
opposite the heavens). This accords with one common etymology for
the word *Sheol* (שָׁחַת) , the Hebrew root meaning "hollow" or "pit."
Henry P. Smith notes "the Rabbinical conceit that Samuel appeared
standing upright, while in ordinary cases shades present themselves
feet upwards."[13] Whether Smith's judgment suggests that the dead
descend to Sheol headfirst and continue in that orientation is not
altogether clear.

Fourth, he is perceived as a god or supernatural being (אֱלֹהִים) who
knows the future and may be asked about it. This accords with
another common etymology for *Sheol* (שָׁאַל), the root "to ask," suggest-

ing that Sheol is a "place of inquiry" (i.e., judgment). In keeping with Hebrew prophecy, Samuel here as elsewhere knows the future in covenant terms—unlike necromancers, ecstatics, and trancers, who merely predict the future. Saul and the Israelites will be punished (defeated) on the morrow because they have disobeyed God, essentially the same message Samuel had delivered as a "live" prophet at his last earthly meeting with Saul.

Fifth, he is angry at being disturbed, indicating a kind of rest in Sheol—if not peace, at least not torment—and he prefers to remain so. In this connection, Rowley cites a passage in the Intertestamental Apocalypse of Moses where Adam, already buried in Paradise (according to this text), also has a counterpart body buried in "a Paradise in the third heaven."[14]

Sixth, he has company in the state from which the medium has summoned him, and he will return to it forthwith, for he tells Saul that "tomorrow you and your sons shall be with me." The notion of some kind of corporate afterlife is also to be inferred from the most common Old Testament report of death: so-and-so is "gathered to his fathers." It often becomes, of course, a kind of euphemistic cliché for "he died." But a moment's reflection on, say, the report of Abraham's death in Genesis 25—that he died in old age and was gathered to his father's kin, and his sons, Isaac and Ishmael, buried him in the cave at Machpelah—makes it clear that there are two destinations for Abraham's remains: one is Machpelah, which Abraham in the past had carefully purchased from the Hittites; the other is wherever his father's kin affords corporate existence. The latter is certainly not Machpelah, and one can only conclude that it must be Sheol.

The term *Sheol*, as far as my eye tells me, first occurs in the Old Testament (as it stands sequentially) in the Jacob/Joseph sequence, where Jacob, assuming that Joseph is now dead, laments, "I shall go down to Sheol to my son, mourning" (Gen. 37:35).[15] The same point is made in 2 Samuel 12:23, where David, recovering from the death of the first child of the adulterous relationship with Bathsheba, clearly has Sheol in mind when he exclaims: "Can I bring him back again? *I shall go to him*; he will not return to me" (emphasis added).

In this one scene, 1 Samuel 28, it seems to me, there is ample evidence that the Hebrews had some fairly specific views of life beyond earthly existence. Samuel is dead, but he can return from some sort of continuous fellowship in a form Saul recognizes, bearing the truth: the Urim are loaded in favor of David, and tomorrow Saul with his sons will join Samuel in Sheol. And it was so.

A final note on the ending of the seance at En-dor. It may seem strange that the writer should give over one-fourth of the entire unit to details of Saul's hunger and the final taking of food; but the literary strategy here, I believe, is to give perspective to the tragedy of Saul by embedding it in the simple, mundane details of grief and nourishment. Saul had apparently fasted in keen anticipation of the seance, and being now weak after the devastating outcome, he is portrayed as the object of the witch's kindness. In fact, there is something genuinely elegaic about introducing food to conclude the somber denouement. We might recall that when David's first child by Bathsheba died, he washed, put on fresh clothes, and went home and had a meal, saying, "While the child was still alive, I fasted and wept; for I said, 'Who knows whether the Lord will be gracious to me, that the child may live?' But now he is dead; why should I fast?" (2 Sam. 12:21ff.). So Achilles to Priam: "Now let us think of supper. . . . Even Niobe in her extremity took thought for bread . . . being weak and spent."[16]

Thus the witch of En-dor insists that Saul and his servants, now in total despair, must take some nourishment. At first Saul refuses, but finally he agrees, and the account concludes on a simple diminuendo of touching literary art: "When they had eaten, they arose and departed that night" (1 Sam. 28:25b). The tragedy of Saul's life has now narrowed his options to one: Sheol.

Notes

All quotations from the Bible are from the Revised Standard Version, chapter and verse being cited parenthetically in the text.

1. Theodore Gaster, in *Interpreter's Dictionary of the Bible* (Nashville, Tenn.: Abingdon Press, 1962), 6:787.

2. G. W. Caird, in *The Interpreter's Bible* (Nashville, Tenn.: Abingdon Press, 1953), 2:1029.

3. W. O. E. Oesterley, *Immortality and the Unseen World* (New York: Macmillan, 1921), p. 2.

4. H. H. Rowley, *The Faith of Israel* (Philadelphia: Westminster Press, 1956), p. 153.

5. See Oesterley, *Immortality*, p. 119.

6. Ibid., p. 141.

7. Homer, *The Odyssey*, trans. Robert Fitzgerald (Garden City, N.Y.: Doubleday, 1961), 11.542–46.

8. N. J. Tromp, *Primitive Concepts of Death and the Nether World in the Old Testament* (Rome: Pontifical Biblical Institute, 1969), p. 211.

9. Ibid., p. 23.

10. 1 Samuel, trans. P. Kyle McCarter, The Anchor Bible (Garden City, N.Y.: Doubleday, 1980), pp. 421, 423.

11. T. Hertzberg, in *The New Bible Commentary*, ed. D. Guthrie et al. (London: Intervariety, 1970), p. 301.

12. E. Rust, in *The Layman's Bible*, ed. B. H. Kelly et al. (Richmond, Va.: Knox, 1959), 6:119.

13. Henry Preserved Smith, *International Critical Commentary* (New York: Scribner, 1899), 9:241.

14. Rowley, *Faith of Israel*, p. 156.

15. In some translations, including King James and the New English Bible, "Sheol" is translated "grave," while Douay gives "nether world," and Jerome renders *in infernum*; but both Speiser in Anchor Bible and Revised Standard Version correctly give "Sheol," as it occurs in the Masoretic text.

16. Homer, *The Iliad*, trans. Robert Fitzgerald (Garden City, N.Y.: Doubleday, 1974), 24.722ff.

The Dialogic Discourse of Psalms

Herbert J. Levine

Franklin and Marshall College

THE prevalence of quotations in Psalms is remarkable with respect to any comparable body of lyric poetry, ancient or modern. Like other ancient languages, Hebrew had no orthographic means for representing quotation marks, and furthermore, its poets often omitted the *verbum dicendi* in introducing quoted direct speech. Thus, every translation that includes quotations is positing two or more centers of consciousness where one alone will not suffice to explain an apparent shift in perspectives.[1] The new Jewish Publication Society version of Psalms, which is conservative in this regard, places quotation marks in no fewer than sixty-six of the one hundred and fifty poems in the collection.[2] The quoted speakers include generalized groups—the righteous, the wicked, the nations, and more particularized ones— pilgrims en route to Jerusalem, women witnessing the outcome of a battle. The individual speakers quoted are God, the King, oneself, and also, representative types—a fool, a self-reliant individual, a wicked person. Quotations are found in all the genres that Psalms scholarship has recognized.[3]

It is apparent, then, that quoting another's word, the concept so central to the discourse theory of Mikhail Bakhtin, is one of the stylistic hallmarks of the biblical Psalms. In Bakhtin, quoting another's word embodies the essential dialogic principle of prose fiction, which allows for the interplay of many voices in all their sociolinguistic diversity and stratification. In poetry, by contrast, Bakhtin claims that another's word does not have an independent existence, but is subject to the control of a unitary lyric voice. "Poetic style is by convention," he wrote, "suspended from any mutual interaction with alien discourse, any allusion to alien discourse."[4] Even where there is more than one voice in a poem, for Bakhtin, these voices tend to partake of the speaker's unitary language. In Bakhtin's monologic view of poetry, where he finds double-voicedness, he attributes it to the speaker's polemical strategy, not to a mutually fructifying interaction between one's own and another's word.

Even if we grant Bakhtin his premise that the dialogic elements in poetry are part of a unitary language (not a true social *heteroglossia*), we ought not to concede so quickly that all poetic attempts at double-

268

voicedness are always rhetorical or polemical. A famous critical dictum of Yeats's is helpful here: "We make out of the quarrel with others, rhetoric, but of the quarrel with ourselves, poetry."[5] In the Psalms, the quarrel with others and the quarrel with oneself both lead to quotation. In the first case, the quoted words pertain to an external, often political, struggle for dominance, and, in the second, to an inner dialogue, in which the speaker may seem to be quarreling with another's word, but is really quarreling internally over the nature and power of God.

In both the externally and internally oriented Psalms, the poets struggle to reconcile what other people say with their own sense of what is real. In struggling toward what Bakhtin calls an "internally persuasive discourse" (p. 345), the psalmists find themselves intimately involved with the words of others. Their religious tradition has taught them that God saves the people of Israel from its enemies and cares especially for the faithful, such as these very Levitical psalmists serving in the Temple. Contrary to these catechistic truths are the pronouncements of the atheists, who deny such claims for a providential God. And the psalmists take pains to include both sorts of statements within their own discourse. Some men are quoted as saying, "'there is, then, a reward for the righteous; / indeed God does judge on earth'" (58:12), while others say, "'How could God know? / Is there knowledge with the Most High?'" (73:11). Through this contest of quotations, we witness in the Psalms what Bakhtin calls "the ideological becoming" of human beings, seen in the "process of selectively assimilating the words of others" (p. 341).

In this ideological process, no word is more central than what Bakhtin calls "the authoritative word" of the culture. Stalinism was "the authoritative word" that Bakhtin could not address directly in his writings, but his definition applies equally to a voice representing political or religious orthodoxy. "The authoritative word demands that we acknowledge it, that we make it our own; it binds us, quite independent of any power it might have to persuade us internally; we encounter it with its authority already fused to it . . . One must either totally affirm it, or totally reject it" (pp. 342–43).

The "authoritative word" of God is quoted in sixteen Psalms, comprising several different contexts. Some quote God recalling past promises made to the Davidic king (2, 89, 110, 132). Others quote God recalling the founding events of the nation (68, 81, 95, 105). Still others quote God delivering exhortations, judgments, and promises to individuals in distress (12, 35, 91), to the nation and its enemies

(46, 50, 75, 90), and to other gods (82). Where there are quarrels in such Psalms, they are usually quarrels with others—the wicked who deny God's Providence, the nations that oppose Israel, and, once, a quarrel with God, who seems to have forgotten past promises in support of the Davidic dynasty (132).

How are we to take such instances of divine speech? Are they oracles delivered through an individual psalmist, as a kind of cultic prophet, as argued by some?[6] We might just as easily see God's speeches as being fictive representations of how God *might* speak. From our vantage point, we cannot know whether the psalmists who spoke the God-voice, or the worshipers who heard it, thought of this authoritative word as a human or divine creation or as some sort of partnership betwen the two. Whatever the provenance of the God-voice, we can learn a great deal from looking at the boundaries of such discourse about how human speakers interacted with the authoritative word of God in this poetic culture.

In describing the role of authoritative discourse in the European novel, Bakhtin comments that because of its absolute nature, "authoritative discourse permits no play with the context framing it, no play with its borders, no gradual and flexible transitions" (p. 343). To remain authoritative and timeless, such a word—whether it be religious, political, or scientific—must not enter into the novelistic dialogue and so must be set apart stylistically from the dialogizing interplay of contemporary voices. The case is rather different in the poetry of the Psalms, where the authoritative word is fused with the sacred context framing it. Thus, at a chosen moment, the human narrator simply begins quoting God in the first person, shifting into third person descriptions of God's actions and then back into first person recitations in the voice of God. Here is an example from Psalm 81, which recalls God's providential care for the formative Israelite generation. The reader should attend carefully to the pronouns in the following excerpt:

> He imposed it as a decree upon Joseph
> when he went forth from the land of Egypt;
> I heard a language that I knew not.
> I relieved his shoulder of the burden,
> his hands were freed from the basket.
>
> [vv.6–7]

> Those who hate the Lord shall cower before Him;
> their doom shall be eternal.
> He fed them the finest wheat,
> I sated you with honey from the rock.
>
> [vv.16–17]

In these lines, a modern reader is likely first to find incoherence and then may wonder how it it that "He, God" and "I, God" are interchangeable locutions. An ancient listener would presumably have understood that a psalmist's discourse exercised authority precisely because of this blurred line between personal speech and speech of divinity.

As Bakhtin notes, the authoritative word is "indissolubly fused with its authority—with political power, an institution, a person—and it stands and falls together with that authority" (p. 343). The prophets, speaking as individuals in search of an audience (in the marketplace and at the city gates), begin their discourse with an introductory formula that authorizes their speech, even as it demarcates divine speech from the surrounding human context. In the prophetic phrase, "thus spoke the Lord," we get a sense of both divine origins and human intermediation. The psalmists, however, are not only individual speakers, but representatives of an institution, the Temple cult, with the authority to recreate theophany, the God-voice speaking in its own Temple home before an appreciative audience. Since their institutional role maintains the ritualistic distance that preserves and enshrines authoritative discourse as such, their literary strategies can minimize any sense of the speakers' distance from the authoritative word they transmit.

For the psalmists, the authoritative word is lodged in the zone of sacred history in order to be retrieved and applied to the present. As Bakhtin explains, "the authoritative word is located in a distanced zone, organically connected with a past that is felt to be hierarchically higher. It is so to speak, the word of the fathers. Its authority was *acknowledged* in the past. It is a *prior* discourse. It is therefore not a question of choosing it from among other possible discourses that are its equal" (p. 342).

In Psalm 95, one of several that retells the founding events of the nation, the voice quoting God moves immediately from the present to the remembered past: "'Do not be stubborn as at Meribah, / as on the day of Massah, in the wilderness, / when your fathers put me to the test'" (vv.8–9a). Even within that zone of sacred memory, the voice cites a prior, and presumably more authoritative, discourse. The Psalm concludes with a series of internal quotations within the quotation of God's speech:

> "Forty years I was provoked by that generation;
> I thought, 'They are a senseless people;
> they would not know my ways.'
> Concerning them I swore in anger,
> 'They shall never come to My resting-place.'"

[vv.10– 11]

The psalmist quotes God quoting earlier discourse (an echo and adaptation of Numbers 14:22–23), in order to bring the authority of sacred history to bear on the present moment, namely, his own exhortation to the people, "if you would but heed His charge this day" (v.7). In this instance, divine authority is completely vested in the vehicle that delivers God's word.

This is indeed a rhetorical use of double-voicedness. The priest uses the hieratic divine voice as an extension of his own monologic control of the worshiping crowd. A similar rhetorical emphasis is present in all the Psalms in which the God-voice is given the last word (50, 75, 81, 91, 95, 132). More interesting are the cases in which the divine voice is quoted in order to quarrel with it. Precisely because the institution of the priesthood allowed for the blurring of boundaries between one's own discourse and God's, psalmists could challenge God with God's own words.[7]

In Psalm 90, this challenge revolves around repetition of forms of the verb "to turn." "You return man to dust; You decreed, 'Return you mortals!'" (v.3). The first "return," in the psalmist's language, signals natural process, while the second is God's call for moral regeneration, delivered through the prophets,[8] and, now, quoted back to God by the psalmist. Toward the end of the poem, the poet picks up God's own quoted language to plead, "Turn, Lord! How long? / Show mercy to your servants" (v.13). The imperative phrases, "Return . . . mortals" and "Turn, Lord," use plural and singular forms of the same verb. Just as God can ask the people to return in repentance, so the psalmist, as the people's representative, can use God's language to enjoin God to turn back to the people.[9] Natural process need not lead quickly to dust, in this psalmist's wordplay, if God chooses to "prosper the work of our hands"(v.17).

In a similar vein, but showing a much bolder freedom with the divine voice is Psalm 82. The psalmist creates a heavenly scenario, in which God assembles "the divine beings," presumably the inferior gods of other nations, to pronounce judgment upon them (or possibly upon earthly judges) for having failed to uphold justice in the world. The audience for the poem, the assembled community of Israel, is acting as collective witness for this heavenly tribunal. I have followed the view of most translators that the poet, as stage manager, takes the first and last lines and in between allows God to conduct the prosecution. An alternative view has the poet interrupting the proceedings, first speaking in an aside (v.5), then to the defendants (vv.6–7), and finally to God (v.8).[10] The new JPS translation avoids the issue by using no quotation marks at all, though clearly the poem displays several pronominal shifts in perspective:

v.1   God stands in the divine assembly;
      among the divine beings He pronounces judgment:

v.2   "How long will you judge perversely,
      showing favor to the wicked? (Selah).
v.3   Judge the wretched and the orphan,
      vindicate the lowly and the poor,
v.4   rescue the wretched and the needy;
      save them from the hand of the wicked.
v.5   They neither know nor understand,
      they go about in darkness;
      all the foundations of earth totter.[11]
v.6   I had taken you for divine beings,
      Sons of the Most High, all of you;
v.7   but you shall die as men do,
      fall like any prince."

v.8   Arise, God, judge the earth,
      for all the nations are your possession.

The psalmist has imaginatively stationed God in a heavenly assembly in order to turn on God from an earthly vantage point at the end of the Psalm. What God asks of the inferior divine beings in heaven is precisely what the psalmist asks of God on earth. When God asks "How long?" (v.2), we hear the "how long" of other psalmic laments (e.g., Psalm 90:13). In the inner dialogism of the poem, God's judgment is reheard through the echo of the final judging line so that the whole poem becomes charged with irony. The poem is a lament for the state of injustice on earth and the seeming absence of God's just government, but until its sharp conclusion, it is presented in the naive guise of a heavenly vision.

While the purpose of this double-voiced strategy is polemical, it proceeds from what is certainly a deep internal quarrel. Having taken the authoritative word of the culture as internally persuasive, this psalmist is acutely sensitive to contradictions to that word. The dynamism of Psalm 82 derives from the poet's willingness to expose this rift in the fabric of authoritative ideology.

The poet's solution is at once literary and theological. The poet summons the energy of both divine and human words, so as to collaborate with God in repairing the world and thereby allowing God's word to become again internally persuasive for the psalmist's generation. That collaboration could not take place without apostrophe, the trope of invocation that defines God as potentially responsive audience for every psalmic speaker. In secular poetry, the object addressed by an apostrophe—whether it be a nightingale, a West Wind, or a season—becomes a potentially responsive subject only by virtue of the poetic act that calls upon it; therefore, apostrophe is preeminently the figure of poetic vocation,[12] that which constitutes the speaker as a visionary poet (and not a madman who talks to birds and trees). In sacred poetry, however, the invocation functions quite differently. There is no need for an openmouthed "O" to allow the speaker to shift into visionary gear. God does not need to be made into a subject by a visionary poet, but rather needs to be brought back into a conversation that God started and human beings feel has been interrupted. This is the reason that the poet speaks God's words of judgment in Psalm 82, words that the people would like to hear God speak and, better still, act upon. With the concluding apostrophe, "Arise, God, judge the earth," the poet deconstructs the fictiveness of the discourse that opened the Psalm, saying, in effect: "my fictionalized words as God have no performative force. But my direct call can reestablish a relation to You. And I know that Your words are supremely able to perform what they say (cf. Genesis 1). Since we all know what You *can* say and do, why not do what is right?"

While the word of God is acknowledged as the most potent in the culture, the word of the wicked is perhaps even more central to the ideological formation of the psalmists. "Consciousness awakens to independent ideological life," Bakhtin writes, "precisely in a world of alien discourses surrounding it, and from which it cannot initially separate itself" (p. 345). The words of the wicked awaken the consciousness of many psalmists, because if what the wicked say about the world is true—that there is no God, no deliverance from misfortune, no accountability for one's actions—then the whole of Israel's collective life is a lie. Just as the psalmists attained potency vis-à-vis the authoritative word of God by transmitting, emulating and even subjecting it to ironic reproof, so must they become potent speakers in relation to the word of God's adversaries. The psalmists quote the words of the wicked in poems addressed to God, yet, presumably, an omnisicient God knows what the wicked say. The psalmists do so in order to challenge God, in the presence of the assembled community, to overturn the words of the wicked.

Yet this process of incorporating an alien discourse inevitably dulls the psalmists' polemical thrust against the wicked. The authoritative word of the culture enters into dialogue with skeptical, alien words that may prove, quite threateningly, to be internally persuasive. The psalmists do not want to be in an open dialogue with the wicked. They prefer the security of monologue, of their own self-sufficient vocabulary, but they are in dialogue with the wicked despite themselves, hoping that God's response will make it possible for them to shut out such atheistic words once and for all. We cannot know whether the words of the wicked provoked the doubts of the psalmists, or whether already existing doubts needed to be objectively represented as another's word. However we construe the origin of these quotations, we shall see their dialogic influence within these prayer-poems, revealing the complexity of the psalmists' representation of their faith.

There are twenty-four Psalms that quote the wicked, both their direct speech and their thoughts, while numerous others allude to the speech of the wicked without quoting them.[13] While the psalmists' mouths and hearts are occupied in prayer, outside the doors of the Temple is a world whose very foundations are shaken by an alien discourse strikingly opposed to the psalmists' statements of faith. Here is a sampling of jibes directed personally at psalmists, followed by denials directed at the psalmists' God:

> "There is no deliverance for him from God." [3:3]

> "When will he die and his name perish?" [41:6]

> "Where is your God?" [42:4,11]

> "God has forsaken him;
> Chase him and catch him,
> for no one will save him." [71:11]

> "God is not mindful,
> He hides His face; He never looks." [10:11]

> "There is no God." [14:1]

> "The Lord does not see it,
> The God of Jacob does not pay heed." [94:7]

> "By our tongues, we shall prevail;
> with lips such as ours, who can be our master?" [12:5]

The Psalms are full of metonymies for speech such as these: mouth, lips, tongue, teeth, throat, and, for unspoken speech, heart. Hiding something in the heart should keep a person invulnerable,[14] but in their linguistic will to power the psalmists infiltrate not only the vocal organs but the hidden self-consciousness of their adversaries as well. We know from the formulaic phrase, "He says in his heart" (Pss. 10:6, 11, 13; 14:1 = 53:2; 35:25; 74:8), that the psalmists represent

some speeches of the wicked as inward, and that these can therefore
be seen as fictive constructions[15] and, possibly, as projections of the
psalmists' own thoughts.[16] Similarly, with respect to the outward
speech of the wicked, we recognize a thematized consistency in their
deliberate negations of Israel's central beliefs. We cannot know exactly what words the psalmists heard some wicked individuals say before
inventing these stylized words for them; we can see clearly, though,
that their poems conceptualize the speech acts of the wicked in relation to their own. The wicked and the psalmists both want to prevail
with their tongues. But where the wicked insist on the autonomy of
human speech, the psalmists make their speech acts contingent on
acts of God. The Psalms that quote the wicked do not seek a mere
recitation of authoritative words, as we have seen in some historically
oriented Psalms. Instead, to revalidate the sacred history of the past,
they seek resolution of internal conflicts in external deeds: God's
powerful and persuasive acts of salvation and justice.

In their struggle against the discourse of the wicked, the psalmists
represent their antagonists by quoting their speech and by depicting
their deeds. The doubling is apt, since the wicked do not merely
speack unjustly but also perpetrate all manner of evil deeds against
the poor and the weak. We can seize on an important link between the
representation of the wicked's speech and actions. They are depicted
as hunters of the lowly, devising nets that they pull shut when the
hapless fall into their power (10:9–10). The same Psalm that depicts
them as hunters, not surprisingly, wishes that they be "caught in the
schemes they devise" (v.2). Two verses later, this word for schemes is
used in apposition to the quoted thought of the wicked, "there is no
God'" (literal translation v.4b). These clever links in the psalmist's
diction point to the conclusion that the atheistic thoughts of the
wicked *are* the net in which they will be caught. "Let the net they hid
catch them" (Ps.35:8) is the way another psalmist reflects on their
fate.

To catch the wicked in the net of their own thoughts is what Bakhtin would describe as conducting experiments and getting "solutions
in the language of another's discourse" (p. 347). In order to use
another's word thus dialogically, according to Bakhtin, that word
must first be announced in the speaker's own discourse. Psalm 10,
which we have just been considering, opens by announcing the speaker's theme: "Why, O Lord, do you stand aloof, / heedless in times of
trouble?" (v.1). This sense of distance between God and human
beings is echoed and extended in the more radical words of the arro-
gant one who thinks, "'He does not call to account; there is no God'"
(v.4). The wicked speaker is characterized through further quotation:

> "I shall not be shaken,
> through all time never be in trouble." [v.6]

> "God is not mindful,
> He hides His face, He never looks." [v.11]

When the words of the wicked are quoted for a fourth and final time, the words are reaccentuated by the psalmist. "Why should the wicked man scorn God, / thinking You do not call to account?" (v.13). In the previously quoted speeches, the wicked one spoke of God only in a distant third person; this final quotation, rendered in free indirect discourse, is in the second person, because the psalmist has transposed the words of the wicked into a new context, a direct interrogation of God.

The words of the wicked are alien to the psalmist, and yet, since they are also possible conclusions to be drawn from the Psalm's opening lament over the aloofness of God, these alien words exercise a "capacity to further creative life" (Bakhtin, p. 346) in the psalmist's ideological consciousness. "The internally persuasive word," Bakhtin writes, "is half ours and half someone else's. It . . . awakens our own independent words . . . it organizes masses of our words from within, and does not remain in an isolated and static condition. . . . The semantic structure of an internally persuasive discourse is *not finite*, it is *open*; in each of the new contexts that dialogize it, this discourse is able to reveal ever new *ways to mean*" (pp. 345–46).

A closed issue for the wicked becomes an open question for the psalmist. Thus, "He never looks" (v.11) becomes "You do look!" (v.14). "He does not call to account" (v.4), reaccentuated as the interrogative, "Why should the wicked . . . think You do not call to account?" (v.13), becomes the speaker's entree for calling God to account and thereby opening up the very possibility that the wicked have foreclosed. By freely adapting the alien word of the wicked, the psalmist "conducts experiments and gets solutions in the language of another's discourse" (Bakhtin, p. 347).

In the remainder of the poem, the psalmist speaks of God hearing the pleas of the lowly; the speaker thus reactivates internally persuasive words that had been suspended in the terrifying perception of God's aloofness. Three modern translations offer quite different readings of the closing lines of this Psalm, which suggest that there is room for questioning the psalmist's affirmations. Artur Weiser offers an already completed action, "O Lord, Thou hast heard the desire of the meek."[17] Equally firm, but deferring God's response to the future is the JPS version,which reads "You will listen to the entreaty of the

lowly, O Lord." Mitchell Dahood uses an imperative to represent the
psalmist's urgency, "Hear, O Yahweh, the lament of the poor"
(v.17).[18] Underlying the psalmist's sense of having arrived at an internally persuasive solution, there may yet linger a tone of entreaty, since
the justice the psalmist desires has not yet come to pass. However we
choose to interpret the ideological closure of the poem, it is undeniable
that much has changed between speaker and addressee in these final
lines. As a result of the Psalm's inner dialogue, the authoritative
words of Israel's faith can once again be spoken by the psalmist. The
absent God no longer stands aloof, "heedless in times of trouble"
(v.1).

Consciousness, Bakhtin tells us, cannot initially separate itself from
alien discourse, but when it begins to do so, it turns "persuasive discourse into speaking persons," especially when "a struggle against
such images has already begun, where someone is striving to liberate
himself from the influence of such an image and its discourse by
means of objectification" (p. 348). We can see the history of a struggle
to liberate oneself from a compelling but alien discourse in Psalm 73, a
poem that objectifies the wicked, even as it expresses the psalmist's
guilty attraction to their image and words. In Psalm 73, this struggle
is presented to us as a completed action, told through the hindsight of
one who has escaped great peril:

> As for me, my feet had almost strayed,
> My steps were nearly led off course,
> for I envied the profligate,
> I saw the wicked at ease.
> Death has no pangs for them;
> Their body is healthy.
> They have no part in the travail of men;
> They are not afflicted like the rest of mankind.
>
> [vv.3–5]

Given this idealizing envy, we can imagine the psalmist's suscepti-
bility to their words, when they said, "How could God know? / Is
there knowledge with the Most High?" (v.11). "Had I decided to say
these things, / I should have been false to the circle of Your disciples"
(v.15). To have said them, would have turned the poet into one of the
wicked. To have considered saying them, but resisted (until this
Psalm, that is), reveals the inner struggle into which this psalmist has
been led. And it was at this point in the struggle, the psalmist tells us,
that "I entered God's sanctuary and reflected on their fate"(v.17).
The radical shift in perspective that ensues is illuminated by a re-

mark of Bakhtin's. "A conversation with an internally persuasive word that one has begun to resist may continue, but it takes on another character: it is questioned, it is put in a new situation in order to expose its weak sides, to get a feel for its boundaries, to experience it physically as an object" (p. 345). The psalmist reexperiences the existence of the wicked in the context of God's sancturary to gain a totally new vision of their claims for invulnerability:

> You surround them with flattery,
> make them fall through blandishments.
> How suddenly are they ruined,
> wholly swept away by terrors.
> When You are aroused You despise their image,
> as one does a dream after waking, Lord."

[vv.18–20]

Earlier in the poem, it was the tangible solidity and physicality of the wicked's bodily ease ("fat shuts out their eyes," v.7) that made their image and discourse seem incontrovertible to the psalmist. But in the Temple, with its specialized access to visionary states, the image of their discourse is replaced by a vision of divine reality, and the wicked become as insubstantial as "a dream after waking." Awakened from the common materialistic dream, the poet recants the earlier idealization of the wicked: "I was a dolt, without knowledge; / I was brutish toward You" (v.22).

In this Psalm, we see the poet in dialogue not only with the words of the wicked, but also with the almost-spoken words and thoughts of an earlier self. Insofar as "the ideological becoming of a human being" is, as Bakhtin has said, "the process of selectively assimilating the words of others" (p. 341), it extends quite naturally, I would add, to selecting among the words of the various selves that we have been.

There are two distinct groups of Psalms where we note an internal conversation with past selves. One such group offers a reaffirming discourse, in which the psalmists remind God of their pious words spoken in the past (31, 32, 40, 41, 94, 140). Such words are requoted to ensure deliverance, just as they did in the past. These are liturgical formulas, not really the interposition of another's word, since the quoting and quoted selves are continuous. In the second group, however, the dialogic dimension is quite pronounced. The psalmists recant what they said in the past, because they presumed something that they now see was an inadequate representation of reality. They mistakenly thought of the self as being unshakable (30), or unsavable (31), or, contrarily, that one could find refuge by one's own power (55), or that human beings were not to be trusted (116).

These recantatory Psalms sizzle with the energy of transformation, as can be seen from a brief glance at Psalm 30. "When I was untroubled, I thought, 'I shall never be shaken'" (v.7), a phrase also spoken by the wicked interlocutor of Psalm 10.[19] The rest of the Psalm goes on to dramatize the nadir and zenith of the speaker's experience: the psalmist on the verge of death, praying not to "descend into the Pit," and, afterward, the psalmist redeemed: "You turned my lament into dancing, / You undid my sackcloth and girded me with joy, / that [my] whole being might sing hymns to You endlessly" (vv.12–13a). The quotation from an earlier self is the hinge on which the experience of transformation turns. If one's words ("I shall never be shaken") can be proven so wrong by the turn of events from mourning to dancing, then that transforming experience can teach one to use words properly: "O Lord my God, I will praise You forever" (v.13b).

The dialogic discourse of Psalms does not conclude in this anthology of one hundred fifty poems. The psalmists were not only in dialogue with God, the wicked, and themselves, but also with other important speakers of their culture—prophets, teachers of wisdom, writers of sacred history; from those dialogues comes the polyphony of echoing voices throughout this rich poetic corpus. By turning their inner quarrels into speaking voices, the psalmists created an image of a voice that continues to live in our culture, just as, Bakhtin argues, great novelistic images continue to be creatively transformed by succeeding generations of writers. We continue to encounter the image of that voice in the poetry of latter-day psalmists, believers and agnostics, from medievals to moderns.[20] Whether it be in Karl Shapiro's ironic interrogation and challenge, "Are You looking for us? We are here. . . . Follow us"[21] or in Irving Feldman's affirmation and entreaty, "There is no singing without God. . . . Do not deny your blessing, speak to us,"[22] we hear a contemporary reaccentuation of the psalmists' words of petition and praise. From such reaccentuations of another's word, we make up the history of our collective discourse.[23]

Notes

1. Meir Sternberg, "Point of View and the Indirections of Direct Speech," *Language and Style* 15 (1982): 67–117.

2. With some slight modifications, I have followed the translation of Psalms in *Tanach: A New Translation of the Holy Scriptures* (Philadelphia: Jewish Publication Society of America, 1985). This translation (hereafter, JPS) has not put quotation marks around most of the instances of quoted indirect discourse enumerated in Robert Gordis, "Quotations as a Literary Usage in Biblical, Oriental, and Rabbinic Literature," *Hebrew Union College Annual* 22 (1949): 157–220.

3. The topic of quotation is strikingly absent from the Psalms bibliography, perhaps because literary investigation in the form-critical tradition has followed generic lines—individual laments, communal laments, thanksgivings, hymns etc.—and has therefore failed to address liter-

ary features that cut across genres; for a survey of this scholarly tradition, see Erhard Gerstenberger, "Psalms," in *Old Testament Form Criticism*, ed. John H. Hayes (San Antonio, Tex.: Trinity University Press, 1974), pp. 179–224, and for recent developments, Patrick D. Miller, *Interpreting the Psalms* (Philadelphia: Fortress Press, 1986), pp. 3–17.

4. Mikhail Bakhtin, "Discourse in the Novel," in *The Dialogic Imagination: Four Essays*, trans. Caryl Emerson and Michael Holquist, ed. Michael Holquist (Austin: University of Texas Press, 1981), p. 285; subsequent quotations from Bakhtin are from this volume and will be cited parenthetically in the text.

5. William Butler Yeats, *Mythologies* (New York: Macmillan, 1959), p. 336.

6. Aubrey R. Johnson, *The Cultic Prophet and Israel's Psalmody* (Cardiff: University of Wales Press, 1979).

7. On a similar blurring of boundaries where Moses dialogizes and internalizes the monologic, authoritative Word of God, see Robert Polzin, "Dialogic Imagination in the Book of Deuteronomy," *Studies in Twentieth-Century Literature* 9 (1984): 135–43.

8. The imperative "return" is a fundamental prophetic word, found in the major prophets, Isaiah, Jeremiah, Ezekiel, as well as in the minor prophets, Hosea, Joel, Zachariah, and Malachi.

9. Robert Alter, *The Art of Biblical Poetry* (New York: Basic Books, 1985), p. 127, makes similar points about wordplay in this Psalm.

10. Mitchell Dahood, S. J., trans., *Psalms II (51–100)*, The Anchor Bible (Garden City, N.Y.: Doubleday, 1968), p. 268.

11. Matitiahu Tsevat, "God and the Gods in Assembly: An Interpretation of Psalm 82," in *The Meaning of the Book of Job and Other Biblical Studies* (New York: Ktav, 1980), p. 137, argues convincingly that verse 5 should be regarded as an aside by God, spoken *in camerra* before pronouncing final judgment; if this verse were taken as an interruption by the narrator, it would, in my view, greatly diminish the ironic force of the apostrophic conclusion.

12. Jonathan Culler, "Apostrophe," *Diacritics* 7 (1977): 59–67.

13. The wicked speak as enemies of the psalmist in Psalms 3, 11, 13, 22, 35, 40, 41, 42, 70, 71 and as enemies of God in 10, 12, 14 = 53, 64, 73, 94; allied to these is the self-reliant individual quoted in 49. As enemies of Israel and Israel's God, they are quoted in 59, 74, 79, 83, 115 and 137.

14. Jean Starobinski, "The Outside and the Inside," *Hudson Review* 28 (1975): 336.

15. Hans Walter Wolf, "Das Zitat im Prophetenspruch," in *Gesammelte Studien zum Alten Testament* (Munich: Kaiser, 1964), p. 73.

16. Othmar Keel, *Feinde und Gottesleugner: Studien zum Image der Widersacher in den Individualpsalmen* (Stuttgart: Katholisches Bibelwerk, 1969), pp. 179–80.

17. Artur Weiser, *The Psalms: A Commentary* (Philadelphia: Westminster Press, 1962), p. 148.

18. Mitchell Dahood, S. J., trans., *Psalms I (1–50)*, The Anchor Bible (Garden City, N.Y.: Doubleday, 1966), p. 61.

19. The phrase is bivalent, depending on who speaks it and in what conditions of faith or faithlessness; see the opposite sense in Psalms 16:8 and 62:3.

20. Of the many poets that come to mind—John of the Cross, Halevi, Traherne, Watts, Hopkins, Dickinson, Amichai, to name but a few, the relation of Herbert to the Psalms is the best documented, for which see Chana Bloch, *Spelling the Word: George Herbert and the Bible* (Berkeley: University of California Press, 1985), and Michael Marx, "The Church with Psalms Must Shout: The Influence of the Psalms on George Herbert's 'The Church'" (Ph.D. diss. University of Michigan, 1984).

21. Karl Shapiro, *Poems of a Jew* (New York: Random House, 1958), p. 6.

22. Irving Feldman, *New and Selected Poems* (New York: Penguin Books, 1979), p. 69.

23. I am grateful to my students at the National Havurah Committee's Summer Institutes, with whom I have been able to share these Psalms in both Hebrew and English.

How to Read the Hebrew Prophets

David Lyle Jeffrey

University of Ottawa

THE literature of the Hebrew prophets has been the subject of strikingly divergent types of interest and corresponding textual analysis. The most influential of these perhaps concentrates on the eschatological material in the texts. Especially within Western Christian exegetical tradition, interest in the eschatological element has been subsumed under a general pattern of typological reading and messianic interpretation. In early Western Christianity the focus was on the kerygma: Jerome is representative of this interest when he says of Daniel's author that "not only did he assert that He [the Messiah] would come, a prediction common to the other prophets as well, but he also set forth the very time at which he would come."[1] It is typical of the typological shaping of this material that in Western medieval drama, both Latin and vernacular, the prophets are exclusively represented as messianic heralds, and this tradition extends into Christian sermon literature of later periods.[2] Partly, at least, it is for this reason that the subgenre apocalyptic, associated with Daniel and chapters 24–27 of Isaiah, for example, has often tended to overshadow and distort the exegesis of the other prophetic texts.[3] A typical feature of this type of reading is that of apocalyptic itself—the periodization of history and creation of temporal correlatives for prophetic images, visions, and even symbolic numbers. In terms of the four-level stratification of medieval exegesis in which this approach became firmly codified, the emphasis from Jerome and Augustine to Aquinas or Wyclif and the protestant commentators of a later period such as Matthew Henry, has fallen largely upon the allegorical and anagogical possibilities of textual reference.[4]

The second tradition, better known to contemporary biblical scholarship, is early modern and is a product of late-nineteenth- and early-twentieth-century higher criticism. The central tools of this approach are linguistic, stylistic, and textual, and its effect has been to create a formal analysis which probes deeply beneath the surface of the *textus receptus* to suggest the layering of composition, interrelationships among schools of redaction and, among other things, implications of multiple authorship for our sense of unity (and authority) of the text. The scholar approaching the text from this point of view is likely to be as highly self-conscious concerning method as any scholastic exegete, and technically—especially in linguistic matters—much more sophisticated. And whereas the working assumptions of traditional exegesis had been not merely of a unified text but, indeed, of a unified canon, modern criticism has tended to assume that it works with an assortment of fragmented texts, in which much apparent unity is actually the product of efforts by editors and compilers. In contrast to the earlier, eschatologically oriented exegesis, it has accordingly focused largely on the historical level of the text, its context and historical transmission.

More recently, in the wake of renewed literary interest in the Bible, a third approach has emerged. In it the writings of the prophets have been studied for their use of literary techniques. Discussion of prosody, genre, and various specific rhetorical devices highlights the aesthetic achievement of the text as a work of literature that is considered, for these purposes, more or less apart from its own history. Where aesthetic interest predominates, as in the work of Northrop Frye or Robert Alter, for example, the tendency of higher criticism in its extreme of historical orientation to fragment the text has, without being rejected, been more or less surreptitiously bypassed en route to reestablishing (for aesthetic rather than religious reasons) a more unified view of the received text. It should be stressed that this type of approach represents itself, as the first two did not, as quite detached from sectarian motives and has become the province largely of literary scholars as distinct from traditional biblical scholars or theologians. The character of these literary approaches may vary from New Criticism to structuralism to poststructuralist deconstruction, but rhetorical analysis in one form or another is a central concern of current literary criticism of the Hebrew prophets.[5]

This development, as will be clear, has the potential to make the reading and study of the Hebrew prophets distinctly more attractive and accessible to the general student. At the same time, in its return to focusing on the way in which the text makes its own argument, or in which the authors present their concerns, it opens up the possibility that these powerful and literarily rich works will be once again read more straightforwardly in terms of their own most evident level of engagement—which is, after all, that of ethical challenge. It is the tropological character of prophetic rhetoric—its unswerving determination upon a wide-ranging and trenchant criticism of moral praxis—which infuses these works with their special tone and atmosphere.[6] Confronting this in literary analysis, we begin to see that if the analytical power of the Hebrew prophetic writings as cultural and ethical criticism is often blunted or obscured by preoc-

cupation with questions of text and composition, it can be badly dis-
torted or even lost altogether to popular misconceptions based upon
an extravagant interest in "traditional" typological or messianic interpretation.

THE PROPHET AS AUTHOR

It is the most sensational representations of this literature, of course,
which tend to color the preconceptions some modern students bring to
the text. In the discourse of our time, a "prophet" or someone to
whom we are likely to attach that name is essentially a kind of forecas-
ter. He or she may be a student of politics or economics or a popular
journalist who consults the right polls and collects the right samples
so as to be able to "call" an election, predict a coup, or plot the ups
and downs of the stockmarket. Such nomenclature might attach itself
as easily to a gossip columnist clairvoyant, a popular entertainer with
an eye and ear for Hollywood careers, or the *National Enquirer*. Or even
an individualistic minister of the electronic gospel, with his eye in a
fine frenzy rolling. From the point of view of the Hebrew Scriptures, of
course, all of these would more likely be seen as subspecies of the
"false prophet."

In ancient Israel, a true prophet could be none of these things.
Instead of being defined in terms of political sensitivity or entertain-
ment value, the vocational worth of a prophet twenty-six hundred
years ago stood directly in proportion to his or her detachment from
politics, obtuseness to what was popular, and separation from formal
institutions of religion. That is to say, a prophet was "a voice crying in
the wilderness" by definition, not by some accident of bad career
management.

It is essential to the character of a true Hebrew prophet that he
himself has never sought the job. He is a *nabhî* (נביא)—"one who is
called" (Deut. 18:15ff; 34:10). Often, in fact, as in the case of Moses,
Jonah, and Ezekiel, the prophet is not at all sure he wants the job.
Moses pleads inadequacy, Jonah is revolted by his itinerary, and the
astonished Ezekiel is forced to swallow his marching orders whole like
medicine. And when appointed, or "called," the prophet is required
to submit his own skills and conscious imagination utterly, permitting
himself to be seized by the Spirit of God and given directly whatever
words he has to speak—or indeed, as in the case of Ezekiel (3:25–
5:5) and Hosea (1:2–9; 3:1–3), ordered whatever alarming symbolic
acts to perform.

The prophet has no prophetic training because none is necessary,
and none is available. He is not a sorcerer because he deals not so
much with hidden things as with that which has been revealed (Deut.

29:28–30:3). He is not a shaman. He is simply a mouthpiece, an amanuensis, a voice. His own previous vocation is, to this purpose, irrelevant. He may have been a shepherd, a householder, a civil servant, a priest. He may even stay in his initial line of work for his daily bread. But he must be ready always to be interrupted for a burst of the divine imperative upon him without so much as a moment's notice. We may consider the call of Jeremiah as good an illustration as any:

The word of Yahweh was addressed to me, saying,

> "Before I formed you in the womb I knew you;
> before you came to birth I consecrated you;
> I have appointed you as prophet to the nations."

I said, "Ah, Lord Yahweh; look, I do not know how to speak: I am a child!"

> But Yahweh replied,
> "Do not say, 'I am a child.'
> Go now to those to whom I send you
> and say whatever I command you.
> Do not be afraid of them,
> for I am with you to protect you—
> it is Yahweh who speaks!"

Then Yahweh put out his hand and touched my mouth and said to me:

> "There! I am putting my words into your mouth."
> [Jer. 1:4–9][7]

The authors of Hebrew prophetic literature consistently represent the prophet himself as, in effect, a nonauthor. The prophet is but one who has words put in his mouth.[8] Yahweh God will be always the author, and to his authority the prophet will be as an actor on the stage is to his playwright/producer. For that is just the point these texts make about the genesis of prophecy—it is an authorial intervention into the unfolding script of history, editorial, critical, and invariably pedagogical. The prophet is one forced to stand at the flashpoint, where the current is grounding and the sparks fly, as the divine author comments definitively on his people's performance. He is one in time who stands for a terrible moment also outside of temporal order: one foot in the *chronos*, the other in *chairos*, his ear to eternity and mouth toward the city, he speaks as he is directed. And the proclamation is usually a judgment, bad news for the hearers.

It is a notoriously unpopular thing to be the bearer of bad tidings, and it usually incurs considerable risk for the messenger. But there is not much the prophet can do about this. Consider the case of the prophet Micaiah in 1 Kings 22, where he is brought against his will to confront the unregenerate despot, King Ahab. Ahab's four hundred flattering court prognosticators, led in their raving dance by a chief shaman called Zedekiah dressed up in a mask with iron horns (22:11), have already been entertaining the king with what they perceive he wants to hear:

> The messenger who had gone to summon Micaiah said, "Here are all the prophets as one man speaking favorably to the king. Try to speak like one of them and foretell success." But Micaiah answered, "As Yahweh lives, what Yahweh says to me, that will I utter!" When he came to the king, the king said, "Micaiah, should we march to attack Ramoth-gilead, or should we refrain?" He answered, "March and conquer. Yahweh will deliver it into the power of the king." But the king said, "How often must I put you on oath to tell me nothing but the truth in the name of Yahweh?" Then Micaiah spoke: "I have seen all Israel scattered on the mountains like sheep without a shepherd. And Yahweh said, 'These have no master, let each go home unmolested.'" At this the king of Israel said to Jehoshaphat, "Did I not tell you that he never gives me favorable prophecies, but only unfavorable ones?" Micaiah went on, "Listen rather to the word of Yahweh. I have seen Yahweh seated on his throne; all the array of heaven stood in his presence, on his right and on his left. Yahweh said, 'Who will trick Ahab into marching to his death at Ramoth-gilead?' At which some answered one way, and some another. Then the spirit came forward and stood before Yahweh. "I," he said "I will trick him." "How?" Yahweh asked. He replied, "I will go and become a lying spirit in the mouth of all his prophets." "You shall trick him," Yahweh said "you shall succeed. Go and do it. "Now see how Yahweh has put a lying spirit into the mouths of all your prophets here. But Yahweh has pronounced disaster on you.
> Then Zedekiah son of Chenaanah came up and struck Micaiah on the jaw. "Which way" he asked "did the spirit of Yahweh leave me, to talk to you?" "That is what you will find out," Micaiah retorted "the day you flee to an inner room to hide." The king of Israel said, "Seize Micaiah and hand him over to Amon, governor of the city, and to Prince Joash, and say, 'These are the king's orders. Put this man in prison and feed him on nothing but bread and water until I come back safe and sound.'" Micaiah said, "If you come back safe and sound, Yahweh has not spoken through me."
> The king of Israel and Jehoshaphat king of Judah went up against Ramoth-gilead. The king of Israel said to Jehoshaphat, "I will disguise myself to go into battle, but I want to wear your royal uniform." The king of Israel went into battle disguised. The king of Aram had given his chariot commanders the following order: "Do not attack anyone of whatever rank, except the king of Israel." When the chariot commanders caught sight of Jehoshaphat, they said, "That is obviously the king of Israel." And they wheeled to the attack. But Jehoshaphat shouted his war cry and the chariot commanders, realizing that he was not the king of Israel, called off their pursuit.

Now one of the men, drawing his bow at random, hit the king of Israel between the corslet and the scale-armor of his breastplate. "Turn about" the king said to his charioteer. "Get me out of the battle; I have been hurt." But the battle grew fiercer as the day went on; the king was held upright in his chariot facing the Aramaeans, and in the evening he died; the blood from the wound flowed into the bottom of the chariot. At sundown a shout ran through the camp, "Every man back to his town, every man back to his country; the king is dead!" They went to Samaria, and in Samaria they buried the king. They washed the chariot at the Pool of Samaria; the dogs licked up the blood, and the prostitutes washed in it, in accordance with the word that Yahweh had spoken. [1 Kings 22:13– 38]

Back in the court, the false prophets are nowhere to be seen. And the throne is empty. In the stark, swift contours of this powerful narrative, the reader is made to see the main point: Ahab's court has been judged by another court, tried and found wanting. Heaven and earth have both witnessed against the tyrant. Judgment has been pronounced and executed. Of the bearer of the summons we hear nothing more; Micaiah may be rotting somewhere in a dungeon, left to the rats. Or freed. But from the writer's point of view the role of the prophet has been played out consummately: the word from out of time has been proclaimed in time, giving an agenda for true justice and integrity by which Ahab's greed and false balances are swept from the stage and his royalty reduced to dog food and gutter wash. The announcer of the justice is as apparently unlooked for as its instrument: a nameless archer who, "drawing his bow at random, hit the king of Israel between the corslet and the scale-armor of his breastplate" (a place about the size of a good coin). Un-self-intended, perhaps, the narrator implies, but not unbidden. And so the shaft, like the rhetoric, hits right on its intended target.

The raving four hundred, Ahab's shamanistic vizers, are among those called ro'eh (ראה)—from the active participal form of the verb "to see" (Isa. 30:10; 1 Chron. 29:29) or hozeh (חוזה, 1 Sam. 9:9). Persons called by these names could be merely diviners or clairvoyants of an unexalted sort. These terms are likely to mean something better than that only if the character of a true nahbî has first been established, that is, when the "call" has been authenticated.

Nabhim are not thus restricted to the "authors" of the major and minor prophetic books, or even their chief protagonists. In fact, the first to receive this denomination was Abraham (Gen. 20:7), even though prophetism as such really begins with Moses (Deut. 18:15; 34:10). We are to recognize, then, that the prophetic vocation has a long tradition in Hebrew history and literature and that the nature of the divine transmission to which the prophets are prompted is pretex-

tual; it may appear as symbolic act (a mime, a sacrifice, a life journey), as proclamation of divine judgment (bad news about the up-
coming wilderness or a sentence of death), or as prediction of the
future (the promise of Canaan, the fall of Jerusalem). The pattern of
prophetic activity is thus already well established in Israel's history
and chief literature, and this pattern is one which reflects—in the
Torah as in the time of the divided kingdoms—God's insistence on
maintaining a conversation with his people Israel. When they will not
incline their ear to hear what he is saying in a soft voice, or when they
have forgotten the character of his conversation with their parents, or
lost the book which records it, then he calls out a chosen *nahbî* to shout
in their ears and obtain attention. For that is the whole end of Hebrew
prophecy—to restore conversation with the ultimate author.

THE RHETORIC OF THE PROPHETS

In some of the situations in which the prophets find themselves, it
seems almost as though God's people have forgotten the very language of that conversation. That is to say, they have forgotten the
Torah, the five books of Moses, and the other Scriptures. It is thus
that the basic drive of prophets like Isaiah, Jeremiah, Amos, and Ezekiel is to carry the fragmenting memory of Israel back to its roots in
that source. And for this very reason, both in the object and the rhetorical form of their discourse, the prophetic books require most of all
for our understanding that we know and refer them to the Torah, to
the history of the conversation. We see this quite readily, I think, in
the prologue to Isaiah:

> The vision of Isaiah son of Amoz concerning Judah and Jerusalem which
> he saw in the reigns of Uzziah, Jotham, Ahaz, and Hezekiah, kings of
> Judah.

> Listen, you heavens; earth, attend
> for Yahweh is speaking,
> "I reared sons, I brought them up,
> but they rebelled against me.
> The ox knows its owner
> and the ass its master's crib,
> Israel knows nothing,
> my people understands nothing."

> A sinful nation, a people weighed down with guilt,
> a breed of wrong-doers, perverted sons.
> They have abandoned Yahweh, despised the Holy One of Israel,
> they have turned away from him.

Where shall I strike your next,
since you heap one betrayal on another?
The whole head is sick, the whole heart grown faint;
from the sole of the foot to the head there is not a sound spot,
wounds, bruises, open sores
not dressed, not bandaged,
not soothed with oil.

Your land is desolate, your towns burnt down,
your fields—strangers lay them waste before your eyes;
all is desolation, as after the fall of Sodom.

The daughter of Zion is left
like a shanty in a vineyard,
like a shed in a melon patch,
like a besieged city.
Had Yahweh not left us a few survivors,
we should be like Sodom,
we should now be like Gomorrah.

Hear the word of Yahweh,
you rulers of Sodom;
listen to the command of our God,
you people of Gomorrah.

"What are your endless sacrifices to me?"
says Yahweh.
"I am sick of holocausts of rams
and the fat of calves.
The blood of bulls and of goats revolts me.
When you come to present yourselves before me,
who asked you to trample over my courts?
Bring me your worthless offerings no more,
the smoke of them fills me with disgust.
New Moons, sabbaths, assemblies—
I cannot endure festival and solemnity.
Your New Moons and your pilgrimages
I hate with all my soul.
They lie heavy on me,
I am tired of bearing them.
When you stretch out your hands
I turn my eyes away.
You may multiply your prayers,
I shall not listen.
Your hands are covered with blood,
wash, make yourselves clean.
"Take your wrong-doing out of my sight.
Cease to do evil.
Learn to do good,

search for justice,
help the oppressed,
be just to the orphan,
plead for the widow.

"Come now, let us talk this over,"
says Yahweh.
"Though your sins are like scarlet,
they shall be as white as snow;
though they are red as crimson,
they shall be like wool.

"If you are willing to obey,
you shall eat the good things of the earth.
But if you persist in rebellion,
the sword shall eat you instead."
The mouth of Yahweh has spoken.

[Isa. 1:1–20]

We may readily divide this prologue into three rhetorical movements, each having a binary construction.

I. Presentation of the problem:
    a) Rebellion against the fatherhood (authority) of God the
       Creator (1:2–4)
    b) Result: sickness in the body—creature and creation (5–9)
II. Disparate analysis:
    a) Human response: more rebellion or meaningless sacrifices
       (10–15)
    b) The author's prescription: ethical obedience (16–17)
III. Presentation of options:
    a) To see history and the book as a conversation to set things
       in perspective (18)—or reject it
    b) To choose enactment of the Word—or to deny it (19–20)

The predominance in Hebrew of the short phrase lends itself naturally to parallelism, a feature much noted in the discussion of Hebrew
poetry. Here, in its basic dyadic form, it suits perfectly the larger
ethical oppositions which the argument of Isaiah is concerned to
elaborate. When reenforced by the rhetorical ordering of argument
observed here, the effect of the alternating elements is to force the
reader almost relentlessly toward a personal engagement of the ethical
imperative. As Luis Alonso Schökel has aptly observed, here in verses
16 and 17, "two alliterative verbs and nouns say it all: *limdu heytev,
dirshu mishpat*, 'cease to do evil, learn to do good.'"[9] Such parallelism

echoes the movement of the main argument throughout the text; patterns of metaphorical elaboration, cryptic judgments, and gentle encouragement all formally anticipate a stark either/or ethical moment to which they draw. Thus, in powerful contrasts such as those between desert and garden, Babylon and Jerusalem, harlot and bride, the element of suggestion or suasion can be as pointed as the imperative itself:

> "Though your sins are like scarlet,
> they shall be as white as snow;
> though they are red as crimson,
> they shall be like wool."

Though many of Isaiah's tropes are broadly referential to a moral ecology in which the whole of creation is implicated, the force of the rhetoric is always to present implications for the ethical responsibility of each reader/hearer of the text:

> "If you are willing to obey,
> you shall eat the good things of the earth.
> But if you persist in rebellion,
> the sword shall eat you instead."
> The mouth of Yahweh has spoken.

As a whole, the Book of Isaiah is evidently an anthology, an orchestration of several genres on many aspects of a plurality of themes. There are tone poems, songs, dirges, oracles, recitations of judgment, even a section of narrative. Yet throughout this whole anthology, whose sixty-six chapters have sometimes been seen as a synechdoche for the shape and movement of the whole scriptural anthology,[10] runs this unifying pattern of discourse—problem/analysis/options—an implied rhetoric repeating itself over and over again as in a motet or canon, or a majestic fugue (chaps. 1–5; 6–12; 13–24; 25–27; 28–35; [36– 39]; 40–55; 56–66).

In Isaiah we see a book concluded over two generations, possibly by several hands, as Isaiah's faithful successors concluded the task after his untimely execution. But the overall result is beautifully symphonic, a text, as generations of critics have observed, of astonishing literary unity. How, given such a complex of features and circumstances, does it achieve this apparent unity? The simple answer is that Isaiah, as a book of prophecy, is itself a powerful "reading" of another book, the Torah, and that its unity comes from the established shape of the canonical transmission of Hebrew Scripture and history—the implied as well as explicit rhetorical patterning of its foundational texts. And this, then, is an essential perspective for reading Hebrew prophetic literature: one must read it with one eye on the first five books of the Bible. And this is true—even most particularly true— when one is reading prophets such as Daniel and Ezekiel who seem to be speaking of the far future, of events that have not yet come to pass.

THE GRAMMAR OF THE PROPHETS

It is of the essence of the predictive as well as proclamatory character of these books that we read Yahweh God's judgments on the future in terms of what he has already said and done in the past. Or, to put it another way: we are to understand that "future" and "past" are going to be like each other in content, even as the content of the divine author's character is eternal—his justice and integrity, his jealous love, his insistence on the conversation. And in fact the Hebrew language of the text makes this point clear to us in its distinction, effectively, between only two orders of time or tenses in respect to our epistemological starting point as mortal readers.

As readers, of course, or as hearers, we stand circumscribed by our limit in time present, what the text calls *hayyom hazzeh* (תיום חֲגָח). But our problem is at least to some degree simplified when we come to the next step. What we read is either of the past, *bayyom hahu* (בְּיום החוא) or the future, *bayyom hahu*.[11] That is, "this day," the "today" of our reading, is distinguished from the "that day" of the text. But the phrase "in that day" is the same whether the prophetic text is speaking of God's action in the past or what he says he will do in the future. (This phrase is used largely in the prophetic books, especially Isaiah, but see also Exod. 8:22; Deut. 31:17ff.; 1 Sam. 3:12). When applied to the future, we know it by the context, since of course the Hebrew verb does not make our distinction of future tense. Thus, in Isaiah 2:11 and again in 2:17:

> Human pride will lower its eyes,
> the arrogance of men will be humbled.
> Yahweh alone shall be exalted
> on that day [*bayyom hahu*].

References to time past, "in that day" (*bayyom hahu*) are to moments of revelatory confirmation, as of God's eternal character of the character of his promise, the covenant with his people (Exod. 14:30; Josh. 24:25; Gen. 15:18; 1 Sam. 7:10; 2 Sam. 23:10). In this "past" context, the phrase "in that day" is often used as an epitome, a summarizing characterization concerning a particular day in which Israel's

God was in some way seen to be active in a crucial confrontation with his people.

"That day," the recurrent prophetic reference, is then a reference to the larger divine conversation, a conversation with the reader which is having now its present aspect as we read. *Bayyom hahu*, past or future as we should try to think it, is really all one in God's perspective of eternity, and it is indeed all one at least in the sense that both past and future are beyond our immediate experience. *Bayyom hahu* is book time; *hayyom hazzeh* is reader time, or hearer time. But *hayyom hazzeh* is of crucial importance for the response we make as readers to our text; indeed, the dramatic conscriptions of prophets like Jeremiah, Isaiah, and Ezekiel are put in the text partly to model this point. "This day," "today," is the day which is really always being appealed to by the prophetic books because it is only in "this day" that the reader's response can be relevant. *Hayyom hazzeh* is, in effect, the moment of ethical decision, such as is captured in the challenge of Joshua: "Choose you *this day* whom you will serve: as for me and my house, we will serve the Lord" (Josh. 24:15). The culminating point of prophetic rhetoric is thus an insistence on the reader's option, as well as a reminder of what is at stake in the choosing.

The framework of prophetic discourse—the interspersed relation of vision and prophetic dream to the flow of historical events—is a simulacrum of this "grammar" of the text, point-counterpoint. It is indeed as though one is confronted in a prophetic book with two texts, or a text within a text. The first text, or "surface" text, is the one with which we have least difficulty. It is the general narrative, the historical context in which the prophetic utterance suddenly comes as an interruption. The predictable and topical syntax of this narrative is characterized by causal relationship. In the decline and fall of an empire, the logic of cause and effect is apparent enough even to the chronicler: the syntax of history is the normative, conscious syntax of our language of observation and critique. The encroachments of Babylon, the dissipation of Ahab's kingdom, the aggrandizements of Nebuchadnezzar—all these are the stuff of narrative order as we expect to find it on the reader's side of the page.

But there is in the prophetic books another text, the text within the text. This text is not, in any wooden way, the literal codex of the Torah, but its incorporated substance as ethical vision. It is the psychological commentary, the story within that comments upon and interprets the story without. It is not simply the record of unfolding present historical events but rather the playbook of sacred memory and dream. And this other text, juxtaposed upon the surface narrative of history in such a way as to confound and redirect its expected flow, exhibits another syntax all its own. For the syntax of memory and dream does not abide by causal logic, nor does it follow strict temporal governance. Here the temporal, the *chronos*, is confounded by a continuum of accessible past and future, a *chairos* which startles and overflows the temporal imagination. The prophet is one who is called repeatedly into this second flow of syntax and whose speaking is thus according to the grammar and logic of eternity admonishing the finitude of the temporal, causal perspective. The visions and interpretation of dreams in Daniel (interspersed with his patient stewardship as a high bureaucrat in the governments of two empires) or Isaiah's divine ambassadorship, interpreting fateful signs to the kingdom of Hezekiah, are the stuff of visionary order, and they wash across and reinterpret the "surface" or historical text (and context) of the prophetic books in which they occur. In the case of the parallel courts in the confrontation of Micaiah and Ahab, it is in the prophet's access to the syntax of memory and dream that we see the special advantage of his "book." For it is in this "syntax" that the divine conversation is clearly heard from the author's side.

STYLE AND MOOD IN THE PROPHETS

There are of course many different kinds of style exhibited by the prophets. Close to popular stereotype is the haranguing style of Amos; Jeremiah's style is verbally volatile, ranging from euphoric and ecstatic reverie to sarcastic, even vitriolic, taunting (he is the Mercutio of the prophets); the style of Daniel (part 1) is as balanced, measured, and temperate as that of a seasoned scholar; Hosea's is passionate, lyrical, and, appropriate to his situation, dramatic. Ezekiel and Isaiah, like Micaiah, are no strangers to irony. And all of them use devices of patterning and rhythm, repetition and refrain, to build up a sense of interrelatedness and emphasis in their message.

Beyond these differences, however, there is a stylistic feature more or less common to the prophets which is so part and parcel of the character of Hebrew prophecy that it deserves our careful attention. What I am referring to, from the point of view of philological analysis, is really a matter of tone and mood. As even the character of the few examples given here will illustrate, most readers are inclined to think first of the accusatory voice in prophetic literature and to think of the style of the prophets as being largely in the line of Jeremiah's and Amos's condemnations and predictions of doom. This is natural and, to a point, entirely appropriate. For it is the prophet's vocation after all to announce God's judgment of his people for their sins and to proclaim his Law and obedience to it as the only remedy against sin's consequences.

The tone and mood of such proclamations is thus not to be imagined as a matter of high dudgeon on the part of the prophet; indeed, the tone and mood are attributable to Yahweh in his character as an offended Lord, a betrayed lover, a slandered judge: the tone is that of an offended party to a covenant and expresses anger for breaches and turning away, for breaking off the relationship. Since the offended party is God, the aggrievement is not an idle matter. The prophets spend much of their time proclaiming corruption and predicting disaster.

But this is far from a complete picture. Indeed, if it were, one should find reading them almost too much to bear. In fact, the style of prophetic books has also two sides, two moods—even in the grammatical sense—to match the two-aspected nature of the conversation to which they are enjoined by their author. This is well illustrated in Isaiah. An early example comes at the beginning of chapter 11, where after several chapters of condemnation in which God's judgment is seen always in its condemnatory character, there comes a refreshing wind (*ruah*, v.2) of transformation. Suddenly, the prophet's testimony to God's judgment is presented in a compassionate, hopeful tone. Until chapter 11, the concept of this witness of judgment against the people has been expressed only in the imperative and indicative mood (*adah*). It is a "testimony of accusation." In this context, the reader or hearer is driven to despair at the coming of such bad news. Now, there is a new breath; that other side of the Spirit of Yahweh speaks, and the expectation of judgment is transformed into a hope of remission, release, and comfort. The announcement of judgment is now not *adah* but *teudah*—the mood no longer imperative and indicative but subjunctive and optative.[12] Not only God's justice, but his integrity (vv.4,5) are expressed, and in this word, the tyranny of that purely causal syntax of history is subverted. In such a vision of life, "the wolf lives with the lamb . . . the calf and the lion cub feed together, with a little boy to lead them." The mood is one of play—in a world where all things are possible—a harkening back to that very first conversation, Adam and Eve and God in the garden. The shift from imperative and indicative order to subjunctive and optative possibility is a movement from the world in which things "just are" and "we must accept the consequences" to a new world in which "we may" become something other, and in which "we can" rejoin the divine conversation. That is, the dramatic shift of tone and mood which so characterizes a book like Isaiah mirrors the shift from one order of meaning, or syntax, to another—from the determinism of the surface text to the open world of the text within, "reading" as it writes the syntax of memory and dream. It is a reminder, as Martin Buber puts it, that behind every proclamation of disaster a message of consolation lies hidden.[13]

It is this feature then, at every level—rhetoric, grammar, logic, and

style—which is finally the special contribution of the prophets to
Hebrew literature, the central content of the unfolding "conversation" in which they participate. For it is not their proclamation of
warning alone which privileges their place in the canon of Scripture or
in the great tradition of Western literature. Rather it is their con-
veyance of a promise of consolation that signals both their faithful
relationship to the book, and their commitment to the reader's need
for an avenue of hope and peace—hope beyond the despair we feel
and peace beyond the tyranny of marching history.

After the rhetoric of the divine conversation has been played for
thirty-five chapters over the pattern of a crumbling kingdom's refusal
to learn from history, Isaiah includes a three-chapter narrative from
the regency of Hezekiah which illustrates, in précis, the whole sad
course of forgetfulness which Yahweh God, through the mouths of his
prophets, is lamenting. At the end of it, well begun though he was,
Hezekiah is so preoccupied with himself and so obtuse to the hearing
he has had of Yahweh that it is enough for him merely that destruction will fall on his children and not upon himself. "Oh good," he
says, when hearing Isaiah's prophecy of the destruction soon to come,
"at least peace and security will last through my own lifetime" (29:8).
In Hezekiah's very response we see why it is that doom is falling. And
we know that the jig is up. Despair lies heavily over the text.

But then comes that other mood, that shift in the tone of the author's voice. It is a reiteration of the prophet's call, his call to be a
nabhî. And what it says we hear gladly the world over whenever we are
overwhelmed with any kind of imperative, indicative reading of our
sorrowful world:

> "Console my people, console them"
> says your God.
> "Speak to the heart of Jerusalem
> and call to her
> that her time of service is ended,
> that her sin is atoned for,
> that she has received from the hand of Yahweh
> double punishment for all her crimes."
>
> [Isa. 40:1– 8]

When we read the Hebrew prophets we are reading in the ebb and
flow, the give and take, of a conversation between earth and heaven. If
we are to read well, the writers suggest, we will apprentice ourselves
to the larger conversation as we find it in the scriptural canon. For
their point is everywhere the same: though men and women forget,
though they lose the language or stop their hearing, the divine author

does not forget. His Word remains forever, and even in the midst of
the ruins of Babylon his voice is speaking still: "Did you not know?"
"Had you not heard?" (Isaiah's voicing of Yahweh is both a plea and
a taunt.) "Was it not told you from the beginning?" "Have you not
understood how the earth was formed?" (Isa. 40:21).

The message of the prophets remains accordingly the message of
the Torah:

> Things hidden belong to Yahweh our God, but things revealed are ours
> and our children's for all time; so that we may observe all the words of the
> Lord. And when all these words come true for you, the blessing and the
> curse I have set before you, if you meditate on them in your heart wherever
> among the nations Yahweh your God drives you, if you return to Yahweh
> your God...then [he] will bring back your captives. [Deut. 29:28–
> 30:3]

> I call heaven and earth to witness against you today. I set before you life or
> death, blessing or curse. Choose life, then, so that you and your descen-
> dents may live. [Deut. 30:19]

So ends the reading of the Torah and also of the prophets. It is
purposefully fitting that the collection of the twelve minor prophets
summarizes the concern of all Hebrew prophetic literature in a characteristic appeal for ethical praxis and for seeing that praxis as having
its roots in the Law:

> Remember the Law of my servant Moses to whom at Horeb I prescribed
> laws and customs for the whole of Israel. Know that I am going to send
> you Elijah the prophet before my day comes, that great and terrible day.
> He shall turn the hearts of fathers towards their children and the hearts of
> children towards their fathers, lest I come and strike the land with a curse.
> [Mal. 3:22–24][14]

Notes

1. Jerome, *Commentarii in Danielem ad Pammachium & Marcellam*, PL 25.491. In the Hebrew
canon, Daniel is not classified as one of the major works of prophetic literature, but is assigned to
the *Kethubhim*, or "Writings."

2. For example, the celebrated phrase often ascribed to Daniel, "When the Holy of Holies
shall come, your anointing shall cease," enters medieval apocalyptic commentary as well as the
Latin liturgical drama from the misconstrual (cf. Dan. 9:24) of a pseudo-Augustinian sermon.
See Karl Young, *Drama of the Medieval Church* (Oxford: Clarendon Press, 1933; reprint, 1962),
2:126–27. In the Middle English Townley play, *Prophets*, as in the *ordo prophetarum* of the Anglo-
Norman *Jeu d'Adam*, Daniel is made to expand upon this phrase in the vernacular. In John
Donne's sermon on Daniel 9:24, he still reads the prophecy of the seventy weeks as having to do
with the birth of Christ. Among Christian typological exegetes of later periods, notably since the

numerological and mathematical speculations of Sir Isaac Newton, it has been more common to apply prognostication to the Parousia, or "Second Coming." See Isaac Newton, *Observations upon the Prophecies of Daniel and the Apocalypse of St. John* (London, 1773).

3. Unsurprisingly, it is apocalyptic interest which leads Josephus (*Antiquitates judaicum* 10.11.7) to categorize Daniel as "the greatest of the prophets . . . for he not only prophesied of future events, as did other prophets, but he also determined the time of their accomplishment." (Jerome, cited above, is evidently indebted to Josephus for his own formulations concerning the importance of Daniel.) Equally unsurprising is Philo's complete avoidance of the book, as of apocalyptic generally.

4. The trend away from these emphases becomes pronounced in the eighteenth century among deist and rationalist commentators such as Anthony Collins, *The Scheme of Literal Prophecy* (London, 1726).

5. This is representatively evident in the volume of essays collected in *The Literary Guide to the Bible*, ed. Robert Alter and Frank Kermode (Cambridge: Harvard University Press, 1987).

6. "Atmosphere" is used here with the sense given it by Wesley A. Kort, *Story, Text, and Scripture: Literary Interests in Biblical Narrative* (University Park: Pennsylvania State University Press, 1988), pp. 35–40.

7. This and all subsequent biblical references are to The Jerusalem Bible (Garden City, N.Y.: Doubleday, 1966).

8. A case can be made that Jeremiah is atypical. He adds considerably to Yahweh's utterances with his own complaint: he is aggrieved with the insensitivity of his hearers, and takes their rejection of God personally. In his case, as Joel Rosenberg has put it, to some degree "the lavishness of prophetic pathos flows more from the breakdown of missionary purpose than from an enactment of it." See *Literary Guide to Bible*, p. 187.

9. Luis Alonso Schökel, ibid., p. 169.

10. One of the more interesting discussions is afforded by John Wyclif: see D. Jeffrey, "John Wyclif and the Hermeneutics of Reader Response," *Interpretation* 39 (1985): 272–87.

11. General students will find helpful the discussion by Simon John DeVries, *Yesterday, Today, and Tomorrow: Time and History in the Old Testament* (Grand Rapids, Mich.: Eerdmans, 1975).

12. George Steiner's observations concerning this shift in *After Babel: Aspects of Language and Translation* (Oxford: Oxford University Press, 1975), pp. 146–47 are here more useful to the reader's sense of the rhetorical power of the text than conventional efforts to account for the shift of mood in chap. 11 by appeal to another author for the second half of the chapter.

13. Martin Buber, *The Prophetic Faith* (New York: Harper & Row, 1960), p. 103.

14. It is the rhetorical coherence of the Bible which, despite the parsing of modern form criticism, has continued to characterize its literary appreciation. In the principles of reiteration and envelope structure, illustrated here, we see why it is that a literary critic such as Northrop Frye can rightly claim, for his purposes, that the Bible "has influenced Western imagination as a unity" and that "wherever we stop, the unity of the Bible as a whole is an assumption underlying any part of it." See *The Great Code: The Bible and Literature* (Toronto: University of Toronto Press, 1982), pp. xiii, 62. Frye attributes this to what he calls "implicit metaphor"; I have here characterized the ground of unity as explicit and rhetorical, the result of a reiterated ethical vision.

Isaiah the Poet

Theodore L. Steinberg
State University of New York at Fredonia

THERE has been, in recent years, a tremendous growth of interest in the Bible as a literary work (or, more precisely, as a collection of literary works), as evidenced not only by the present volume but in books by Terence Collins, Stephen Geller, M. O'Connor, Adele Berlin, James Kugel, Robert Alter, and in the recently released *Literary Guide to the Bible*.[1] Whether this trend represents a secularization of the Bible or a recognition of the Bible's influence on secular life is perhaps a matter for theologians and sociologists to consider, but that the Bible can and should be considered from a literary standpoint is indisputable. Still, there seems to be some confusion over what constitutes a literary standpoint. Several of the authors mentioned above, for example, are theologians and linguists, and while they make valuable contributions to biblical studies, it is questionable whether those contributions are in the literary realm. Thus Collins, Geller, and O'Connor seem to operate from Roman Jakobson's stance that "the terminological confusion of 'literary studies' with 'criticism' tempts the student of literature to replace the description of the intrinsic values of a literary work by a subjective, censorious verdict."[2] Consequently their books are in the field that Jakobson calls "literary studies," that is, descriptions of quantifiable elements in biblical writing. Berlin, although she touches on what is usually called "literary criticism," still maintains a strong linguistic outlook. Kugel presents some of the best evidence for the literary status of the Bible, but then, perversely, he denies his own evidence and argues against that status. From the above list, only Alter and some of the contributors to the *Literary Guide* take a real literary approach to the texts.

This is not, I stress, to deny the valuable contributions made by these scholars, who have added immeasurably to our understanding of how Hebrew verse works. But it is essential that we recognize the distinction between verse and poetry, a distinction which does not appear in these "literary studies."

I

Although it's now a year that we have been apart.
Let me assure you certainly that you live in my heart.

Those lines are verse—in fact they are in Poulter's measure, a form that was very popular in the sixteenth century—but they are not poetry. They are, at best, doggerel; and if we think of them as anything but doggerel, we may find ourselves having to consider the Hallmark or American Greetings schools of poetry. In other words, not all verse is poetry; or, as Earl Wasserman used to say in class, poetry is not simply literature that goes halfway across the page. Surely this point seems obvious, but many of the studies of biblical literature seem unaware of it. Thus Jakobson writes that "verse always implies poetical function"[3] and Collins calls his study *Line-Forms in Hebrew Poetry*, though his focus is strictly on the workings of the verse, without any consideration of whether the verse is poetry. And while O'Connor more accurately calls his work *Hebrew Verse Structure*, he, too, confuses verse and poetry, as when, citing other scholars, he says that "poetic structure has been suggested for a number of Hebrew texts, including the Gezer Calendar" and a number of other inscriptions.[4] Such texts may well employ verse, but verse by itself does not make them poetic.

So what does make poetry? That question, of course, probably should not be answered here, because any answer short enough to fit into an article would be incomplete and would unnecessarily limit our conception of poetry, just as Renaissance definitions of epic severely limited the critics' ability to deal with works like Ariosto's *Orlando Furioso*. Nonetheless, if we are to think of the prophets as poets, we must have somewhere to start. One way to determine the poetic status of the texts is by seeing whether they use what have usually been considered poetic genres. So J. Lindblom lists among the rhetorical and literary modes in the prophets satire, lamentation, hymns, allegories, and lyric poetry.[5] Such a list suggests at the very least that there is poetry, not just verse, in these texts.

Alter provides another starting point when he says that "poetry is a particular way of imagining the world" and he adds "that poetry as such has its own logic, its own ways of making connections and engendering implications."[6] Poetry is, he says, "our best human model of intricately rich communication, not only solemn, weighty, and forceful but also densely woven with complex internal connections, meanings, and implications."[7] Such poetry may or may not be in verse, though, as in the case of the prophets, it usually is. In what follows I shall focus on Isaiah's use of imagery in parallelistic verse to create a kind of "intricately rich communication" in chapters 1–39.

First, however, two points must be made. One is that despite the obviously piecemeal composition (or redaction) of the book, I treat it as a unified whole because, at some point in its history, that was how it was intended to be treated. The second, and more important point, is a justification for treating the prophets as poets. Geller states the problem succinctly: "A prophet is . . . the mouthpiece of a god. A poet is a 'maker,' a craftsman in words. The former is a medium, the latter an artist. A prophet who consciously molded his prophecy would be false. A poet whose verse did not reflect his personality would be no true artist."[8] Certain books of the Bible, such as Psalms, Lamentations, Job, and others, have traditionally been considered poetic, but the controversy over the poetic status of the prophets has ancient roots. The third-century *Didascalia apostolorum* forbad the reading of pagan literature but suggested, "If you wish to read histories, take those of the Book of Kings: if you want poetry and wisdom, take the Prophets . . . if you desire songs, you have the Psaltery."[9] On the other hand, Jerome, who laid out his translation of the prophets in verse form, warned in his preface to Isaiah that except for such obviously poetic passages as Isaiah 5, which declares itself to be a song, the prophets should not be thought of as poets. As Lindblom points out, however, citing Isaiah 5, Amos 5, and Ezekiel 14, 19, 27, and 32, "sometimes the prophets chose to appear as poets or minstrels rather than speakers or preachers."[10] Furthermore, as Alter says, given the richness of poetry, "it makes sense that divine speech should be represented as poetry."[11] In their attempt to make the divine message as effective as possible, the prophets used the most effective language they knew, the language of poetry.

II

The basic teaching of the prophets is rather simple to understand, though difficult to carry out. As stated most clearly by Isaiah, it is "Cease to do evil; learn to do good" (1:17). Even if we allow for extensive elaboration, that teaching is fairly clear, and yet the prophets find hundreds of striking ways to say it, to make it vivid, to make it enter the consciousness of their audience. One of their techniques—one of their poetic techniques—is the use of dense clusters of imagery in which seemingly disparate images are brought together to reenforce or comment on each other. This clustering is especially effective because of the nature of parallelism: an image will be used in an *a* line and somehow expanded in the *b* line. Then a new image will be used in a subsequent *a* line and expanded in the *b* line, but that second set of images will somehow be an expansion of the first. Prophetic poetry is a perfect example of Jakobson's dictum that "similarity superimposed on contiguity imparts to poetry its through-going [sic] symbolic, multiplex, polysemantic essence."[12]

Part of the first chapter of Isaiah provides one of the best examples of this aspect of prophetic poetry:

> 4. Ah, sinful nation,
>   a people laden with iniquity,
>   offspring of evildoers,
>   sons who deal corruptly!
>   They have forsaken the Lord,
>   they have despised the Holy One of Israel,
>   they are utterly estranged.
> 5. Why will you still be smitten
>   that you continue to rebel?
>   The whole head is sick,
>   and the whole heart faint.
> 6. From the soul of the foot even to the head,
>   there is no soundness in it,
>   but bruises and sores
>   and bleeding wounds;
>   they are not pressed out, or bound up,
>   or softened with oil.
> 7. Your country [literally "your land"] lies desolate,
>   your cities are burned with fire;
>   in your very presence
>   aliens devour your land [literally "your earth"];
>   it is desolate, as overthrown by aliens.
> 8. And the daughter of Zion is left
>   like a booth in a vineyard,
>   like a lodge in a cucumber field,
>   like a besieged city.[13]

This piling on of images has its source partially in the prophet's anger, which leads him to castigate the people in a variety of ways; but it also originates in parallelism, which Kugel describes as consisting "not of stringing together clauses that bear some semantic, syntactic, or phonetic resemblance, nor yet of 'saying the same thing twice.'" Rather it is a style in which the second half of the line both continues the first half and yet is separated from it in "a typically emphatic, 'seconding' style.[14]

We can see this style in Isaiah's use of imagery. The images in 1:4–8 are not disparate expressions of the prophet's anger, although they may appear so. They are, instead, complementary. Verse 4 begins with Isaiah calling Israel a "sinful nation," as straightforward a phrase as we are likely to find. He then moves to a metaphoric plane when he calls it "a people laden with iniquity." This is not merely a restatement of the first phrase. It illustrates that phrase; it gives us almost a visual perception of that first phrase. Then Israel becomes "offspring of evildoers, sons who deal corruptly." "Evildoers" is straightforward but vague. In what way do they do evil? By dealing corruptly. Furthermore, the nation has suddenly become "offspring" (literally "seed") and "sons." Whose sons? The Lord's. By yoking these images together, the prophet has not simply said the same thing in five different ways. Instead he has intensified his condemnation, establishing that the people of Israel are God's children whose corruption, evil in itself, has led them to be even more sinful, laden with iniquity.[15]

At this point the prophet abruptly shifts to a whole new metaphor that describes Israel as a body that is sick and wounded. This metaphor, unlike those in verse 4, is carried through two verses and almost becomes a minor allegory, describing the rottenness of the country. It also continues the movement from nation to children that began in verse 4 by now comparing the entire nation to an individual, thereby helping to focus the earlier images more clearly and to hint at the relationship between the individual and the society. Verses 5 and 6 complement verse 4 by means of thematic continuity, made more striking by the juxtaposition of metaphors. This juxtaposition continues in verse 7, which begins with another clear statement, "Your country lies desolate." This phrase marks a transition from the body metaphor back to the nation, providing an application of the metaphor from the previous two verses by implying the comparison between desolated land and desolated body and focusing the audience's attention on the specific problem of an invading army. (It is likely that this prophecy was delivered during a siege, possibly that of Sennacherib in 701 B.C.E.) Strangers devour the country and it will be wasted.

After these bleak words, we hear of the daughter of Zion. This metaphor returns us to the ungrateful sons of verse 4 and the individual person of verses 5 and 6. This daughter of Zion will be left "like a booth in a vineyard, like a lodge in a cucumber field," that is, she will be isolated, visible but alone, in a field of comestibles. In these similes, Isaiah introduces yet another of his major themes, that despite their wickedness and despite the trials that they will face, the people of Israel will survive—or at least a remnant will survive. The country may be devoured, like the grapes in the vineyard or the cucumbers, but the daughter of Zion, like the booth and the lodge, will survive. Furthermore, the daughter of Zion will also be like "a besieged city," which seems to clash with the similes of the booth and the lodge. But this third simile returns us to verse 7, "Your country lies desolate, your cities are burned with fire," and reminds the audience that while the daughter of Zion will survive, it will be at great expense, both of individuals and of the society as a whole.

In these five verses, then, Isaiah, by yoking together so many seemingly disparate similes and metaphors, has not only warned the people but has also introduced a number of the themes that will run through the book; and the abrupt shifts, along with the vehemence of the speech, force the audience to be aware of the wider implications of the prophet's message, so that he can then proceed to his famous condemnation of empty ritual, culminating in the advice, "Learn to do good." In addition, in these few verses the prophet has used six different images for Israel, images that ordinarily have no other relationship to each other. And the metaphoric "daughter of Zion" is itself the subject of the series of similes involving the booth, the lodge, and the city. In order to convey the reality of Israel's situation, the prophet operates simultaneously on a number of imagistic levels.

If the people do indeed learn to do good, what will be the result?

> 18. Come now, let us reason together,
>   says the Lord:
>   though your sins are as scarlet,
>   they shall be as white as snow;
>   though they are red like crimson,
>   they shall become like wool.
> 19. If you are willing and obedient,
>   you shall eat the good of the land;
> 20. But if you refuse and rebel,
>   you shall be devoured ["eaten"] by the sword;
>   for the mouth of the Lord has spoken.

Here and throughout the prophets, key themes and images appear in a kaleidoscopic way. The reward for repentance will be dialogue with God and purification. And since the people have just been told, "Your hands are full of blood. Wash yourselves; make yourselves clean" (vv.15–16), the purification consists, imagistically, of turning the redness of their sins to white. The next verse promises that, if the people repent, they will "eat the good of the land," which recalls the earlier description of the land as desolate and then as a place devoured by strangers, an image which is picked up again in verse 20, where the prophet's (and God's) anger shows again, contrasting the healthy eating of Israel with the devouring done by strangers. (It is noteworthy that in Hebrew the root for the words translated as "eat" and "devour" are the same, which relates the verses even more closely.)

Verse 21 continues and expands the pattern we have seen developing: "How the faithful city has become a harlot, she that was full of justice! Righteousness lodged in her, but now murderers." In an image that the prophets use frequently (e.g., Jermiah 2:2; Ezekiel 16; and most famous of all, Hosea 1), Israel, here represented by Jerusalem, is depicted as a harlot or an unfaithful wife, an image that refers back to verse 4, "they have forsaken the Lord," and to the chapter's opening verses. Then, in an abrupt shift, the city that has become a harlot is said to be inhabited by murderers, which may recall the sword of verse 20 and surely recalls the blood-covered hands of verse 15. Thus, what appears at first as a mixed—or at least confused—metaphor in verse 21 actually combines in a new way elements that have already been used, sharpening both the prophet's condemnation and his picture of the ideal relationship between God and Israel. The images do not have to make perfect logical sense in order to be effective. There is no sense here of a strictly logical argument. Isaiah's point is really a simple one: the people have been behaving badly and they need to repent. Each of the images that he uses reenforces this message, revealing new facets either of the people's evil or of the possible good that could exist; and the images recur and are expanded, albeit in no special order, throughout the chapter and the book.

After the metaphor of verse 21, Isaiah becomes more literal in verse 23: "Your princes are rebels and companions of thieves: Everyone loves a bribe, and runs after gifts. They do not defend the fatherless; and the widow's cause does not come to them." Ordinarily this verse might have followed verse 17, "Learn to do good; seek justice, correct oppression, defend the fatherless, plead for the widow," for it indicates exactly how the leaders do not "do good," but the intervening five verses, with their promise of forgiveness and their metaphoric picture of what Israel has become, make verse 23 more striking and more effective. It is not simply that the leaders have money and ignore justice or that they favor the strong over the weak. These are only examples of a greater evil, that the leaders—and all of Israel—have been unfaithful to God. The multitude of sins is symptomatic of the problem as Isaiah expressed it in verse 3: "The ox knows its owner, and the ass its master's crib; but Israel does not know, my people does not understand." The ox and even the ass know to whom they owe their well-being; but Israel, which stands in the relationship of a beloved child or wife to God, does not understand. Thus the prophet's task is to teach the people and to move them so that they will both understand and do what they should, and he approaches that task through poetic prophecy.

The first chapter of Isaiah closes with the promise, both hopeful and terrible, that if the people do not repent, God will purge them, another of Isaiah's favorite images, and will then reestablish the nation in justice: "Afterward you shall be called the city of righteousness, the faithful city" (v.26). When justice is reestablished, when the people have learned to do good, the city, which has been a harlot, will be faithful once again. This promise, which might be called apocalyptic, is based on the imagery that has informed the whole chapter and seems like a fitting conclusion to the opening prophecy; but there are still five verses left, verses that describe briefly the "faithful city" but that then return to the theme that between now and then there will be hard times:

> 30. For you shall be like an oak
>   whose leaf withers,
>   and like a garden without water.
> 31. And the strong shall become tow
>   and his work a spark,
>   and both of them shall burn together,
>   with none to quench them.

If the people repent, conditions will improve. If they do not repent, conditions will deteriorate and then improve. Clearly the first way is preferable, but Isaiah knows that the people are not likely to repent, and he therefore concludes the chapter not with a consoling picture of the city restored but with an image of the destruction that will necessarily precede the restoration. His object here is not to console. It is to disturb, and so he concludes with a chilling picture.

This first chapter of Isaiah is typical of many chapters in the prophets, chapters that are crammed full of various images which seem either to be unconnected or to clash with each other but that in fact complement each other, building up an emotional picture which the prophets hope will stir the people to repentance. We can look briefly, for example, at Isaiah 17:10–14, part of a poem condemning idolatry. These five relatively long verses contain a cluster of images, including images of rock, planting, rushing waters, rushing nations, chaff, and spoliation. Most of these images, like those in the first chapter, are fairly common and must have been traditional, but what is striking is the way in which the prophet manipulates and combines them to give his pronouncements the fullest possible force in this oracle directed specifically at Damascus but also at Israel:

> 10. For thou hast forgotten the God of thy salvation,
>   And thou hast not been mindful of the Rock of thy stronghold;
>   Therefore thou didst plant plants of pleasantness,
>   And didst set it with slips of a stranger;

11. In the day of thy planting thou didst make it to grow,
    And in the morning thou didst make thy seed to blossom—
    A heap of boughs in the day of grief
    And of desperate pain.
12. Ah, the uproar of many peoples,
    That roar like the roaring of the seas;
    And the rushing of nations, that rush
    Like the rushing of mighty waters!
13. The nations shall rush like the rushing of many waters;
    But He shall rebuke them, and they shall flee far off,
    And shall be chased as the chaff of the mountains before the wind,
    And like the whirling dust before the storm.
14. At eventide behold terror;
    And before the morning they are not.
    This is the portion of them that spoil us,
    And the lot of them that rob us.[16]

One thing that strikes the reader of this passage in Hebrew is the poet's elaborate wordplay, common in the prophetic writings but most effectively employed here. Part of verse 10, for example, reads

על כן תטעי נטעי נעתנים
וזמרת זר תזרענו

'Al keyn tit'ay nit'ay na'amanim
u'zmorath zar tizra'enu

and verse 12 compares the peoples ('amim) to the seas (yamim) and the nations (umim) to water (mayim), so that the similes, which are already reenforced by the verse structure, are further emphasized by the wordplay.[17]

Furthermore, the images themselves operate according to a poetic logic. Thus verses 10 and 11 contain imagery of planting and fruitfulness (possibly in reference to rites associated with the worship of Adonis) surrounded by an opening mention of the people's neglect of God and a closing prediction of grief and pain. These verses are followed by two verses in which the image of water predominates. In the Middle East, water is often a symbol of life and fruitfulness, and here, coming after verses 10 and 11, this might well be our expectation; but Isaiah undercuts that expectation by making the rushing waters a simile for the destructive onslaught of other nations against Israel, so that in these verses, as in the preceding verses, the focus is on a false appearance of fruitfulness, a point that Isaiah makes even clearer by concluding verse 13 with the rushing waters transformed into chaff and dust, a transformation whose speed is the subject of the chapter's final verse. What we have, then, is two images of potential fertility— gardens and waters—undercut by images of destruction and aridity;

but undercutting this whole complex of images is a further irony in the image by which the poet speaks of God, "the Rock of thy stronghold." It is the lack of belief in this Rock, not usually an image of fertility, and the transference of faith to the apparent fertility of the gardens that results in destruction and aridity. This realization makes the possible association of the garden with the Adonis cult even more appealing, as Isaiah contrasts the productiveness of the Rock with the sterility of the resurrection god. God, the Rock, allows his people to flourish by reducing the adherents of a fertility cult to chaff and dust.

This complex of images relies on yet another image that appears often not only in Isaiah but in the other prophets, though Isaiah's use of it is most striking, the image of the vineyard. This image, which Isaiah first uses in chapter 5, differs from those we have been examining. Whereas we have been looking at image clusters, chapter 5 develops one image into an allegory, an allegory that the poet explains for us. First Isaiah describes in detail the planting of a vineyard and the planter's disappointment that the vineyard has produced only wild grapes. Then he provides an exposition:

> 7. For the vineyard of the Lord of hosts
>   is the house of Israel,
>   and the men of Judah
>   are his pleasant planting;
>   and he looked for justice,
>   but behold, bloodshed;
>   for righteousness,
>   but behold, a cry!

This short allegory is clear and effective, but it does not end with Isaiah's exposition, for Isaiah continues to describe what will happen to the vineyard, then shifts to consider the people's drunkenness ("Woe to those who rise early in the morning that they may run after strong drink," 5:11) and the people's unwillingness to regard their proper labor ("They have lyre and harp, timbrel and flute and wine at their feasts; but they do not regard the deeds of the Lord," 5:12), and he adds that part of the appropriate punishment consists of thirst. Much of Isaiah 5, then, is based on the symbol of the vineyard, which is drawn out to illustrate God's potential as a source of fertility as well as God's disappointment in the people, their sins, and the nature of their punishment.

Chapter 5 is not the end of the vineyard, however. In Isaiah 27 we read

    2. In that day [the day when Leviathan will be punished]:
       A pleasant vineyard, sing of it!
    3. I, the Lord, am its keeper;
       every moment I water it.
    Lest anyone harm it,
       I guard it night and day.

Here, after twenty-two chapters, the vineyard reappears with its original allegorical meaning intact. God, the Rock, is the keeper of the vineyard, its protector and the source of its fruitfulness. Regardless of the order of composition in the book, the imagery remains intact. There is a constancy here that is even carried over into other prophets. Thus both Jeremiah (2:21) and Ezekiel (17:1–10) use the image of the vineyard, as do several of the minor prophets. The image continued to exert power even into Greek Testament times as a result of its poetical development.

There are, of course, other ways of examining Isaiah and the other prophets as poets: we could consider their allegories, for example, or various genres. But a study of their imagery—its imaginativeness, its development, its logic—even in a brief article like this one, shows the prophets were not versifying polemicists. They were, as part of their divine function, poets who used poetry to make their pronouncements vivid and rich so that they resonate even into our own time.

Notes

1. Terence Collins, *Line-Forms in Hebrew Poetry* (Rome: Biblical Institute Press, 1978); Stephen Geller, *Parallelism in Early Biblical Poetry* (Missoula, Mont.: Scholars Press, 1979); M. O'Connor, *Hebrew Verse Structure* (Winona Lake; Minn.: Eisenbrauns, 1980); Adele Berlin, *The Dyanamics of Biblical Parallelism* (Bloomington: Indiana University Press, 1985); James Kugel, *The Idea of Biblical Poetry* (New Haven: Yale University Press, 1981); Robert Alter, *The Art of Biblical Poetry* (New York: Basic Books, 1985); *The Literary Guide to the Bible*, ed. Robert Alter and Frank Kermode (Cambridge: Harvard University Press, 1987).

2. Roman Jakobson, "Linguistics and Poetics," in *Style in Language*, ed. Thomas A. Sebeok (Cambridge: MIT Press, 1960), p. 351.

3. Ibid., p. 359.

4. O'Connor, *Hebrew Verse Structure*, p. 26.

5. J. Lindblom, *Prophecy in Ancient Israel* (Philadelphia: Fortress Press, 1962), p. 155.

6. Alter, *Art of Biblical Poetry*, p. 151.

7. Ibid., p. 141.

8. Stephen Geller, "Were the Prophets Poets?", *Prooftexts* 3 (1983): 211.

9. Kugel, *Idea of Biblical Poetry*, p. 151.

10. Lindblom, *Prophecy in Ancient Israel*, p. 154.

11. Alter, *Art of Biblical Poetry*, p. 141.

12. Jakobson, "Linguistics and Poetics," p. 370.

13. In Revised Standard Version; unless otherwise indicated quotations from Isaiah are from this edition of the Bible. Both Berlin and Alter examine this chapter as well. While my interpretation differs in some ways from theirs, I hope that all three readings will be seen as complementary rather than exclusive.

14. Kugel, *Idea of Biblical Poetry*, p. 153.

15. As Rémi Lack indicates in *La Symbolique du Livre d'Isaïe* (Rome: Biblical Institute Press, 1973), the words for nation (*goy*), people (*'am*), offspring (*zera'*), and sons (*banim*) form a pattern of increasing intimacy, which by itself contributes to the intensification.

16. I have used the Jewish Publication Society of America's translation here.

17. For a detailed examination of the complex wordplay in Zephaniah, whom the author calls a "prophet-poet" (p. 367), see Lawrence Zalcman, "Ambiguity and Assonance at Zephaniah II 4," *Vetus Testamentum* 36 (1968): 365–71.

In Praise of The Wisdom of Solomon

John Bligh
University of Guelph

TO describe a book as apocryphal and pseudonymous is a poor way of commending it to the attention of readers. The Wisdom of Solomon is, alas, one of the Apocrypha, and it was written not by Solomon but by an unknown scholar of Alexandria. Yet the author or editor who chose the bold title was not making an idle claim; the book does contain the essential wisdom of the Solomon of 1 Kings. It also develops some of the principal themes of the Old Testament; it introduces new ideas and new questions; and a strong case can be made for the view that it was used by Luke, John, and Paul.[1] It may even have been known to Jesus himself.[2] These are some of the reasons why it deserves a place in courses on the Bible as literature.

Taken together, the books of the Bible constitute a literature comparable to the Greek literature or the Roman. Each of these ancient literatures is of mercifully restricted compass, so that within a few years of hard work students of the Bible, without renouncing their reading of other literatures, can master their primary sources and begin to debate on a fairly equal footing with those who have worked much longer in the field. But biblical literature has this advantage over the Greek and Roman: it is more compact and coherent. All its books are woven into a single tapestry by certain recurring themes, the chief of which is the justice of God. Hebrew thought on this topic develops throughout the Old Testament books, coming to a climax but not a resolution in the Book of Job and is continued in the New Testament, where the main thesis of Paul's theology is that the righteousness (or justice) of God is revealed in the gospel (Rom. 1:17). The Wisdom of Solomon makes an important contribution to the slowly evolving debate: it is a missing link between the Old-Testament and the New-Testament phases of this unending discussion. If we treat the Bible as a literature, The Wisdom of Solomon deserves to be included within the *literary* canon of this literature, even though it has been excluded from most synagogal and ecclesiastical canons.

To treat the Bible as literature means, among other things, to read each book in the light of the whole, attending to what each author says and how he says it, and identifying his own contributions to the stream of biblical thought, *without passing judgment on the truth or falsity of what is said*, and without searching for evidence in support of any pre-determined thesis or dogma. That is why the Bible as literature fits so well into the curriculum of a modern, secular university. The instructor, if he is wise, never tells the students what he believes and never allows them to disclose what they believe. The aim is simply to discover what the biblical authors are saying and how their thought develops and to experience the power of the noble language in which these thoughts are clothed. The position to be developed here is that the Bible *as a literature* is a more complete whole if it is allowed to include The Wisdom of Solomon, and that a course entitled "The Bible as Literature" will have greater cohesion if this valuable book is included.[3]

First, some observations on the form and structure of the book. The text is divided into nineteen chapters, the first nine of which form a unit apart. If the book does indeed contain the wisdom of King Solomon, it is to be found in these nine chapters. (Hereinafter, the speaker in The Wisdom of Solomon will always be called simply Solomon, while the royal son of David will always be called King Solomon.) The remaining ten chapters are inferior, and their relationship to the first nine is problematic. They are, however, deserving of attention because Paul is indebted to them in various ways, and they raise an important question about the relationship of natural to supernatural or biblical revelation.

The first nine chapters taken alone constitute a treatise on kingship, which can be usefully compared to a group of Pythagorean specimens of the same genre by Ecphantus, Diotogenes, and Sthenidas.[4] Hellenistic kings like Antiochus Epiphanes IV (who provoked the Wars of the Maccabees) habitually claimed to be epiphanies of some deity and as such did not enjoy being admonished by their merely human subjects. One tactful and safe way of admonishing such a king, without directly criticizing his administration, was to write a treatise on kingship, offering a description of the ideal king, to serve as a mirror in which the particular king could see, by comparison, his own shortcomings. The Pythagorean authors went a long way toward justifying the Hellenistic kings' claim to be epiphanies of divinity: their ideal king is a being of superior nature who contemplates and imitates God directly, whereas his subjects imitate God by contemplating and imitating their king. Therefore, while a treatise on kingship offers an ideal directly to the king, it is also indirectly offering a similar moral ideal to his subjects.

The author of The Wisdom of Solomon, desiring no doubt to admonish the rulers of Alexandria, presents as his ideal king an idealized Solomon, whom he does not simply describe. Instead of speaking in his own person about Solomon, he makes Solomon himself the speaking persona throughout. (If the title, "The Wisdom of Solomon," comes from the author, the reader may be intended to recognize from the start that the speaker is Solomon; the reference becomes fully apparent in chapter 8.) Tactfully, therefore, he admonishes kings and rulers through the persona of a king.[5] The result is that this biblical treatise on kingship resembles, in some interesting ways, the literary form known to students of English Literature as the "dramatic monologue," developed by Robert Browning, in which a persona other than the poet addresses a silent listener or listeners, and the reader is cast in the role of overhearer. Through this device the poet is able to convey his lessons to the reader unobtrusively, or "by indirection," as Browning liked to say. Solomon addresses fellow kings, and readers who are not kings can apply his lessons to themselves if they have ears to hear. Jewish and Christian readers can also claim the instruction as their own on the grounds that kingship is a charisma imparted by God to all men in some degree (see Gen. 1:20; Rev. 1:10).[6]

The second half of the book (chapters 10–19) is a meditation on the miraculous interventions of God at the time of the Israelites' Exodus from Egypt and entry into Canaan. It has been suggested that this may be a Hellenistic Passover Haggadah, that is, a devotional narrative of the Exodus composed to give glory to God at the Paschal meal for his goodness in leading Israel out of Egypt into the promised land.[7] But it is better to regard these chapters as constituting, along with the litany of Wisdom in 7:22–30, as an example of the Hellenistic literary form known as the "aretalogy," that is, a list (*logos*) of the excellences and good works (*aretai*) of a goddess (such as Isis) or of a personified abstraction (here Wisdom; in Heb. 11, Faith). The whole book is a "protreptic," that is, a hortatory discourse, urging kings and subjects to seek Wisdom and yield themselves to her guidance.[8]

The book is not unworthy of its title. It really can claim to expound the wisdom of the King Solomon known to history from 1 Kings 3–8. In the author's opinion, the wisdom of King Solomon consisted in his recognition that kingship is a gift given by God to persons of his choice, and that the charisma of kingship is not complete in itself: a king needs and must pray for the additional gift of wisdom, so that he may exercise his kingship according to God's will, that is, with "justice"—which includes compassion for the weak and the poor (cf. 12:18–19). All this is in agreement with 1 Kings 3, where King Solomon, who is already enthroned, prays for the gift of wisdom, and having received it, shows it in his saving-justice (*sedaqah*) by providing a loving home for the weakest of his subjects, the newborn son of a harlot.

The author has rightly seized upon the substance of King Solomon's wisdom, namely, his concept of responsible and compassionate rulership. This is also one of the most important ideas in the teaching of Jesus, who, like Solomon, develops it with the aid of a contrast. Salome, the mother of James and John, asks Jesus to give her anything she asks for, but he refuses to make a rash promise and requires her to specify her request (Matt. 20:20; Mark 10:35–36). When she asks that her sons be appointed the chief grandees in his kingdom, he tells her that it is not for him to grant; though a king, he is dependent on God's will (Mark 10:40). When the other disciples become indignant about the request, Jesus admonishes them:

> You know that those who are supposed to rule over the Gentiles lord it over them, and their great men tyrannize over them.[9] But it shall not be so among you; but whoever would be first among you must be slave of all. For the Son of Man also came not to be served but to serve, and to give his life as a ransom for many. [Mark 10:42–45]

The whole passage should be read as a comment on the execution of John the Baptist. To please Salome the dancer, Herod Antipas, surrounded by his grandees, makes a rash promise to give her whatever she asks for, up to half his kingdom (Mark 6:23). When she asks for the head of the Baptist, Herod, defying God's law and his conscience, destroys a prophet. The true king, respecting God's will, is a savior; the seeming king (who in reality is no king, since he is ruled by the women of his court) defies God's will and is a destroyer. This is the wisdom of King Solomon and of Jesus alike.

The author agrees with King Solomon that divine wisdom is available to man; God is not jealous of his wisdom; he gives it to those who seek it by prayer:

> Radiant and unfading is Wisdom;
> she is not coy about being seen by those who love her
> and found by those who seek her.
> She anticipates their desire,
> revealing herself first.

> [6:12–13]

Surprisingly, the Gospels do not contain the idea that the gift of the kingdom (*basileia*) imparted to believers needs to be supplemented with the gift of wisdom. In Matthew 6:33, Jesus says: "Seek first the kingdom of God and its justice and all these things [food, drink, clothing] will be given you in addition"—which is strongly reminiscent of 1 Kings 3:11–13 and of The Wisdom of Solomon 7:11: "All good things came to me along with her, and in her hands uncounted wealth." We might have expected Jesus to say, "Seek first the kingdom of God and its wisdom." The meaning of his phrase, "the kingdom and its justice," is perhaps not too dissimilar, since the wisdom of the kingdom translated into action is saving-justice (*sedaqah*). However, the advantage of praying explicitly for wisdom is that such a prayer implies acknowledgment of one's present limitations. Christians are perhaps too inclined to believe that they already have the solutions to the world's problems.

When Solomon urges rulers to pray for wisdom, he is in fact calling them to repentance, to a change of heart and the following of a new way of life. To assure them that conversion is possible, he narrates his own life story: he shows that he was not born wise; he first desired wisdom, then prayed for it, then received it—and others can do the same. He even repeats the prayer he made for wisdom (based on the prayer of King Solomon in 1 Kings 8), so that it may serve as a model for the prayer of other kings:

> O God of our fathers and Lord of mercy,
> who madest all things by thy Word [*Logos*]
> and by thy Wisdom [*Sophia*] didst form man
> to have dominion over the creatures made by thee,
> to rule the world in holiness and righteousness,
> and pronounce judgment in uprightness of soul:
> give me that Wisdom who sits by thy throne,
> and do not reject me from among thy servants.
> I am thy slave and the son of thy maidservant,
> a man weak and short-lived,
> wanting in understanding of judgment and laws.
> ·
> With thee is Wisdom, who knows thy works
> and was present when thou wast making the world;
> she understands what is pleasing in thy sight
> and what is right according to thy commandments.
> Send her forth from the holy heavens,
> send her from thy glorious throne,
> that she may work with me at my side
> and I may know what is pleasing to thee.
>
> [9:1–5, 9–10]

The author does not explicitly call upon wicked kings to "repent," but any ruler using Solomon's prayer, or any lesser mortal adapting it to his own situation, would in fact be turning away from his past life and seeking God's grace to help him follow a different way for the future. The prayer itself would be a kind of baptism, a death to one sort of existence, "an appeal to God for a clear conscience" (1 Pet. 3:21), and a transition to another and better life.

While the nucleus of Solomon's wisdom can be traced back to King Solomon, the author in developing and expanding it has attributed to Solomon ideas of later origin, derived in part from Greek philosophy, about survival after death and about the operations of the divine Spirit.

On the sound rhetorical principle that juxtaposed opposites illuminate each other, Solomon illustrates his idea of kingship by means of a contrast with the thinking of kings who do not believe in the justice of God. Solomon himself creates a speaking persona, an unbelieving and ungodly ruler who gives voice to his secret thoughts. At first he sounds like the Solomon of Ecclesiastes. "Short and sorrowful is our life," he says,

> there is no remedy for death
> and from Hades there is no release.
> We were born by mere chance,
> and hereafter we shall be as though we had never been.
> The breath in our nostrils is smoke,
> and reason a spark kindled by the beating of our hearts,
> which extinguished, the body will turn to ash,
> and the spirit dissolve like yawning air.
> Our name will be forgotten in time,
> and no one will remember our works;
> our life will pass away like the traces of a cloud,
> and vanish like a mist
>   chased by the rays of the sun
>   and overcome by its heat.
> For our allotted time is the passing of a shadow,
> and there is no putting back the date of our death:
> it is sealed and settled, and none can reverse it.
> Come, then, let us enjoy the good things that are to hand,
> and enjoy creation with the zest of youth.
> Let us take our fill of costly wine and perfumes,
> and not miss out on the flowers of spring.
> Let us crown ourselves with rosebuds before they wither.
> Let every meadow share in our revelry.
> Everywhere let us leave signs of our mirth,
> for this is our portion, and this our lot.

[2:1–9]

But from this point on, the speaker diverges from Ecclesiastes. Having no faith in the justice of God (and, it seems, no experience of the self-respect that comes from acting justly), he thinks he can commit injustices with impunity:

> Let us oppress the righteous poor man;
> let us not spare the widow
> nor regard the gray hairs of the aged.
> Let our strength be the norm of justice,
> for we know the weak cannot do a thing.
>
> [2:10–11]

Next, the unrighteous ruler turns his attention to prophets and preachers who dare to admonish him. To test the truth of a prophet's words, he puts God to a test, saying in effect: "This prophet trusted in God; let us see if God will protect him!":

> Let us lie in wait for the righteous man;
> he is a nuisance to us and opposes our actions;
> he reproaches us for sins against the law,
> and accuses us of lapses of taste.
> He professes knowledge of God,
> and calls himself a child of the Lord.
> He is a standing reproach to our ways of thinking;
> the very sight of him is a burden to us,
> because his manner of life is unlike that of others,
> and his ways are strange.
> We are reckoned as dross by him,
> and he avoids our ways as unclean.
> "Blessed is the latter end of the righteous," he says,
> and he boasts that God is his father.
> Let us see if his words are true,
> and test what will happen at the end of his life;
> for if the righteous man is God's son indeed,
> God will help him
> and deliver him from the hand of his adversaries.
> Let us tempt him with insult and torture,
>   to test out his meekness
>   and make trial of his endurance.
> Let us condemn him to a shameful death,
> for, if what he says is true, he will be protected.
>
> [2:12– 20]

So the unjust king puts the prophet to torture and death: God does not intervene, the prophet dies a martyr's death, and the unjust ruler thinks he has proved his point—that there is no just God who vindicates the upholders of his law.

Solomon proceeds to tell such unjust rulers that they are wrong. To defend the justice of God, he proposes his doctrine of survival after death: because God is just, there *must* be, and therefore he confidently asserts there *is*, judgment after death. Unjust rulers have made themselves unworthy of the enlightenment that wisdom would have given them on this point. After the speech just quoted, he comments:

> Thus they reasoned, but they went astray,
> for their wickedness had blinded them.
> They did not know the secret purposes of God,
> they had no hope of the wages of holiness,
> and no notion of the prize awaiting the souls of the blameless.
> God created man for incorruption
> and made him in the image of his own eternity;
> the devil's envy brought death into the world,
> and those who join his party experience death.
> But the souls of the righteous are in the hand of God,
> and torment shall not touch them.
> In the eyes of the foolish they seemed to die;
> their departure was reckoned an evil end,
> and their going from us a wiping out.
> And yet they are at peace.
> For though in the sight of men they were punished,
> their hope of immortality is complete.
>
> [2:21–3:4]

Unjust rulers have blinded themselves to the true meaning of Genesis 3, where the "serpent" is the devil, and "death" is not physical death but spiritual ruin, which, for those of the devil's party, begins in this world (v.24) and lasts after physical death. The just do not experience "death": their souls remain living in the hand or protection of God and will be glorified. The closing phrase, "their hope of immortality is complete," is unfortunately obscure. It seems to mean: "they still live in hope, but their hope is untroubled by any fear." Its future fulfillment is described in 3:7–8:

> In the time of their visitation they will shine forth,
> and will run like sparks through the stubble.
> They will govern nations and rule over peoples,
> and the Lord will reign over them for ever.

To complete his argument, Solomon summons up a picture of judgment: when the unjust rulers see the vindication of the righteous martyr, they will confess how foolish they were:

> This is the man whom we once held in derision
> and made a byword of reproach—we fools!
> We thought his life madness
> and his end without honor.
> See how he has been numbered among the sons of God,
> and his inheritance is among the saints!
> Then it was we who strayed from the way of truth!
> The light of righteousness did not shine on us,
> and its sun did not rise upon us.
> In paths of lawlessness and destruction we disported ourselves,
> and through trackless deserts we journeyed,
> but the way of the Lord we did not know.
> What did our arrogance profit us?
> And what good has our wealth and boasting brought us?
>
> [5:4–8]

As they contemplate the reversal of roles, the wicked see that they have learned wisdom too late, when they can no longer profit by it. Their hope of vicarious immortality is vain. Solomon, speaking in his own person, sums up:

> The hope of the ungodly man is like chaff carried away by the wind,
> or a light spider's web driven away by a storm,
> or smoke dispersed before a wind,
> or the remembrance of a guest who stays but a day.
> But the righteous live for ever,
> and their reward is with the Lord;
> the Most High takes care of them.
> Therefore they will receive a glorious crown
> and a beautiful diadem from the hand of the Lord;
> with his right hand he will cover them,
> and with his arm he will shield them.
>
> [5:14–16]

The author's confident assertion of survival after death was not, of course, entirely unprepared. Both Jeremiah and Ezekiel had moved in this direction when they individualized the Israelites' relationship to God (Jer. 31:34; Ezek. 11:19). In the end, it is impossible to maintain that God displays his justice in his treatment of each individual Israelite, without asserting sanctions after death. Jeremiah and Ezekiel do not go this far, but their principles point toward the conclusion drawn by the authors of the Book of Daniel and The Wisdom of Solomon. The author of Daniel, reflecting on the fate of the Maccabean martyrs, was convinced that death could not be the end for them or for their unpunished oppressors. Therefore he makes the angel Michael say:

> Many of those who sleep in the dust of the earth shall awake, some to everlasting life, and some to shame and everlasting contempt. And those who are wise shall shine like the brightness of the firmament; and those who turn many to righteousness, like the stars for ever and ever. [Dan. 12:2– 3]

Michael appears to be promising the awakening only of the very righteous and the very wicked.[10] Solomon goes further, perhaps under the influence of Plato.[11] He talks of the immortality of the souls of the just rather than of the resurrection of their bodies, and he thinks of man's immortality as an image of God's eternity, which seems to make it a natural property of the soul. The just look forward to immortal life, the wicked to immortal death. Solomon introduces the ideas of survival and of judgment after death partly to defend the justice of God but partly also to provide a motive for kings and other rulers, to induce them to practice justice and compassion. For the subjects of kings, fear of the law and other social pressures are powerful motives to right conduct, but kings consider themselves above the law and answerable to God alone.[12] If kings are not convinced of the justice of God, they are more likely to be tempted to act capriciously. Fear of God and belief in his judgment are therefore more necessary for kings than for others. For ordinary men and women, fear of judgment can become an additional motive, but for them it is not the only effective motive, nor is it usually the most effective. Forgetting this, later teachers have sometimes talked as if sanctions after death were by themselves sufficient and effective for all. The evangelist who put together the Sermon on the Mount perhaps gave too much prominence to otherworldly sanctions.

The book also contains interesting developments of the idea of the Spirit of God, which Solomon identifies with the wisdom of God (9:17). He represents the Spirit as being on the one hand the agent of divine omniscience through whom men's secret thoughts are known to God, and on the other hand the revealer of God's secrets and the guide or inspirer of moral conduct impelling kings to rule with justice and compassion. The author is doubtless indebted in some measure to the Stoic philosophers, Zeno, Cleanthes, Chrysippus and the rest, who combined the ontology of Heracleitus with the ethics of Socrates and taught that the Word of God, which orders the wheeling heavens, is also the universal law to which human conduct should be conformed. One of the noblest expressions of this philosophy is Cleanthes' hymn to Zeus:

    ...O King of Kings
    Through ceaseless ages, God, whose purpose brings
    To birth, whate'er on land or in the sea
    Is wrought, or in high heaven's immensity;
    Save what the sinner works infatuate.
    Nay but thou knowest to make the crooked straight:
    Chaos to thee is order: in thine eyes
    The unloved is lovely, who did'st harmonise
    Things evil with things good, that there should be
    One Word through all things everlastingly.
    One Word—whose voice alas! the wicked spurn;
    Insatiate for the good their spirits yearn:
    Yet seeing see not, neither hearing hear
    God's universal law, which those revere,
    By reason guided, happiness who win.[13]

The Wisdom of Solomon is one of the channels through which Stoic thought and language passed into Christianity.[14]

Solomon begins his address to the rulers of the earth by warning them against "perverse thoughts [that] separate men from God" (1:3). Whereas the rebellious and hostile thoughts of human subjects are hidden from their kings, the skeptical and irreligious thoughts of kings are not hidden from God because the Spirit of God pervades and explores the whole of creation, gathering information for the divine judge about all that is said and all that is thought:

    The Spirit of the Lord has filled the world,
    the power that holds the universe together has knowledge of every voice.
    Therefore no one who talks wickedness will escape notice.
    Justice, when she punishes, will not pass him by.
    For the counsels of the ungodly man will be investigated,
    and a report of his words will come to the Lord,
    to convict him of his lawless deeds.
    A jealous ear hears all things,
    and the murmur of secret complaint is not hidden away.

                                          [1:7–10]

This all-pervasive Spirit that is Wisdom reappears in the fourth Gospel in Jesus, the Word, who knows the secret thoughts and actions of all men and women (John 1:48; 4:18; 20:27) and does not need to be told what is in man (John 2:24–25).

Second, Wisdom is the guide and helper of kings in the fulfillment of their royal tasks. Solomon follows Proverbs 8 in personifying Wisdom as a female teacher who was present and active in the creation of the world, but he goes further when he makes the daring suggestion that this beautiful bride of God (whom he describes in lyrical terms) can become the bride of men:

In her there is a spirit that is intelligent, holy,
one in origin, many in effects,
subtle, mobile, clear, unpolluted,
distinct, invulnerable, loving the good, keen,
irresistible, beneficent, humane [*philanthropon*],
steadfast, sure, free from anxiety,
all-powerful, overseeing all,
and penetrating through all spirits
that are intelligent and pure and most subtle.
For Wisdom is more mobile than any motion;
in her pureness she pervades and penetrates all things.
She is a breath of the power of God,
and a pure emanation of the glory of the Almighty;
therefore nothing defiled gains entrance into her.
She is the radiance [*apaugasma*]¹⁵ of Light eternal,
the spotless mirror of the working of God,
and the image of his goodness.

I loved her and sought her from my youth,
and I desired to take her for my bride,
and I became a lover of her beauty.
She glorifies her noble birth by living with God,
And the Lord of all loves her.

[7:22–26; 8:2–3]

Here is a remarkable anticipation of John's portrayal of Jesus as "the Bridegroom" (3:29): divine Wisdom comes into the world to enter into a covenant comparable to marriage. But what is more important is that the author is subtly and perhaps unconsciously modifying the Jewish picture of God.¹⁶ Sophia embodies his humane attributes, his saving-justice, his love of frail man, and the universality of his love (she is *philanthropos*, which means all these three things). The Lord is shown to be a God who delights in Wisdom and is willing and eager to share her with those who love her. The figure of the dangerous God who appeared at Sinai in thunder and lightning recedes into the background. One effect, whether intended or unplanned, of such commendations of Sophia is to present the God of Israel in a gentler and more humane light; whereas earlier generations pictured him as a masculine warrior God, or as the remote, incalculable source of both good and evil, he is now seen in his more attractive female *ikon* or image. The change is a method of justifying God: he is commended to the reader as a Lord who is well disposed to mankind and eager to guide individual men and women, through the teachings of his heavenly consort, to virtue, prosperity, and peace.

The wisdom or knowledge that Sophia imparts is mainly moral instruction to enable kings to rule justly, but since she knows the secrets of God and pervades the whole of creation, there is no reason why she should not communicate every form of knowledge to the human mind (7:17–22). Solomon agrees with the author of Job that man cannot by his own efforts discover the secret counsels of God (Job 28:20–28), but he believes (as Job does not) that the Spirit or Wisdom of God can and will reveal divine mysteries to the devout:

> With difficulty we conjecture the truths of earth,
> and what is at hand we discover with toil.
> The truths of heaven who has traced out,
> and who has learned thy counsel,
> unless thou hast given Wisdom and sent thy holy Spirit from on high?
> [9:16–17]

This is exactly the view of Paul:

> "What no eye has seen, nor ear heard, nor the heart of man conceived, what God has prepared for those who love him," God has revealed to us through the Spirit. For the Spirit searches everything, even the depths of God. [1 Cor. 2:7–10]

In general, there is remarkable continuity between the teachings of Solomon and of Paul and John. All three warn their hearers of impending judgment, urge them to renounce the perverse thoughts that separate them from God, and bid them seek the Spirit or Wisdom of God while they still have time. The difference is by way of development and addition, not by way of contradiction or correction: Paul and John see the same Wisdom as incarnate in Jesus (Col. 1:15–20; John 1:1–14), who imparts his Spirit to those who believe in him and ask for the Spirit by seeking baptism. They add that Jesus himself will be the future judge of all (Rom. 2:16; John 5:27), and they introduce concepts of vicarious expiation and intercession not to be found in The Wisdom of Solomon (Rom. 3:24–25; John 12:50–52).

In chapters 1–9, Solomon has not explained on what grounds he is convinced of the proposition that God is just, which is the major premise of his argument for immortality. In the second part he appears to do so. He argues from history as recorded in the Pentateuch, first, that in the time of the patriarchs the wisdom imparted to men who believed in the justice of God protected them, while men lacking that wisdom perished; and second, that at the time of the Exodus God was just both in his punishment of the Egyptians and Canaanites and in his lenience to the Israelites. In the devout and reverential tone befitting a religious celebration, the author is developing an argument: he is trying to prove from biblical history that God is just and merciful. In an atmosphere of worship such arguments may be accepted uncritically, but a reader taking a cool, detached view of what is said can hardly fail to notice that Solomon's version of the Exodus story is highly selective, imaginative, and biased.

The argument concerning the Egyptians, Canaanites, and Israelites is, moreover, curiously defensive. The author may be replying to skeptical critics who wonder whether God *was* just in his treatment of those early peoples, or he may be replying to doubts that have arisen in his own mind. The apologetic tone is clear in the following passage:

> For who shall say, "What hast thou done?"
> Or who shall resist thy judgment?
> Who will accuse thee for destroying nations which thyself didst make?
> Or who will come forward to denounce thy treatment of the wicked?
> For apart from thee there is no God caring for all
> to whom thou shouldst prove that thou hast not judged unjustly;
> nor can any king or monarch bandy looks with thee about those whom
>   thou hast punished.
> Righteous art thou and rulest all things righteously,
> deeming it inconsistent with thy rule
> to condemn him who does not deserve to be punished.
>
> [12:12–15]

Solomon attempts to show that God combined mercy with justice in his treatment of the Canaanites: he destroyed them gradually, so as to leave them time for repentance:

> Those who dwelt of old in thy holy land
> thou didst hate for their detestable practices,
> their works of sorcery and unholy rites,
> their merciless slaughter of children,
> and their sacrificial feasting on human flesh and blood.
> These initiates from the midst of a heathen cult,
> parents who murdered helpless babes,
> thou didst will to destroy by the hands of our fathers,
> that the land most precious of all to thee
> might receive a worthy colony of servants of God.
> But even these [the Canaanites] thou didst spare, since they were but
>   men,
> and didst send wasps as forerunners of thy army,
> to destroy them little by little.
> Not that thou wast unable to give the ungodly into the hands of the
>   righteous in a battle,
> or to destroy them at once by dread wild beasts, or by thy stern Word,
> but judging them little by little thou gavest them space to repent.
>
> [12:3–10]

The Egyptians deserved "the utmost condemnation" because they rejected God's self-revelation through nature and fell into idolatry, which was the beginning of fornication and of every form of corruption (14:13). Having adopted the worship of animal-idols, they were justly punished "through such creatures" in the plagues. Meanwhile, God protected the Israelites, feeding them with quails and miraculously curing them of snakebites—this in spite of the making of the golden calf at Sinai (Exod. 22) and the idolatry of the Israelites at Baal-Peor (Num. 25), which are passed over in silence.

Solomon's argument from history is too selective to be convincing even to readers disposed to accept the Pentateuch as history, and, what is more, it places him in the awkward position of holding that whereas in the past God's justice was revealed in this world, in the present it is not; one must now look to another world and to a judgment beyond death. It is hard to believe that the pentateuchal narratives are the real basis of the author's belief in the justice of God. More probably the real basis is disclosed in his passage about natural revelation:

> Foolish by nature were all men, living in ignorance of God;
> from the good things that are seen they failed to know him who is;
> they did not discover the Craftsman by paying heed to his works.
> But fire, or wind, or the swift air,
> or the circle of stars, or turbulent water, or the luminaries of heaven,
> they thought to be gods that rule the world.
> And if through delight in their beauty they took them for gods,
> let them know how much better is the Lord of these things,
> for the source of all beauty created them;
> but if through astonishment at their power and influence,
> let them infer how much more powerful is he who created them.
> For from the greatness and beauty of creatures
> one ascends to the contemplation of their creator.
>
> [13:1–5]

The author sees the beauty and order of the natural world as a revelation of God's wisdom, which all men ought to be able to see, though most do not. Solomon debates with himself whether or not to blame them for their failure (13:6 and 8). Since he himself sees it, his present experience gives him grounds to believe in the goodness of God—and he is thereby disposed to believe in the interventions of God in past history. The real ground of his faith is his present response to the natural revelation of God. His revisionist history of the Exodus from Egypt and entry into Canaan is convincing only to others who like himself already believe in the goodness and justice of God on other grounds. Another awkwardness in Solomon's explanation of why so many men fail to recognize the justice of God (13:1) is that if all men are foolish by nature, how can they be blamed for the results of their folly? Who is responsible for this congenital defect? The author has no answer. Paul supplies one—by developing further this author's reinterpretation of Genesis 3.

For the modern student, The Wisdom of Solomon raises three or four questions to be carried over into the study of the New Testament. First, what are we to think of Solomon's attempt to defend the justice of God by invoking a doctrine of survival? Hasn't the author of Job shown that the wisdom of God is so far beyond human comprehension that we cannot use our conception of his justice as the premise of any argument?

Second, how is the supernatural revelation of the Bible related to God's revelation of himself in nature and through the consciences of good men? Does the supernatural revelation supersede and render superfluous the natural revelation? From Paul's practice we might infer that it does. When addressing a Gentile audience in Athens (Acts 17:22–31) or in Rome (Rom. 1–2), he speaks of God's self-revelation in nature; when, however, he is addressing Jews (Acts 13:26–41), he argues exclusively from the Bible. Perhaps Jews and Christians have always tended to underestimate the value of present revelation through nature and through conscience, whereas in fact it is always needed as a corrective and as a supplement to what can be learned from the Bible. Just as the author of The Wisdom of Solomon may have been mistaken about the basis of his own faith, supposing it to rest on the miracles of the Exodus, so too modern theologians who attempt to construct an academic apologetics based on the miracles of the Gospels may have failed to discern the true basis of their own faith. Self-analysis is never easy.

Third, once Jews and Christians have admitted belief in sanctions after death, are they wise to give so little attention to sanctions in this world? Social approval and self-respect are powerful sanctions of morality, in addition to which, as Matthew Arnold pointed out, there are supernatural sanctions in this world: in the fourth Gospel Jesus declares that if any man will put his teaching to the test of practice, "he shall know whether the teaching is from God" (John 7:17).[17] The moral teaching of Jesus has power to commend itself, independently of supernatural sanctions and apart from miracles: "If a man loves me, he will keep my word, and my Father will love him, and we will come to him and make our home with him" (John 14:23). This is one aspect of John's realized or inaugurated eschatology: the reward for Christian conduct is here and now, or at least begins here and now.

Fourth, whether or not Jesus read The Wisdom of Solomon, the whole of his ministry appears to be based on acceptance of the conclusion reached for the first time in this book, that the soul of every man and woman survives death, is judged, and is then rewarded or punished. His gospel is addressed to individuals, to help them prepare for judgment. Paul and other preachers of the first century did not try to initiate social reform here on this earth; they were concerned with the salvation of individuals out of this world. Unless they misunderstood Jesus, that is what he intended. What then is the role and purpose of the churches today? When a Western missionary goes into China, can his mission be to preach social justice to a people who already look after the poor and the sick better, and are more willing to share what they have, than the European country that sends him out? Or is he sent to prepare them one by one for judgment?

Notes

1. See Samuel Holmes in R. H. Charles, *The Apocrypha and Pseudepigrapha of the Old Testament* (Oxford: Clarendon Press, 1913), 1:526–27; C. Larcher, *Études sur le Livre de la Sagesse* (Paris: Gabalda, 1969), pp. 12–26; C. H. Dodd, *The Epistle of Paul to the Romans* (London: Hodder & Stoughton, 1932), p. 27; G. Ziener, "Weisheitsbuch und Johannesevangelium," *Biblica* 38 (1957): 399–418; 39 (1958): 37–60.

2. The possibility that the Wisdom of Solomon (hereafter, Wis) was somehow known to Jesus is taken seriously by C. Larcher, *Études sur le Livre de la Sagesse*, p. 26. He observes "with a certain astonishment" that the Jesus of the fourth Gospel throws into high relief two Old Testament types to which the author of Wis had already given special prominence, the brazen serpent (Wis 16:6–12) and the manna (16:20–26). David Winton, trans., The Wisdom of Solomon, The Anchor Bible (Garden City, N.Y.: Doubleday, 1979), pp. 20–25, conjectures that Wis was written in the reign of Gaius Caligula (31–41 c.e.), that is, after the death of Jesus, but his main argument is unconvincing, namely, that Wis 5:16–23 "could only be called forth" by the desperate situation of the Jewish community of Alexandria under Caligula.

3. Quotations from the Bible are from the Revised Standard Version, but I have departed from it whenever I saw reason to do so. The language of Wis is often finer than this version allows the English reader to see.

4. These fragments are preserved in Stobaeus, *Anthologia*, 4.7.61–66. According to W. W. Tarn, *Alexander the Great* (Cambridge: The University Press, 1948), 2:409, the surviving fragments of these authors are the debris of an abundant literature: "kingship after Alexander became so important that there was hardly a philosopher who did not write a treatise upon it." See further E. R. Goodenough, "The Political Philosophy of Hellenistic Kingship," *Yale Classical Studies* 1 (1928): 55–102; L. Delatte, *Les traités de la royauté d'Ecphante, Diotogène et Sthénidas* (Paris: Droz, 1942); James M. Reese, *Hellenistic Influence on the Book of Wisdom and Its Consequences* (Rome: Biblical Institute Press, 1970), pp. 72–79.

5. Shakespeare does the same: he reminds kings of their duty to the poor through the persona of Lear, and, for the benefit of King James and his brother-in-law King Christian of Denmark, he lists the king-becoming virtues through the persona of Malcolm.

6. The participation of every believer, Jew or Christian, in the kingship of God means that each is, to some extent, responsible for others as God's representative, with a duty to serve them

and to care for the weak. The obligation to make the heavens seem just is recognized equally by King Lear and by his subject, the Earl of Gloucester, in *King Lear*, 3.4.36 and 4.1.66–76.

7. Thus G. H. Box, *Judaism in the Greek Period* (Oxford: Clarendon Press, 1932), p. 174, following J. G. Eichhorn, *Einleitung in die apokalyptischen Schriften des Alten Testaments* (Leipzig: Weidmann, 1957), p. 89.

8. See A. J. Festugière, "À propos des arétalogies d'Isis," *Harvard Theological Review* 42 (1949): 209– 34; É. des Places, "Hymnes grecs au seuil de l'ère chrétienne," *Biblica* 38 (1957): 113–39; J. M. Reese, *Hellenistic Influence on the Book of Wisdom*, pp. 43 and 103. An early protreptic, in dialogue form, is included in Plato's *Euthydemus*, 278e–282d. Plato's argument is that wisdom leads to happiness in this world; Solomon's, that it leads to happiness both in this world (when kings rule wisely) and in the next. Plato thinks that wisdom can be learned from human teachers; Solomon thinks it is to be sought by prayer. So does Cleanthes (see n.13).

9. As the context shows, the rare word *katexousiazousin* has a pejorative sense; hence "tyrannize." Luke emphasizes the importance of this passage by transferring it to the context of the Last Supper (Luke 22:24–26) and adding the saying of Jesus, "I am among you as one who serves." This is illustrated in the fourth Gospel by the washing of feet, after which Jesus says: "I have given you an example, that you also should do as I have done to you" (John 13:15).

10. Box, *Judaism in the Greek Period*, p. 217.

11. Solomon makes a real distinction between soul and body and appears to accept the Platonic doctrine of preexistence when he says: "I was a comely child, and a good soul fell to my lot—or rather, being good, I entered an undefiled body" (8:19–20). But perhaps he no more intends to assert preexistence than Wordsworth in his "Intimations" Ode.

12. See Shakespeare, *King John*, 3.1.147–48, "What earthly name to interrogatories / Can task the free breath of a sacred king," and *Richard II*, 4.1.121, "What subject can give sentence on his king?" In *The Complete Works*, ed. Peter Alexander (London: Collins, 1985).

13. The complete text of this translation by James Adam is reprinted in F. C. Copleston, *A History of Philosophy*, vol. 1, pt. 2 (1946; reprint ed., Garden City, N.Y.: Doubleday, 1962), pp. 137–38. For the Greek of Cleanthes' hymn see A. C. Pearson, *The Fragments of Zeno and Cleanthes* (1891; reprint ed., New York: Arno Press, 1973), pp. 274–75.

14. The influence of Stoicism was sometimes more direct. Paul at Athens quotes a tag from a Stoic poet, Aratus: "For we are indeed his offspring" (Acts 17:28). The context of the quotation is preserved in Eusebius, *Praeparatio evangelii*, 13. 26–27: "Let us begin from Zeus, whom never, O men, let us leave unmentioned. Full of God are all roads and all the meeting places of men, full are the sea and harbours; everywhere we have experience of God. For we are indeed his offspring. And he is kindly to mankind." W.L. Knox, *St. Paul and the Church of the Gentiles* (Cambridge: The University Press, 1939), p. 24, suggests that perhaps Paul knew the tag but not the context.

15. This word reappears in an important christological passage at the beginning of the Epistle to the Hebrews (1:3). In the Greek, the nouns "reflection," "mirror," and "image" have no definite article because they are in the predicative position.

16. See Carl G. Jung, *Answer to Job* (Princeton: Princeton University Press, 1958), #563.

17. Matthew Arnold, *Literature and Dogma* (New York: Macmillan, 1906), pp. 98, 142–43, 203, 223.

Johannine Myth and the New Trinity

John Maier
State University of New York College at Brockport

NOT too many years ago I was invited to attend a meeting of a business and social club in the town where I live—the kind of club whose emblem welcomes us into virtually every town and village in the United States. My heart sank when I espied a certain business-man of the town, who, I was sure, had just cheated me on a car repair deal. My depression deepened when, as the first order of business, the group was called to attention and asked to rise and in unison pronounce the club's creed. The rest of the evening is now—as it was then, actually—a blur. I was forced to confront my own abhorrence of creeds.

I mention this in a volume devoted to the contemporary interest in literature and the Bible to warn the reader that I am wont to take deep delight in the overcoming of creeds. That particular business-man's creed was probably pretty innocuous; no one else in the group seemed to care much about it at all. It has long been considered desirable to turn texts—stories and discourses especially—into creeds. No doubt a good bit of my personal and then professional interest in literary texts is the resistance those texts put up to very strenuous efforts at substituting the "meaning" or "essence" of a work for the work itself.

The task was somewhat easier in an earlier day, before "text" and "work" and "literature" itself became difficult and problematic concepts. Even to consider the Bible as a "text" or parts of the Bible as "texts" is to invite, today, vigorous—not to say rancorous—debate. And well it should. I do not have the solution to many of the problems raised by modern theorists; but I do tend to welcome the questions they raise. Indeed, I think we can agree, this is a day in which all notions of literature are put into question.

My remarks here, I have to admit at the outset, are prompted by two works that discuss the Gospel of John from the standpoint of Jacques Derrida.

Not the least of the ironies emerging from recent forays in literary theory is that even deconstructionists can be read in more than one way. The intellectual leader of the movement, Jacques Derrida, has been interpreted in strikingly different fashion by theologians and biblical scholars who have made use of his work. Werner Kelber, in the new journal *Oral Tradition*, takes what is by far the majority position on Derrida in a brilliant article whose title captures the spirit of the Derridean enterprise: "The Authority of the Word in St. John's Gospel: Charismatic Speech, Narrative Text, Logocentric Metaphysics." A very different Derrida emerges in Joseph S. O'Leary's *Questioning Back* (1985), a book whose subtitle also reveals the imprint of the French thinker: *The Overcoming of Metaphysics in Christian Tradition*. Between them Kelber and O'Leary map out very different trails for students of literature who want to read the "master" work of the Western tradition, the Bible.

According to Kelber, a "visualist language" permeates the Gospel of John "alongside its oralist language," yet visionary experience, seeing God and seeing the Risen Christ, is restrained in the Gospel. The spoken word—the sayings of Jesus and the activity of the paraclete, for example—is more efficacious, perhaps, than heavenly visions. This is important in view of the "status of the Logos as determiner of the text." No other aspect of the Gospel of John has received as much detailed scrutiny as its Logos doctrine. Kelber makes the connection with Derrida explicit when he points out that the Johannine Logos is "a typical, and perhaps the leading, case of *logocentrism*."[1]

Once he summarizes Derrida's position on logocentrism, Kelber makes a turn away from the text and from grammatology and back to an older way of reading (or hearing) the gospel, a way that is logocentric.

> Again, what is unthinkable in the age of *grammatology* is not altogether alien to historical periods when linguistic properties were defined largely in oral terms. The privileging of the *Logos* in a time still dominated by orality should not surprise us any more than the privileging of writing in our own present. That the *Logos* incarnates itself in textuality and texts emanate from orality constitutes common thinking in antiquity about the relations of speech and writing. By oral standards, not even the personification of the *Logos* is entirely baffling, for what typifies oral verbalization is the inseparable unity of speaker and message.[2]

Kelber is able, finally, to reaffirm the *Logos* as "the appropriate metaphor for transcendence." By acknowledging what scholars of oral traditions have told us about an understanding of the Word in antiquity, Kelber is able to use the despair of the age of grammatology against itself—to use the emptiness of Derrida's textcenteredness as a way to rethink ourselves back to an acceptable (and traditional) Johannine *Logos*.

A very different view of Derrida, one that as yet has few advocates, is offered by theologian O'Leary's *Questioning Back*, whose subtitle, as we have seen, is *The Overcoming of Metaphysics in Christian Tradition*. You can imagine, with my aversion to creeds, just how great my delight was to be see a book that attempts the overcoming of metaphysics in Christian tradition. It is a brilliant book. My expectations were, for the most part, fulfilled when I read it. In one—and for us a key—area I was disappointed. In O'Leary's deconstruction of certain key texts in the Western tradition he eventually reaches back to the Gospel of John. The preparation for that final chapter was superb, but I came away with some reservations about the chapter once it was reached.

My aim here is to summarize very briefly O'Leary's method of "questioning back" and indicate its importance for "the Bible and Literature." In a very sketchy way I will suggest a way O'Leary's method could be pushed back further than he does: from the Gospel of John through that brilliant Hellenistic work, the Book of Wisdom, to earlier texts in the Hebrew Bible and to texts much earlier even than those, namely works in the ancient Sumerian and Akkadian languages.

O'Leary bases his method on the thinking of Martin Heidegger and Derrida, whom he considers mainly "an acolyte to Heidegger." Before he attempts a deconstructive method of reading "the Christian classics," an attempt that is of great interest to students of literature, O'Leary takes pains to show that Derrida has been much misunderstood of late. "It is entirely inaccurate," he writes, "to speak of deconstruction as the abolition of the objective referentiality of discourse. Derrida is close to Heidegger in his understanding of the rapport between speech and world, except that his understanding of language is more complex than Heidegger's." Deconstruction, rather, "brings about a new opening on the world." The relation between context, text, and commentary is "rendered ungovernable," he claims, but commentary is not abolished. Rather, commentary becomes "part of the play of intertextuality in which no authoritative hierarchy can be established." "Reading as mastery must cede to reading as rewriting."[3]

O'Leary also claims that for Derrida, "the other aspect of *differance*, the differentiation of meaning, no more reduces meaning to randomness than the deferral of the referent constitutes its abolition." The *re*construction of the "textual field" relocates "that objectivity in an ongoing process of articulation rather than in propositions whose meaning is fully fixed" (pp. 41, 42).

> Deconstruction is not the reduction of meaning to a mere nothingness, or to the empty space lit up by the play of signifiers. It is a wrestling with the metaphysical tradition of meaning which, to use Heidegger's terms, it appropriates in a more originary way, by bringing to light the play of dissemination which the stable hierarchies of metaphysics occlude. [P. 44]

Of course, as these remarks from O'Leary suggest, the enemy is "metaphysics." The "overcoming of metaphysics" is a project of Heideggerian thinking. (It is perhaps worth noting that O'Leary restricts his Heideggerian project to the "truth of revelation," and does not attempt the Heideggerian "truth of being" or "clearing," though O'Leary seems certainly to approve that project.) Metaphysics is the enemy, first, because historically it is a kind of thinking originating in Greek that plays "a determining role in Western culture through a series of historical epochs culminating in contemporary technology." Where Heidegger had sought in the pre-Socratic fragments confirmation of a premetaphysical understanding of being, O'Leary takes a tack that leads us back to biblical texts. "The Semitic world," O'Leary claims, "had no notion of metaphysics, before the advent of hellenization in the later books of the Bible" (p. 10). Clearly O'Leary wants to break the domination of Greek metaphysical thought on Western theology; and he finds a method in deconstruction for "reading back" and "questioning back" to the fissures that break down mainstream theological thought, such as one finds in the Nicene Creed.

This historical domination of Western thought is one side of it; the "Greek problematic of the being of what-is," which Heidegger called the "onto-theo-logical" pattern of metaphysical thinking, a systematic side of the question, is the other. O'Leary follows Heidegger in condemning the mistake of locating "being" in a "logical way," that is, "as the ground or cause of beings, either in the sense of that which beings as such have in common (ontology) or that source of being which grounds the unity of being as a whole (theology) (p. 11).

O'Leary's method of "questioning back" to "overcome" metaphysics will, he thinks, enable us to have a renewed dialogue with Judaism, and will dewesternize our thinking, preparing us for our "next adventure," the "full-scale confrontation with the traditions and mentalities of the East" (p. 207). Instead of the hierarchical oppositions that characterize metaphysical thought, O'Leary will find, if a little tentatively, "emptiness, phenomenality and immediacy" (p. 224). A countermetaphysical reading will also, he suggests, prepare us to respond in a compassionate way to the great questions of peace, justice, and freedom so important today.

For us—since our interest is not so much theological and ethical as literary—what is most immediately fruitful in O'Leary's project is the way he reads texts. His method, now understood not in a purely destructive way, is deconstruction, the method of Derrida and, before him, Heidegger. O'Leary begins his attack on texts with those which have appeared most recently, modern theological works (especially Barth and Rahner). He then reads back to (or through) Martin Luther, and then to the church fathers. (His treatment of Negative Theology is particularly striking, since he finds even there the dominance of metaphysics, pp. 156–61.)

For me, the most intriguing chapters are those in which he approaches more directly the kinds of texts we as students of literature are keen to study. In chapter 4, called "Overcoming Augustine," he masterfully deconstructs certain strongly narrative sections of Augustine's *Confessions*, reading the text, as he says, "backwards."

In his last chapter, O'Leary breaks down that very Nicene Creed, so central to the hellenization of Western Christianity. He ends his "questioning back" with a very brief account of the fourth Gospel.

As he moves back through Augustine's *Confessions* to the Gospel of John, O'Leary considers the Nicene Creed, in whose second article alone he differentiates some fourteen "layers of language." So basic is this creed to Western thought that O'Leary assumes—like a good many others—we know it going in. What the Council of Nicaea formulated in 325 c.e. is the following. The text in *Enchiridion symbolorum* is given in Greek and Latin. The Latin runs as follows:

> Credimus in unum Deum Patrem omnipotentem,
> omnium visibilium et invisibilium factorem.
> Et in unum Dominum nostrum Iesum Christum
> Filium Dei, natum ex Patre unigenitum [monogene],
> hoc est de substantia [ousias] Patris,
> Deum ex Deo, lumen ex lumine, Deum verum de Deo vero,
> natum, non factum, unius substantiae cum Patre
> (quod Graece dicunt homousion),
> per quem omnia facta sunt,
> quae in coelo et in terra,
> qui propter nostram salutem descendit,
> incarnatus est et homo factus est et passus est,
> et resurrexit tertia die,
> et ascendit in coelos,
> venturus iudicare vivos et mortuous.
> Et in Spiritum Sanctum.

Eos autem, qui dicunt: "Erat, quando non erat," et "Antequam nasceretur, non erat," et "Quia ex non existentibus factus est aut ex alia subsistentia vel essentia," dicentes esse aut "convertibilem aut mutabilium filium Dei," hos anathematizat [anathematizei] catholica et apostolica Ecclesia.[4]

(Note the clear statement of wrong positions and their explicit condemnation.)

It is the second article (and not the condemnation) that O'Leary breaks down according to different speech acts: assertive and commissive acts; confessional naming; bare statement of fact (where, though, is Pontius Pilate, mentioned by O'Leary?); "stylized diction in which credal coloration of fact becomes manifest"; "quasi-historical statements whose texture is permeated by numinous references"; interpretative clauses; a statement of the ontological significance of the Incarnation; a narration of a celestial prehistory; the celestial posthistory; "theological notes appended to ward off heretical misreadings of the mythic narration" (where in the text?); a second set of "theological notes imposing a new logical precision on the mythic narration"; a doxological supplement" (light from light); a "second layer of logical clarification using the notion of 'substance'"; and a phrase from the narrative of creation (pp. 215–17). O'Leary concludes that the creed "offers an exhaustive toplogy of the being and function of Jesus Christ, within a horizon which embraces Creator and creation, the being and manifestation of God, the origin and destiny of the world, eternity and time, past, present, and future" (p. 217). Quickly, though, he hastens to point out that "it seems that this comprehensive horizon is no longer accessible to us." "The mythical concern with origins, the metaphysical concern with grounds and an anthropological valorization of paternity" that define "eternal sonship" are, for us, "obsolete." In the creed we notice the "tensions of Christian tradition" and we are sent back to the Scriptures once the deconstruction is carried out (p. 217).

One would hope that the questioning back would lead O'Leary to that most tantalizing feature of the Gospel of John, the persistence of "I AM" formulas that reach back to the Hebrew Bible and its Greek translation in the Septuagint. For example,

"Before Abraham even came into existence, I AM" [8:58]
"*Ego eimi*; do not be afraid" [6:20] or
"I am the bread of life" [6:35][5]

Raymond Brown distinguishes three different types of I AM formulas in the three examples above: the absolute use with no predicate; the use where a predicate may be understood even though it is not expressed; and the use with a predicate nominative.[6] (Brown also sees certain borderline cases in John; the point here is that I AM is a particularly striking feature of the Gospel, carefully introduced in the discourses and narratives that make up the well-designed work.)

Brown examines other, often earlier, pagan uses of "I am" in sacred texts, but tends to dismiss their possible impact on John. The Book of Wisdom, on the one hand, and the prophets (Deutero-Isaiah in particular) are within a tradition that stretches back to "I am Yahweh" pronouncements, especially in the story of the revelation of the divine name (Exod. 3:13–15).

The passage is worth recalling here. The most sacred of divine names is revealed to Moses when the "angel of Yahweh" appears to Moses in the shape of a flame of fire coming from the middle of a bush. Moses is commissioned to offer worship on the mountain after the people have been liberated from Egypt.

> Then Moses said to God [*'elohim*], "I am to go, then, to the sons of Israel and say to them, 'The God of your fathers has sent me to you.' But if they ask me what his name is, what am I to tell them?" And God said to Moses, "I Am who I Am [*'ehyeh 'asher 'ehyeh*, better "I Am what I Am," according to some scholars].[7] "This," he added, "is what you must say to the sons of Israel: 'I Am [*'ehyeh*] has sent me to you.'" And God also said to Moses, "You are to say to the sons of Israel: 'Yahweh, the God [*'eloha*] of your fathers, the God of Abraham, the God of Isaac, the God of Jacob, has sent me to you.' This is my name for all time; by this name I shall be invoked for all generations to come."[8]

The Septuagint will come to translate the "I AM" as *ego eimi*.

Between the early "I Am who I Am" of Exodus and the Johannine "I am the food of the full-grown" one can see what stands behind the passage in Augustine O'Leary finds so intriguing (and in need of deconstruction):

> Thee when I first knew, Thou liftedst me up, that I might see there was what I might see, and that I was not yet such as to see. And Thou didst beat back the weakness of my sight, streaming forth Thy beams of light upon me most strongly, and I trembled with love and awe: and I perceived myself to be far off from Thee, in the region of unlikeness, as if I heard this Thy voice from on high: "I am the food of grown men; grow and thou shalt feed upon Me; nor shalt thou convert Me, like the food of thy flesh, into thee, but thou shalt be converted into Me." And I learned that Thou for

iniquity chastenest man, and Thou madest my soul to consume away like a spider. And I said, "Is Truth therefore nothing because it is not diffused through space finite or infinite?" And Thou criedst to me from afar: "Yea verily, I AM that I AM." And I heard, as the heart heareth, nor had I room to doubt, and I should sooner doubt that I live, than that Truth is not, which is clearly seen, being understood by those things which are made.[9]

O'Leary's deconstruction of Augustine's passage is masterful. He considers the Exodus 3:14 allusion "the king-pin of the ontological interpretation of the contrast between the reality of God and his own weak state. The 'region of dissimilitude' is the Plotinian terminology for the lowest degree of being, verging on non-being (*Ennead* I 8.13). Augustine has not yet being, cannot yet participate in the fullness of being which is God: this ontological reading underlies the food-image" (p. 186). Yet the *Confessions* is an "inherently troubled and instable composition, as is every text which attempts an original synthesis of faith and metaphysics," for, according to O'Leary, there is another reading of the passage at odds with Augustine's Platonic-metaphysical God. O'Leary's attempt to "draw out the more primordial biblical sense of God from the prevailing metaphysical discourse about God" requires a close attention to the tone and narrative movement of the text (p. 186).

To the apparent metaphysical reading of the text O'Leary opposes a "phenomenological reading which takes the *failles* in the text as indications of the unthought, invitations to deeper questioning" (p. 191).

Augustine's text is surely a remarkable, post-Nicene, highly individualistic (if troubled) metaphysical text, one that yokes together the Old Testament and New Testament "I AM" formulas in a striking way. On *this* side of the Nicene Creed, once the metaphysical formulation is struck, the creed can act as a kind of fixed point around which the imagination can play. On *that* side of the Nicene Creed, though, the biblical text opens to a different kind of reading. In this I am in agreement with O'Leary.

I am bothered, though, by two—I think related—concerns in the questioning back that leads to the overcoming of metaphysics O'Leary offers. He is keen to save "faith," which becomes very problematic not only in his treatment of "faith" (especially in his consideration of the Gospel of John, pp. 221–25), and he has certainly found in the Gospel of John the right text. The "new kind of language" to be found in the New Testament[10] is particularly in evidence in John. Those key words, "faith," "hope," and "love," appear in enormous excess over their equivalents in the Old Testament. Perhaps the most striking example is that the term "believe" [*pisteuein*] is used about one hundred times in the Johannine writings—more than in the whole of the Old Testament.[11]

O'Leary is anxious to press back to the earlier Semitic formulations in order to provide a countermetaphysical reading of the Gospel. He does not really show how that is to be done. The Gospel of John, with its massive concern for "belief" is really the end of O'Leary's task. What particularly interests me in the pre-Nicene, premetaphysical texts is precisely the absence of creeds. In the absence of creeds we seem, the further back we question, to have stories. This is really what should spark the interest of the literary critic. If the Nicene Creed attempts (and, if O'Leary is right, ultimately unsuccessfully) through metaphysical language to reduce the many stories of the Bible to something approaching a purely conceptual language of faith, that well-designed Gospel of John stands as a crucial test of an old way that has not yet given way to a new way of reading.

What is striking is the thickening of the text with its "key words"— not exactly concepts. The thickening of the text is the capture of key words by story. Brown treats eleven such keys words in the Johannine writings (*agape* "love," *alethia* "truth," *blepein* and others "see," *doxa* "glory," *entole* "command," *zoe* "life," *kosmos* "world," *menein* "remain," *pisteuein* "believe," *phos/skotia* "light/darkness," and *hora* "hour").[12] Even more than that very tricky task biblical scholars delight in, distinguishing "discourse" from narrative in the biblical texts, we are now faced with the task of accounting for the presence of the very language that seems to give rise to metaphysical creeds in nonmetaphysical stories.

This is the task we face. A deconstructive reading of Exodus 3:13–16 would be most useful here. I am not really capable of doing that in this paper (perhaps at all). But I would like to include a few pointers. The pointers are texts that are, historically, much older than Exodus 3. It is possible the literary "stream of tradition" that kept the texts alive in Mesopotamia for several thousand years might have influenced the composition of the biblical text. It is not necessary that such an influence (as, say, Chaucer influenced Shakespeare) actually took place. It is only important that the Mesopotamian texts provide something of a countertext that will, eventually, allow us to deconstruct the Exodus 3:13–16 story.

The "I Am what I Am" (*'ehyeh asher 'ehyeh*) is in some way even more sacred than the unpronounced "He Is" that appears to derive from it, YHWH. Especially with the way the name translates into

Greek, "I Am" would seem to be the very rock upon which Greek ontology can grasp hold and, eventually, build a system of the world.

The kind of text that names the god in a powerful way, I Am, is much older than the examples usually given (e.g., Gnostic and Hellenistic examples from Isis magical texts, the Hermetic corpus, and Mithra.[13] A Sumerian poem, "Enki and Inanna: The Organization of the Earth and Its Cultural Processes," for example, which may go back to the third millennium B.C.E., includes a long litany in the form:

> I am the true offspring, sprung from the wild ox.
> I am a leading son of An.
>
> I am the great storm that breaks over the "Great Below":
> I am the great lord over the land.

In a second speech in the same story, the god proclaims, "I am lord. I am the one whose word endures. / I am eternal." What in a way sums the whole series of epithets is the last one to appear in the speeches of the god, the line in which he names himself:

> I am Enki.

Enki is a rather peculiar god, whose cult and whose myths were widespread in the Ancient Near East.[14] He is the god who is the creative word, the god of the waters below. Because he is identified as cunning and because he is "the word," there was, I think, a great tendency to play with his name, which in Sumerian could mean *en*, usually translated by "lord" but really a more powerful term than that, or *ki*, sometimes "earth" and sometimes the world below, often just "place," the *en* of *ki*.

There is a beautiful example of the play on his name in a Sumerian incantation that begins

> The *en* was going around the holy sheepfold,
> the great *en*—Enki—was entering the holy sheepfold,
>
> where the mother licked her lamb,
> where the she-goat circled her kid.[15]

The incantation provides a delightful example of ring composition, returning at the end to the kid and its drinking-spot, the sheep and its sheepfold. The most powerful part of this incantation in the form of a narrative is the passage in which Enki speaks to his son.

A very tricky text in which the narrative line is almost swallowed up in the key words naming Enki is a poem called "Enki and His Word: A Chant to the Rider of the Waves." One section brings out the fiercely destructive capability of Enki's word. (Enki is more often the one who brings the healing or saving word.)

> His word is the venom of a lion that does not come out
> for the sake of a man.

> His word is a floodwave,
> a floodwave that breeds fear.

An unusual feature of this long chant is that in the tenth and last section there appears to be a complex play on words that can hardly be translated. One half line is repeated several times:

> Eh! Ah! the king's house! Eh! Ah! the king's house![16]

The section is probably meant as a magical blessing called down on the Sumerian king. In Sumerian it reads

> *e-a é-lugal e-a é-lugal.*

There is a play on two cuneiform signs used to represent the homophone *é*, which means "house" in "house of the king" and also the nonsignifying sigh, *e-a.*

What is most curious about this is that the sigh *e-a* pronounces the name of the god Enki, though his *Akkadian name*, É-a, is usually written Ea. An intriguing bilingual pun.

This Akkadian Ea is a major character in a great many of the literary works that have survived from Mesopotamia. In most of these stories Ea is the god to whom appeal is made when all else fails, and Ea manages to have just the right words and advice to resolve the conflict in the story. The one example I will cite is the text closest to our purposes. At the end of the so-called Babylonian Creation Epic (*Enūma Elish*), Ea's son, Marduk, has been exalted over all of the other gods in the pantheon. With his father's help, Marduk has defeated the great goddess in battle and has built upon her body a cosmos. The gods pronounce a litany of fifty sacred names that now constitute the exalted Marduk. At the very end Ea brings the epic to a close by emptying himself in Marduk.

> When the Igigi exhausted their store of names
> and Ea heard the names, his spirit sang out jubilantly

thus: "The one whose names his father have glorified—
he is the same as I am! Ea is his name!
He is the only one to manage my decrees,
          the whole collection,
                    every one of them!
He alone carries out the total of my oracles!"[17]

Note particularly in this that the "I am" is a formulation that includes
a pun on Ea's name: *šu-u ki-ma ia-a-ti*, "he is the same as I am," and
é-a lu-u šum-šu, "Ea is his name!"

The power of names is usually brought up—since it is so widespread
in the ancient world—only to be dismissed, as magic is usually dismissed. We know about the protection afforded the divine name
YHWH (which has its own history, according to M. H. Segal).[18] The
names obviously have, in a sense, an existence independent of any
context; by themselves the names have magical force. And, having
force by themselves, they may give rise to transparent concepts. In the
absence of creeds, proclaiming names may lay the groundwork for a
premetaphysical ontology (if such a thing makes sense).

What is most striking, though, is the opposite: the key words in
these old texts are so completely integrated into the texture of the
work in which they appear that they resist the reduction into purely
conceptual language.

O'Leary's final section in *Questioning Back* is called, simply, "The
Fourth Gospel," but it is, as O'Leary makes clear, a sketch that
consists—with "violence," note—in a reading of John "exclusively in
the key of phenomenality." O'Leary considers the Johannine writings
"the most highly reflected articulation of the phenomenality of revelation in the New Testament" and therefore "the most promising source
for the primordial understanding of faith to which the dogmatic,
metaphysical tradition has referred us back" (p. 221).

In that final section O'Leary presents us with a new trinity. The
"mythic structure" of the fourth Gospel can be "burst open" with a
threefold "phenomenological retrieval" that O'Leary names emptiness, phenomenality, and immediacy. Ultimately, O'Leary calls these
"makeshift" terms and "only pointers" to show "the kind of questioning to which New Testament language must be subjected when its
mythical terms are suspended and it can no longer be subsumed into
metaphysical frameworks" (p. 224). He hopes that a "credible contemporary naming of Father, Son and Spirit" will aid in a dialogue
with other religions. Since this is as close to a positive claim for New
Testament faith as O'Leary makes, his deconstructive reading is
worth considering here.

O'Leary is careful not to reduce his three terms to a precise correlation with either of the two trinities favored by the tradition: Father, Son, Spirit; or faith, hope, love. Still, the names of god guide the phenomenological retrieval, and the threefold of faith, hope, and love that has been subjected to such intense metaphysical transformation by the Christian tradition is given a kind of renewal in O'Leary's new trinity.

"Emptiness" is the term O'Leary uses to show that the phenomenality of Jesus Christ is "one with the phenomenality of God." The Johannine texts are only mentioned in passing: 1:48–49, 2:11, 4:53, 6:69, 9:1–7, 9:38, 11:27, 11:43, 19:35, 20:28. (O'Leary's method turns out not to be one of close examination of the biblical text, certainly not the most obvious characteristics of the fourth Gospel, that is, a text made up of discourses and a narrative.) The last reference, though, would seem to have greatest weight for O'Leary. It is Thomas's post-Resurrection declaration, once Thomas no longer doubts but believes: "My Lord and my God" (20:28). Brown refers to this as the "ultimate confession" and "the supreme christological pronouncement" of the Gospel.[19] Although one would do well to regard the pronouncement, coming as it does at the very end of the Gospel (and the last words spoken by a disciple in the Gospel), as the climax of a carefully developing narrative, O'Leary is not really concerned with that.

In view of O'Leary's aim to prepare a return to earlier Semitic formulations, it is striking that he does not consider the evidence offered, e.g., by Brown, that "My Lord and my God" is very likely (though not entirely a precise) formula used in the Septuagint to translate the divine names YHWH (=*kyrios*) and Elohim (=*theos*). (A second possibility is that contemporary paganism understood the phrase *Dominus et Deus noster* as a title of the Emperor Domitian.[20] The historical complexity of the formula has been considered by Segal.[21]

What O'Leary sees is "the divine emptiness." The form of Jesus "is correctly apprehended only as divine Logos (the phenomenality of God); and this form itself subsists on the basis of the divine emptiness with which it is coterminous. . . . God is intrinsically unseen (1:18), yet to see Christ in faith is to see God (8:19, 14:9)" (p. 222).

The second term O'Leary uses is "phenomenality." The language of Father and Son, he thinks, is not a matter of "blind hope," but rather of love. The "phenomenological ground" of the language of Father and Son is the experience of God "as love." The texts O'Leary cites, again with little connection to a narrative, are these: 10:18, 10:38, 13:31–32; 14:10, 17:5, 17:21–23. Combining the two terms, emptiness and phenomenality, O'Leary arrives at the following formulation: "through love the humanity of Jesus (and of the believers in dependence on it) is shaped into that form which is fully transparent to the emptiness of God" (p. 223).

Because, however, "the form of the pneumatic Christ can never be fully grasped in this life," O'Leary sees a third element, the Spirit, involved in Johannine faith. "The Spirit," he claims, "might be defined as the immediacy of God, that aspect of God which vitally touches our existence" (p. 223). Once again O'Leary points to a few texts in the Gospel, but does not set them in a narrative context: 3:8, 4:23, 14:16.

Thus he offers a phenomenological reduction of the Johannine language—Father, Son, and Spirit—to emptiness, phenomenality, and immediacy. O'Leary goes further in claiming that his phenomenological reduction "is a continuation of the reductive movement of the Gospel itself." One quite useful point in this is O'Leary's suggestion that the reduction is in line with the use of figurative language in the Gospel to "abolish" the very statements they appear at first to serve. But O'Leary does not develop this potentially rich idea. He mentions, in passing, the figure of the Good Shepherd (10:30, 10:38) as an example of what he means, but he does not pursue it.

O'Leary offers a final comment about his method:

> Talk of the emptiness, phenomenality, and immediacy of God might lead to a colorless, modalist image of God, a danger which the biblical names ward off; but on the other hand, the repetition of these biblical names without a constant effort to realize their meaning at the level of phenomenality can be equally damaging. [P. 224]

The reader of this enormously useful book, *Questioning Back*, may well feel a sense of disappointment with O'Leary's brief and sketchy discussion of the one biblical text—the fourth Gospel—he discusses to arrive at a premetaphysical understanding of Christianity. Among the dust-jacket claims for the book, Harvey Cox's is perhaps the one that best summarizes the importance of O'Leary's enterprise. It "delivers theology from its centuries-old captivity to metaphysics."

For the student of literature, especially biblical literature, O'Leary's work is likely to prove very important. There are a number of ways the enterprise might have been extended without, I think, weakening its foundation. I offer these as suggestions for further work.

It is a little disconcerting to see a work dealing with the Trinity, as O'Leary's does at the end, with nothing to say about the trinity of

Father, Mother, and Son that the recently translated documents of *The Nag Hammadi Library* proposes. True, the Gnostic documents from Nag Hammadi present enormous historical problems, many of them being composed much later than the canonical biblical texts. And Gnosticism may well be dominated by the same metaphysical tradition O'Leary is anxious to see "overcome"; indeed, its very intellectuality may impede the recovery of a premetaphysical understanding of Christianity. The fact that the earliest commentaries on, e.g., the Gospel of John, were part of the Gnostic movement does not make dealing with the fourth Gospel, the Johannine tradition, and the primitive understanding of the Trinity any easier than it was before.

In view of the importance these days—one might even say the urgency—of a feminist rethinking of early Christian formulations of, say, the Trinity (and with the possibility that the canon may have to be reconsidered as well), one would certainly like to see a deconstructionist reading of the Nag Hammadi texts. And such an enterprise would seem to be related to O'Leary's desire to see the Christ of faith coming to be "known in a new way as Christians become more compassionately responsive to the questions of peace, justice, and freedom which press on them so urgently" (p. 225). One thinks, for example, of what Father, Son, and Spirit might mean in the light of Elaine Pagels's chapter, "God the Father/God the Mother," in her book *The Gnostic Gospels*.[22]

The disappearance of the feminine in the concept and representation of the divine was an extremely complex historical process. While it is most evident in the orthodox theological (and credal/metaphysical) formulations of Christianity, the very tradition O'Leary seeks to overcome, the disappearance of the feminine (or the obscuring of the feminine) is much older than the Christian theologians, the New Testament, and even the Hebrew Bible. These are not mere historical questions, and it is possible that deconstructive readings like those advanced by O'Leary will prove to be extremely useful in acknowledging the divine feminine in our time. Recall that the documents of *The Nag Hammadi Library* were themselves, at times, engaged in deconstruction, retelling, e.g., the Flood story to show the importance of Barbelo, Sophia, and Noah's wife—and critcizing Moses at the same time (as in "The Apocryphon of John").[23]

One would certainly like to know if a deconstructive reading of Hebrew Bible narratives, the ones drawn upon by the fourth Gospel in particular, would yield, as O'Leary seems to suggest, a premetaphysical understanding of a formula such as YHWH *Elohim*. Fortunately the materials are in place to trace, by way of Brown's commentary on the fourth Gospel and Segal's study of the names of God in the

Hebrew Bible—to take but one of many studies of the divine names —both the feminine in the godhead and different historical understandings of the divine names.

Another direction the study should take is a serious look at the ancient works that constitute the "stream of tradition" most influential in the development of biblical literature, namely, the Sumero-Akkadian tradition of literature. Since the suggestion was followed up briefly in an earlier section of this paper, I will not repeat the point here. If a Semitic premetaphysical tradition stands behind the Christian tradition, as O'Leary points out, and should be considered in the overcoming of metaphysics in Christian tradition, it is worth acknowledging that the Semitic tradition is considerably older than even the earliest biblical texts.

For students of literature, though, the most useful approach to a text like the fourth Gospel is one that leads not just to a phenomenological reduction of the language of faith but to a fuller engagement with the text itself. It strikes me that O'Leary's best insight in *Questioning Back* is that deconstruction (if he is correct in seeing a genuine connection between Derrida and Heidegger) does not *simply* do violence to the text in an anarchic and a nihilistic way (p. 37). Deconstruction ought not, then, simply return to the demythologizing postures of Rudolf Bultmann when it regards the New Testament. This is what seems to me to happen to O'Leary's otherwise brilliant and useful enterprise. His phenomenological reduction of the language of the Trinity to emptiness, phenomenality, and immediacy is not, I think, essentially different from Bultmann's enterprise. This may be a beginning, but surely not an adequate deconstruction of the text.

Fortunately, an article in the *Journal of Biblical Literature* offers a more promising method, at least for the investigation of the Gospel of John. Gail R. O'Day, in an article entitled "Narrative Mode and Theological Claim: A Study in the Fourth Gospel," pursues the highly influential work of Rudolf Bultmann (who was, by the way, deeply indebted to Martin Heidegger) to show that the attempt to distinguish the "that" (*Dass*) of revelation from the "what" (*Was*) of revelation, at the basis of Bultmannian theory of revelation, "falls short," in her words, "of capturing the nature of Johannine revelation because those categories fail to take into account the ways in which the literary and narrative characteristics of the Fourth Gospel shape the Johannine portrait of Jesus as revealer and communicate the Johannine theology of revelation."[24] Following the Johannine scholars P. D. Duke and R. A. Culpepper, and critics such as D. C. Muecke, Wayne Booth, and Wolfgang Iser, O'Day insists that the revelation at the heart of the fourth Gospel cannot be divorced from a reading of the text. I might add here that, if O'Day is correct, at least with regard to the Gospel of John, the reduction of the Gospel's revelation to dogma is completely suspect, and O'Leary's deconstruction of the dogmatic tradition even more useful. Students of literatrue will note in O'Day's assertion a familiar theme in twentieth-century literary study, which, in its crudest form, insisted that "content" could not be, finally, separated from "form."

According to O'Day, the fourth Gospel is constructed in such a way that the reader "participates" in the "revelatory dynamics." As the reader interacts with the text, the traditional subject/object dichotomy is overcome. The fourth Gospel is not, she claims, just a "report" of Jesus as revealer. Rather, the text "allows the reader to *experience* Jesus' revelation" for himself or herself. The narrative told in the Gospel of John, far from being destroyed in a process that robs names, characters, and story of their work in a literary text, "does not just mediate the revelation . . . but *is* the revelation."

With the deconstruction of texts in the Christian tradition made possible though O'Leary's method and with the reader's response to the text preserved, the literary critic and the biblical scholar can look ahead to a very fruitful exchange of readings in the near future.

Notes

1. Werner Kelber, "The Authority of the Word in St. John's Gospel: Charismatic Speech, Narrative Text, Logocentric Metaphysics," *Oral Tradition* 2 (1987): 114, 119.

2. Ibid., p. 129.

3. Joseph S. O'Leary, *Questioning Back: The Overcoming of Metaphysics in Christian Tradition* (Minneapolis: Winston, 1985), pp. 38, 39, 41. Further page references to this work will be cited parenthetically in the text.

4. *Enchiridion symbolorum*, ed. Henrici Denzinger (Barcelona: Herder, 1960), pp. 29–30.

5. See Raymond Brown, trans., *The Gospel According to John I–XII*, The Anchor Bible (Garden City, N.Y.: Doubleday, 1966), pp. 533–38.

6. Ibid., pp. 533– 34.

7. A. van den Born, *Encyclopedic Dictionary of the Bible*, trans. Louis F. Hartman (New York: McGraw-Hill, 1963), col. 2614. The translation of the Hebrew used here is The Jerusalem Bible, ed. Alexander Jones (Garden City, N.Y.: Doubleday, 1968), p. 536.

8. For the Hebrew text, see *Biblia Hebraica Stuttgartensia*, ed. A. O. Alt, O. Eissfeldt, P. Kahle, and R. Kittel (Stuttgart: Deutsche Bibelstiftung, 1967–77), p. 89. On the self-references of the divine, see also R. A. F. MacKenzie, S. J., "The Divine Soliloquies in Genesis," *Catholic Biblical Quarterly* 17 (1955): 277–86.

9. Augustine, *Confessions* 7.10–16, in the Pusey translation, *The Essential Augustine*, ed. Vernon J. Bourke (New York: New American Library, 1964), p. 129. O'Leary uses a somewhat different translation.

10. Paul Auvray, Pierre Poulain, and Albert Blaise, *Sacred Languages*, trans. J. Tester (New York: Hawthorn, 1960), p. 96.

11. Ibid., p. 98.

12. Brown, trans., *Gospel According to John*, pp. 497–518.

13. Ibid., p. 535.

14. Samuel Noah Kramer and John Maier, *Myths of Enki: The Crafty God* (New York: Oxford University Press, forthcoming), chap. 3.

15. Ibid., chap. 7.

16. Ibid., chap. 6.

17. Ibid., chap. 8.

18. M. H. Segal, "El, Elohim, and YHWH in the Bible," *Jewish Quarterly* 46 (1966): 100–102.

19. Brown, trans., *The Gospel According to John*, pp. 1046–47.

20. Ibid., p. 1047.

21. Segal, "El, Elohim," p. 114.

22. Elaine Pagels, *The Gnostic Gospels* (New York: Vintage Press, 1979), chap. 3.

23. E. g., "The Apocryphon of John," trans. Frederik Wisse, in *The Nag Hammadi Library*, gen. ed. James M. Robinson (San Francisco: Harper & Row, 1977), pp. 98–116.

24. Gail R. O'Day, "Narrative Mode and Theological Claim: A Study in the Fourth Gospel," *Journal of Biblical Literature* 105 (1986): 657. See also Lynn M. Poland, *Literary Criticism and Biblical Hermeneutics: A Critique of Formalist Approaches* (Chico, Calif.: Scholars Press, 1985).

The Literary Unity of the Book of Revelation

Leonard L. Thompson
Lawrence University

IN the Western battle of the "-taxes," hypotaxis has usually won over parataxis. We learn early on not to write "run on" sentences connected by "and." We learn to subordinate clauses in a sentence so that its form reflects the priority of our thoughts. If parataxis is to be allowed at all, then it should occur in connection with a strong narrative line so that the unconnectedness of the sentences is overpowered by the plot development. Hemingway is often pointed to in this connection.

Given these predispositions, readers may find that the Book of Revelation does not meet the canons of their expectations, for it is written in a paratactic style without a strong plot. No Hemingway here, and no philosophical treatise either. That is, the parataxis cannot be ignored in favor of a strong plot or a strong line of argument. Therefore, the unity of the Book of Revelation hangs in jeopardy. Critics may refer to it as "visionary" literature which has no coherence: one vision is connected to another vision with little attempt to provide a literary or linguistic unity. Or source critics can have a field day in the Book of Revelation as they sort out which pericope belongs in what source and damn implicitly the final redactor as having done a pretty lousy job. More recent critics have discovered that the paratactic style of the Book of Revelation can be given a structuralist interpretation with the various unconnected units becoming mythemes forming binary oppositions which reflect fundamental conflicts in life and society, especially conflicts between harsh social, political realities and the claims of Christian faith.

In what follows, I examine some of the ways that the seer of the Book of Revelation has unified his work. The seer's language does not simply flow in narrative or logical sequence; it plays on formal, thematic, metaphoric, symbolic, and auditory levels of association. Moreover, the various levels overlap in such a way that breaks occur at different points among the different levels. Series of seven define units throughout the work, yet other numbering systems overlap these units; for example, the numbering of the three woes (9:12; 11:14;

12:12) helps to unify the series of seven trumpets which ends at 11:19 and the seven visions which begin at 12:1. Different sections of the Revelation are also connected and unified by repeated metaphors, symbols, and motifs. In brief, the organization of the Book of Revelation is more complex than may first meet the eye, and it engages in more "literary complexity" than its paratactic style may suggest. I shall conclude by suggesting that the language of the Book of Revelation is mythic language in the way that it unifies paratactic units.

NARRATIVE UNITY

The unity of the Revelation is established in part through various kinds of narrative or sequential linkage. In tracing out its narrative unity we shall be following the horizontal threads which break at different points so that at every break there are also continuous threads which unify the narrative and create a seamless weave.

Contrasting Units

Commentators often call attention to contrasting oppositions in the Revelation as indication of the tension which exists between God and the world or Christian faith and social, political realities.[1] So, for example, the sealing of the 144,000 and the salvation of the innumerable multitude (7:1–17) contrast with the vengeance which God delivers upon earth in the opening of the six seals (6:1–17). The celebration of God's kingdom at the blowing of the seventh trumpet (11:15–19) contrasts with God's punishment of those members of an apostate kingdom which occurs in the blowing of the six previous trumpets (8:7–9:20). Similarly the two beasts in Revelation 13 represent a false kingdom in contrast to the community of the Lamb in Revelation 14. The hope of Christians is assured in the scene on Mt. Zion (14:1) in spite of the dangers of the beast standing on the seashore from the primordial abyss (12:18). Christians will rest from their labors (14:13) in contrast to those who succumb to the pressure of political servitude (14:11). If Christians are to feast at the marriage of the Lamb (19:9) rather than be feasted upon by the birds of the air (19:17–18), they will receive the seal of the Lamb (14:1) and withstand the stamp of the beast (13:16).

    Contrasting units can be traced through the Revelation to illustrate its binary character and to point to conflictual elements in its vision of the world; if contrast and conflict are sought out, then the Revelation can be segmented into contrasting units. But contrasting units are only one of several kinds of relations which organize the flow of the seer's language. Other sorts of relations need to be traced out if the unity of the Revelation is to be fully appreciated. In the final analysis, binary contrasts unfold from an unbroken unity which enfolds the apparent tensions in the seer's vision.

Equivalence of Measure

A fairly simple unifying device consists of equivalence in numerical measurement. For most people, numbers in the Revelation probably evoke 666, the number of the beast (13:18), which according to the seer can be calculated by anyone having some intelligence. Through gematria whereby a number signifies a letter, many different identifications of that number have been made, the earliest of which is probably the Emperor Nero. My interest here in equivalences of measure has a different focus: how recurring numbers of equivalent values contribute toward the unity of the Revelation.

As previously noted, apocalyptic disasters tend to be organized around the number 7: seven seals, seven trumpets, seven bowls.[2] Themes in the pouring out of the seven bowls are strikingly similar to those of the blowing of the seven trumpets: in each series the first four describe disasters to earth, seas, rivers and fountains, and the sun, respectively. The fifth refers to the kingdom of the beast (16:10, cf. 9:11), the sixth refers to the Euphrates, and the seventh to a heavenly scene that includes theophanic sky phenomena of lightning, thunder, earthquake, and hail. In each series this repetitive unfolding, which occurs again at the pouring out of the seven bowls, culminates in heavenly worship.[3] Those repetitions create a kind of déjà vu, a sense that one can step in the same river twice.[4]

Within the series of the seven trumpets (8:2–11:19) two references are made to the same time span. In the first instance, in connection with a command to measure the temple of God and the altar and those who worship there, John is told that the nations will trample the holy city for forty-two months (11:2). In the next verse, which introduces rather abruptly the two witnesses (although it is part of the same speech addressed to John), the two witnesses are granted power to prophesy for 1,260 days (=42 months). In the next series of seven visions (12:1–14:20) a story is told about a pregnant woman about to give birth to a male child endangered by a great red dragon. After the birth, the child is caught up to God and the throne, and the woman flees into the wilderness to be nourished there for 1,260 days (12:6).[5] In the third vision of that same series a beast comes forth from the sea and is allowed to exercise authority for 42 months (13:5). Thus through equivalence of measure, trampling the holy city by the Gen-

tiles and the witness of the two prophets—scenes in the series of the
seven trumpets—are brought into synchrony with the woman's
nourishment in the wilderness and the authority of the beast—scenes
in a later series of visions.[6]

Visions throughout the Revelation are linked through the number
12. The number itself appears regularly in connection with the New
Jerusalem: 12 gates of 12 pearls (21:21), inscribed with 12 names of
12 tribes, accompanied by 12 angels (21:12); a wall with 12 foundations on which are the 12 names of the apostles (21:14); the city measures 12,000 stadia (21:16); and in it the tree of life produces 12 kinds
of fruit, one for each of 12 months (22:2). Twice 12 elders sit on their
24 thrones surrounding the throne in heaven (4:4). Twelve thousand
times 12 are sealed from the 12 tribes of Israel (7:4) and the same
number later appear with the Lamb on Mt. Zion (14:1).[7]

Reversed Relationships

Sometimes the elements in one scene are transformed in such a way
that relationships and actions are reversed when compared to a previous scene. For example, in 7:1–2 John sees four angels standing
upon the four corners of the earth, holding back the four winds of the
earth so that they do not blow and harm. Another angel coming up
from the rising of the sun cries out to the four angels not to harm the
earth until the servants of our God are sealed. The only other reference to four angels occurs at 9:13–15, the blowing of the sixth trumpet. John hears a voice from the four horns of the altar saying: loose
the four angels bound at the great river Euphrates. Those angels are
loosed so as to kill one-third of the people. The two passages form
mirror images. In chapter 7 an angel from the East (the rising of the
sun) commands the angels on the four corners of the earth not to harm
the earth, and they do not. In chapter 9 a voice from the four corners
(horns) of the altar command that angels in the East (Euphrates) be
loosed to harm the earth, and they do.[8] Reversal of subject and object
results in reversed consequences.

The scene in chapter 10 involving the little scroll (βιβλαρίδιον)
reverses several elements in chapter 5, which describes the scroll
(βιβλίον) sealed with seven seals. In chapter 10 a mighty angel,
crying out as a lion, holds in his hand an open scroll (βιβλαρίδιον
ἠνεωγμένον), the contents of which are presumably recited by the
angel and the seven thunders (10:3).[9] John is about to write down
the contents of this "open scroll" when he is ordered to "seal
(σφράγισον) what the seven thunders spoke, and do not write these
things" (10:4). Later he is ordered to eat his words (10:9). In contrast to chapter 10, the scroll of chapter 5 is sealed (βιβλίον

... κατεσφραγισμένον σφραγῖσιν ἑπτά) so that no one can open (ἀνοῖξαι) it until it is handed over to the powerful "lion of the tribe of Judah." The sequence of the action in chapter 10 thus reverses that in chapter 5.

After eating the bittersweet scroll, John is ordered to prophesy again to people, nations, tongues, and kings (10:9–11, cf. 5:9). This commission to prophesy (see Ezek. 2:8; 3:1–3) harks back to the inaugural vision of 1:19–20 where John is ordered to write down the things which he sees, both those things which are and will be. In both instances the commissioning is associated loosely with "mystery" (10:7; 1:20) and with things to come (1:19; 10:7). Because of those connections with chapter 1, some have understood the little scroll in chapter 10 as a new prophetic commissioning introducing another set of visions.[10] The commission in chapter 1, the unsealing in chapter 5, and the little scroll in chapter 10 are interconnected through these various elements.

Accumulation of Images

Sometimes images occurring at different places in the Revelation are accumulated in a later scene. This type of unfolding gives a cumulative affect, as images recurring at different points in the Apocalypse are gathered together at a later point. A retrospective review of the images in Revelation 19:11–16 illustrates this. At 19:11 John sees heaven open (cf. 4:1) and then a white horse with a rider called Faithful and True who judges justly and makes war. The rider's eyes are as a flame of fire; on his head are many diadems; and he has a name written which no one knows but himself. He wears a garment dipped in blood and he has a name, The Word of God. An army in heaven follows him on white horses; they are clad with white, pure linen. From his mouth issues a sharp sword with which to smite the nations, and he will rule them with an iron rod; and he will trod the wine press of the fury of the wrath of God the Almighty. On his blood-dipped garment and on his thigh he has a name written, King of Kings and Lord of Lords.

These six verses make up a clearly defined unit introduced by the stereotyped formula, "And I saw."[11] This vision is linked closely with the two following (19:17–18; 19:19–21) by a returning in verse 21 to the warring of the rider with a sword issuing from his mouth. Revelation 19:11–16 is also the first of seven final visions of judgment, victory, and salvation.[12] Thus Revelation 19:11–16 is a narrative unit which links in several ways to the narrative, visionary units immediately around it.

At the same time, however, Revelation 19:11–16 accumulates im-

ages from earlier scenes, especially those describing the ultimate judgment and victorious rule of God and his Christ. The rider of a white
horse occurs elsewhere only at the opening of the first seal in 6:2
where the first of the four horsemen of the Apocalypse is introduced.
There the rider has a bow, is given a crown, and goes forth to conquer
(6:2); the language in both visions (6:2; 19:11–16) thus unfolds a
warring, conquering king, the first introducing and the second concluding the apocalyptic disasters described by the seer.[13] The phrase
"eyes like a flame of fire" relates the rider of the white horse to the one
who speaks to the angel of the church of Thyatira (2:18) and to the
one like a son of man whom John sees in his inaugural vision (1:14).
That figure also shares with the rider of the white horse a "sharp
sword issuing from his mouth" (1:16, cf. 2:12; 19.15). The diadems
(19:12), shared only with the dragon (12:3) and the beast from the
sea (13:1), are a sign of royalty as is of course the title, King of kings
and Lord of lords (19:16, cf. 17:14). So also "ruling with a rod of
iron" (19:15) is a royal image (Ps. 2:9) that links the rider to the male
child endangered by the dragon (12:5). As the Lamb conquers
through his blood (5:5, 9), so here the royal garment is "dipped in
blood" (19:13), probably alluding to the crucified king, though the
garment may simply be bloody from battle.

     Four times the rider's name is referred to: in 19:11 he is called
"Faithful and True," in 19:12 he has a written name that only he
knows; in 19:13 his name is The Word of God; and, as discussed
above, in 19:16 his written name is "King of Kings and Lord of
Lords." A name written on a person establishes identity (13:16–17;
14:1, cf. 3:12; 22:4). That the name is unknown probably identifies
the rider of the white horse as outside the human sphere, for mystery
also surrounds the name of the land-beast (13:17) and the woman
riding the scarlet beast (17:5).[14] The name Faithful and True (19:11)
links this final revelation of the Word of God (19:12) to the one
addressing the angel of the church of Laodicea, who calls himself "the
Amen, The Faithful and True (Witness), The Beginning of God's
Creation" (3:14, cf. 1:5).[15] The Faithful and True Word of God riding the white horse also parallels "the faithful and true words of God"
given to John and authenticated by God himself (21:5; 22:6). In fact,
The Faithful and True Word of God riding the white horse is transmitted as part of those "faithful and true words of God." The words
that transmit and The Word on the white horse transmitted merge
into one. Form and content, signifier and signified, syntax and semantics are united in the sign of The Word.

     The rider goes forth to make war. Except for Jesus' threat to war
against those at Pergamum (2:16), warring occurs only between di-

vine and evil forces: Michael and the dragon (12:7), the dragon and
the woman's seed (12:17), the Lamb and the beast with 10 kings
(17:14), the two witnesses and the beast (11:7), Armageddon
(16:15), and Satan and the saints (20:8). Here the rider on the white
horse, along with his army wearing white linen and riding white
horses, do battle with the beast, the kings of the earth, and their army
(19:19).

Thus Revelation 19:11–16 consists of transformations of a series of
linguistic elements that appear earlier in the Revelation. Some of
those elements first appear in John's inaugural vision of the Christ
(1:12–16). Others appear in introductions to the letters, in the description of the first of the four horsemen of the Apocalypse, in the
fighting Lamb who conquers the beast and 10 kings, in the newborn
male child threatened by the dragon, and in the blood of the wine
press of the wrath of God. That final transformation also takes into
itself elements previously formed around the demonic figures of the
dragon, the beast from the sea, and the whore on the scarlet beast. If
we were to read the Revelation aloud with this cumulative process in
mind, we would notice similarities and differences, on various levels,
as structures, motifs, images, and perspectives form and unform
diachronically. Each element has a different shape and a different
location in the stream, but each is also a transformation of the other
within the pliable medium of the seer's language. Where there is
cumulation, the perspective gained through one image of the Christ
enters into all other perspectives so that the final scene of 19:11–16
does bring a kind of climax—not in the narrative line but in the concentration of images.[16]

Circularity

Circularity refers to concentric development of a passage so that the
ending reflects the beginning.[17] A simple example occurs in 4:1: "*After this* I looked, and lo, in heaven an open door! And the first voice
...said...I will show you what must take place *after this*."[18] On a
different level, the pregnant woman and dragon ring chapter 12, for
that chapter begins with their conflict, shifts to a battle in heaven, and
then ends with another version of the woman/dragon conflict. Revelation 17:1–19:10 is enclosed by an antithetical ring consisting of the
Great Whore clothed in purple and scarlet at the beginning and the
bride of the Lamb clothed in bright, pure fine linen at the end. Or an
even larger unit, 12:1–19:10, is ringed by another set of feminine
images: the pregnant woman clothed with the sun and the bride of the
Lamb clothed with pure linen. Circularity consists of repeated words,

syntactical forms, or motifs. As with all analysis, as location of circularity becomes the more ingenious, the more removed it is from the actual language of the Revelation.

The seer tends to develop his material concentrically into ever-widening rings. So, for example, several of the eschatological promises to those who conquer, an element in the seven letters of chapters 2–3, reappear in the vision of the New Jerusalem in chapters 21–22. At the beginning of the vision of renewal, God makes the link to the letters by saying "He who conquers shall have . . ." (21:7, cf. 2:11). The tree of life promised to those victorious at Ephesus (2:7) appears in the city (22:2).[19] The victorious at Smyrna will not be harmed by the second death, a phrase which is made clear in 21:8 (cf. 20:6, 14). Those conquering at Sardis will not have their names wiped from the book of life (cf. 21:27). And to those conquering at Laodicea, Jesus promises a seat with him on his throne, while at 22:5 his servants reign forever in the city with the enthroned God and the royal Lamb.[20]

The final section of the Apocalypse (22:6–21) circles back to the beginning to create one grand circularity. At Revelation 22:8 John once again identifies himself as the seer who hears and sees what he writes (cf. 1:9). At 22:13 Jesus calls himself the "first and last" (1:17), but also creates a cumulative affect by including as well, "alpha and omega" (cf. 1:8) and "beginning and end" (cf. 3:14; 1:5).[21] The chain of command and blessing in 1:1–3 are repeated in 22:6–7, and the assertion that "the time is near" (1:3) is repeated in 22:10.

In the processes of circularity and accumulation, placement in the narrative sequence is a significant factor, for earlier occurrences of a term, an image, or a motif become a given in the narrative line to be drawn on in the development of a later scene. Thus, the first vision which focuses upon Christian life in Asia Minor provides the "givens" which the seer loops back upon in the heavenly visions. Such recursive activity—to use a phrase of M. H. Abrams—whereby something given is taken up into a later, more complex operation, grounds the seer's visionary scenes in the social life of the Asian province.[22]

METAPHORIC UNITY IN THE REVELATION

In contrast to the narrative unity of the Revelation which interconnects scenes through horizontal threads that run sequentially throughout the work, metaphoric unity interrelates elements of the seer's language "vertically." In narrative sequence, time is always involved in moving from one scene to another. Metaphoric unity, on the other hand, occurs all at once; that is, a metaphor consists of simultaneous "vertical" layers of language analogous to a musical chord. Metaphoric phrases such as "crown of life" or "wine press of the wrath of God" must be grasped instantaneously; the metaphor cannot be traced through the letters or the words. The seer unifies his work as much through figurative or metaphoric language as through narrative devices.

Similes and Metaphors

A simile compares two different objects through particles such as ὡς, ὥσπερ, and ὅμοιος, all of which may be translated as "like" or "as." An angel cries with a loud voice like a lion roars (10:3); unclean spirits like frogs come from the mouth of the dragon (16:13); one of the four living creatures around the throne was like an ox (4:7). At 6:14 the seer sees the heavens split which he links in simile to a scroll rolled up.

As though to highlight the importance of figurative speech, the seer often introduces some of the most basic elements in his landscape through a simile. The "sea," for example, used throughout the Apocalypse as an element coordinate with "land," "earth," and "heaven," first occurs as a figure in the throne scene: "and before the throne there is as it were a sea of glass, like crystal" (4:6).[23] So, also, "fire" first appears metaphorically as a simile in a description of eyes in John's inaugural vision (1:14). Later, as an independent element "fire" describes various catastrophes and punishments.[24] "Trumpet" describes metaphorically the voice in the inaugural vision (1:10) and the voice calling John into heaven (4:1), while later (8:2–11:19), trumpets are blown by angels to bring different kinds of eschatological revelations. Several animals are also introduced first through metaphoric speech. The first living creature around the throne is "like a lion" (4:7). In the next chapter, the seer declares that the "lion from the tribe of Judah has conquered" (5:5).[25] "Serpent," a significant animal in the action of the Apocalypse, first appears as a simile describing the tails of the horses released at the blowing of the sixth trumpet (9:19). "Serpent" then appears in its own right as an independent object in conflict with the woman (12:9, 14, 15) and as the one bound for a thousand years (20:2). Before an eagle is seen flying in midheaven crying woes (8:13), it has been introduced in a simile describing the fourth living creature (4:7). So also the activity of warring first occurs in a simile (9:9). The two witnesses wear sackcloth (11:3), but earlier "the sun became black as sackcloth" (6:12). These transformations from similes to independent entities exemplify pliability in the seer's language, and they contribute toward unifying elements in the seer's world. By using key terms as similes, elements in nature, animal life, human activity, and forces from both heaven and the underworld are woven together in the seer's work.

A metaphor identifies rather than compares two elements: in 12:1 the clothing of the woman is said not to be like the sun; her clothing is the sun. Throughout the Revelation, similes and metaphors appear together. For example, in the seer's inaugural vision, a figure of awe is created through similes and metaphors combining human and inanimate spheres (1:13–16). The awesome manifestation becomes present visually as "one like a son of man, clothed with a long robe and with a golden girdle round his breast." The white color of his head and hair is as wool or snow. His eyes are as a flame of fire, his feet like bronze fired in a furnace, and his voice sounded like many waters. His face was like the sun shining in full strength. From his mouth issued a sharp two-edged sword, and more striking, he held in his right hand seven stars. This portrait is drawn from traditional images in the Old Testament, but it nonetheless combines metaphorically spheres of everyday experience to produce a creature of awesome, divine proportions.

Later, in the first throne scene, the creator God who sits upon the throne is described by means of images of precious stones, jasper and carnelian, and by a rainbow that looks like an emerald (4:3). Once again the inorganic becomes the means of revealing the divine. In contrast, animal similes become the means of envisioning the heavenly figuresaround the throne. One is like a lion, another like an eagle, an ox, and a man—all with six wings and full of eyes (4:6–8). There are as well twenty-four elders with white garments and golden crowns (4:4). Atmospherics, sea, and fire combine to fill out the rest of the presentation (4:5–6). Celestial objects frequently combine to characterize divine forces: a mighty angel comes down from heaven wrapped in a cloud, with a rainbow over his head, with a face like the sun and legs like pillars of fire (10:1). Or a woman appears in heaven clothed with the sun, with the moon under her feet and twelve stars on her head (12:1).

The seer also envisions suprahuman evil forces by breaking the categories of everyday experience through metaphor and simile. The monstrous beast from the sea has ten horns and seven heads. It is like a leopard, its feet like a bear's, and its mouth like a lion's. The locusts who come up through the opening from the bottomless abyss combine a stinger like a scorpion, an appearance like horses, though with human faces, women's hair, and lions' teeth (9:7–10).[26]

Irony

Irony is another trope which occurs in the Apocalypse. That is, dis-sembling and concealing occur so that true meaning reverses what appears.[27] Ironic language sometimes appears with words that play on different meanings: the Smyrnians are poor but are rich, while the Laodiceans are rich but are wretched and poor (2:9; 3:17). Structural irony—where a *form* effects duplicity—appears in the dirges over Babylon in chapter 18, especially the dirge by the angel (18:2–3) who uses that form to rejoice.[28] Kerygmatic irony occurs frequently throughout the Revelation, whereby the Christian proclamation and imitation of the "crucified king" is expressed in various ways.[29] The irony of Christian redemption comes out in the language of 5:5–10. John is assured there that the sealed scroll would be opened, for "the lion of the tribe of Judah, the Root of David, has conquered, so that he can open the scroll and its seven seals." At that point John sees in the midst of the throne "a Lamb standing as though it had been slain," and heavenly creatures sing about the Lamb's worthiness to open the book "because you were slain." Here the seer, albeit in his own dis-tinctive language, alludes to the irony in the Christian proclamation that the one on the cross reigns as king.[30] Because of the powerless condition of being slain, the Lamb has power and is worthy of receiv-ing "power, strength, honor, and glory" (5:6–9). Life, victory, and power come through crucifixion.

As with the Lamb, so with those Christians who follow the Lamb. Those at Smyrna are exhorted to "be faithful unto death, and I will give you the crown of life" (2:10). For the Christian, life also comes through death. So also Christians gain power through being power-less. To the Philadelphians it is said: "I have placed before you an open door which no one has the power to close because you have little power and you kept my word and you did not deny my name" (3:8). Here there is both a wordplay on δύναται/δύναμιν and an ironic display of powerlessness, for their "little power" is celebrated as a partial reason why no one has power to close the door.[31] In a similar, ironic vein Jesus urges the Laodiceans, who think that they are rich but are actually poor, to buy from him who purchased them by his blood fired gold, white garments, and eye salve (3:18).[32]

The irony of Christian proclamation and imitation occurs in a more subtle form in the message to the Ephesians where those conquering are promised to eat from the "tree of life." Reference to the tree of life occurs again at 22:2–3 where it is linked clearly to the cross: "and the

leaves of the tree were for the healing of the nations. There shall no
more be anything accursed."[33]

Puns and Wordplays

The seer often creates puns and plays on different meanings of a word.
To the Ephesians the speaker says, "I know your works... how
you cannot *bear* [βαστάσαι] evil men... [and are] *bearing up*
[ἐβάστασας] for my name's sake." Also the speaker knows their
"toil" [κόπνο] and that they *"have not grown weary"* [κεκοπίακεν]. In
the Sardis letter "name" at one point represents external, superficial
reality, "You have the *name* of being alive" (3:1), whereas later he
declares that he will not blot out the *name* of the one who conquers
(3:5) from the book of life, i.e., here *name* represents the deepest reality. Assurance is given the Philadelphians: "Because you have *kept*
[ἐτήρησας] my word... I will *keep* [τηρήσω] you from the hour of
trial." The "after this" which rings 4:1 serves as a "superficial connector" at the beginning, but as a temporal referent at the end.[34]
Earth and serpent create a wordplay with their *mouths*, as "the earth
opened its mouth and swallowed the river which the dragon had
poured from his mouth" (12:16). At 1:17 John falls down "as a corpse"
before the one who was "alive, became a corpse, and again alive"
(1:18). At 19:20 it is stated that "the beast is caught." Through a
play on the action of the verb, the beast is "caught" like an animal
(e.g., John 21:3), but the verb also carries here the meaning of
"arrest" or "take into custody" (e.g., Acts 12:4). Prepositions sometimes create verbal plays: the difficult proverb in 13:10 probably
means that if a person goes away for the *purpose of* [εἰς] captivity, he
goes *into* [εἰς] captivity.[35] In the second part, there is a play on
another preposition: "If someone goes forth *with* [ἐν] a sword to be
killed, he will be killed *by* [Ἐν] a sword." Prepositional playfulness
also occurs at 16:11 where those suffering under the fifth bowl cursed
God *because of* [ἐκ] their pain and did not turn *from* [ἐκ] their deeds.
On occasion a phrase is used to refer blatantly to different referents.
So, in the throne scene of chapters 4 and 5 the seer casually identifies
the "seven spirits of God" with the "seven torches of fire" (4:5) and
later with the "seven eyes" of the Lamb (5:6); or "the seven heads" of
the beast are both "seven hills" and "seven kings" (17:9).

Other verbal playfulness can be seen in the reversals of the Ephesians and those at Thyatira: the Ephesians should do their *first works*
(2:4), whereas the "latter works" of those at Thyatira exceed their
first (2:19). Those at Laodicea must open the door (3:20), but the

Philadelphians have an open door set before them (3:8). Those at Smyrna are poor, but rich (2:9), while those at Laodicea are rich, but poor (3:17). While the scroll is being unsealed (6:12), the 144,000 are being sealed (7:3).

When considering the meaning of a word at any specific instance, its range of meanings may also be present. Consider, for example, the meaning of "blood" (αἷμα) in the Book of Revelation. A primary meaning is fixed early on in the doxology following the epistolary greeting at 1:5: "to the one loving us and loosing us from our sins by his blood" (cf. 5:9; 19:13). Christian martyrs who follow the pattern of Jesus offer their blood in witness of the gospel (6:10), and are saved by blood. So, those who come through the great tribulation wash and make white their garments in the blood of the lamb (7:14), and the brethren endangered by the dragon fallen from heaven are victorious through that same blood (12:11). Blood can also refer to disasters and destruction, especially in association with bodies of water: at the second trumpet, a third of the sea became blood (8:8);[36] the two witnesses had power to turn water into blood (11:6); in a scene where earth is "harvested," blood from the wine press came up to the bridles of the horses (14:20).

In certain passages those different meanings of "blood" play together. Babylon the Great Whore is drunk with the blood of the saints and of the witnesses of Jesus (17:6, cf. 18:24), and that blood is exacted from her hand by judgment (19:2) and destruction (18:21–24). In connection with the pouring out of the third bowl of wrath, rivers and streams turn into blood (16:4). Then the angel of the waters declares God just and explains with a *lex talionis* playing on different meanings of "blood": " you are just . . . because they poured out the blood of the saints and prophets, and you have given to them blood to drink" (16:5). Saving blood involves destruction and death; martyrs follow Jesus in pouring out their blood, but that blood brings with it judgment—salvation or destruction. Perhaps in every instance, "blood" carries both its positive and negative meanings.

In sum, figures of speech abound in the Revelation as comparisons, similes, metaphors, and wordplays weave into ever-changing patterns. Syntactical shifts and grammatical changes break into novel connections and disclose new associations. The seer writes a language of metaphor, symbol, brief narration, and cultic cries. It illustrates what some would call the primary language of religious experience.[37] At times, that "writing style" seems to be in tension with the subject matter of commitment, judgment, and hope; it borders on a facile lightness reminiscent of Ovid's compilation of myth in which—in contrast to tragedy—the most horrifying content is presented in a light style.[38] Whatever else may be observed about that language, it spins another set of threads which unify the Revelation.

The Mythic Unity of the Book of Revelation

The references to "primary religious language" and Ovid suggest that the language of the Revelation can be viewed as mythic language in that it takes the shape of metaphor, simile, wordplay, and symbol. As with characters in all myths, characters in the Book of Revelation are creatures of awesome and monstrous dimensions, "hybrids" created from inorganic, animal, and human components. In the Revelation there is also the metaphoric transgression of boundaries that normally divide aspects and dimensions of the everyday world: dwellers on earth become drunk with the "wine of fornication" (17:2) or Great Babylon is drunk "with the blood of the saints" (17:6). The New Jerusalem forms a complex boundary with sacred space on earth, eschatological time, and heaven above—a boundary that cannot be charted in an ordinary space-time grid. Finally, the metamorphoses which occur at the opening of a door in heaven in chapter 4 occur simultaneously in several dimensions. The spatial movement "up" (4:1) becomes synonymous with the psychological state of "being in the spirit" (4:2), and the spatial/psychological is in turn linked closely to the temporal future: "come up here and I will show you what must take place after this" (4:1). Through the identification of metaphor, to go up is to go forward in time and to change psychological states.

Sequential arrangements in the Book of Revelation also reflect mythic patterns. The threads crisscross in different ways, sometimes tracing a path forward, sometimes backward, or sometimes through overlays creating metaphoric simultaneity. By the time that the reader reads the last chapters in the Book of Revelation, he or she notices an increased intensification and a more fully developed "end" than was present in earlier chapters. Yet it is difficult to trace out a plot line in the Book of Revelation with a climax at the end. Even narrative progression as a conic spiral moving from the present to the eschatological future can be traced only at the expense of other crisscrossing threads of fulfillment which occur throughout the Revelation.[39] Throughout the book there is a mythic redundancy, a repetition of the message in order to assure communication. For example, at the blowing of the seventh trumpet "the mystery of God, as he announced to his servants the prophets," is fulfilled (10:7). The

Apocalypse could end with chapter 11 in the heavenly celebration of God's just judgment of the dead and his eternal reign (11:17–18). Or after the battle of Armageddon, the heavenly theophany brings eschatological fulfillment. Terms such as "climax," "interruption," or "interlude" help to simplify the complex web by subordinating certain elements, but they inevitably distort the wholeness of the Apocalypse. Even an understanding of the Apocalypse through the metaphor of a web distorts its wholeness, for that metaphor suggests that there are strands that exist throughout the work. The language of the seer is probably more pliable and fluid than that.

That fluid quality of mythic language which unfolds and enfolds narrative and metaphoric connections calls into question any structural analysis of the Revelation which easily divides the text into binary oppositions. Further, the interconnectedness of the surface language of the Revelation suggests a vision of the world that does *not* see fundamental conflicts between religious promises and social disappointments, bodily mortality and spiritual hopes of immortality, or natural impulses and cultural demands. Rather, the fluidity of the language—its narrative reiterations and metaphoric identifications— points to a vision in which religious promises, social encounters, biological givens, and cultural demands undergo mutual adjustments, form metaphoric relations, and finally enter into alliances that create coherence, integrity, and wholeness.

That is—and here I can only suggest a direction for consideration—mythic signification in the Book of Revelation does not hold together oppositions and conflicts; rather it speaks from unbroken wholeness to unbroken wholeness. Signifiers, signifieds, deep structures, and surface structures form metaphoric alliances not contradictory oppositions. Both the surface language (with which this essay has been concerned) and the vision of the world created and articulated through that language can best be visioned as flowing liquid: the seer's language flows into and out of images, figures, reiterations, recursions, contrasts, and cumulations as whorls, vortices, and eddies in a stream. That image captures the literary unity of the Revelation.

Notes

1. E.g., John Gager, *Kingdom and Community* (Englewood Cliffs, N.J.: Prentice-Hall, 1975), pp. 54–55; Adela Yarbro Collins, *Crisis and Catharsis* (Philadelphia: Westminster Press, 1984), pp. 141–42.

2. Note also how the seven angels with the seven bowls reappear at 17:1 and 21:9 as another device unifying segments of the Revelation.

3. Revelation 8:1; 11:15; 16:17. This assumes that the "silence" in heaven at the opening of

the seventh seal reflects worship. Note the heavenly worship which precedes it in Revelation 7:10–17. For the importance of heavenly worship in the seventh item, see Leonard L. Thompson, "Cult and Eschatology in the Apocalypse of John," *Journal of Religion* 49 (1969): 330–50.

4. See J. Lambrecht, "A Structuration of Rev 4, 1–22, 5" in *L'Apocalypse johannique et l'apocalyptique dans le Nouveau Testament*, ed. J. Lambrecht (Gembloux: Louvain University Press, 1980), pp. 89–90, for a synoptic tabulation of the two series. The sixth in the series of seals, trumpets, and bowls are also interrelated through structural reversals and cumulative images; see below.

5. The "time, and times, and half a time" in Revelation 12:14, a parallel passage, probably refers to the three and a half years of Daniel 7:25 which also of course equals 42 months or 1,260 days. Compare also the time of the exposure of the bodies of the witnesses (11:9, 11).

6. For a discussion of what these "times" may mean in a larger context, see J. P. M. Sweet, *Revelation* (Philadelphia: Westminster Press, 1979), pp. 182–83.

7. Three and four, factors of 12, appear regularly in the Book of Revelation, e.g., 6:6; 8:7, 13; 9:18; 16:13, 19; 21:13; 4:6; 7:1; 9:13, 14; 14:20; 20:8.

8. At Revelation 16:12, "the rising of the sun" and "Euphrates" appear together as references to the East. That is the only other passage in which those terms occur. On the altar as microcosm, see for example, Mircea Eliade, *Patterns in Comparative Religion* (Cleveland, Ohio: World, 1963), pp. 371–74.

9. The content of the open scroll and the message of the seven thunders are somehow interrelated in this scene.

10. See G. B. Caird, *The Revelation of St. John the Divine* (New York: Harper & Row, 1966), p. 126; Elisabeth Schüssler Fiorenza, *Invitation to the Book of Revelation* (New York: Doubleday, 1981), pp. 107–8.

11. καὶ εἶσον. See Leonard L. Thompson, "Cult and Eschatology in the Apocalypse of John," *Journal of Religion* 49 (1969): 332.

12. 19:11–16; 19:17–18; 19:19–21; 20:1–3; 20:4–10; 20:11–15; 21:1–8.

13. Later at 20:7–10 there is the "warless" battle between Satan and the saints.

14. With sufficient cleverness, one is supposed to be able to figure out the number of the name of the beast, for it is human (13:18); for the woman, "mystery" is only one of several names written on her forehead (17:5). Those victorious at Pergamum are promised a share in Christ's mystery (2:17).

15. Note how easily the seer transforms Christ as "the first from the dead" (1:5) to "the first of God's creation" (3:14).

16. If notated as an elaborate score, those Christ images could be seen in the structuralist language of Lévi-Strauss as synchronic mythemes. Like music, a piece of language can be viewed both statically as a score or dynamically as performance. The best literary critics—whatever their school—assume that.

17. Ring composition and inclusion are other terms used for this phenomenon.

18. See also οὐκ ἔτι in 18:11, 14; οἱ πλουτήσαντές and πλουτος in 18:15, 17; γράψον in 1:11 and 1:19.

19. The new city also shares characteristics with the throne in chapter 4, cf. 21:11, 18–20 and 4:1.

20. That cluster of similarities is only one of several links between the letters and the visions indicating that the former cannot be isolated from the latter, e.g., at Revelation 4:1 the "first voice" speaks to John again; or the throne scene in 4–5 reflects vocabulary in the letters (throne, white clothes, gold crowns).

21. Revelation 22:16 repeats several elements in the introduction at 1:1–2.

22. M. H. Abrams uses "recursive" in a way that seems almost synonymous with typology. See "Apocalyse: Theme and Variations," in *The Apocalypse in English Renaissance Thought and Literature*, ed. C. A. Patrides and Joseph Wittreich (Ithaca: Cornell University Press, 1984), p. 343. Jerome Bruner defines it more precisely as "the process whereby the mind or a computer

program loops back on the output of a prior computation and treats it as a given that can be the input for the next operation." In *Actual Minds, Possible Worlds* (Cambridge: Harvard University Press, 1986), p. 97.

23. See 5:13; 7:1, 2; 12:12; 14:7. With the new heaven and new earth, the sea passes away and is no more (21:1).

24. See 8:8; 9:17; 11:5; 14:10; 16:8; 17:16; 19:20; 20:9.

25. The other instances of "lion" are metaphoric: 9:8, 17; 10:3; 13:2.

26. Contrast the "horses" of the sixth trumpet which have heads like lions from whose mouths come forth fire, smoke, and sulphur and whose tails are like serpents with heads (9:17–19). Only evil forces seem to have tails (9:10; 12:4; 9:19).

27. In a sense all language is ironic, for all conceals. See Frank Kermode, *The Genesis of Secrecy: On the Interpretation of Narrative* (Cambridge: Harvard University Press, 1979). Sometimes, however, the "concealing" is called attention to in an explicit manner and invites the audience to join in collusion with the author. Irony thus contributes to the community which John shares with his audience. The irony in the Revelation is stable, to use a term of Wayne Booth. In *A Rhetoric of Irony* (Chicago: University of Chicago Press, 1974); that is, it operates from a definite standpoint. For example, reigning through suffering is itself not susceptible to ironic manipulation.

28. Note especially verse 3 where the motivation for the fall is given: "drunk the wine of her impure passion," "committed fornication," and "wantonness." This is not the language of lament. See also Adela Yarbro Collins, "Revelation 18: Taunt-Song or Dirge?", in *L'Apocalypse johannique*, p. 138.

29. See Leonard L. Thompson, *Introducing Biblical Literature* (Englewood Cliffs, N.J.: Prentice-Hall, 1978), pp. 224–26.

30. See also 19:13 where the Word of God is soaked in blood and 1:7 where the "pierced one" comes on the clouds.

31. The ὅτι clause could be linked to οἰδά σου τὰ ἔργα, with the intervening words a parenthetical comment, but as it stands, the play on δύναται / δύναμιν cannot go unnoticed. So also the καὶ after δύναμιν may be taken as adversative ("and yet"), but καὶ connects ἔχεις, ἐτήρησάς, and δήρνήσω in a series. To read the sentence with a parenthetical phrase and an adversative καὶ complicates the syntax unnecessarily.

32. On the white garments, see 7:14 where they are made white in the blood of the Lamb.

33. See Galatians 3:13; Acts 5:30; 10:39; Polycarp, Philippians 8. At Revelation 13:3 there is a parody of the crucifixion of Jesus in the "healing" of the wound of the beast.

34. Ernst Lohmeyer, *Die Offenbarung des Johannes* (Tübingen: Mohr, 1953), p. 42. It is used as a connector for example in 7:1, 9; 15:5; 18:1, and with a specific temporal meaning in 9:12; 11:11; 20:3.

35. ὑπάγω with εἰς is a common idiom for "purpose."

36. See 16:3 at the pouring of the second bowl, 16:4; 6:12; 8:7.

37. For example, David Tracy's comment that "all authentic limit-language seems to be initially and irretrievably a symbolic and a metaphorical one." In "Religious Language as Limit-language," *Theology Digest* 22 (1974): 295.

38. Irving Massey, *The Gaping Pig: Literature and Transformation* (Berkeley: University of California Press, 1976), pp. 24–25.

39. E.g., Elisabeth Schüssler Fiorenza, *The Book of Revelation: Justice and Judgment* (Philadelphia: Fortress Press, 1981), p. 26.

Voice, Metaphor, and Narrative in the Book of Revelation

Michael Payne
Bucknell University

IN his magnificent recent book *Pagans and Christians* Robin Lane Fox provides an immensely helpful clue to understanding the apocalyptic visionary experience in the Book of Revelation. He observes that whereas "among pagans the gods still 'stood beside' mortals and 'held their hand' over individuals and their cities; among Christians, meanwhile, an unseen presence was a guide and guardian."[1] Between Jesus' death and Constantine's time there was no significant Christian architecture, no visual art to reenforce the idea of Christ's presence at a service, and no memory of what Jesus looked like in life. Even in early Christian dream literature there is a general condemnation of the clarity and vividness of pagan dreams, and dream interpreters were actually denied the rite of Christian baptism. Good dreams were reenactments of scenes from Scripture and were direct, straightforward messages offering correction and discipline. By the beginning of the third century when he first appears in visual art, on early Christian sarcophagi, Jesus is given the pagan image of a philosopher among his pupils or a sheperd among his flock.[2] John Beckwith in his *Early Christian and Byzantine Art* further emphasizes this need of the earliest Christian artists to take their images of Christ from pagan and Old Testament sources. In one of the earliest known series of Christian vault and wall mosaics the vine of Dionysos becomes the True Vine of Christ, Jonah's falling into the whale's mouth appears as an emblem for the Christian belief in the body's resurrection, and a solar charioteer merges with the risen Christ[3] (Figure 1). Fox argues that the consequence for the imagination of early Christians' emphasis on singing and listening to texts rather than gazing, as pagans did, on idealized images of their gods was a greater reliance on the "eye of the soul" than on the physical eye.

This shift in emphasis, Fox concludes, is clearest in the Book of Revelation. There

> God appears in the abstract, like a precious stone, blazing in brilliant red and white. Only in the "new heaven and new earth" is he visible directly:

Figure 1. Christus-Sol. 3rd.-C. mosaic in the necropolis under St. Peter's. (Rome, Grotte Vaticane)

we may aspire, Irenaeus believed, to the vision of God, but only at the end of this world. As for Christ, he is revealed symbolically, as "one like a son of man." He is imagined through his supernatural attributes, not through features fixed in art.[4]

Indeed, the essential features of the Book of Revelation may now be seen as having a place in the general aesthetic view Fox has provided.

First of all, the Book of Revelation is in many ways a book about books, and the voice of John is that of a highly self-conscious author who wrestles with problems of textuality and inspirational authority. Revelation opens with seven letters to the churches of Asia dictated to John by "one like unto the Son of Man" who appears in the midst of "seven golden candlesticks." Later, major portions of the text are devoted to the book with seven seals (chaps. 5–10), opened for John by "the Lion of the tribe of Judah." With the opening of the seventh seal, seven angels are heard in turn, the last holding "in his hand a little book open" (chaps. 10–15:4). The last verses of Revelation's final chapter explicitly bring to a close not only the Book of Revelation itself but also the Bible as a whole, with extensive references to The Book of Life. Although the texts are to remain unsealed, available for all to read, the canon is said to be closed; nothing is to be added or taken away. John's voice, then, serves primarily as a textual mediator for the divine word; and when God is revealed in heaven at the climactic end of chapter 11, the focal point is still a text, "the ark of his testament" (11:19).

Second, the major metaphors in the Book of Revelation have the two qualities Fox and Beckwith identify as characteristic of the early Christian imagination: they are abstract, tending toward the symbolic rather than the allegorical, and they retain their Judaic and pagan identity. The ubiquitous numerology of Revelation has no mimetic function in pointing to specific events in history or prophecy but serves instead to provide symmetrical structure to the text and to define a reality beyond numerical definition. When the last becomes the first and the first the last, calculation ceases. The imagery of the Hebrew Bible is similarly invoked to be transcended. The menorah becomes Christ, the light of the world; Sion becomes the place of the Lamb; Babylon is "fallen" to become the place of Christian martyrdom; Jerusalem is transformed into the holy city sent from a new heaven to a new earth that has replaced the first creation. These typological transformations are complete to the point that it becomes virtually impossible to judge whether the Christian antitype has fully complemented the Hebrew type or whether in a colossal act of cultural appropriation all of the image's original significance is simply lost, as Spinoza claimed.

Figure 2. Romans with Temple menorah and other spoils of Jerusalem on the arch of Titus in Rome. (Tel Aviv, Government Archives)

Third, the narrative of Revelation defies even those structured forms it invokes. At first the book appears to have a shape similar to the Book of Job or Ecclesiastes, with a framing device enclosing the central material in a way that defends the reader against what is radically new. Likewise, the vision of the new heaven, new earth, and New Jerusalem seems to conclude both Revelation and the Bible as a whole in the way Psalm 150 provides simultaneously a doxology for the fifth book of Psalms and a conclusion to the entire collection. Each of these framing devices, however, is unable to contain the vision of Revelation. Taken together, the narrative forms in Revelation suggest a process of semiotic overloading in which significance always overwhelms the sign. Throughout Revelation the personal voice of John is taken over by angelic and divine speech; the vehicles of conventional metaphors are made to convey tenors that overburden them; and the temporal and spatial coordinates of narrative art are used to map events that are beyond time and space.

Although this text seems designed to frustrate the attempt of any explanatory or interpretative strategy to frame its fearful symmetry, its apocalyptic dynamics can be seen fully displayed in the image of the menorah, the "seven golden candlesticks" of the King James Version (1:12), which is the first in a succession of visionary images of divinity in the book (Figure 2). In his use of the menorah John is adapting an image from the vision of Zechariah: "I have looked," Zechariah says to his angel, "and behold a candlestick all of gold, with a bowl upon the top of it, and his seven lamps thereon, and seven pipes to the seven lamps, which are upon the top thereof: And two olive trees by it, one upon the right side of the bowl, and the other upon the left side thereof" (4:2–3). In a later passage in the fourth chapter of Zechariah (4:12), it is revealed that the two olive branches empty their oil into the golden pipes of the stand. In the earliest known stone representations of the menorah, dating from the third century C.E., the olive branches are sometimes kept distinct from the lampstand and sometimes they are joined with it so that its branches come alive with leaves, blossoms, and fruit. Carol Meyers points out that the language in Hebrew Scripture used to describe the menorah has "a vegetal origin, indicating the translation of plant forms into architectural features," which is clearly preserved in the King James Version of the specifications for the menorah in Exodus 37:17–24. Tracing these features back to conventions of ancient Near Eastern iconography, Meyers concludes that

> By far the most common theme expressed by branched forms of any kind is that of fertility and the sustenance of life . . . The menorah in the tabernacle is singled out (Exod. 25:40; cf. Num. 8:4) as having its pattern revealed "on the mountain." This invocation of the mountain paradigm, along with the epithet "pure" (Exod. 31:8; 39:37) as an indication of cosmic brightness, serves to place the menorah within the realm of indicators of sacred space, the dwelling of the Lord in his heavenly abode or its earthly counterpart. As a visual expression of an arboreal form, within a culture in which the fertility and immortality themes associated with life trees are negated, it is transformed into a symbolic assurance of God's presence.[5]

The symbolic image of the menorah is not only the first and most powerful image of Christ's divinity in the Book of Revelation, it also provides a dynamic force in the text for unifying voice, metaphor, and narrative.

The surface narrative of Revelation is condensed almost to the point of extinction. John hears, he sees, he writes what his heavenly voices tell him. Who John was probably cannot any longer be determined, though it seems certain he was not John the apostle, since he derives his authority from his prophetic vision (1:3, 9–20) rather than from knowing Jesus in life. Whether he is on the island of Patmos because of Christian persecution or because he had withdrawn there for purposes of prophetic meditation is not clear from the text, although the New English Bible translation eliminates the ambiguity. Despite the apparent reference to John's own time in the angel's commentary on the iconography of the Whore of Babylon (17:9–16), scholars have reached no consensus on what historical chronology may be relevant to the passage: "they do not agree whether or not to begin with Caesar, Augustus, Caligula, or Nero."[6] Revelation begins on a note of personal intimacy, but John quickly becomes little more than a mediating voice once he hears Jesus speak from the midst of the golden candlesticks.

In place of a narrative that moves from an Aristotelian beginning to a middle and then to an end, Revelation has a structure that can be described as concentric or intercalated.[7] The architectonics of the text resemble the structure of the menorah, linking the first branch with the seventh, the second with the sixth, the third with the fifth, leaving a central unpaired fourth branch. The function of this structure is to reveal Christ as the beginning and the end, alpha and omega, the first word and the last word. Indeed, most of the physical details of Christ's first appearance in the text are identified with the seven golden candlesticks: "his eyes were as a flame of fire" (1:14), "his feet like unto fine brass" (1:15),[8] and "his countenance was as the sun shineth in his strength" (1:16). Christ's appearance is both apocalytically abstract and derived from the Old Testament image of the menorah as the symbol of God's presence.

Having identified the menorah with Christ, John proceeds to construct his book according to the method of intercalation, which Elisabeth Fiorenza has described in this way: "He narrates two formal units or two episodes (A and A') that essentially belong together. Between these two formal units or episodes he intercalates another form or scene (B) and thus requires the reader to see the combined text as a whole"[9] (Figure 3). The first branch of the text (1:1–11) consists of John's preface in which he identifies himself with his reader, calling himself a "brother" and a "companion in tribulation" (1:9). This section concludes with John's vision of Christ, who identifies himself as "the first and the last" and who commands John to record his visions "in a book" (1:11). The counterpart to this first branch (22:6–21) is John's report of the final words of the angel and of Jesus, including John's insistence that he saw and heard the things he has reported (22:8) and that his text is a complete whole from which nothing should be taken away (22:19). The second branch (1:11–3:33) begins with the appearance of Christ in the midst of the meno-

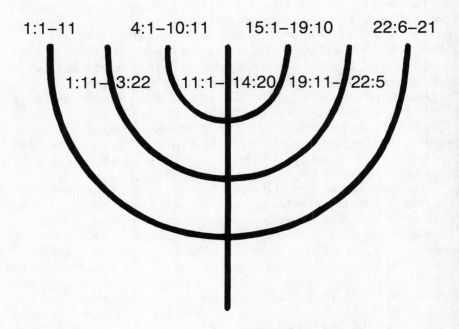

| 1:1–11 | 4:1–10:11 | 15:1–19:10 | 22:6–21 |

1:11–3:22   11:1–14:20 19:11–22:5

Figure 3. Possible structure of Revelation based on the model of the menorah.

rah and his identification of the seven golden candlesticks with the
seven churches (1:20) to whom he directs John to send the formulaic
letters with their warnings and promises to the churches of Asia. The
counterpart to the second branch (19:11–22:5) foresees the vision of
the Last Judgment in which those who were martyred "for the word of
God" (20:4) are rewarded with the "first resurrection," while those
whose names are not written "in the book of life" are cast into a lake
of fire (20:15). In the new heaven and earth of the holy city Jerusalem, personified as the bride of the Lamb, there is neither church
nor temple, "for the Lord God Almighty and the Lamb are the temple
of it" (21:22). Similarly in place of the letters directing the churches'
activities there is "the Lamb's book of life" (21:27) in which the
names of those are recorded who will be a part of the second resurrection. The third branch (4:1–10:11) begins with John's vision of the
throne of God and includes the opening of the book with seven seals
and John's devouring the angel's "little book." It is complemented
(15:1–19:10) by the account of the seven angels with seven plagues
and the defeat of the Whore of Babylon, who is a demonic parody of
Jerusalem as the bride of the Lamb. The central branch (11:1–14:20)
begins with a renewed reference to the two olive trees and the candle-

sticks that stand before God (11:4) and includes the opening of God's temple in heaven with "the ark of his testament" in the midst of it (11:19), as well as the woman clothed with the sun, the war in heaven with the defeat of Satan, the appearance of the beast with the number 666, and the vision of the Lamb followed by the harvest of the earth.

In his posthumously published *Apocalypse*, D. H. Lawrence finds his general antipathy to the Bible strongest in his reaction to the Book of Revelation, which he calls a "repulsive" book of revenge and death. In opposition to it, he declares, "What man most passionately wants is his living wholeness and his living unison."[10] Dante, Milton, and Blake, on the other hand, found vital imaginative stimulus in the book, all three attracted to its climactic center. For the conclusion of *Paradiso* Dante borrows from Revelation the image of God identified with his testament; for book 7 of *Paradise Lost* Milton takes from John's visions the account of the war in heaven; and for the conclusion to *The Four Zoas* Blake appropriates the image of the great harvest that ends John's chapter 14. Lawrence's "living wholeness . . . and living unison" are precisely what these three poets find in Revelation, recognizing, as Lawrence did not, that the abstract structure of the book has a dynamic, unifying force that runs through it, just as the olive trees give life to the menorah. Lawrence's attention to the text was, he confesses, deflected by the childhood religious circumstances in which he first encountered it. Those circumstances fragmented the text for him, just as many practicing Christians are exposed to the text mainly through the lectionary calendar. Furthermore, the modern biblical scholarly tradition, inspired by the important documentary discoveries concerning some of the earliest texts in the Hebrew Bible, has carried over into studies of Revelation, further fragmenting the text. The Anchor Bible editor, for example, has totally disassembled and rearranged the text. Biblical studies are, however, now at a point at which both documentary analysis and appreciation for the traditional unity of the biblical books can be accommodated to each other. The student of literature is in a position to profit from the exacting standards of modern biblical scholarship while bringing to the text also a respect for the perception that the Bible is a dynamically unified text. That perception of the Bible has been an important component in the history of literature and the visual arts.

Notes

1. Robin Lane Fox, *Pagans and Christians* (New York: Knopf, 1986), pp. 390–91.
2. Ibid., pp. 392–93.
3. John Beckwith, *Early Christian and Byzantine Art* (New York: Viking, 1979), p. 19 and accompanying illustrations.

4. Fox, *Pagans and Christians*, p. 394.

5. Carol Meyers, *Interpreter's Dictionary of the Bible* (Nashville, Tenn.: Abingdon Press, 1976), pp. 586–87.

6. Elisabeth Schüssler Fiorenza, *The Book of Revelation: Justice and Judgment* (Philadelphia: Fortress Press, 1985), p. 20. Professor Fiorenza provides an excellent review of research on all aspects of Revelation (pp. 12–34).

7. See Fiorenza, ibid., p. 175, whose structural analysis differs slightly from mine. She sees the text as falling into the following units.:

A   1:1–8
B   1:9–3:22
C   4:1–9:21; 11:15–19
D   10:1–15:4
C'   15:1, 5–19:10
B'   19:11–22:9
A'   20:10–22:21

8. Concerning the controversy over the base of the menorah occasioned by its depiction on the arch of Titus, see *Encyclopedia Judaica* (Jerusalem: Keter, 1971), 11:1365–66 and accompanying illustration.

9. Fiorenza, *Book of Revelation*, p. 172. She later comments: "The golden candelabra which appears on the arch of Titus in Rome consists of a centerpiece paralleled on either side by three pieces and thus exhibits the pattern ABCDC'B'A'" (p. 176).

10. D. H. Lawrence, *Apocalypse* (Harmondsworth: Penguin Books, 1974), p. 125.